In Defence of Labour Market Institutions

The International Labour Organization

The International Labour Organization was founded in 1919 to promote social justice and, thereby, to contribute to universal and lasting peace. Its tripartite structure is unique among agencies affiliated to the United Nations; the ILO's Governing Body includes representatives of government, and of employers' and workers' organizations. These three constituencies are active participants in regional and other meetings sponsored by the ILO, as well as in the International Labour Conference – a world forum which meets annually to discuss social and labour questions.

Over the years the ILO has issued for adoption by member States a widely respected code of international labour Conventions and Recommendations on freedom of association, employment, social policy, conditions of work, social security, industrial relations and labour administration, among others.

The ILO provides expert advice and technical assistance to member States through a network of offices and multidisciplinary teams in over 40 countries. This assistance takes the form of labour rights and industrial relations counselling, employment promotion, training in small business development, project management, advice on social security, workplace safety and working conditions, the compiling and dissemination of labour statistics, and workers' education.

In Defence of Labour Market Institutions

Cultivating Justice in the Developing World

Edited by

Janine Berg and David Kucera

First published in 2008 by
PALGRAVE MACMILLAN
Houndmills, Basingstoke, Hampshire RG21 6XS and
175 Fifth Avenue, New York, N.Y. 10010
Companies and representatives throughout the world.

ISBN-13: 978–0–230–53805–4   hardback
ISBN-10: 0–230–53805–3   hardback

And

International Labour Office
CH-1211 Geneva 22, Switzerland

ISBN-13: 978–92–2–119319–7   hardback
ISBN-10: 92–2–119319–5   hardback

A catalogue record for this book is available from the British Library.

Library of Congress Cataloging-in-Publication Data

In defence of labour market institutions : cultivating justice in the
developing world / edited by Janine Berg and David Kucera.
     p. cm.
  Includes index.
  ISBN 0–230–53805–3 (alk. paper)
  1. Labor market—Developing countries.   I. Berg, Janine.   II. Kucera,
  David, 1960-
  HD5852.I5 2007
  331.1209172'4—dc22

                                                                          2007050218

10   9   8   7   6   5   4   3   2   1
17 16 15 14 13 12 11 10 09 08

Printed and bound in Great Britain by
CPI Antony Rowe, Chippenham and Eastbourne

If you wish for peace, cultivate justice
—ILO motto

Contents

List of Tables and Figures

Tables

Boxes

Figures

Acknowledgements

In November 2005, the ILO's Policy Integration Department and Economic and Labour Market Analysis Department held a two-day technical staff seminar on Labour Market Institutions and Employment in Developing Countries at ILO headquarters in Geneva. The objective of the seminar was bring together ILO staff working on the employment effects of labour market institutions in developing countries in order to improve our work in this area as well as reflect on the ongoing debate on labour market 'rigidities'. We are grateful to the participants of the seminar, from ILO headquarters and the field, as well as the outside experts, for a very engaging and lively discussion of the issues. We would also like to thank those participants whose contributions appear as chapters in this volume.

We are extremely grateful to Peter Peek for initiating the seminar and for his ongoing support of our work in putting together this volume. We would also like to thank Peter Auer for his support, including his participation in the seminar and for his valuable comments on our draft chapters.

The seminar and volume were financed by funds from the Follow-Up to the World Commission on the Social Dimensions of Globalization and by the Economic and Labour Market Analysis Department of the ILO. We are grateful to Duncan Campbell, Riswanul Islam, Peter Peek and Peter Auer for help with arranging financing.

The completed manuscript benefited from a detailed and extremely helpful review of the text by Professor Chris Tilly of the University of Massachussetts-Lowell. We would also like to thank Sukti Dasgupta and Gyorgy Sziraczki, for valuable comments and suggestions on improving the draft. We hope we have done justice to their comments.

Finally, we would like to thank Charlotte Beauchamp, the ILO's Editor, for her continuous support of this volume. Besides being a pleasure to work with, Charlotte read over the text numerous times and provided valuable advice and suggestions for its improvement. Along with her colleagues, Alison Irvine and Lauren Elsaesser, to whom we are also thankful, she also worked closely with our co-publisher, Palgrave Macmillan.

Janine Berg
David Kucera

Notes on Contributors

Janine Berg is Senior Labour Economist in the Economic and Labour Market Analysis Department of the International Labour Office, Geneva, Switzerland. She received her PhD in Economics from the New School for Social Research.

José Luis Daza Pérez is Director of the Subregional Office for the Andean countries, International Labour Office, Lima, Peru. He received his Masters in Law from the Universidad de Salamanca.

François Eyraud is Director of the ILO Training Centre in Turin, Italy, and is former Director of the ILO Conditions of Work and Employment Programme. He received his Doctorat d'Etat en Sciences Économique from the Université d'Aix, Marseille.

Jesus Felipe is Principal Economist with the Central and West Asia Department of the Asian Development Bank, Manila, Philippines and Research Associate at the Centre for Applied Macroeconomic Analysis, Australian National University and at the Cambridge Centre for Economic and Public Policy, University of Cambridge. He received his PhD in Regional Science from the University of Pennsylvania.

Rosanna Galli is Professor of Macroeconomics at the Università Svizzera Italiana in Lugano, Switzerland. She received her PhD in Economics at Birkbeck College, University of London.

David Kucera is Senior Research Economist in the Policy Integration Department, International Labour Office, Geneva, Switzerland. He received his PhD in Economics from the New School for Social Research.

Sangheon Lee is Senior Research Officer with the Conditions of Work and Employment Programme, International Labour Office, Geneva, Switzerland. He received his PhD in Economics from Cambridge University.

Deirdre McCann is Research Officer with the Conditions of Work and Employment Programme, International Labour Office, Geneva, Switzerland. She received her DPhil in Labour Law from the University of Oxford.

J.S.L. McCombie is Reader in Applied Economics and Director of the Cambridge Centre of Economic and Public Policy, Department of Land Economy,

University of Cambridge and Fellow in Economics, Downing College, Cambridge. He received his PhD in Economics from the University of Cambridge.

Irmgard Nübler is Senior Skills and Training Policy Specialist, Skills and Employability Department, International Labour Office, Geneva, Switzerland. She received her PhD in Economics from the Free University of Berlin.

Catherine Saget is Senior Research Officer with the Conditions of Work and Employment Programme, International Labour Office, Geneva, Switzerland. She received her PhD in Economics from the European University Institute.

Matthew Salerno is a graduate of the School of Industrial Relations, Cornell University and a former intern at the International Labour Office, Geneva, Switzerland.

Zafiris Tzannatos is currently Advisor at the World Bank Institute, World Bank. He previously served as Advisor to the World Bank's Managing Director for Human Development, Manager for social protection in the MENA region, and Leader for the child labour programme. He received his PhD in Economics from the University of London.

María Luz Vega Ruíz is Senior Specialist in Labour Administration and Industrial Relations, Department of Social Dialogue, Labour Law and Labour Administration, International Labour Office, Geneva, Switzerland. She received her MPhil in Labour Law from the Université de Genève.

1
Introduction

Janine Berg and David Kucera

1.1 The labour market flexibility debate

Debates on labour institutions and regulations have taken on new urgency in the current era of globalization. Disappointing job growth and poor-quality jobs continue to characterize the labour markets of many developing countries, even in those countries that have experienced high rates of economic growth. Some critics argue that labour laws are overly burdensome, making it difficult to hire workers and costly to dismiss them. Indeed, since 2003 the International Finance Corporation, the private sector arm of the World Bank, has ranked countries according to their 'ease of a doing business', including regulations associated with 'employing workers'. The belief is that onerous regulations concerning hiring workers on temporary contracts, paying large amounts of severance on dismissal, restrictive working hours and too high payroll taxes have hampered investment and stalled job growth, causing the poor to suffer more than they already do. But are rigid labour markets really to blame? Is deregulation therefore the answer?

This book argues that the answer to both questions is, no. There is only weak evidence for the negative impacts of labour market regulations. Moreover, labour laws and labour market policies are needed to ensure social justice for workers in developing countries. In labour markets where labour is in surplus, there must be a minimum statutory protection for workers. The scope and enforcement of the law should be broadened rather than chipped away. Furthermore, new laws and policies should be designed and advanced to address new trends in the world of work, brought about by shifting social norms, technological advancements and economic integration.

This volume seeks to remind readers of the importance of labour market institutions – including labour market regulations – as well as improve our understanding of how these institutions evolve. We address the labour market flexibility debate through a series of studies of different labour institutions in developing countries. The chapters span a diverse group of institutions that reflect the nature of work itself in developing countries, extending well beyond labour markets to include many forms of informal employment as well as household production for own use. The diversity and uniqueness of this volume also results from the range of disciplines of the contributors, particularly in law and economics, as well as the historical perspectives taken by a number of authors.

The debate on labour market regulations and employment is incomplete without a consideration of the legal and economic aspects of labour market regulations. Most economists have much to learn from lawyers in terms of understanding what the implementation of labour law actually means in a concrete sense, and we believe this volume benefits from including contributions from both disciplines. Labour law developed out of the need to correct the imbalance between employers and workers in the employment relationship. Economic debates, however, often begin from the starting point of market efficiency, sometimes assessing whether the benefits of the labour laws and policies in place to protect workers do more harm than good. And even within economics, the debate has been too narrow, based on a theoretical abstraction of downward-sloping labour demand that is not particularly representative of reality. Any discussion of labour markets must consider asymmetries in bargaining as well as the endogeneity of many institutions.

Thus, one approach we use in this debate is through a historical analysis of institutions. We demonstrate that many labour institutions were developed to meet the social demands of both workers and employers. Rather than being imposed from without, the development of labour institutions and regulations more often reflects the playing out of dynamics of a more homegrown nature. The endogenous nature of labour institutions is also reflected in their embeddedness within law, production systems and social norms. Indeed, even such core workings of labour markets as wage setting and wage flexibility reflect social norms, particularly norms of fairness. Social norms may also provide the underpinnings of minimum wage and employment protection laws, codifying that which is already practiced. This view suggests that even when labour laws are changed, practice may not change, or at least not so readily.

It is one thing, of course, to understand the origins of labour institutions and regulations and quite another to argue for their contemporary relevance or that they do not give rise to unintended negative consequences – including for those they are intended to benefit. This concern is at the heart of debates on labour market flexibility and the calls for the deregulation of labour markets, which this volume addresses from several angles. Chapters in this volume argue that the theory on which deregulation advocates base their views is fundamentally flawed, for instance as regards the neoclassical theory of labour demand and the conception of working time regulation. Several chapters in this volume also provide critical surveys of prior empirical evidence as well as new evidence on the impact of labour institutions, both micro- and macroeconomic, particularly regarding minimum wages, hours of work, unemployment insurance, trade union rights and civil liberties more generally. Our reading of this evidence suggests that the negative effects of labour institutions and regulations are – at the very least – overstated and are too readily accepted as truths without having undergone sufficient critical scrutiny. This evidence, in turn, reinforces the value of historical perspectives on labour institutions, reminding us that the goals these institutions serve are still valid today: improving workers' health and family life in the case of working hours, reducing poverty and inequality in the case of minimum wages, providing support to displaced workers in the case of unemployment benefits, and giving voice to workers in the case of freedom of association, collective bargaining rights and civil liberties.

Though labour market institutions are important for developing countries, this does not mean, however, that there is no room for improvement. As some of the contributions to this volume point out, too many workers in developing countries are excluded from recourse under the law as well as social security benefits because labour administrators tend to limit inspection to registered medium and large firms. In addition, the minimum wage has lost ground in some developing countries as an effective instrument in defence of the lowest-paid wage-earners because of the practice of linking pension and other government benefits to minimum wage adjustments. This has kept governments from limiting increases in order not to strain their budgets. Similarly, many workers are without access to unemployment benefits or government work programmes during unemployment because a portfolio of programmes has not been developed to meet the competing needs of different workers.

We argue that addressing policy challenges in the world of work must be done through the revision and adoption of national, as well as international, labour laws and policies. Policy-makers should respond proactively to the challenges of globalization through re-regulation, rather than de-regulation. We recognize, however, that many of the policy solutions for the challenges that face developing countries, such as the persistence of the working poor, underemployment and precarious work, lie outside the realm of labour regulations and involve development policy more broadly, particularly regarding macroeconomic policy, the development of the domestic market and strategic engagement with the global economy. These broader debates, however, are beyond the scope of this already wide-ranging volume. It is our hope, nonetheless, that this volume might provide a useful contribution to these debates, if only by shedding light on potentially dangerous paths as well as by affirming the value – both social and economic – of 'good' labour institutions and regulations.

1.2   Overview of the chapters

The chapter that follows is a historical and theoretical analysis of labour institutions. Labour institutions are comprised of labour market institutions – for example, laws regulating working hours, dismissal or collective bargaining – but also non-market institutions such as social norms that affect our decision to enter the labour force and what jobs to pursue. The chapter argues that the labour market flexibility debate has been argued too narrowly, without a sufficient understanding of how labour markets operate and thus the effects as well as limits that regulations can have in influencing the labour market. The chapter includes a historical analysis of the development of labour standards and national and international labour law, its purpose and its effectiveness. The theoretical and historical analysis provides a background to the more detailed critique of the contemporary debate on labour market flexibility that is given in the last part of the chapter.

This analytical chapter is followed by three chapters that address specific labour market institutions – Chapter 3 on working hours regulations, Chapter 4 on training institutions in the informal economy, and Chapter 5 on unemployment insurance. These are followed by Chapters 6 and 7 on wages and, in particular, minimum wages; Chapter 7 also providing a theoretical critique of the labour demand function that is the foundation of neoclassical labour market theory, including theories of (private and social) wage determination and unemployment. Chapters 8 and 9 address trade unions and freedom of association and collective bargaining rights more generally, with Chapter 8 providing a comprehensive survey of the relevant empirical literature and Chapter 9 focussing on employment in informal establishments. Chapters 10 and 11 give legal perspectives on labour institutions in developing countries, with implications for informal employment the central concern of Chapter 10.

In putting together this volume, we hoped to arrive at a collection of chapters that gave adequate representation to all developing regions, but in this we have had mixed success. A disproportionate share of these studies address evidence for Latin America and, indeed, for developed countries. To some extent, this reflects a research bias in the literature itself, particularly the empirical literature on the impact of labour market regulations. That said, the authors of these chapters are careful to suggest lessons and implications for the developing world as a whole, making the limited geographic coverage of the volume less problematic.

In Chapter 3, Sangheon Lee and Deirdre McCann provide a critique of the labour market flexibility debate concerning working time laws and their implementation in the context of debates on labour market rigidities as a cause of poor labour market performance. The authors provide a critical assessment both of influential studies arguing for labour market deregulation and of existing indicators of working time regulation. In addition, the authors construct a preliminary indicator of the 'effective regulation' of working hours, based on legislated hours and the observance rate for legislated hours. The main message of the chapter is that arguments for deregulating labour markets – in this case working time regulations – have been based on overly simplistic indicators that do not adequately address fundamental distinctions in regulations. Moreover, these indicators tend to ignore the original social and economic objectives that led to the development of working time regulations and that remain valid. The authors also find that existing indicators of working time regulation do not provide a good sense of actual working time and that there is a need to better address the *de jure* and *de facto* aspects of working time and the relationship between them.

Chapter 4, by Irmgard Nübler, is a theoretical and empirical analysis of the development of informal training institutions. The critical problem addressed is under what conditions informal entrepreneurs would undertake general skills training for their workers given the risk of being unable to recoup training investments should these workers leave the establishment and possibly even take up work in a competing establishment. This issue is of particular policy importance given current shifts in training responsibilities from the public to the private sector. The theoretical analysis builds on the insights of new institutional economics and, in particular, on game theory to address how informal rules govern the workings of informal labour institutions. The theoretical analysis is illustrated by what the author argues to be failed and successful examples of the provisions of general skill training in informal establishments in Kenya and Togo. The author finds that informal establishments in Togo are willing to finance broad-based apprenticeship training and argues that this results from the existence of informal institutions that provide incentives for employers and workers to cooperate. This contrasts with the case of Kenya, where such informal institutions do not exist and employers generally provide training only in a narrow set of skills.

Chapter 5, by Janine Berg and Matthew Salerno, is an analysis of the development and evolution of unemployment insurance and its applicability to developing countries. The authors discuss the historical reasons behind the adoption of unemployment insurance systems in today's industrialized countries and the lessons that can be gleaned for developing countries surrounding their adoption and evolution. In particular, the authors compare certain characteristics of the economies of the OECD countries at the time of establishment – GDP per capita as well as an economic breakdown by sector – with that of today's middle- and lower-income developing countries. The authors address some of the criticisms often raised concerning establishing such systems, particularly whether developing countries can afford them and whether the high incidence of informal employment makes them too difficult to administer. The authors argue that many middle-income developing countries are well-suited to the adoption of unemployment insurance or other programmes of compensation in case of job loss. Nevertheless, the schemes should be designed in accordance with existing labour institutions and labour market characteristics. This analysis is undertaken in response to the debate on unemployment insurance and severance pay in developing countries as well as the recent policy trend of advancing *flexicurity* systems.

Since the mid-1990s, there has been a renewed interest in the minimum wage as a social and economic policy instrument after decades of heavy criticism. In Chapter 6, François Eyraud and Catherine Saget survey the theoretical and empirical debate on the effect of minimum wages on employment as well as providing an overview of minimum wage setting institutions and a brief summary of their impact in developing countries. Using the ILO database on minimum wage legislation for more than 100 countries, the chapter documents the diversity of the minimum wage setting mechanisms, both in terms of how they are administered and their stated objectives. They also explain the relationship between state wage-fixing policies and collective bargaining in determining minimum wages as well as the potential role of the minimum wage in reducing poverty and inequality. One important point made by the authors is that the two ILO Conventions on minimum wages (No. 26 from 1928 and No. 131 from 1970, the latter with specific reference to developing countries) do not specify a level of minimum wages nor that there be a national minimum wage but rather advocate procedures that are highly flexible to accommodate different levels of economic development, with both Conventions having in common the requirement that all ILO social partners – employers, workers and governments – be consulted in this regard. Based on a review of empirical studies of the effects of the minimum wage, the authors also argue that the negative effect of the minimum wage on employment is often overestimated by standard econometric methods, while its positive effects in reducing wage inequality, sustaining the demand for goods and services and contributing to social cohesion have tended to be ignored in policy debates.

Chapter 7, by Jesus Felipe and J.S.L. McCombie, is a critique of the method typically used to estimate the employment effects of changes in wages, including changes resulting from wage policies and other labour institutions that influence wages, such as the structure of collective bargaining. The studies, which are based on the neoclassical theory of labour demand, nearly always find an inverse relationship between wages and employment, leading to the policy conclusion that wage increases (and increases in labour costs more generally) negatively affect employment. The authors argue that the theory on which this conclusion is made is flawed. Their argument is based on prior theoretical work critiquing the derivation of the neoclassical aggregate demand function, in which the neoclassical labour demand function is embodied. The chapter also shows that an expression identical to the neoclassical labour demand function can be obtained by simply rewriting an accounting identity. This poses a fundamental problem of interpretation of the empirical evidence on effects of changes in wages on employment and, more specifically, of the inverse relationship between wages and employment. The authors illustrate these arguments with an evaluation of minimum wage policy in the Philippines, where it has been argued, based on estimates of the labour demand function, that raising the minimum wage would negatively affect employment. The authors' critique has far-reaching implications given the preponderance of studies based on estimates of the neoclassical theory of labour demand.

In Chapter 8, Zafiris Tzannatos provides a comprehensive review of the empirical literature on the economic effect of unions and collective bargaining, summarizing over a thousand published articles on the topic. Though the author finds that collective bargaining does affect economic performance, the effect is too complex to allow simple positive or negative conclusions. As the author explains, there are over thirty performance indicators, at both microeconomic and macroeconomic levels, that have been used to evaluate performance. And how collective bargaining affects these indicators will depend on whether an economy is closed, open, competitive or monopolistic; the relationship between the government and the trade unions; how collective bargaining is coordinated among social partners; as well as the scope and power of unions and firms. The analysis reveals the complex interaction between formal and informal institutions, and demonstrates that a sole labour market institution or policy cannot be expected to improve economic performance. Rather, what is needed is a complementary 'package' of institutions and policies designed with local conditions in mind.

Chapter 9, by Rosanna Galli and David Kucera, is an empirical study of the relationship between trade union rights and the extent of formal employment. Based on a panel data analysis of 14 Latin American countries, the authors test competing hypotheses of how trade union rights, proxied by 'civic rights', and wage shares in formal employment affect shares of formal and informal employment. Stronger civic rights have been argued to affect economic and social stability both negatively and positively, with attendant implications for investment, economic growth and the growth of formal employment. Higher wage shares in formal employment might also affect formal employment either negatively or positively, with microeconomic effects possibly offset by macroeconomic effects. The analysis of wage shares is also intended to shed light on the employment effects of labour market institutions affecting wage setting, such as the centralization of collective bargaining. The chapter's most important finding is that countries with stronger civic rights have higher shares of formal employment and lower shares of informal employment. In other words, the chapter provides evidence that countries can reach a long run position of stronger civic rights and more formal and less informal employment.

Chapter 10, by José Luis Daza Pérez, is a study of labour administration and the informal economy. The author distinguishes between the legal versus the socioeconomic definition of informality, making the distinction between informality due to the limited scope of legal coverage versus illegality. Workers can be informal because the labour laws of a country exclude certain groups of workers, such as agricultural workers or domestic servants or workers in micro- and small enterprises. At other times, workers are informal not because of exemptions in the law but because employers evade the law. The distinction is important since labour administration systems are based solely on the legal definitions embodied in that country's labour code, thus policies to deter informality and improve enforcement must reflect what is in the law. The study provides an important starting point for developing solutions to mitigate informality in the developing world.

Chapter 11, by María Luz Vega Ruíz, offers a critique of the labour law reforms undertaken in Latin America in the 1990s in pursuit of greater labour market flexibility. The author reviews the principal reforms undertaken in the region with respect to employment contracts, conditions of work, salaries, exclusions for micro- and small enterprises, and collective negotiation. As the author demonstrates, a good number of the reforms were ill-conceived, as evidenced by the 'counter-reforms' that have since taken place in the region, many of which reversed the original policy changes. Moreover, the reforms did not achieve their stated objective of creating employment. But, as the author points out, these reforms were flawed from the outset, as basic labour rights were sidelined in pursuit of greater competitiveness. The author makes clear that there is sufficient scope for flexibility in labour law as international labour conventions are inherently flexible, being the outcome of tripartite negotiations and being subject to periodic review and updating in order to reflect the times. Vega Ruíz argues that the biggest challenge in Latin America concerning labour law is not the extensive regulation of the labour market, but its lack of application, and the need for administrative and judicial reform to ensure its greater coverage.

2
Labour Institutions in the Developing World: Historical and Theoretical Perspectives

Janine Berg and David Kucera

2.1 Introduction

Labour institutions structure all forms of work, rural and urban, formal and informal, from the most visible to the most remote. The rules, practices and policies that are inherent in labour institutions influence almost every aspect of our working lives – how we enter a job, the training we receive to qualify for the job and while on the job, the conditions under which the job is performed (the employment contract including the hours, pay, benefits and safety measures associated with the work), as well as what happens when the job ends. Consider four examples of work in developing countries, two rural and two urban, and the differences in labour institutions among them. These differences reflect the system of production, prevailing social norms, and the substance and reach of the law. The character of our lives, both at home and at work, is shaped by these institutions.

In the Gokwe region of Zimbabwe, one of the most important cotton-growing regions in the country, sharecropping has expanded along with the growth of cotton production and the rapid, internal migration of landless workers.[1] Many of these migrants are from other rural areas, but in the late 1980s and early 1990s, there was also a large influx of migrants displaced from the state-owned iron and steel mills that were restructured in the wake of the country's Economic Structural Adjustment Programme. In this example, the central labour institution is the sharecropping contract and the form it takes: whether it is oral or written, whether it is between family members, its duration, and, of course, how the crops are shared between tenants and landlords. Tenants and landlords determine their shares depending upon who ploughs the land, who provides inputs of fertilizer and seeds, and who is responsible for weeding and harvesting – as well as their respective bargaining power. Disputes over contracts are fairly common and are generally resolved informally by village heads or by the tenants and landlords themselves, though occasionally such disputes result in more formal legal action. The terms of sharecropping contracts evolve over time between tenants and landlords.

9

These changes come about partly in response to lifecycle factors: as land-lords grow older, they tend to become less actively involved in production and cede increasing responsibilities to tenants, who are in many cases family members. This creates dynamism in the system, in that tenants have the prospect to become landlords over time.

On cattle ranches in Paraguay, ranch workers are paid in cash, in credit and in kind (primarily food and housing).[2] Credit payments are redeemable at the ranch store and although the proportion of payment in cash versus credit is fixed by Paraguayan law, these laws are often violated, and ranch workers are commonly charged inflated prices for goods, causing ranch workers to become indebted to their employers. While some ranches pay their workers on a monthly basis, consistent with Paraguayan labour law, others do not. Wages are also higher for non-indigenous workers. Ranches that pay the legislated minimum wage tend to make social security payments, with social security supposing to provide health care, paid sick leave, disability benefits and pensions. Nonetheless, these ranches are relatively isolated and self-contained communities in which the availability of health and education facilities is scarce. There is a gendered division of labour on the ranches, with, for instance, indigenous women working as cooks and maids in the homes of both ranchers and non-indigenous ranch workers. Indigenous persons also rely on traditional subsistence activities such as hunting and fishing.

In India's brassware industry, large, formal enterprises have modern factories and produce for the international as well as the domestic market. But much of the production comes from households which produce intermediate or final goods for the larger, formal manufacturers and traders.[3] The homeworkers earn piece-rates, with piece-rates differing among households depending upon the job performed. The flow of goods among households and larger manufacturers and traders is usually mediated by jobbers, who may also monitor the progress and quality of work. But the jobbers do not mediate labour conditions since household producers lack protection under India's labour laws.[4] Production in the household relies on a variety of labour sources. When demand is high, temporary workers, some of whom are migrants, aid with production. Child labour is also common and helps to supplement family incomes, with piece-rates offsetting children's generally lower productivity.

Working at a maquila in the northern Mexican town of Matamoros has its own set of institutions, many of which are formal.[5] In this town, maquila jobs are allocated by the SJOI, the Union of Industrial Workers and Day Laborers, which screens on a daily basis the hundreds and sometimes thousands of newly arrived migrants according to the profiles demanded by the foreign assembly factories – typically young women in their late teens and early twenties with a secondary education. The women selected for work are hired on a 30-day probation, which shifts to a formal job if the trial is successfully completed. Because these are formal jobs, the workers benefit from regulated working hours, including the payment of overtime, approximately two weeks' paid vacation, as well as severance equal to 20 days for each year of service. All workers are automatically members of the local union, which in contract negotiations managed to negotiate a 40-hour working week as opposed to the legal maximum of 48 hours. The union, however, conceded the employers' legal obligation to pay social security payments on the workers' behalf in 1991 negotiations. The minimum wage serves as a floor to workers' earnings, though its precipitous fall since the early 1980s has meant that workers with families struggle to keep out of poverty. Competition for foreign investment by other maquila towns on the Mexican border as well the threats made by the factories to shift operations to Central America or China, where labour is cheaper, has weakened the ability of workers to bargain for higher wages.

As these four examples illustrate, labour institutions are the outcome of a complex system of social relations, production, and national labour laws. In this chapter, we define labour institutions and discuss their significance for developing countries. As many national labour laws and policies are governed by international standards promulgated by the International Labour Organization (ILO), we provide a history of their formation as well as the past and present role of the ILO in setting and promoting labour standards. This analysis provides a backdrop to the present debate on labour market flexibility, which we summarize and critique. The aim of this chapter is to deepen our understanding of labour institutions, through a discussion of its origins, workings and outcomes. We hope that this will inform the current debate on labour market flexibility, much of which we feel has been based on an evangelical and somewhat irresponsible quest to limit 'rigidities', without due consideration of the workings of labour institutions.

2.2   What are labour institutions?

Labour institutions comprise rules, practices and policies – whether formal or informal, written or unwritten – all of which affect how the labour market works. They are as explicit and long-standing as certain labour laws that we have come to consider as universal rights, but also span the scope of informal practices that reflect the views of society, as well as short-term laws and policies that fade and resurge depending on the policy mood. All countries, irrespective of their level of economic development, have labour institutions. The distinction between countries lies in the degree to which they are embedded in law, whether the law is applied in practice, and the extent that government policies are used to pursue certain objectives. To argue that labour institutions are pervasive is not to argue that they are all desirable or defensible. After all, forced labour is a labour institution and discrimination in employment is sustained by various labour institutions. The point, rather,

Box 2.1 Labour institutions

1. Employment contracts.
2. The mechanisms for controlling and regulating employment contracts.
3. The organization and representation of labour: trade unions, or trade or craft associations.
4. The organization and representation of employers: employers' associations, business associations.
5. The dominant procedures for job search and rules for access to jobs of different types.
6. The methods by which wages are paid.
7. The process of wage fixing.
8. Training and skill institutions.
9. The organization of jobs within the firm.
10. The structure of ownership and control over production.
11. The social and state regulation of self-employment.
12. Social security and income guarantee systems.
13. The conventional standard of life – aspirations regarding consumption, leisure, savings and work.
14. The organization of labour supply, both within and outside the household.

Source: Abridgement of Rodgers (1994).

is that labour institutions – whether good or bad – appear in manifold forms as historically specific outcomes.

Labour institutions encompass labour market institutions – for example, employment protection legislation, hiring halls, and collective bargaining – as well as non-market institutions, such as trade unions and employers' organizations and the work ethic.[6] Box 2.1 gives a list of the dominant labour institutions that condition our working lives, both within and outside of the labour market. Some of the institutions listed are clearly market institutions, but others are not, or are a combination of the two. For example, social security can be provided by the State, the enterprise or through institutionalized private networks, but can also be based on family and communal obligations. Similarly, our decision to leave the labour market may stem from a lack of job opportunities, but may also be due to family commitments.

These 14 labour institutions are determined by, and comprised of, social norms, national labour laws and policies, as well as the system of production. Figure 2.1 is an abstraction of this interplay. The three axes of the triangle affect, but also form part of, labour institutions. For example, trade unions and employers' associations are labour institutions. These institutions bargain over national labour laws and policies. How they bargain and what they

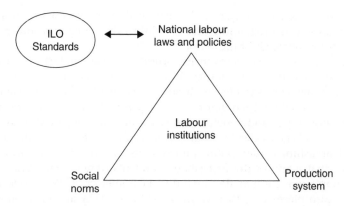

Figure 2.1   Determining labour institutions

bargain over will depend on underlying social norms as well as on the constraints or demands of the production system, as well as national labour laws on freedom of association and collective bargaining. Similarly, the organization of jobs within the firm is a labour institution that is determined by the production system and perhaps national laws, but that can also reflect underlying social norms, such as occupational sex segregation.

National labour laws and policies are formal labour institutions, often embodied in a nation's labour code, and subject to revision over time. Their origin reflects the contested ambitions of different groups of society, chiefly the rights demanded by workers as well as the demands of businesses according to their production needs. National laws are sometimes a 'formalization' of what already occurs informally, though most often they are a remedy to correct that which exists: most fundamentally, the bargaining power disadvantage that workers have vis-à-vis employers.[7] Legal statutes (on, for example, maximum hours, vacations, minimum wages, health and safety regulations), as well as laws protecting freedom of association and collective bargaining, which are considered process rights, serve to strengthen the bargaining power of workers.[8]

Production systems are associated with their own particular labour institutions. The work codes developed are 'sometimes embodie[d] in national law, [or] sometimes left to more local and less formally instituted processes, which govern work relations.'[9] These work codes are part of larger enterprise dynamics including access to capital, relationships with suppliers and competitors, as well as technological development. The actions of businesses do not just reflect one particular labour law, such as employment protection legislation, but rather are a gamut of laws, policies and practices including industrial relations, schooling and training systems, promotion within the firm, and corporate governance.[10] Thus, for example, a company may develop a promotion system based on seniority to ensure loyalty and protect intellectual property, or an industry-wide employers' association may develop a training programme that establishes skill categories and training protocols for the needs of the sector.[11]

Whereas production systems create corresponding labour institutions, they can in turn be constrained by these institutions, particularly if they are formalized in law. For example, the limits on payment in credit in Paraguay, recourse to formal legal action for sharecroppers in Zimbabwe, and regulated working hours, pay and benefits among maquila workers in Mexico, serve to protect workers' weaker bargaining position. Laws can also be instrumental in demolishing certain production systems and creating new ones. Piore explains that many of the first labour standards were directed against the 'sweatshop' production model and industrial homework.[12] When sweatshop workers earn piece-rates, their earnings will fall if they are less productive. Poor working conditions, such as cramped and poorly ventilated work spaces, lower productivity, but since workers are paid piece-wages, only they suffer the cost of the poor conditions. They also suffer the cost of fluctuations in market demand as well as industrial accidents when safety and health standards are ignored. But by regulating working conditions, through provisions on health and safety, child labour, minimum wages, and employment protection, labour standards alter the incentives of employers. Under a system of minimum wages, it becomes in the employers' interest to improve workforce productivity, thus firms are more likely to adopt safety and health standards in their workplaces. Similarly, by making dismissal more difficult, firms have more incentive to train their workers, thereby replacing numerical flexibility with functional flexibility. Mass production is preserved, but the sweatshop, at least in this form, is displaced.

Institutions and policies are also modelled around predominant, or at least perceived, social norms. For example, social security systems that are based on continual contributions over the work life have typically been structured on the 'male breadwinner' model. This system is biased against women as it punishes workers who exit the labour market to care for family members.[13] Moreover, because women typically earn less than men, they also receive lower pension and unemployment benefits – in those instances when they are entitled. Similarly, the gendered division of labour, as described in the above examples, reflects prevailing views about what constitutes women's work and men's work. Homework, paid on a piece-rate system, is a production system that exploits women's responsibilities for homecare and childcare. Laws and policies can be useful tools for countering social norms that disadvantage particular workers. For example, laws to prevent discrimination in hiring and mandating equal pay, as well as training policies for disadvantaged groups, have been helpful in transforming social norms by improving access to the labour market.

Although laws and policies respond to business needs, the concerns of workers and general social norms, the process is constantly evolving and there are often delays in appropriate legal responses. For example, the trend to replace stable, long-term employees with subcontracted workers, often under civil as opposed to labour contracts, has meant that these workers are not privy to the protections of labour law (for example, workers' compensation in case of industrial accidents) and have also encountered difficulty in participating in the social security system. There have been a myriad of policy proposals on how to respond to this trend, including the often-heard argument that the labour market should be further deregulated to make room for the needs of firms operating in a highly competitive, global economy. In June 2006, the International Labour Conference (ILC) of the ILO passed a Recommendation on the Employment Relationship with the purpose of clarifying international definitions of dependent relationships. The Recommendation stated that Members should periodically review relevant laws and regulations 'in order to guarantee effective protection for workers who perform work in the context of an employment relationship'. Governments are to implement national policies to 'combat disguised employment relationships' including the 'use of contractual arrangements that hide the true legal status' of the worker.[14]

Though labour laws and policies are derived from the contested ambitions of different groups, the laws and policies that a nation pursues are also influenced by the Conventions and Recommendations issued by the ILC as well as the technical cooperation and advocacy work done by the International Labour Office. At the same time, these Conventions and Recommendations are also influenced by the experiences of ILO member States in the course of ILC discussions, including experiences with national labour laws and policies. The two-headed arrow in Figure 2.1 reflects this mutual causation. In the next section, we discuss the history of the ILO's formation, its mechanisms for promulgating and supervising the implementation of standards and recommendations on labour rights, as well as debates over its efficacy. We hope that this section will help deepen understanding of the relationship between international labour standards and national labour laws as well as serve as a historical anchor for our later discussion on the current debate on labour market regulations.

2.3 History of labour standards and the ILO

While the first forms of labour regulation concerned the regulation and abolition of slavery and master and servant laws, it was the Industrial Revolution that spawned the modern labour movement and the development of labour law as its own regulatory branch. National laws regulating labour were passed in response to the demands of social reformers and the collective action of trade unions to remedy the 16-hour days without breaks or weekly rest, rampant use of child labour, and barriers to collective action that were typical of the working conditions of early industrialization. The first laws concerned working hours and child labour and though the advances were small, there was widespread conviction that unless all industries in all countries were subject to similar legislation protecting workers, competition would undermine whatever protections were put in place.

By the turn of the nineteenth century a movement had surfaced to establish international labour standards. Trade unions had advocated for international standards since the meetings of the First International in 1866, but it was a group of socially minded academics, the International Association for Labour Legislation, that convened the first diplomatic conference to consider international labour legislation. This conference, assembled in 1905 and 1906 and attended by industrial experts from 15 European countries, passed Conventions prohibiting the use of white phosphorus in the manufacture of matches and restricting night work for women. With some delay, most of the nations attending the conference adopted the Conventions as national legislation. A second conference was then planned for 1914 to consider two more Conventions, one prohibiting night work for children and the other limiting hours of women and children, yet the outbreak of the First World War prevented it from occurring.

Nevertheless, the momentum for international labour standards had emerged. As a result of the efforts of the International Association for Labour Legislation, the International Federation of Trade Unions, and various social movements throughout Europe and the United States to establish international labour standards, one of the first acts of the plenipotentiaries at the 1919 Peace Conference at Versailles was to establish, along with the League of Nations, a Labour Commission with the 'mandate to elaborate a scheme for world labour regulation'.[15] The political interest in regulating labour internationally varied in motive – from humanitarian, to concern over socialist uprising, to concern over unfair competition.[16] Moreover, many delegates to the commission held the belief championed by President Wilson of the United States that by making competition fairer, labour standards would encourage nations with higher standards of living to reduce their trade barriers, thus promoting world trade.[17]

But the task of the Labour Commission was not to catalogue labour conditions necessary for peace, it was to elaborate a 'scheme of an organisation which, in days to come, would enable those who operated it to draw up many charters and apply them to various countries according to different and differing circumstances'.[18] Thus the 36 meetings of the Labour Commission held in the spring of 1919 tackled issues of organization and representation of such an organization, as well as national responsibility in adopting labour legislation. After much debate, it was agreed that the proposed International Labour Organization should include a legislative organ, the International Labour Conference, which should convene annually to draft and adopt Conventions and Recommendations. It was decided that there should be tripartite representation of each country, with employer and worker delegates each having one vote and government representatives having two, based on the recognition that implementation laid with national governments.[19] It was also decided that there should be a Governing Body of the Organization, representing 24 members (12 governments, six employers and six workers)[20] to prepare the agenda for the Conference and under which the International Labour Office would serve. The Office would serve as the secretariat of the Organization and was endowed with the responsibility of collecting information on issues discussed at the Conference.

After much debate, the Commission set a majority of two-thirds for approving Conventions and Recommendations, which States then had to submit to the national authority and, if ratified, embody directly in national legislation.[21] Governments were to report on application of Conventions at regular intervals and those governments that had ratified Conventions but then failed to implement them would be subject to investigation and public denunciation. Non-ratified Conventions and Recommendations were also subject to reporting upon request of the Governing Body, the extent to which 'effect has been given' to the standard in the member State's law and practice, and in the case of a Convention, an explanation of the difficulties that prevented or delayed ratification.

The Commission also attached nine guiding principles for the new organization that member nations were to abide by, with due reference to the stage of a country's industrial development and its 'climate'. These were: that labour 'should not be regarded as merely a commodity or article of commerce', that employers and workers have the right to association, that workers should earn a minimum living wage, that working hours should be limited to an eight-hour day or 48-hour week, that there should be a day of weekly rest, that child labour should be abolished, that there should be equal pay for work of equal value, that laws should not discriminate among workers, and that countries should establish a system of labour inspection.[22] The Labour Commission submitted the general principles of the ILO to a plenary session of the Paris Peace Conference and it was accepted 11 April 1919, thus marking the ILO's establishment.[23]

The first meeting of the International Labour Conference took place that October in Washington, DC, and was attended by delegates from 39 nations from across the globe. Six Conventions were drafted establishing a 48-hour week, creating public administration agencies to monitor unemployment, prohibiting night work for women, mandating six weeks' maternity leave, setting a minimum age for work, and prohibiting night work for young people. In keeping with the Organization's stated recognition of differences between countries' industrial development, the Conventions and Recommendations drafted at the early sessions of the International Labour Conference either noted the exceptions granted to certain member countries or were flexible enough to allow member States to pass national legislation that reflected 'cultural conditions', while improving conditions of work.

Thus, for example, a young person was understood as finishing school and therefore eligible for work at the age of 14 in the Northern European countries but at the age of 12 in Southern Europe and the East.

In the years following, the ILC continued to convene annually, including for special sessions on the maritime industry, adopting standards on a wide range of issues concerning conditions of work and labour administration. Yet there was a growing recognition within the ILO, particularly with the onset of the Great Depression, that labour conditions were affected by economic policies that were beyond the purview of labour legislation. As a result, following the Second World War, the scope of the ILO was expanded to consider the social and economic problems that confronted labour, entrusting the Organization with the 'responsibility ... to examine and consider all international economic and financial policies and measures in light of this fundamental objective [of attaining social justice]'.[24] The 1944 Declaration of Philadelphia, which was annexed to the ILO Constitution in 1946, gave the Organization a renewed purpose, expanding its mandate to consider the fundamental issue of how to create more jobs alongside its original directive of upgrading working conditions through labour standards.

In the wake of a campaign to galvanize ratification of Conventions and commitment to the principles of the Organization which had come out of the 1995 Social Summit in Copenhagen, the ILO adopted the Declaration on Fundamental Principles and Rights at Work. The Declaration states that by virtue of their membership of the Organization, member States have a constitutional obligation to respect and abide by the principles concerning four fundamental rights: freedom of association and collective bargaining, the elimination of forced labour, the abolition of child labour, and the elimination of discrimination at work; these 'core' labour rights are expressed in eight fundamental Conventions.[25] The Declaration also mandates an annual review of member States that have not yet ratified all eight Conventions, which is carried out by a specially constituted body. In addition, as part of the follow-up to the Declaration, each year the Office publishes a Global Report on one of the four fundamental rights, assessing challenges in attaining universal compliance of the principle and identifying those areas that require greater attention and could be advanced through technical cooperation.

As of January 2007, 180 countries were Members of the ILO, 187 Conventions and 198 Recommendations had been adopted and there had been over 7,400 ratifications. Most fields of labour law, as well as guidance on an array of labour market policies, are covered by the ILO Conventions and Recommendations. These standards have become a reference for countries that are establishing and revising their labour codes as they are flexible enough to be applied to member States with different legal systems and at different levels of economic development. The flexibility of the standards is not surprising, given that member States have tripartite representation at the ILC, which drafts and approves Conventions and Recommendations.

Thus, the workers' and employers' delegates at the ILC give their perspective on the likely impact of Conventions and Recommendations, which ultimately influences the form the instrument takes.

Conventions and Recommendations are not designed to impose a standard appropriate for industrialized countries onto developing countries. For example, the Minimum Wage Fixing Convention, 1970 (No. 131), discussed by Eyraud and Saget in Chapter 6, asks member States to establish minimum wages, specifies that social partners should be consulted in the process of fixing minimum wages and delineates certain elements to be taken into consideration in determining the minimum wage levels, such as the needs of workers and families as well as economic factors such as productivity. But the Convention does not advocate a specific wage. Member States that ratify it have the obligation to create minimum wages in those trades that are not governed by collective agreements and ensure that they are enforced, but the wage can be set at a level that the national authorities, in consultation with the social partners, deem appropriate. Moreover, many Conventions and Recommendations concern policies for improving labour market administration, including standards on tripartite consultation, employment services, and labour inspection. For example, the Labour Inspection Convention, 1947 (No. 81), calls for the establishment of a system of labour inspection to ensure enforcement of the legal provisions of the country. Labour inspectors should be independent and well-trained and an annual general report of the work of the inspection services must be made available to the ILO.[26]

Another indication of the flexibility of ILO Conventions and Recommendations, as Vega Ruíz notes in Chapter 11 of this volume, is that they are subject to periodic review and updating in order to reflect changes in the world of work. Some of the more recent Conventions and Recommendations reflect emerging issues such as part-time work and private employment agencies, while many are revisions of earlier standards, for example on child labour, night work for women, and the minimum age for work.[27] Conventions that are no longer considered relevant by the ILC have been 'shelved', meaning that they are no longer open to ratification and countries that had ratified the Convention (but have not 'denounced' it) no longer have to report on implementation.[28] Most of these shelved Conventions date from the 1930s. Periodically the Governing Body convenes working groups to assess the relevance of the labour standards, with the most recent working group concluding its assessment in March 2002.[29]

2.4   International labour standards: Are they relevant?

One of the biggest controversies about ILO Conventions concerns their application and enforcement. Member States are not obligated to ratify ILO Conventions; ratification is voluntary. And although ratification entails certain obligations – specifically to adopt national legislation that meets the standards set forth in the Convention, enforce these laws or policies nationally, as well as report on their application to the ILO – the ILO is limited in its ability to sanction those countries that are in breach of their obligations. There is no enforcement mechanism, but neither is there for any international human rights supervisory mechanism. Rather there are tools of moral suasion. Most noticeably, there is the Committee of Experts on the Application of Conventions and Recommendations. This independent committee, which was established by the Governing Body in 1926, is composed of 20 high-level jurists and meets annually to assess the conformity of national law and practice with the provisions of the ILO Conventions. The experts issue a report documenting countries that have compliance problems and a number of these governments are then summoned to appear at the ILC Committee on the Application of Standards. Through persuasion, and some embarrassment, the committee propels countries to remedy the problem. More detailed 'shaming' mechanisms are the complaints procedures under articles 24 and 26 of the ILO Constitution.[30] A final, more radical 'enforcement' mechanism, which has only been used once by the ILO – in 2000 against Myanmar and its non-compliance with the Forced Labour Convention, 1930 (No. 29) – is article 33 of the ILO Constitution. This article authorizes the Governing Body to recommend to the ILC undertaking action 'as it may deem wise and expedient to secure compliance therewith', including seeking a binding resolution by the International Court of Justice that would be enforceable by the United Nations Security Council.[31]

Since its origins, the relative lack of enforcement mechanisms for international labour standards has been a source of great debate. During the drafting of the labour charter in 1919, the Italian delegate had proposed that conference decisions be binding on national legislatures and that automatic economic sanctions apply to countries who had failed to comply with the standards, unless an exception had been granted. But this was vehemently opposed by the other delegates who disdained the idea of a 'super-parliament' and argued that if such a system were to be adopted States would hesitate to join the ILO.[32] It was thus decided that rather than detailing specific commercial or economic sanctions, the possible sanction and its use would not be specified. Nevertheless, some critics responded that 'leaving the question of sanctions optional rendered the system of penalties illusory'.[33]

In the 1990s, the debate on enforcing labour standards re-emerged with the formation of the World Trade Organization (WTO). Advocates of sanctions argued that a social clause should be attached to international trade agreements to ensure respect for international labour standards, particularly the core standards on freedom of association and collective bargaining, prohibition of forced labour, abolition of child labour, and non-discrimination in employment.

But at the WTO Singapore Ministerial Round in 1996, the Ministers rejected attaching a social clause, as a result of opposition from developing countries that a social clause was a disguised form of protectionism. Nevertheless, the declaration issued at the Ministerial Round acknowledged commitment to the core labour standards as well as to the work of the ILO. Following the ILO's passage in 1998 of the Declaration on Fundamental Principles and Rights at Work, numerous bilateral and multilateral trade agreements have stipulated adherence to the eight fundamental Conventions.

Still, the lack of binding enforcement power of the ILO continues to raise concerns about the Organization's effectiveness. Although some critics contend that the monitoring mechanisms of the ILO operate well and that about 80 per cent of violations that are reported by the Committee of Experts are resolved satisfactorily, others criticize the process by which the complaints chosen for review are selected and bemoan the Organization for not doing more to publicize the Committee's findings. Nevertheless, there is much agreement that the tripartite structure of the Organization is a source of strength. Worker and employer delegates have the opportunity to comment on the reports of their governments, thus aiding assessments of compliance and providing a highly visible check on national activities. Countries are also very reluctant to appear before the ILC Committee on the Application of Standards, attesting to the finding that 'shaming' is one of the more effective methods for assuring compliance for international regulations or agreements.[34]

The ILO thus plays an important function in advocating international labour standards, as well as in providing guidance on the development of standards and their application at the national level. As the legal scholar Brian Langille argues, 'the object of international labour law is not to constrain nations from acting in their own self-interest but to show them where it lies in the first place, and to assist them in achieving it'.[35] For this reason, technical assistance is an important component of the Organization's work, as is advocacy. Advocacy, in fact, is the main vehicle by which international organizations influence national policies. This is true as well of the Bretton Woods Institutions, despite the greater leverage that they have in influencing policy because of their ability to lend money. As explained in an analysis of the advocacy efforts of Robert McNamara, former President of the World Bank,

> the Bank's total lending to developing countries financed roughly less than one percent of the development expenditures of [developing] countries ... [McNamara] understood that one percent cannot change the profile of poverty in these countries, except by setting the right signals. That's why he put so much emphasis on economic sector work, on his policy speeches, on country dialogue, and on signals.[36]

But the important role that the ILO must play in promoting policies to improve social justice does not impair it from also monitoring countries' compliance with standards. Advocacy, guidance and monitoring are complementary approaches for achieving social justice.

2.5   The debate on labour market flexibility

Despite the instrumental role that labour laws and policies play in improving social justice, an important debate has arisen on the effects of labour institutions on economic performance and whether greater 'labour market flexibility' is needed through deregulation. General definitions of labour market flexibility typically are based on dichotomies: *flexibility in work* versus *functional flexibility*; and *external* versus *internal flexibility*.[37] *Flexibility in work* and *functional flexibility* refer to flexibility in production processes, typified by just-in-time production and the ability of workers and machines to change quickly between different tasks and product types. *Internal flexibility* (meaning internal to firms) encompasses the definitions of *flexibility in work* and *functional flexibility*, but also refers to the mobility of workers across a firm's facilities and to the flexibility of payment systems within firms. *Flexibility in employment* and *numerical flexibility* refer to hiring and firing, the use of part-time and temporary workers, hours worked, and the organization of shifts. *External flexibility* encompasses those aspects of *flexibility in employment* and *numerical flexibility* involving the labour market at large and also includes labour mobility across regions, sectors and occupations and wage flexibility.

Many aspects of labour market flexibility such as labour mobility and functional flexibility, are desirable and worth promoting. In practical terms, however, the debates on labour market flexibility have focused on a very specific set of institutions that have played an important role in providing workers with social protection and voice, but that have nonetheless been the targets of 'structural reform' of labour markets. These are employment protection legislation, unemployment insurance, the regulation of working time and working arrangements, and the nature of wage-setting institutions, including their centralization and coordination, as well as the role of unions and collective bargaining.

The basic view of one school of thought – at present the hegemonic school of thought among academics and policy-makers alike – is that protective labour institutions impede the workings of the labour market. This school of thought is described by David Howell as the 'OECD–IMF orthodoxy', reflecting the important role these two institutions played in its promulgation.[38] The OECD's position has undergone a formal reassessment in recent years, with its new empirical analyses leading it, for example, to argue against the negative effect of employment protection legislation and to emphasize the positive effect of 'highly centralized and/or coordinated wage bargaining systems' on aggregate employment, as well as to note that the negative effects of generous unemployment benefits might be offset by active labour market policies. The view to which Howell refers, however, is embodied

in the influential 'OECD Jobs Strategy' of 1994, with four of the ten recommendations advocating greater flexibility with respect to 'working time',
'wages and labour costs', 'employment protection legislation', and 'social
security benefits'.[39] For this 'orthodoxy', labour institutions are argued to
create market inefficiencies and particularly, in this context, to lead to higher
unemployment. This reasoning is based on an abstractly conceived theoretical labour market, defined by an upward-sloping supply curve and a
downward-sloping demand curve for labour. Under conventional supply and
demand analysis, jobs are allocated in a fair exchange between two equal parties that, if left unrestricted, will result in full employment. This framework
does not incorporate the recognized inequality in bargaining that prompted
the creation of labour law. As we discussed earlier, the purpose of labour
law is to address an imbalance in bargaining through protective and process rights, that otherwise lacking, would result in an unfair outcome for
employees.[40]

This conventional supply and demand framework provides the foundation
for a range of theories of unemployment, including the unadorned neoclassical theory of unemployment as well as its offshoots: the theory of the natural rate of unemployment, efficiency wage theory, and job search theory, for
which the 'social wage', which includes unemployment insurance benefits,
is argued to be the key determinant of unemployment. The neoclassical theory of unemployment also provides the foundation for the so-called 'unified
theory' aiming to link patterns of unemployment and earnings inequality,
which are argued to trade off against each other.[41] For the adherents of the
unified theory, the United States is commonly regarded as the archetype of
the lower unemployment–higher inequality model and France and Germany
the archetypes of the higher unemployment–lower inequality model. The
basic argument of the unified theory is that there has been a relative demand
shift away from less-skilled workers in all the advanced countries, resulting
from a combination of skills-biased technical change as well as increased
trade with developing countries having large relative supplies of unskilled
labour. From the viewpoint of less developed countries, the presumption is
that trade expansion would increase the demand for unskilled labour. Yet
the extent of these benefits is also linked to labour market flexibility insofar
as rigidities lead to higher labour costs that in turn hinder the comparative trade advantage of less developed countries. In this sense, debates about
labour market flexibility are also tied up with debates about globalization,
international competitiveness, international labour standards and a 'race to
the bottom'.

In the view of the unified theory, in countries with greater labour flexibility, the relative demand shift away from less skilled workers is argued
to express itself in a fall in wages, though full employment is maintained.
In countries with less labour market flexibility (or so-called rigid labour
laws), this same relative demand shift is argued to express itself in the

inverse – unemployment. But the few, and lucky, low-skilled workers that are able to keep their jobs are higher paid, as a result of an artificially imposed wage floor. These differences in labour market flexibility are attributed largely to differences in labour institutions, particularly minimum wages, but also state-supported institutions such as unemployment insurance. Thus, the differences in unemployment–earnings inequality patterns are argued to reflect a policy choice. Yet the policy choice is generally not held to be neutral, in the sense that the higher unemployment–lower inequality model is commonly held to be an expression of the interests of relatively protected workers versus more vulnerable workers, or the interests of 'insiders' versus 'outsiders' in which insider status is typically associated with full-time, regular employment for males of prime working age, as well as with union membership.

These varying theories of unemployment share common theoretical foundations but are also akin in the sense that they attribute unemployment primarily to microeconomic rather than macroeconomic causes. This shift from macro to micro reflects the retreat from the so-called Keynesian consensus that dominated state policy from the post-Second World War years until the mid-1970s, when traditional Keynesian policies faced difficulty countering rapidly rising unemployment without giving way to inflation. Keynesianism was thus abandoned in favour of macro-stabilization and policies to address perceived deficits in labour supply. For developing countries, the rise of free market orthodoxy was also reflected in the policy shift from import substitution industrialization and its associated state policies limiting trade, controlling exchange rates and using monetary and fiscal policy to stimulate demand, to a policy of free trade, privatization, and a reduced role of the state, based on the belief that unhindered international trade was best able to absorb the abundant surplus labour of these countries.

This orthodoxy has been challenged on two main grounds, theoretical and empirical. One example of the theoretical challenge is provided in this volume by Felipe and McCombie, who provide a criticism of the interpretation of econometric estimates of the demand curve for labour. The authors show how the inverse relationship between wages and employment embodied in the neoclassical labour demand function can be derived by manipulating an accounting identity and argue that this poses a fundamental problem for the interpretation of empirical estimates of employment effects of changes in wages.

Regarding empirical evidence on the effects of labour institutions on economic performance, we do not attempt a survey of the literature,[42] but it is worth highlighting the results of a few seminal and widely-cited studies, considering first country-level and then micro-level econometric studies. While much of this debate and the empirical evidence for it focuses on the (pre-1990s) OECD countries, particularly on the contrast between the United States and 'core' Europe, the micro studies address developing countries, mainly in Latin America.

In 2003, the IMF published a chapter in its *World Economic Outlook* titled 'Unemployment and Labor Market Institutions: Why Reforms Pay Off'.[43] The most definitive results of the study (based on change over time) are, however, contrary to the title of the paper, and provide evidence that labour market institutions 'hardly account for the growing trend [in unemployment] observed in most European countries and the dramatic fall in US unemployment in the 1990s'.[44] Baker *et al.* re-evaluate the findings of prior studies that provided evidence of the negative impact of labour institutions on economic performance for OECD countries.[45] Based on a number of tests of the sensitivity of the findings of these prior studies, the authors conclude that 'the empirical case has not been made that could justify the sweeping and unconditional prescriptions for labour market deregulation which pervade much of the policy discussion'.[46] Their conclusion is supported by the finding that among the wide range of unemployment experiences and labour institutions in Europe, it is those countries with the strongest institutions and welfare states that have performed the best.[47]

In a useful overview of the debates on labour market flexibility, Richard Freeman gives a central role to the IMF and Baker *et al.* studies.[48] He argues that debates on labour market flexibility have been clouded by the 'priors' of the participants, who tend to selectively present empirical evidence that accords with what they wish to believe. Freeman argues that further country-level econometric studies are of limited value and suggests two ways forward to deepen our understanding of the economic impacts of labour institutions. The first is to develop new theoretical understandings of the effects of labour institutions through 'experimental economics lab findings and artificial agent simulations of markets'.[49] Such approaches have yielded useful insights on how wage rigidity is determined by norms of fairness.[50] Freeman notes, however, that 'ultimately it is evidence that ends scientific debate', and in this regard he argues for a second approach centred on microeconomic analyses, specifically studying the behaviour of workers and firms.[51]

Further microeconomic analyses would no doubt shed light on the debates on the economics of labour institutions and flexibility. Yet it is not obvious that microeconomic analyses are less vulnerable to the prejudice of 'priors' than macroeconomic analyses, particularly regarding the interpretation of results and the emphasis with which ambiguous or contrary results are presented. An example of this is provided by the collection of studies in the volume *Law and Employment: Lessons from Latin America and the Caribbean*, edited by J. Heckman and C. Pagés.[52] For instance, summarizing studies on the effects of 'job security provisions' on average employment and unemployment, Heckman and Pagés write: 'The available evidence for LAC countries shows a consistent, although not always statistically significant, negative impact of job security provisions on average employment rates.'[53] Elsewhere in the volume, the authors are less qualified, writing, 'While the aggregate evidence on the effects of job security on the level of employment is incon-clusive, the microstudies assembled here find a large and negative effect of job security on employment.'[54]

There are six studies based on micro data surveyed in the volume, analysing eight countries in the region. Yet for five of these countries – Barbados, Brazil, Chile, Jamaica, and Trinidad and Tobago – Heckman and Pagés find that the studies show no statistically significant relationship found between 'job security provisions' on average employment or unemployment.[55] Summa-rizing the study of Columbia by Kugler, Heckman and Pagés write, that a 'Decline in JS [job security] in 1990 brings a decline in unemployment rates. This is based on computing the net effect of changes in hazard rates, in and out of unemployment, induced by a reduction in JS.'[56] The study, however, assesses the impact of the change in 1990 until the mid-1990s, during which there was an overall decline in unemployment rates in the country. That is, it addresses the impact of weakening job security on unemployment only during a period of macroeconomic expansion, but the effects of job security on hazard rates into and out of unemployment are likely to be asymmetrical over expansions and recessions and possibly offsetting in the long run. This is the view suggested by Kugler, who concludes her study writing that 'the greater flexibility in hiring and firing after the reform is likely to translate into increased hiring relative to firing during expansions but in increasing firings relative to hiring during recessions'.[57]

The two studies for which there is statistically significant evidence of a negative effect of job security provisions are concerned with Argentina and Peru.[58] In sum, only two of the eight country analyses surveyed by Heckman and Pagés show a statistically significant negative relationship between job security provisions and average employment or unemployment; the other six do not. This is not to argue that microeconomic analyses cannot provide a useful way forward in understanding these relationships. Rather the point is that the findings of microeconomic studies are not necessarily less ambigu-ous than findings of macroeconomic studies nor is their interpretation less malleable to shaping by 'priors'.

In addition to microeconomic analyses, what other approaches might yield useful evidence on the economics of labour market institutions? One important avenue is further research on the historical development of labour institutions, addressing the context in which these institutions arose, the problems they were intended to address, and the extent to which they are still viable in the current era of globalization. Useful insights regarding labour institutions and the welfare states more generally are provided by Howell regarding the OECD countries. He writes:

> Notably, the case for the welfare state has been made on efficiency as well as equity grounds. The Great Depression helped teach the lesson that too much poverty, inequality, economic insecurity, and lack of access by

large parts of the population to basic needs ... can cripple economic efficiency. ... With the early postwar period, the efficiency implications of the argument were extended. ... The right to join a union and bargain collectively can increase worker voice, encourage stability in industrial relations, promote on-the-job training, and reduce the pressure on taxpayers to maintain acceptable standards of living. ... The provision of unemployment insurance and assistance would not only help workers in times of need but would facilitate job search.[59]

Several chapters in this volume argue on behalf of labour institutions from such historical perspectives, shedding light on their role in contributing to both economic efficiency and social justice. These include Berg and Salerno on unemployment compensation, Daza Pérez on informal employment, Eyraud and Saget on minimum wage setting institutions, Lee and McCann on working time regulations, Nübler on training institutions, and Vega Ruiz on labour law reform. It would seem, nonetheless, that our understanding of labour institutions and employment in developing countries would benefit from further studies having a consistent emphasis on their historical development and addressing a wide range of institutions for countries at different levels of development.

2.6 Conclusion

In this chapter, we have sought to define labour institutions and address their historical origin and evolution. Our purpose is to illustrate that labour institutions are embedded in social norms as well as in prevailing systems of production. Labour laws and policies respond to this context with the intent of improving social justice for workers by levelling and limiting bargaining through laws that protect freedom of association and collective bargaining as well as mandating standards on conditions of work, many of which are not subject to international agreement. As such, labour institutions should not be envisaged as a cost on the economy that slows economic growth. Yet the view that countries, particularly developing countries, cannot afford laws and policies to protect workers has unfortunately dominated policy debates. It is based on the neoclassical labour market theory and the conventional supply and demand framework, which does not consider asymmetries in bargaining or account for the endogeneity of labour institutions. By addressing the array of institutions that influence the labour market, we hope to have improved readers' understanding of how the labour market functions and, in doing so, contribute to shifting the policy debate away from a 'deregulate or not' discussion to one that promotes enacting labour laws and policies that respond to the evolution of social norms and production needs, while upholding the pursuit of social justice.

Notes

1   P. Nyambara (2003) 'Rural Landlords, Rural Tenants, and the Sharecropping Complex in Gokwe, Northwestern Zimbabwe, 1963–79', in M. Roth and F. Gonese (eds), *Delivering Land and Securing Livelihoods: Post-Independence Land Reform and Resettlement in Zimbabwe* (Harare: CASS).

2   Anti-Slavery International and International Working Group for Indigenous Affairs (1997) *Enslaved Peoples in the 1990s: Indigenous Peoples, Debt Bondage and Human Rights* (London and Copenhagen: Anti-Slavery International and International Working Group for Indigenous Affairs).

3   Based on R. Ghosh Singh, N. Raj and H. Sekar (eds) (2002) *Hard Labour at a Tender Age: Child Labour in the Home-based Industries in the Wake of Legislation* (Noida: V.V. Giri National Labour Institute), as well a visit to the industry in India in 2004.

4   Ibid., p. iii.

5   Based on W.M. Adler (2000) *Mollie's Job: A Story of Life and Work in the Global Assembly Line* (New York: Touchstone Press) and M.L. Vega Ruíz (2004) *La Reforma Laboral en América Latina: 15 años después* (Geneva: ILO).

6   This discussion is based on G. Rodgers (1994) 'Institutional Economics, Development Economics and Labour Economics', in G. Rodgers (ed.), *Workers, Institutions and Economic Growth in Asia* (Geneva: International Institute for Labour Studies).

7   A useful notion in this regard is J.K. Galbraith's concept of the 'countervailing power', that, with the rise of powerful employers, markets function best when countervailing institutions exist, most relevantly workers' organizations and governments and law. Galbraith argues that workers are 'highly vulnerable' with respect to employers because of their 'comparative immobility', an asymmetry which if anything has increased in the current era of globalization. For Galbraith, when workers are unable to develop sufficiently strong countervailing institutions, the role of governments and law becomes particularly important (see J.K. Galbraith (1952) *American Capitalism: The Concept of the Countervailing Power* (Boston: Houghton Mifflin Company)).

8   B. Langille (2005) 'What is International Labour Law For?' (Geneva: International Institute for Labour Studies).

9   M. Piore (2004) 'Rethinking International Labor Standards', in William Milberg (ed.), *Labor and the Globalization of Production: Causes and Consequences of Industrial Upgrading* (Baskingstoke: Palgrave), p. 262.

10   P.A. Hall and D. Soskice (2001) 'An Introduction to Varieties of Capitalism', in P. Hall and D. Soskice (eds), *Varieties of Capitalism: The Institutional Foundations of Comparative Advantage* (Oxford: Oxford University Press).

11   Ibid.

12   Piore (2004).

13   S. Deakin (2001) *Renewing Labour Market Institutions* (Geneva: International Institute for Labour Studies).

14   International Labour Conference Provisional Record 21A, 95th Session (2006) (Geneva: ILO).

15   G.N. Barnes (1926) *History of the International Labour Office* (London: Williams and Norgate), p. 38. Barnes was the head of the English delegation to the Labour Commission.

16   These sentiments would be reflected in the preamble to the ILO Constitution written by the Commission, which recognized the 'injustice, hardship and privation' of large numbers of people and how it could 'produce unrest so great that the peace

and harmony of the world are imperilled' as well as become 'an obstacle in the way of other nations which desire to improve the conditions in their own countries'.

17 E. Lorenz (2001) *Defining Global Justice: The History of U.S. International Labour Standards Policy* (Notre Dame: University of Notre Dame Press).

18 Barnes (1926), p. 42.

19 Another source of debate concerned the status of the colonies. The Commission decided that self-governing colonies should have independent representation and voting rights, similar to other member States. Regarding non-self-governing territories, it was decided that 'Conventions adopted by the metropolitan country should be applicable to its non-self-governing territories "subject to such modifications as local conditions may render indispensable"' (A. Alcock (1971) *History of the International Labour Organisation* (London: Macmillan), citing Shotwell, p. 33).

20 The Governing Body has since been expanded to 56 members: 28 government, 14 employers and 14 workers.

21 An important source of contention concerned national responsibility for adopting and abiding by the international Conventions. Samuel Gompers, president of the American Federation of Labor, and chair of the Commission argued that the federal system of the United States precluded it from ratifying Conventions as social policy was the domain of state governments. On these grounds, the commission decided that federal governments could regard Conventions as Recommendations.

22 Appendix II General Principles (The Labour Charter).

23 After the League of Nations ceased its activities, the ILO continued as an independent agency until it became a specialized agency of the United Nations in 1946.

24 *Declaration of Philadelphia*, 1944, Annex to the Constitution of the ILO. See E. Lee (1994) 'The Declaration of Philadelphia: Retrospect and Prospect' in *International Labour Review*, 133(4), for an analysis of the origins and purpose of the Philadelphia Declaration.

25 The eight fundamental Conventions are Freedom of Association and Protection of the Right to Organize Convention, 1948 (No. 87); Right to Organize and Collective Bargaining Convention, 1949 (No. 98); Forced Labour Convention, 1930 (No. 29); Abolition of Forced Labour Convention, 1957 (No. 105); Minimum Age Convention, 1973 (No. 138); Worst Forms of Child Labour Convention, 1999 (No. 182); Equal Remuneration Convention, 1951 (No. 100); and Discrimination (Employment and Occupation) Convention, 1958 (No. 111). The Worst Forms of Child Labour Convention, 1999 (No. 182) was adopted by the ILC one year following the adoption of the Declaration and added to the list of fundamental Conventions.

26 A useful typology of labour standards, provided by Sengenberger, distinguishes among protective, participatory and promotional ILO Conventions. For example, Conventions addressing working time, employment protection and minimum wages are protective; Conventions addressing freedom of association and collective bargaining are participatory; and Conventions addressing training, employment and the establishment of labour administrations are promotional. See W. Sengenberger, 'Protection–Participation–Promotion: The Systematic Nature and Effects of Labour Standards', in W. Sengenberger and D. Campbell (eds) (1994) *Creating Economic Opportunities: The Role of Labour Standards in Industrial Restructuring* (Geneva: International Institute for Labour Studies).

27 L. Swepston (1994) 'The Future of ILO Standards', *Monthly Labor Review*, 117(9): 16–23.

28 As of 2006, 24 Conventions had been shelved and five had been withdrawn. Withdrawal means that the Convention never entered into force because an insufficient

number of states ratified it. ILO Conventions include denunciation clauses, which give countries the right to denounce their obligations to that convention, after a specified period of time, usually ten years. Thus, the country no longer has to uphold the commitments entailed by ratifying that convention, including conformity with national law or reporting requirements.

29   For a listing of the 75 ILO Conventions that are considered 'up-to-date', see: http://www.ilo.org/ilolex/english/index.htm

30   Article 24: 'In the event of any representation being made to the International Labour Office by an industrial association of employers or of workers ... the Governing Body may communicate this representation to the government against which it is made, and may invite the government to make such statement on the subject as it may think fit.' Article 26: 'Any of the Members shall have the right to file a complaint with the International Labour Office if it is not satisfied that any other Member is securing the effective observance of any Convention which both have ratified in accordance with the foregoing articles.'

31   See ILC Provisional Record 95th Session, Geneva 2006, Agenda Item 2, for a discussion of the case against Myanmar and the options available to the ILC (www.ilo.org).

32   A. Alcock, *History of the International Labour Organisation*, p. 31. It was also argued, moreover, that the different levels of economic development and different forms of government, particularly federal systems, did not permit such a system.

33   Ibid. Alcock is summarizing the objections of Fontaine, French delegate to the Labour Commission.

34   J. Braithwaite and P. Drahos (2005) *Global Business Regulation* (New York: Cambridge University Press), p. 239.

35   Langille (2005), p. 17.

36   Interview of Mahbub ul Haq given for the World Bank Oral History Program, 3 December 1982 and cited in D. Kapur *et al.* (1997) *The World Bank: Its First Half Century*, vol. 1 (Washington: Brookings Institution Press), p. 271.

37   Cf. M. Brodsky (1994) 'Labor Market Flexibility: A Changing International Perspective', *Monthly Labor Review*, 117(11); J. Curry (1993) 'The Flexibility Fetish: A Review Essay on Flexible Specialisation', *Capital & Class*, 50(2).

38   D.R. Howell (2005) 'Introduction', in D.R. Howell (ed.), *Fighting Unemployment: The Limits to Free Market Orthodoxy* (New York: Oxford University Press), p. 6.

39   OECD (1994) *The OECD Jobs Strategy: Facts, Analysis, Strategies* (Paris: OECD). For a reassessment of the 'OECD Jobs Strategy', see, for example, the 2006 *OECD Employment Outlook: Boosting Jobs and Incomes* (Paris: OECD), particularly the summary of main findings on pp. 208–9.

40   Langille (2005).

41   F. Blau and L. Kahn (2002) *At Home and Abroad: US Labor Market Performance in International Perspective* (New York: Russell Sage).

42   In this regard, see D. Baker, A. Glyn, D.R. Howell, and J. Schmitt (2005) 'Labor Market Institutions and Unemployment: A Critical Assessment of the Cross-Country Evidence', in D. Howell (ed.), *Fighting Unemployment: The Limits of Free Market Orthodoxy* (New York: Oxford University Press).

43   IMF (2003) *World Economic Outlook* (Washington, DC: IMF).

44   Ibid., p. 134.

45   Baker *et al.* (2005).

46   Ibid., p. 109.

47   Howell, op. cit. and P. Auer (2000) *Employment Revival in Europe* (Geneva: ILO).

48 R. Freeman (2005) 'Labour Market Institutions without Blinders: The Debate Over Flexibility and Labour Market Performance', NBER Working Paper 11286 (Cambridge, MA: National Bureau of Economic Research).

49 Ibid., p. 17.

50 J. Agell (1999) 'On the Benefits from Rigid Labour Markets: Norms, Market Failures, and Social Insurance', *The Economic Journal*, 109(453).

51 Freeman (2005), p. 19.

52 J. Heckman and C. Pagés (eds) (2004) *Law and Employment: Lessons from Latin America and the Caribbean* (Chicago: University of Chicago Press).

53 Ibid., p. 62.

54 Ibid., p. 85. Cf. also J. Heckman, M. Ljunge, and K. Ragan (2006 (1 June draft)) 'What are the Key Employment Challenges and Policy Priorities for OECD Countries'. Paper for Presentation on Boosting Jobs and Incomes: Lessons from OECD Country Experiences, Toronto, 15 June 2006, p. 3.

55 See the summary table in Heckman and Pagés (2004), pp. 58–9.

56 Ibid.

57 A. Kugler (2004) 'The Effect of Job Security Regulations on Labor Market Flexibility: Evidence from the Columbian Labor Market Reform', in Heckman and Pagés (eds) (2004), p. 226.

58 Neither are these studies without their ambiguities. Most strikingly, the study for Peru does not show a statistically significant relationship between a measure of job security provision ('expected severance payments') for three of six specifications looking at three sub-periods from 1987 to 1997 by sector and firm level data and two of these six specifications show a statistically significant *positive* relationship between labour cost and labour demand (J. Saavedra and M. Torero (2004) 'Labor Market Reforms and Their Impact over Formal Labor Demand and Job Market Turnover: The Case of Peru', in Heckman and Pagés (eds) (2004), p. 155).

59 Howell, 'Introduction', p. 8.

3
Measuring Labour Market Institutions: Conceptual and Methodological Questions on 'Working Hours Rigidity'

Sangheon Lee and Deirdre McCann[1]

3.1 Introduction

Research on the effects of labour market institutions on employment performance has recently been extended from industrialized to developing countries, using institutional indicators far more extensive in their coverage than those at the core of the OECD debates. These indicators extend to the regulation of working conditions, including working time, and are being used as the basis for the contention that 'rigid' regulation of employment conditions is to a large extent responsible for aspects of poor labour market performance such as low productivity and high unemployment and informal employment.

Among the efforts that have been made towards quantifying, comparing and assessing the impact of these kinds of laws, the most prominent are those carried out by Botero *et al.*[2] and the World Bank.[3] Their assessment of the existing regulations in developing countries has been overwhelmingly negative. The World Bank has argued that 'beyond adopting and enforcing [the ILO's fundamental principles], governments struggle to strike the right balance between labour market flexibility and job stability. *Most developing countries err on the side of excessive rigidity*, to the detriment of businesses and workers alike.'[4]

Such views have been the subject of severe criticism from trade unions. The ICFTU and Global Unions, for example, have suggested that the World Bank index is 'based on the simplistic premise that any kind of labour regulation, other than those strictly limited to the core labour standards, is inherently bad for development and should be removed'.[5] Despite the significance of this debate, however, few research attempts have been made to evaluate these indexes. One notable exception is that by Bertola *et al.*, which used the World Bank's Employment Rigidity Index but questioned its premises.[6]

This research does not, however, examine the quality of the Index, except to indicate its potential problems, based on the experiences of Latin American labour markets.

There is, then, an urgent need to broaden the research towards investigating the existing indicators and the claims being made for their policy implications, and evaluating the role of labour regulations from a perspective that takes into account the policy rationales that underlie them.[7] Since the adoption of the ILO Declaration of Fundamental Principles and Rights at Work in 1998,[8] this kind of research has in the main been devoted to laws related to these fundamental principles (freedom of association; freedom from forced labour and child labour; and non-discrimination in employment).[9] The risk of confining the research to the core standards, however, is that, as Alston and Heenan have argued, the kinds of measures mandated by these instruments could come to be viewed as the central features of acceptable labour market regulation, rather than an absolute minimum of protection.[10] Excluded are the much more extensive range of protections that constitute the international labour code, including those on working conditions such as health and safety, wages and working time.

This chapter represents a modest and preliminary attempt to investigate the quality of the existing institutional indicators that relate to the ILO's 'technical' or working conditions standards. It focuses exclusively on working time laws, considering the extent to which working time indicators are conceptually and methodologically sound and questioning their relevancy to understanding actual working time patterns. While this study considers only working time, we believe that the conceptual and methodological questions raised have broader application to the measurement of labour market regulation.

The rest of the chapter is constructed as follows. After reviewing the existing indicators on working time regulation in section 3.2, the conceptual and methodological questions underlying these indicators are examined in section 3.3, where it is argued that they lack a proper consideration of the rationales for working time regulation, so that these indicators risk regarding any form of regulation as 'rigid'. It will also be suggested that what is required is a sound understanding of how different elements of working time regulation are articulated in the context of country-specific conditions. Section 3.4 investigates another critical issue, the distinction between *de jure* and *de facto* regulation, which is frequently alluded to without any proper analysis or empirical evidence of the influence of working time laws on actual working time arrangements. Based on the notion of 'observance' of labour legislation and the related indicator the 'observance rate', an Effective Regulation Index (ERI) is constructed, which shows that the relationship between working time regulation, income, and the observance of legal measures is not clear-cut, and, especially in low-income countries, often very complex. As a result, it is suggested that the allegedly negative employment effects of working time 'rigidity' are questionable. The chapter concludes in section 3.5 by identifying avenues for future research.

3.2   A review of the indicators

The utility of indicators in evaluating the effect of labour market institutions is apparent. When the required information is either not readily available or too costly, an indicator can be developed as an alternative. By definition, then, an indicator should be directly associated with the required variable such that differences in the values of the variable (called the 'latent' variable) mirror differences in the values of the indicator. In other words, the indicator needs to be valid in the sense that it actually measures what it is supposed to measure. Validity, then, is one of the key properties that an indicator should meet to be used in empirical analysis.[11]

With respect to working time indicators, although the underlying motivation is sometimes unclear, they appear to be intended to measure the constraints imposed on firms in adjusting the duration and timing of their working hours and the impact of working time laws. While it is obvious that effective adjustment of working time is an essential element of enterprise adaptation to changing market circumstances, it is difficult to know what constraints are actually in place at the workplace, and working time regulations can be seen as indicative of these constraints.

To this end, two approaches are being used in the current indicators, which are based on either the ratification of the international standards or on the texts of domestic working time laws.

Ratification of the international standards

The first method for international comparison of working time is to use as a proxy the ratification of working-time-related international standards. This method is widely used for ILO's core labour standards. However, at least with respect to working time laws, its usefulness is rather limited. One illustration is the ratification record of the Hours of Work Conventions (Nos 1 and 30), which include a 48-hour limit on weekly hours for industry, commerce and offices.[12] Ratification of these Conventions appears to have had limited impact on actual working hours. As Figure 3.1 demonstrates, the proportion of paid employees who are working more than 48 hours (19.4 per cent) is equally high in countries that have ratified both Conventions as in those that have ratified neither.[13] Moreover, countries that have ratified only one of the Conventions (for example, Canada, France, and Norway) have a lower incidence of 'excessive hours' than those that have ratified both. It is difficult, then, at least with respect to weekly hours limits, to argue that ratification accurately reflects the actual constraints placed on workers and employers in different countries in organizing working time.

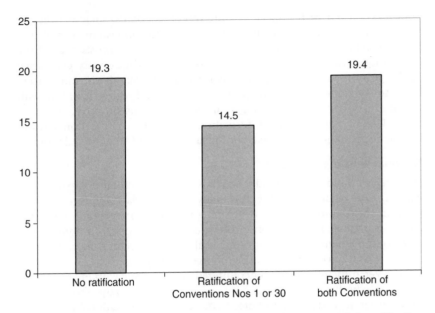

Figure 3.1　Proportion of workers working more than 48 hours per week (by ratification record, % of paid employees: unweighted mean of national averages)
Source:　ILO Working Time Database and ILOLEX.

Reliance on ratification rates also excludes from consideration working hours regulations in countries that have not ratified the Conventions, even when they are broadly in line with the international standards. A recent review of the working time laws of more than 100 countries, for example, found that most have enacted a normal weekly hours limit that matches or exceeds that required by the Forty-Hour Week Convention, 1935 (No. 47), despite this instrument having been ratified by only 14 member States.[14] And only two countries were found to have weekly limits that exceed the 48-hour normal limit of Conventions Nos 1 and 30, despite these standards being ratified by a total of only 55 member States.

Ratification of international Conventions, then, can be a poor indicator of the influence of the standards they contain.[15] It should be noted that ratification can depend on a wide range of factors. For example, Conventions Nos 1 and 30 contain a number of detailed requirements that may curtail their ratification. Most obviously, they require that working hours in principle be arranged in an even 8-hour per day pattern (Convention No. 1, Article 2(b)). And their 48-hour limits can be averaged over a period of longer than a week only in 'exceptional cases'. The degree of flexibility inherent in the working time laws of many countries, then, would prevent them from ratifying these standards, even though their weekly limits are in line with the Conventions.

Moreover, even with respect to more recent standards, such as Convention No. 47, which tend not to have such detailed provisions, ratification may depend on factors as diverse as the current ratification strategy of the International Labour Office, the ILO's standing in the country concerned or the government's attitude towards international standards, rather than being solely a question of whether the national legal regime is in line with the international standards. As a result, although a useful proxy when no more detailed national-level information is available, ratification rates of international standards can be a poor measurement of labour regulation.

National working time laws

National legislation is a more advanced basis for international comparisons of working time regulation and textual analysis of these laws tends to be relied on in the recent work towards developing indicators on working time regulation. It permits a recognition of the specific regulatory techniques being used to implement the Conventions. It also allows account to be taken of countries that have not ratified the international standards.

However, difficulties can be encountered in comparing working time regulations due both to their complexity and to the considerable cross-country variations in regulatory techniques.[16] For example, the relationship between limits on normal hours of work and other elements of working time laws, such as provisions on overtime hours, rest periods and night and weekend work, presents a challenge for establishing a single composite index of working time for statistical analysis.

This has often led researchers to rely on their 'overall' judgements about the 'rigidity' of working time legislation. Such an impressionistic indicator has been used in several studies, including by the OECD[17] and Nickell,[18] both of which concluded that the 'rigidity' of labour standards, including those on working time, has little impact on labour supply and demand across OECD countries.[19]

A more systematic and extensive investigation of national working time standards has been carried out by Rodrik, who compiled data on 'the statutory hours of work in a normal working week in manufacturing or construction', 'days of annual leave with pay in manufacturing', and the ratification of ILO standards.[20] A regression analysis demonstrated that low standards were associated with comparative advantages in labour-intensive goods such as textiles and clothing, but that this correlation was not strong. The only exceptions were the statutory normal hours (the limits beyond which overtime premia are required), which were found to have statistically significant impacts on labour cost advantages. However, the extent to which the statutory provisions were associated with *actual* constraints on enterprises was not investigated.

The most extensive work carried out so far in measuring working time regulation has been that conducted by Botero *et al.* and the World Bank.[21] These cover a range of key aspects of working time regulation and have global geographical coverage. While both seem to share the same data sources and include a working time index as a subset of an 'employment law index'[22] and an 'Employment Rigidity Index',[23] the methods by which they measure 'rigidity' differs. Botero *et al.* measure the cost of increasing working hours, while the World Bank indicators measure five areas in which firms' flexibility in adjusting working time is restrained (night work, weekend work, daily hours, the length of the working week and paid annual leave). Despite these differences, both studies conclude, based on a rather simple bivariate correlation analysis, that 'rigidity' of employment is associated with large informal employment and high unemployment, especially among vulnerable groups such as women and young and older workers. Moreover, it is suggested that this is particularly true of developing countries, which are adopting labour laws better suited to countries at higher levels of development and thereby damaging their development. In the words of a recent World Bank report,

> Many developing countries have adopted far-reaching regulations on [working time] – in some cases going beyond what is on the books in most developed countries. ... Even among countries at similar stages of development, the differences in regulations can be large, with significant effects on labor costs and on the ability of firms to accommodate fluctuations in demand.[24]

While these conjectures and comparisons may appear rather simplistic and even naïve to many development economists, sociologists and labour lawyers, their implications are not trivial. If these observations are correct, 'rigid' working time regulation in particular, and employment regulation in general, are to a large extent responsible for the sluggish labour market performance of many developing economies, and deregulation should be at the top of their priority lists for reform. For this reason, these two sets of indicators will be the focus of the discussion in the rest of this chapter.

3.3 Methodological and conceptual questions on measuring working time 'rigidity'

Working time laws: content and policy objectives

A preliminary point that can be made about the current indicators on working time regulation is that the understandings of the legislative measures being drawn on are flawed in some regards. For a number of countries, the indicators are being miscalculated due to misunderstandings about the structure of working time legislation. Most significantly, there appears to be a degree of confusion as to whether hours limits represent normal limits (on hours worked before overtime payments are due) or maximum limits (on all working hours, including overtime). The World Bank, for example, cites Ireland and the United Kingdom as permitting 48-hour working weeks.[25] However, these limits are *maximums*, imposing a ceiling on both normal working hours and overtime (and therefore mirroring the European Union's 48-hour maximum).[26] Ireland and the United Kingdom cannot, therefore, be grouped with countries that mandate a 48-hour *normal* hours limit, which can be exceeded by overtime hours. Their 48-hour maximums represent a more stringent legal standard. Similar confusion is also reflected in Botero *et al.*[27]

These kinds of methodological issues are minor and can be easily remedied. More significant are the questions that can be raised about the conceptual foundations on which indicators of 'rigid regulation' are grounded. When labour market institutions such as employment conditions laws are measured so as to investigate their effects, careful consideration should be given to the rationales for their existence. However, as Pissarides has pointed out with respect to employment protection regulations, the analysis of these measures 'has been mostly conducted within a framework that does not justify its existence'.[28] In the literature on indicators, it has often been the case that the benefits of labour market institutions are not clearly recognized while a labour market 'without friction', which is to say without regulation, is assumed as ideal, or as having no rigidity.[29] In this work, then, the line between rigidity and protection is rendered very thin.

This point can be made about the indicators on working time. It is our contention that the understanding of the role and purpose of working hours regulation that underlies these indicators does not reflect a proper grasp of the policy goals of working time regulation. The dominant concerns underlying working time laws in many jurisdictions have been the negative externality of long working hours, notably their negative affects on health and hourly productivity.

Individual employers often fail to take these costs into account in determining working hours, with the result that the market fails and working hours are set at a socially inefficient level.[30] Similarly, individuals who are working very long hours are often oblivious to the potentially (in many cases long-term) negative consequences for their health and family life.[31] In some cases, this may be attributed to these workers having insufficient information. However, there is evidence that workers often 'choose' to believe that long hours do not pose any risk in their individual cases, especially when they have no other option but to work long hours.[32] In this situation, where so-called cognitive dissonance exists, legislation is aimed at achieving Pareto improvements in the economic sense.[33]

In the legal arena, these concerns about the protection of workers' health have resulted in reasonable limits on working hours being conceptualized as fundamental social rights and therefore an essential element of labour law regimes, irrespective of their economic implications. This approach is explicit in the European-level measure, the EU Working Time Directive, in its caution that '[t]he improvement of workers' safety, hygiene and health at work is an objective which should not be subordinated to purely economic considerations'.[34] This status accorded to working time protections, however, is not reflected in their treatment in the indicators, as is discussed below with respect to the World Bank's Rigidity of Hours Index.

Of course, some 'benevolent' employers may take initiatives to internalize these costs, but if competition is intensified within a narrow margin of labour cost advantages, this initiative may not be sustainable. This situation is similar, then, to the 'Prisoners' dilemma' game, which requires coordination between players in order to achieve mutually beneficial outcomes. In the field of working time, this coordination has been ensured by statutory regulation (or collective agreements if the coverage is close to universal, as is the case in Denmark).

Certainly, it must be recognized from the outset that this market failure argument simply provides a rationale for working time regulation, but does not justify all existing measures. For instance, the health aspects of working time regulation cannot play a significant role in explaining the 35-hour legislation in France, a measure aimed primarily at boosting employment. The same goal was embodied in the collectively agreed reductions in the working week in Germany in the 1990s, and has been an element of the policy debate more recently in Chile.[35] Moreover, other policy objectives, grounded primarily in social goals, are often absent from the debates in the economic literature. Ensuring workers have adequate time outside of paid labour, which was initially conceived of as permitting them to engage in leisure pursuits and more recently to discharge caring and domestic obligations, has also been part of the debate at the international level and in many countries.[36] And laws mandating a weekly rest period, although they partially embody a health and safety goal, also have the aim of permitting workers to share a communal rest period on the traditional or customary day of rest in their country.

It is also plausible that the costs of certain kinds of working time regulations could exceed their benefits, but that they are nonetheless sustained due to the power of vested interests.[37] Some regulations can be 'good' and others 'bad', in terms of whether they advance the policy goal for which they were introduced. However, the existence of inefficient or ineffective regulation does not justify the extreme but increasingly common view that the regulation of employment conditions is no more than the result of 'rent-seeking' by 'insiders', typically organized and relatively well paid. And further analysis of the relationship between regulatory measures and their impact is needed to assess the balance between their costs and benefits.

The extent to which the rationales of market failure and rent-seeking are applicable to the existing regulations on employment conditions is not always easy to determine, mainly because it is difficult to operationalize them for empirical testing. Botero *et al.*, for example, hypothesized these two as the 'efficiency' and 'political power' theories, respectively.[38] The efficiency theory corresponds to the market failure argument mentioned above, although they argue that its implication would be that rich countries should regulate less because they have fewer market failures. This prediction can easily be rebutted even without much data, as it is obvious that rich countries tend to have developed more sophisticated protection systems. It should be noted that the market failure argument as such does not imply this prediction, as there is little reason to believe that economic growth can reduce the extent of market failures. Agell, for example, observed that among OECD countries, trade openness is correlated with strong labour market institutions and predicted that globalization, which could mean increased risks for workers, would increase demand for labour market 'rigidity'.[39]

The World Bank Rigidity of Hours Index: Measuring 'rigidity' or 'decency'?

The relevance of empirically testing the 'net benefits' of employment conditions regulation is by and large dependent on how these regulations are measured. The existing studies are particularly problematic in this regard. The most vivid example is probably the World Bank's Rigidity of Hours Index (henceforth, RHI). The RHI, which ranges from 0 to 100, is a simple average of five binominal indicators that question, with respect to national working time legislation,

Whether night work is unrestricted[40]
Whether weekend work is allowed[41]
Whether the working week can consist of 5.5 days[42]
Whether the workday can extend to 12 hours or more (including overtime)[43]
Whether the annual paid vacation days are 21 or fewer[44]

From these indicators, then, it is possible to develop a picture of the kind of working time regulation that would score most highly under the RHI. The optimum model would appear to be a legal regime that permits unlimited daily hours and weekly working time of 66 hours or more; no more than 1.5 days of weekly rest; night work of unlimited duration and which is not required to be paid at a premium rate;[45] and annual leave of no more than 21 days. At present, it is difficult to determine precisely how countries are being ranked, since only their overall scores can be consulted: data on the legislation used and the scores under each of the five indicators are unavailable. However, it is notable that a number of the least regulated, and therefore exceptional, working time regimes score maximum points. The index was calculated for more than 150 countries, and the results demonstrated that 13 countries, including Canada, New Zealand, Singapore and USA, enjoy 'complete working time flexibility' (average score 0).[46]

The vast majority of working time regimes, however, including the international standards, do not reflect the model reflected in the RHI. Table 3.1

Table 3.1 Rigidity of Hours Index, ILO standards and national laws

Form of protection	RHI	International standards	National laws
Daily hours limits	12-hour or higher maximum limit (including overtime)	Earlier standards: overtime hours beyond an 8-hour daily limit are permitted, to a reasonable level. (Hours of Work Convention (Industry), 1919 (No. 1), and Hours of Work Convention (Commerce and Offices), 1930 (No. 30); ILO 2005) Later standards: no daily limit (subject to a 40-hour weekly limit). (Forty-Hour Week Convention, 1935 (No. 47) and Reduction of Hours of Work Recommendation, 1962 (No. 116)).	Most impose a maximum limit (including overtime), often of 12 hours.
Maximum weekly hours limits	66 hour or higher limit	Earlier standards: 48-hour limit (with overtime expected to be exceptional). (Hours of Work Convention (Industry), 1919 (No. 1), and Hours of Work Convention (Commerce and Offices), 1930 (No. 30); ILO 2005) Later standards: 40-hour limit on normal hours. (Convention No. 47; Recommendation No. 116).	Most specify a limit between 48 and 60 hours.

(*Continued*)

Table 3.1 (Continued)

Form of protection	RHI	International standards	National laws
Minimum weekly rest period	Permitted, but not on a specified day, as a total prohibition, or subject to an hours limit or premium pay entitlement.	1 day, to be taken on the traditional or customary rest day. (Weekly Rest (Industry) Convention, 1921 (No. 14); Weekly Rest (Commerce and Offices) Convention, 1957 (No. 106)).	Mandated in almost all countries. The vast majority require 1 day of rest, to be taken, in principle, on a Sunday.
Protections for night workers	Unrestricted (no hours limit or premiums)	Specific compensation (in the form of rest or pay). (Night Work Convention, 1990 (No. 171)) 8-hour daily limit; normal hours not to exceed those of equivalent day workers; overtime should be avoided as far as possible. (Night Work Recommendation, 1990 (No. 178)).	Most countries have some form of restriction on night work. Can include wage premiums or prohibitions e.g. for certain sectors, jobs or workers (e.g. pregnant workers, parents).
Minimum period of paid annual leave	21 days	3 working weeks (Holidays with Pay Convention (Revised), 1970 (No. 132)).	Almost all countries mandate a right to paid annual leave. 20–23 days in more than one-third of countries.

* Daily working time of at least 12 hours worked over a maximum of 5.5 days.
Sources: ILO Working Time Database (www.ilo.org/travdatabase); ILO (2005); Lee, McCann and Messenger (2007).

illustrates this point by comparing the index with international and national legislation.

Interrelationships in working time protections

Table 3.1 highlights a number of the problematic elements of the World Bank's method of measuring working time regulation. A preliminary point is that the RHI appears to be internally inconsistent, in that it inadequately captures the relationship between the different elements of working time regulation. As mentioned above, by allowing an unlimited day without requiring a weekly limit, it in effect envisages weekly working time of at least 66 hours (subject only to the requirement that they be performed within a 5.5-day period). In national laws, daily hours are often subject to a maximum limit, the 12-hour ceiling permitted by the RHI as a minimum limit being common. Finland, for example, has a 13-hour upper limit on daily hours and would therefore be expected to score reasonably highly on the daily hours indicator. Moreover, its working time law also specifies 35 hours of weekly rest, and is therefore in line with the workweek indicator, by permitting a 5.5-day working week.

However, Finnish law, like that in the vast majority of countries, also specifies a weekly limit on working hours, in this case of 40 hours. As a result, while it complies with each of the individual indicators of the RHI it embodies a much stricter weekly limit than even the minimum permitted by the RHI (a 66-hour workweek).[47] The lack of recognition of a weekly limit in the RHI has the result that no meaningful distinction can be drawn between legal regimes that permit, for example, 66 hours of work *every* week, or permit them as a *maximum* on a limited number of weeks. This illustrates the risk of failing to consider working time regulatory regimes as an integrated whole. In particular, in national working time laws, weekly hours limits generally function as constraints under which the kinds of indicators embodied in the RHI are articulated and operate in conjunction with each other. The RHI lacks a recognition of this interrelation between different working time provisions.

The RHI and the rationales for working time regulation

More significantly for our present purposes, Table 3.1 illustrates the dissonance between the vision of working hours regulation that emerges from the RHI and that found in the international standards and national laws. From this comparison, it is clear that most of the indicators of 'hours rigidity' in the RHI are in conflict with these measures. The World Bank itself has signalled acceptance that labour regulation can be limited justifiably by 'social goals' beyond those reflected in the core labour standards, specifically referring to workplace safety.[48] This recognition is not, however, integrated into its assessment of working time regulation in the RHI, which is constructed to value most highly those legal regimes that are without meaningful limits on working hours.

Table 3.2 International standards on working time and the World Bank Rigidity of Hours Index

Number of ratifications (Conventions Nos. 1, 14, 30, 106, 132, 171)	No. of countries	GNI		WB Rigidity of Hours Index (0–100)	
		Simple average	Standard deviation	Average	Standard deviation
0	45	6,352	10,850	38.6	25.7
1	37	5,321	9,706	59.5	22.8
2	25	9,917	15,516	53.6	25.6
3	26	8,540	12,574	55.4	22.8
4	18	6,777	9,085	53.3	22.8
5	4	10,420	8,978	70.0	10.0
Total	155	7,202	11,505	51.6	25.2

Note: The Hours of Work (Industry) Convention, 1919 (No. 1); the Weekly Rest (Industry) Convention, 1921 (No. 14); the Hours of Work (Commerce and Offices) Convention, 1930 (No. 30); the Weekly Rest (Commerce and Offices) Convention, 1957 (No. 106); the Holidays with Pay Conventions (Revised), 1970 (No. 132); the Night Work Convention, 1990 (No. 171).
Sources: ILOLEX and World Bank database.

In relation to the market failure rationale mentioned above, then, the criteria related to daily and weekly working hours and night work are in conflict with the policy objectives of most working time regulations, in that working according to the optimum model reflected in the RHI would have negative consequences on workers' health and safety as well as their family life. And with respect to weekend work, the refusal to countenance a specified day on which weekly rest should be taken fails to recognize one of the traditional rationales behind weekly rest measures, which have been intended not only to allow workers to rest but to ensure a period of time that the entire community can spend together.

As a result, countries whose laws best reflect the internationally agreed standards and the national consensus on appropriate hours regulation are classified as 'most rigid'. For example, as shown in Table 3.2, the laws classified as 'rigid' under this index are more likely to be found in countries that have ratified the international working time standards. Therefore it is not surprising that the rigidity of hours index is correlated with the ratification index, although the relationship is weak (coefficient = .24, significant at 0.01 level).

Flexibility through regulation

The other main problem with the RHI is that it equates most forms of working time regulation with 'rigidity'. It has already been suggested that the very concept of rigidity is highly problematic. In fact, the experience in industrialized countries reveals the relationship between flexibility in working time and its regulation to be much more complex than indicated by the RHI. For instance, the most prominent technique through which modern working time regulation incorporates a degree of flexibility is by permitting weekly hours limits to be averaged over a period of longer than a week, through the inclusion of a reference period in the national legislation (hours averaging). The EU Working Time Directive, for example, permits its 48-hour maximum limit to be averaged over a reference period of four months (Article 16(b)). However, this, the most prominent technique for ensuring a degree of flexibility in working time regulation, is entirely absent from the RHI.

Moreover, the RHI is not structured to capture a further, less direct method in which working time regulation can contribute towards promoting flexibility, through what can be termed its 'incentive' function. By limiting recourse to long hours, working time regulation can play the role of encouraging employers to rethink how work is being organized in their firms in order to bring about productivity improvements. Indeed, in Europe, the 40-hour week has, in many jurisdictions, been the starting point from within which work organization changes have taken place.[49]

The uncomplicated depiction of flexibility in the RHI, however, is focused entirely on numerical flexibility rather than on the role of law in promoting functional flexibility, and thus ignores the more complicated relationship between different forms of flexibility and the role of regulation in advancing them. In this regard, and with respect to the employment creation goal used on occasion to justify collective hours reductions, it is interesting to note that the RHI disregards the contribution that working hours laws can make to its stated objectives, to 'influence the opportunities and incentives for firms to invest productively, create jobs, and expand'.[50] Indeed, the contention that 'regulations can reduce incentives to make new investments, adjust the organization of work to take advantage of new technologies or opportunities, or hire more workers' advances arguments often used in *support* of the regulation of working hours.[51]

It is clear, then, that all of these factors have an impact on the adequacy of the resulting indicators, with the result that the Index is unable to identify the basic components of meaningful working time regulations found in the vast majority of regulatory regimes, does not reflect how their different components interact and does not meaningfully value them. As a result, it does not measure the *strength* of the regulation but only its *existence*.

3.4 Legal texts and actual hours: *de jure* and *de facto* regulation

So far, we have concentrated on the inadequacies of the existing indicators in reflecting the 'statutory reality' in different countries. Even if the conceptual and methodological questions raised in the previous section were to be effect-ively addressed, however, the resulting indicators would still be subject to limitations. For although drawing on domestic legislative texts provides a more accurate picture of working time regulation than reliance on ratifica-tion of the ILO standards, the relationship of the statutory provisions to actual working hours cannot be assumed. The legislated standards may be entirely irrelevant to actual working hours or exercise a strong influence on them, depending on the degree to which the legislation is influential in the jurisdiction in question. This issue relates to the point made earlier on valid-ity as the key property of a good indicator. Without a proper understanding of this relationship, any conclusions as to the impact of standards can only be speculative. As Bertola *et al.* have argued with respect to employment protec-tion laws, the role of working time legislation in influencing labour market outcomes is primarily an empirical question.[52]

Botero *et al.*: working hour adjustment costs – real or imaginary?

The RHI does not purport to examine the influence of legislation on actual working time arrangements. Instead, it assumes that the standard is com-prehensively applied, and then further assumes the kinds of impacts the legislation will have on actual practice. However, it is questionable whether the relationship between working time laws and actual working hours is so straightforward. The significance of this relationship is recognized to some degree by Botero *et al.*[53] Their index on 'the cost of increasing hours worked' is intended to reflect 'actual economic costs and not just statutory languages'.[54] However, they appear to assume that countries with different legal standard hours (annual working hours) are competing in the product market with fluctuating demands. The question is then how different adjustment costs would be incurred in increasing working hours to the level of the highest legal standard hours in the world. By estimating these costs, they argue that 'the distinction between what is written down and what it actually costs to do something is minimized'.[55] In their calculation, the lowest standard is 1,758 hours in Denmark and the highest 2,418 hours in Kenya, and the cost of increasing to the Kenyan level is calculated as the ratio of the final wage bill to the initial one.

The main problem with this approach is that the situation assumed is overly hypothetical and does not reflect reality. First, competition via chan-ging working hours, if it occurred, would normally be carried out within a narrow margin. It is therefore misleading to assume that Denmark would increase actual working hours to 2,418 hours. If such a magnitude of change is not envisioned in the law, and has never been contemplated in policy debates in Denmark, it is not useful to calculate it and compare the costs with other countries.

Secondly, these estimated working hours do not correspond to actual working hours. Where the relevant data are available (OECD countries),

Botero *et al.*'s annual hours are often much higher than actual working hours and, in many cases, the gap is considerable (see Annex 3.1). In the case of Germany, for example, Botero *et al.* estimated 2,296 hours while actual working hours stand at 1,446 hours (a difference of 851 hours). What is more important from the perspective of cross-country comparison is that there is no significant correlation between the estimates and the OECD's actual annual working hours (correlation coefficient = 0.089, not significant). Therefore, it is hard to argue that Botero *et al.*'s estimates of annual working hours represent the level of the constraints actually placed on enterprises.

Observance of working time legislation

It appears, then, that the most accurate way of comparing and assessing the impact of labour laws is through a methodology that incorporates not only the provisions in statutory texts but also accurately captures the actual working hours in the country in question. The remainder of this chapter is our preliminary attempt to develop this kind of approach. To do this, we draw on a notion of 'observance' of statutory working time regulation. We intend this concept to be broader than more conventional notions of 'enforcement' of national laws, in that it captures the variety of ways in which legal norms can influence actual practice. It is also more expansive than what is usually meant by 'compliance' with legislation, in that it does not require adherence to the technicalities of national laws (for example, procedural requirements, record-keeping and so on) and also recognizes that legal standards may be influential in firms to which the law does not formally apply (for example, in sectors or firms excluded from the coverage of the legislation) or where it is not enforced (particularly in firms in the informal economy).[56] The notion of observance, then, is intended to capture the enforcement of the standards through the state labour inspectorate or through court decisions in individual cases, but also to comprehend the other ways in which laws can have an effect on practice, in particular through becoming 'seeded' as a cultural norm, influential even in the absence of enforcement.[57]

In the rest of this section, then, we attempt to measure the effective regulation of working time, by measuring the extent to which working time laws are observed. As mentioned earlier, the comparison of working time regulation can be hampered, in particular by differences across countries in the regulatory techniques adopted. However, when the focus is confined to statutory measures, and to their primary standards[58] (daily and weekly hours, weekly rest periods, annual leave and so on), there is a substantial degree of homogeneity among the national legislative regimes and comparisons are possible.[59] In this chapter, we are concerned with only one element of the regulation of working hours – weekly normal hours limits (the number of hours legally permitted before overtime payments are required).

Recent research conducted for the ILO Working Time Database has allowed us to identify statutory normal hours limits.[60] We have also been able to identify the actual normal hours in those countries for which data are available. One useful way of gauging the actual impact of statutory working time regulation is to measure how many employees are working more than the statutory normal hours of work. This excludes self-employed workers, who are typically not covered by such regulations. To the best of our knowledge, no measurement work of this kind has been done due to data limitation until the recent data collection from the national statistical offices of more than 50 countries on 'the number of employed by number of hours' in 2005.[61] These data collection exercises permitted us to compare statutory standard and actual weekly hours.

Statutory normal weekly hours limits

To determine statutory normal weekly hours limits, we relied on the ILO Working Time Database and additional research, allowing a total of 138 countries to be considered for comparison and classified according to their income levels.[62] The results are presented in Figure 3.2. As this figure indicates, while overall the incidence of shorter hours limits is higher in high-income countries, it is interesting to note that about 43 per cent of countries with a gross national income (GNI) of less than US$2,000 also have a legal standard of 40 hours or less. In line with the World Bank's analysis of labour laws discussed earlier, this finding might be interpreted as evidence that many poor countries have 'rigid' working time standards, which do not reflect 'local reality'.

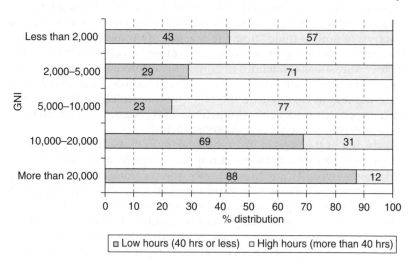

Figure 3.2   Statutory normal hours by national income (total 138 countries)
Note: EU countries that only have a maximum limit including overtime hours (such as the UK) are classified as 'low hours', as some of them have no legal standard of normal hours of work.
Source: ILO Working Time Database.

Before evaluating this claim, however, it is necessary to determine whether these standards are also the actual 'standard' at the workplace.

Observance of the statutory standard

To address this question, Table 3.3(a) provides estimates for the proportion of paid *employees* who are working at or below the statutory standard hours in each country, which we term the 'observance rate'. Note that only employees are considered, as self-employed and family workers are often not covered by working time regulation and labour law in general. A total of 48 countries are considered, excluding those that do not have statutory normal hours (for example, Germany and the United Kingdom, which impose a limit only on maximum hours (including overtime)). In response to the concern that regulations should reflect 'local realities' (see World Bank, 2004a), the gross national income per capita is also considered, and statutory standards are categorized into three groups ('40 hours or less,' '41 to 47 hours' and '48 hours'). Some descriptive statistics are also provided in Table 3.3(b) and scatter diagrams are shown in Figure 3.3.

These efforts reveal, first, that higher statutory hours limits are largely associated with lower national income per capita. While the mean GNI per capita is much lower in countries with higher limits, it is statistically significant only for the '48 hours' group (see Table 3.3(b)). Overall, then, it would be overstated to suggest that working time regulation in developing countries is unnecessarily 'rigid', in the sense of containing overly strict weekly hours limits. Secondly, it is apparent from Figure 3.3 that, overall, a significant proportion of employees are working more than statutory normal hours limits and that in some countries the proportion exceeds 40 per cent of the workforce (see Figure 3.3). This could be taken to imply that the standard hours are not 'standard' in practice. Thirdly, however, it is interesting to note that observance rates are relatively low in those countries that have higher statutory limits, and it can thus be said that low-income countries have lower observance rates *despite* higher statutory hours limits. Therefore, if our finding on statutory weekly hours limits holds true for other elements of labour regulation, any widespread assumption about low-compliance with labour standards in developing countries due to their 'strictness' would need to be reassessed.[63] Finally, when it comes to low-income countries, the relationship between statutory hours, national income and observance rates is much weaker and so remains very unclear.[64]

The Effective Regulation Index

In light of the need to examine both *de jure* and *de facto* regulation in establishing indicators, we have made a preliminary attempt to establish such an indicator for working hours. This 'effective regulation' index for working hours (ERI) was established by *averaging* the normalized values of statutory hours and observance rates, which range between 0 and 10.[65] The results

Table 3.3(a) Statutory hours, observance and working hour regulation index

	GNI 2003	Raw values		Normalized value		Effective working hour regulation index (0 to 10)
		Legal normal hours	Observance rate (employees working no more than legal normal hours)	Statutory-hour strictness (0–10)	Observance degree (0–10)	
Albania	4,710	40	78.4	6.2	7.8	7.0
Armenia	3,790	40	50.9	6.2	5.1	5.6
Azerbaijan	3,390	40	74.6	6.2	7.5	6.8
Bolivia	2,500	48	62.1	0.0	6.2	3.1
Bulgaria	7,260	40	87.8	6.2	8.8	7.5
Canada	29,440	40	88.5	6.2	8.9	7.5
Croatia	11,180	40	67.1	6.2	6.7	6.4
Cyprus	21,250	40	80.5	6.2	8.0	7.1
Czech Republic	17,290	40	84.8	6.2	8.5	7.3
Estonia	12,100	40	85.9	6.2	8.6	7.4
Ethiopia	710	48	57.0	0.0	5.7	2.8
Finland	27,940	40	90.3	6.2	9.0	7.6
France	28,190	35	50.7	10.0	5.1	7.5
Georgia	2,620	41	66.9	5.4	6.7	6.0
Guatemala	4,050	48	69.8	0.0	7.0	3.5
Honduras	2,600	44	64.0	3.1	6.4	4.7
Hungary	14,630	40	90.7	6.2	9.1	7.6
Indonesia	3,270	40	47.6	6.2	4.8	5.5
Israel	22,450	43	59.5	3.8	5.9	4.9
Japan	28,700	40	54.2	6.2	5.4	5.8
Korea, Rep.	19,190	40	24.5	6.2	2.4	4.3
Lithuania	11,530	40	90.3	6.2	9.0	7.6
Luxembourg	57,650	40	98.0	6.2	9.8	8.0
Macedonia, FYR	6,230	40	68.0	6.2	6.8	6.5

Madagascar	800	40	70.9	6.2	7.1	6.6
Mauritius	11,270	45	73.8	2.3	7.4	4.8
Mexico	9,140	48	75.8	0.0	7.6	3.8
Moldova	1,760	40	82.1	6.2	8.2	7.2
Netherlands	30,220	40	97.2	6.2	9.7	7.9
New Zealand	21,040	40	68.5	6.2	6.8	6.5
Norway	36,870	40	92.4	6.2	9.2	7.7
Pakistan	2,040	48	60.4	0.0	6.0	3.0
Panama	6,430	48	85.4	0.0	8.5	4.3
Peru	5,080	48	50.8	0.0	5.1	2.5
Poland	11,750	40	85.9	6.2	8.6	7.4
Portugal	18,660	40	87.1	6.2	8.7	7.4
Romania	7,450	40	82.6	6.2	8.3	7.2
Russian Federation	8,760	40	92.5	6.2	9.3	7.7
Slovak Republic	13,350	40	90.0	6.2	9.0	7.6
Slovenia	19,420	40	84.7	6.2	8.5	7.3
Spain	23,930	40	88.2	6.2	8.8	7.5
Sri Lanka	3,740	45	62.2	2.3	6.2	4.3
Switzerland	34,220	45	81.6	2.3	8.2	5.2
Tanzania, United Rep.	620	45	33.1	2.3	3.3	2.8
Thailand	7,450	48	65.3	0.0	6.5	3.3
Uruguay	7,960	48	79.5	0.0	7.9	4.0
United States	37,610	40	69.1	6.2	6.9	6.5
Zimbabwe	2,180	48	59.4	0.0	5.9	3.0
Total						
Mean	13,842.1	42.1	73.1	4.5	7.3	5.9
Standard deviation	12,455.4	3.5	16.6	2.7	1.7	1.7

Source: ILO Working Time Database; World Bank database.

Table 3.3(b) Statutory hours, observance and working-hour regulation index

Statutory hours	No. of countries	GNI per capita		Observance rate		Correlations between GNI and observance	
		Mean	Standard error	Mean	Standard error	Coefficients	Significance
[40 hours or less]	31	17,398.7	2,312.3	77.5	17.1	0.209	0.260
41 to 47 hours	7	11,074.3	4,809.6	63.0	15.2	0.577	0.175
48 hours	10	4,754.0*	916.6	66.5	10.9	0.657*	0.039
Total	48	13,482.1	1,797.8	73.1	16.6	0.362*	0.012

Note: [ ] refers to the reference group.
*significant at 0.05 level.

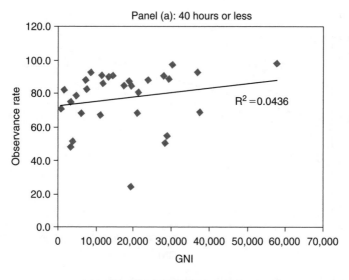

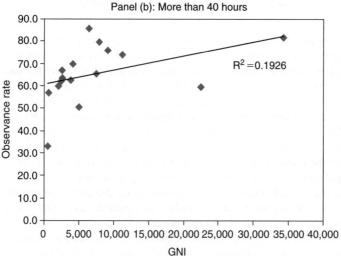

Figure 3.3 Observance rate and income by statutory working hour standards

are provided in the final column of Table 3.3(a). The ERI developed in this table can have a minimum value of 1 (weakest regulation) and a maximum value of 10 (strongest regulation). It should be noted from the outset that such an aggregate index, even when other methods such as nonlinear combination are used, has implicit assumptions which could create bias in the analysis. In our simple method, it is assumed that the length of statutory hours and

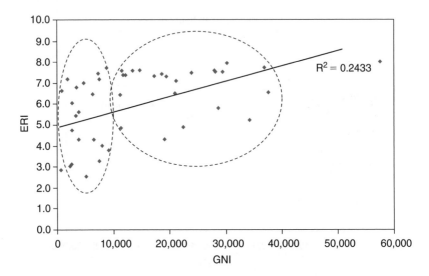

Figure 3.4   Working hour regulation index and national income

the observance rate are *equally* important in determining the effectiveness of regulation in a particular country. What this means in practice is revealed by comparing the Republic of Korea and Panama, which have the same level of regulation (ERI = 4.3): yet Korea has a much lower statutory hours limit (40 hours) and lower observance rate (24 per cent), while Panama's higher statutory limit (48 hours) attracts a higher observance rate (85 per cent). While it is conceivable to introduce other more sophisticated methods (for example, a well-grounded weighting scheme), reliable guidance on this is not currently available, mainly due to the paucity of data and analysis on the regulation of working time in developing countries.[66]

With this caveat, let us turn to the index. Of the countries considered in Table 3.3(a), Peru, the United Republic of Tanzania and Ethiopia have the weakest regulation while the Netherlands and Luxembourg lead the group of countries with strong regulation. Geographical division is clearly present: Europe (including transition economies) tends to have strong regulation, while Africa, Asia and Latin America are, overall, characterized by weak regulation. How then, is economic development associated with the ERI? Is effective regulation associated with economic growth, at least with respect to weekly hours? A positive correlation is conceivable if the benefits of economic growth can be translated into either shorter statutory hours or higher observance rate (for example, through strengthening labour inspection), or both. As Figure 3.4 shows, there is a positive correlation between the index and GNI per capita (significant at the 0.01 level). Yet again, when the sample is separated into two groups of countries by income level (exactly half of the sample have GNI of less than US$10,000), there is no correlation within each group (see dotted circles in Figure 3.4), indicating that weekly hours limits, even when widely observed, are not impacting on economic growth. For instance, Albania and Peru have similar GNI levels of around US$5,000, but contrasting ERI levels (7.0 and 2.5 respectively). Finally, and probably not surprisingly, it is noteworthy that ERI does not have any significant correlation with RHI.

This finding should not be seen as surprising, given the evidence of variations between countries in the way different components of working time regulation are articulated with related labour market institutions. Among high-income countries, it is relatively well established that the impact of statutory working time regulation differs depending on the working time regimes within which they are articulated.[67] If collective negotiations are well organized and the coverage of collective agreements extensive, working time law tends to represent minimum standards, with the result that collectively agreed normal hours tend to be lower than the statutory standard. In this case, the latter represents the upper limit on actual working hours. In some other countries, however, where legal interventions are minimized, the incidence of working hours is relatively high and therefore the statutory standard is often a lower limit on actual working hours.

The challenge now is to examine in more detail why working time, and other laws, appear to be more influential in some jurisdictions than others, even among countries at similar income levels. As we have noted, it is naïve to assert that low compliance in developing countries is due to a strict regulation of working time that does not reflect the local reality. In developing countries, the main problem of working time regulation might be expected to be not its 'rigidity', but its weakness, assuming a strong propensity to bypass the law. In this case, even if a 'rigid' regulation was in place at the national level, the limited resources available for monitoring working hours at the workplace level and enforcing the relevant provisions may create a 'regulation-free' environment. However, further comparative research is needed on the processes of observance of labour law across developing countries; one that does not take into account only enforcement by government agencies, but also the deviations from the principal statutory norms that are permitted by the regulations; the role of unions and collective bargaining; the degree of awareness of labour laws; the indirect influence of labour regulation; and all the other factors that play a part in ensuring that labour laws are observed.

It is impossible to tell from our research whether deviance from weekly hours norms in fact represents a failure to comply with the law. Many legal regimes permit their general hours limits to be exceeded through providing for exceptions, for example for certain sectors or occupations or through collective agreements. As a result, working time standards are sometimes not as strict as they first appear. In Mozambique, for example, the general 48-hour limit can be exceeded by a collective agreement provided it does not result in financial disadvantage or less favourable working conditions for the workers concerned (*Lei do Trabalho*, article 29). And the Slovenian legislation demonstrates flexibility in working time through 'negotiated flexibility': collective agreements are permitted to stipulate a working week shorter than the general 40-hour limit, provided it is not below 30 hours (Labour Relations Act, article 142(2)).[68]

Moreover, a primary factor in the observance of normal hours limits can be expected to be the extent to which overtime hours are worked. It is not possible from the current data to determine the extent to which the deviation from the statutory norm can be attributed to overtime. In this regard, further research is needed to take into account the relationship between wage regulation and overtime work, including to determine the extent to which overtime must be worked in order to secure a reasonable standard of living.

Finally, this kind of work, which is based entirely on statutory regulation, inevitably fails to take into account the role of collective bargaining in regulating working time arrangements.[69] It may be that a high degree of observance in certain countries is an outcome of a strong role for collective bargaining. Alternatively, even when workers are organized, their trade union may actively seek to increase the opportunity for overtime work and premium payments, so as to increase wage earnings for union members.

Working time laws and informal employment

In addition to the above concerns, it is worth singling out a specific argument being made in the research on indicators, that 'rigid' employment regulation in developing countries, including of working hours, is channelling workers into the informal economy. One might argue, for example, that the lack of any significant relationship between income, working time regulation and observance of the law, especially in low-income countries, is simply due to the fact that 'rigidity' of the working time regulation is encouraging informal employment as a way of increasing working hours. This is possible, but difficult to test empirically. One way of doing so would be to determine whether or not informal employment is associated with longer working hours, assuming that employers will take advantage of the 'regulation-free' environment of the informal economy, where labour laws are unlikely to be enforced, to increase working hours beyond those in the formal sector. Due to the paucity of working time data in developing countries, it is not easy to offer a convincing answer to this question. Nonetheless, the data provided in Table 3.4 provide some useful insights. This table presents average working hours in formal and informal employment in Latin American countries, compared with the total averages, and demonstrates that in all of the countries under consideration, working hours in formal employment are significantly *higher* than those in informal employment. This means, then, that the above prediction is not grounded for Latin America and may not be grounded for other regions. Indeed, Table 3.4 suggests that the formal economy, which can

Table 3.4 Working hours by formal and informal employment (base: total average hours = 100.0)

	Argentina 2001	Bolivia 2002	Brazil 2001	Chile 2000	Ecuador 1998	Guatemala 2000	Mexico 2000	Nicaragua 2001	Peru 2000
Formal employment	104.9	104	103.4	102.1	112.2	105.4	104.3	107.9	109.1
Informal employment	93.3	98.4	96.5	97.9	92.3	96.5	95.2	94.6	95.2

Source: Table 10 in Gasparini (2004), 'América Latina: Estudio de la protección social y el empleo sobre la base de encuestas de hogares', in F. Bertranou (ed.) *Protección Social y Mercado Laboral* (Santiago: OIT).

be expected to be more likely to be influenced by working time regulation, tends to have *longer* working hours.

While it is hard to know the precise reasons underlying this difference, there could be two possible explanations. First, data on average working hours in informal employment require great caution, mainly because of the high proportion of time-related underemployment. The typical distributional patterns of working hours in informal employment in developing countries is a dramatic diversification of working hours towards two extremes of very short hours (for example, lack of sufficient work) and very long hours (for example, more than 60 hours per week).[70] Thus, relying on average working hours for the informal economy could be potentially misleading.

Secondly, there could be economic rationales for the relatively long working hours in formal employment, which are related to the 'incentive' effects of working time regulation. 'Doing business' in the formal economy is likely to entail significant investments by employers, which involves relatively high fixed costs. Such investments may encourage employers to increase working hours, even if that involves additional payments for overtime work. This incentive will be stronger and the cost disadvantage weaker if the 'regulated' environment motivates workers and improves labour productivity.

3.5   Concluding remarks

This chapter has investigated the existing institutional indicators for the regulation of working time, with a particular focus on the World Bank's Rigidity of Hours Index and Botero *et al.*[71] Two conceptual and methodological questions were examined. First, do these indicators take into account the reasons that different regulations on working time have been enacted and sustained? In other words, are the potential benefits of these regulations recognized appropriately by these indicators? The second question is one which has rendered many researchers pessimistic about the relevance of institutional indicators concerning the regulation of employment conditions: is the question of *de jure* and *de facto* regulation addressed effectively?

Our overall evaluations provided in this chapter are negative in both areas. The indicators considered appear to lack a sound understanding of working time regulation, so that one might say that the rigidity indicators are based on a 'rigid' concept of regulation. Our preliminary attempt to capture both *de jure* and *de facto* regulation through ERI indeed shows that cross-country variations are substantial, even when income levels are taken into account, thereby making it difficult to establish a meaningful pattern. It has also been indicated that the policy conclusions and implications drawn from the currently available indicators, which do not consider actual practice, do not have solid grounds, and are, in some cases, misleading.

Our research has indicated that the relationship between regulation, employment and economic growth is far more complex than is assumed in the existing indicators. For the development of a more meaningful and valid indicator for working time regulation, further research is required to examine the role and impact of working time laws in developing countries, although we hope that the ERI will offer useful insights for such research efforts. In particular, we need to better understand the conditions under which reasonable hours regulations can be maintained. Rather than assuming that a laxer standard is needed at earlier stages of economic growth,[72] the goal is to identify which factors permit certain economies at the same level of economic growth to maintain more advanced working time standards.

Annex 3.1   Botero *et al.*'s estimates and actual working hours

	OECD data	Botero et al.'s estimates	Difference
Australia	1,814	1,909	−94
Austria	1,550	1,780	−230
Belgium	1,542	1,880	−338
Canada	1,718	1,960	−242
Czech Republic	1,972	1983	−12
Denmark	1,475	1,758	−283
Finland	1,713	1,807	−93
France	1,431	1,859	−428
Germany	1,446	2,296	−851
Greece	1,938	1,907	31
Ireland	1,613	2,331	−718
Italy	1,591	1,873	−282
Japan	1,801	1,947	−146
Mexico	1,857	2,280	−423
Netherlands	1,354	1,900	−546
New Zealand	1,813	1,872	−59
Norway	1,337	1,880	−543
Poland	1,956	1,932	24
Portugal	1,676	1,840	−164
Slovak Republic	1,814	2,028	−214
Spain	1,800	1,808	−8
Sweden	1,564	1,880	−316
Switzerland	1,556	2,123	−566
United Kingdom	1,673	2,080	−407
United States	1,792	2,080	−288

Source: Botero *et al.* (2004); OECD database (2003 data).

Notes

1   The views expressed in this chapter are those of the authors and do not necessarily reflect those of the International Labour Office. We are grateful for comments on an earlier draft of this chapter by P. Auer, J. Berg, I. Campbell, F. Eyraud, C. Fagan,

N. Ghosheh, D. Kucera, S. Lehndorff, J. Messenger, J. Murray, A. Nesporova, P. Peek and the participants at the ILO Technical Staff Seminar on Labour Market Institutions and Employment in Developing Countries, Geneva, 24–25 November 2005.

2 J. Botero *et al.* (2004) 'The Regulation of Labour', *Quarterly Journal of Economics*, 119(4).

3 Rigidity of Employment Index, available in World Bank (2004a) *Doing Business 2005* (Washington, DC: World Bank), and World Bank (2005) *Doing Business 2006* (Washington, DC: World Bank).

4 World Bank (2005), p. 26, emphasis added.

5 ICFTU (2005) 'Comments by ICFTU/Global Unions on the World Bank's *Doing Business in 2005:* "Hiring and firing of workers"'.

6 G. Bertola *et al.* (2005) 'Distribution, Efficiency, and Labor Market Regulation: in Theory, in OECD Countries, and in Latin America', in J. Restrepo and A. Tokman (eds), *Labor Markets and Institutions* (Santiago: Central Bank of Chile).

7 A recent paper that addresses these concerns is J. Berg and S. Cazes, 'Policymaking gone away: The Labour Market Regulations of the Doing Business Regulators,' *Comparative Labor Law and Policy Journal*, 29(3).

8 International Labour Conference, 86th Session (1998).

9 See, for example, D. Kucera (2002) 'Core Labour Standards and Foreign Direct Investment', *International Labour* Review, 114(1–2).

10 P. Alston and J. Heenan (2004) 'Shrinking the International Labor Code: An Unintended Consequence of the 1998 ILO Declaration on Fundamental Principles and Rights at Work?', *New York University School of Law Journal of International Law and Politics*, 36.

11 K.A. Bollen (2001) 'Indicator: Methodology', in N. Smeler and P. Baltes (eds), *International Encyclopedia of the Social & Behavioral Sciences,* vol. 11 (Amsterdam: Elsevier), pp. 7282–7.

12 Hours of Work (Industry) Convention, 1919 (No. 1); Hours of Work (Commerce and Offices) Convention, 1930 (No. 30).

13 These figures are estimated for paid employees only, since they are more likely to be affected by the ratification of these Conventions. The self-employed are excluded.

14 S. Lee, D. McCann and J. Messenger (2007) *Working Time Around the World* (London and Geneva: Routledge and ILO).

15 The lack of correlation between international standards and the actual situation is also reported by P. Belser, (2001) *Four Essays on Trade and Labour Standards*, unpublished PhD dissertation, University of Sussex, M. Busse (2001) 'Do Labour Standards Affect Comparative Advantage? Evidence for Labour-intensive Goods', Centre for International Economic Studies Discussion Paper No. 0142 (Adelaide) and R. Flanagan (2003) 'Labor Standards and International Competitive Advantage', in R. Flanagan (ed.), *International Labor Standards: Globalization, Trade and Public Policy* (Stanford, CA: Stanford University Press).

16 S. Lee (2004) 'Working-Hour Gaps: Trends and Issues' and D. McCann (2004) 'Regulating Working Time Needs and Preferences', in J. Messenger (ed.), *Working Time and Workers' Preferences in Industrialized Countries: Finding the Balance* (London: Routledge).

17 OECD (1994a) 'Labour Standards and Economic Integration', *OECD Employment Outlook* (Paris, OECD), pp. 137–66.

18 S.J. Nickell (1997) 'Unemployment and Labor Market Rigidities: Europe versus North America', *Journal of Economic Perspectives*, 11(3).

19 See, for example, L. Nunziata (2003) 'Labour Market Institutions and the Cyclical Dynamics of Employment', *Labour Economics,* 10(1). In addition, the need for such an indicator appears to be related to the OECD jobs strategy, which calls for 'increased flexibility of working time (both short-term and lifetime) voluntarily sought by workers and employers', although the ambiguity underlying this strategy makes it difficult to develop a valid indicator. The policy intentions are apparent in OECD policy recommendations, which can be characterized by the need for working time determination at decentralized level and the relaxing of relevant legislation, for example 'by allowing longer averaging periods such as annualized hours, by reducing constraints on night work and weekend work' (OECD, 1994b, p. 100). As will be discussed in section 3.3, these policy intentions are made explicit in the World Bank's Rigidity of Hours Index.

20 D. Rodrik (1996) 'Labor Standards in International Trade: Do They Matter and What Do We Do About Them?', in R. Lawrence, D. Rodrik and J. Whalley (eds), *Emerging Agenda for Global Trade: High Stakes for Developing Countries* (Washington, DC: Overseas Development Council), pp. 35–79.

21 Botero *et al.* (2004); World Bank (2004a) *The World Development Report: A Better Investment Climate for Everyone* (Washington, DC: World Bank); and idem. (2005) *Doing Business 2006.*

22 Botero *et al.* (2004).

23 World Bank (2004a).

24 The most vivid example quoted in the report is concerned with paid annual leave: 'Some developing countries have mandated relatively generous annual leave – 30 days in Burkina Faso, 33 in Ethiopia, and 39 in Sierra Leone – but in most other countries paid annual leave is less than 30 days. The United States leaves the decision on annual leave to individual or collective agreements' (ibid., p. 145).

25 World Bank (2004b) *The World Development Report: A Better Investment Climate for Everyone* (Washington, DC: World Bank), p. 145.

26 Directive 2003/88/EC of the European Parliament and of the Council of 4 November 2003 concerning certain aspects of the organization of working time, Article 6.

27 Botero *et al.* (2004). See 'max_hour_w_a' in the data file available at: http://iicg.som.yale.edu/.

28 C. Pissarides (2001) 'Employment Protection', *Labour Economics,* 8(2).

29 As Bertola *et al.* (2005), p. 7, notes, '[t]he literature mostly treats labor market institutions as exogenous determinants of labor market outcomes. Less attention has been directed at explaining and interpreting the motivation behind institutional arrangements in the labor market. Efforts in the latter direction are all the more necessary when researchers study labor market institutions in a heterogeneous group of countries.' See also R. Freeman (2005) 'Labour Market Institutions Without Blinders: The Debate Over Flexibility and Labour Market Performance', NBER Working Paper 11286 (Cambridge, MA: National Bureau of Economic Research).

30 See J. Owen (1989) *Reduced Working Hours: Cure for Unemployment or Economic Burden?* (Baltimore: Johns Hopkins University Press), chapter 4 for details.

31 See A.E. Dembe, J.B. Erickson, R.G. Delbos and S.M. Banks (2005) 'The Impact of Overtime and Long Work Hours on Occupational Injuries and Illnesses: New Evidence from the United States', *Occupational and Environmental Medicine,* 62(9); and A. Spurgeon (2003) *Working Time: Its Impact on Safety and Health* (Geneva: ILO).

32   On the notion of individual choice in working time regulation, see S. Lee and
      D. McCann (2006) 'Working Time Capabilities: Towards Realizing Individual
      Choice', in J.Y Boulin, M. Lallement, J.C. Messenger and F. Michon (eds), *Decent
      Working Time: New Trends, New Issues* (Geneva: ILO).
33   See G. Akerlof and W. Dickens (1984) 'The Economic Consequences of Cogni-
      tive Dissonance', in *An Economic Theorist's Book of Tales* (Cambridge: Cambridge
      University Press), for a discussion of health and safety legislation.
34   Directive 2003/88/EC of the European Parliament and of the Council of 4
      November 2003 concerning certain aspects of the organization of working time,
      Preamble.
35   Lee, McCann and Messenger (2007).
36   J. Murray (2001) *Transnational Labour Regulation: the ILO and EC Compared* (Hague:
      Kluwer Law International), and Lee, McCann and Messenger (forthcoming).
37   World Bank (2004b).
38   Botero *et al.* (2004).
39   Agell (1999) 'On the Benefits from Rigid Labour Markets: Norms, Market Failures,
      and Social Insurance', *Economic Journal*, 109(453).
40   'The answer is: Yes if by law or mandatory collective agreement: (i) there are restric-
      tions on the maximum number of hours of work that can be performed at night;
      and/or (ii) if there are specific premiums for night-time work.'
41   'The answer is Yes if by law or mandatory collective agreement there are restrictions
      on work during the weekly holidays (usually Sunday, Saturday or Friday, depend-
      ing on the country). Restrictions include: (i) complete prohibition; (ii) express
      designation of certain day of the week as weekly holiday, which the employer
      cannot change unless with the worker's consent; (iii) specific maximum hours of
      work on such day; and (iv) special premiums for work on such a day.'
42   The method used is unknown.
43   The method used is unknown.
44   The annual paid vacation day refers to 'the number of days of annual paid leave
      in manufacturing awarded to a worker after twenty years of employment. If there
      is no minimum by law or mandatory collective agreement, the answer is No.'
45   It appears that the other forms of protections for night workers often found in
      national laws are permitted under the RHI e.g. rights to regular health assessments,
      protections for pregnant workers and so on.
46   World Bank (2005).
47   12-hour days worked over a 5.5-day period.
48   World Bank (2004b), p. 141.
49   D. Barnard and R. Hobbs, (2003) 'Opting Out of the 48-Hour Week: Employer
      Necessity or Individual Choice?', *Industrial Law Journal*, 32: 223–52 and G. Bosch
      and S. Lehndorff, (2001) 'Working-Time Reduction and Employment: Experi-
      ences in Europe and Economic Policy Recommendations', *Cambridge Journal of
      Economics*, 25(2): 209.
50   World Bank (2004b).
51   Ibid.
52   G. Bertola *et al.* (2000) 'Employment Protection in Industrialized Countries: the
      Case for New Indicators", *International Labour Review,* 139(1).
53   Botero *et al.* (2004).
54   Ibid., p. 1347.
55   Ibid.

56 On the application of labour laws to the informal economy, see Chapter 10 in this volume.
57 J. Browne, S. Deakin, and F. Wilkinson (2002) 'Capabilities, Social Rights and European Market Integration', *ESRC Centre for Business Research Working Paper 253*, University of Cambridge.
58 These can be defined as the basic entitlements, irrespective of any derogations in the form of exceptions, for example, or permissions to derogate via collective bargaining/individual agreement.
59 Lee, McCann and Messenger (2007).
60 The Working Time Database is an online database of the primary statutory standards on working time in over 100 countries. It is available at www.ilo.org/travdatabase.
61 This data collection exercise was a collaboration between the ILO's Conditions of Work and Employment Programme and Bureau of Statistics.
62 EU countries that do not specify normal hours but only a maximum limit (including overtime) are considered to have a normal hours limit of '40 hours or less'.
63 World Bank (2004a), pp. 145–6.
64 See Lee, McCann and Messenger (2007).
65 The formula used for normalization is $[(10/13 * (48\text{-}SH_i)]$ and $[(1/10 * OR_i)]$ where SH_i is country i's statutory hours and OR_i refers to country i's observance rate.
66 For this, it is essential to better understand the relationship between statutory limits and their observance. Without such analysis, any index on working time regulation, including the one presented in this paper, will remain preliminary.
67 See Lee (2004).
68 On negotiated flexibility in Slovenia see M. Stanojevic (2005) 'Slovenia: Rigidity or "Negotiated Flexibility", in Vaughan-Whitehead (ed.), *Working and Employment Conditions in New EU Member States: Convergence or Diversity?* (Geneva: ILO).
69 See ICFTU (2005) 'Comments by ICFTU/Global Unions on the World Bank's *Doing Business in 2005*: "Hiring and firing of workers"', mimeo.
70 See Lee, McCann and Messenger (forthcoming).
71 Botero *et al.* (2004).
72 World Bank (2004a).

4
Institutions and the Finance of General Skills Training: Evidence from Africa

Irmgard Nübler

4.1 Introduction

The International Labour Organization (ILO) considers investment in training to be the shared responsibility of both the public and the private sector.[1] Enterprises should be committed to the development of skills and competences as skills enhance productivity, adoption of new technologies and competitiveness of firms and the employability of workers. These benefits provide good economic reasons and incentives to firms and workers to invest in skills and training.

In many countries, however, investments in skills are not at the levels needed by society. Three main arguments are provided for the low level of private investment in training. First, economic theory argues that firms face disincentives to finance training as they cannot establish ownership of the human capital in which they invest. They face behavioural uncertainty of trained workers who may leave the firm before it has fully recovered its training costs. The traditional training model of neoclassical economics, distinguishing between firm-specific and general skills, suggests that firms are motivated to finance on-the-job training in firm-specific skills since they are only productive and valuable to the training firm.[2] In contrast, firms will not invest in transferable skills such as general vocational skills and core skills as they can be used productively in different jobs, occupations and enterprises. Financing transferable skills puts the training firm at risk of losing its investment.

A second reason for the low level of private financing of training is poverty among workers, in particular in developing countries. Poor workers are unable to finance expensive skills training and cannot therefore invest in training even when they could expect significant returns.[3] Finally, imperfect capital markets do not provide credit to workers to invest in their human capital. Economic theory concludes that markets fail to provide an efficient level of general skills training due to behavioural uncertainties and the risk of losing the investment, poverty, and imperfect capital markets.

Training policy reforms in the formal economy of many developing countries aim to provide incentives to private firms to invest more in the general and transferable skills of their workers.[4] Policies focus on the funding mechanism and developing levy grant systems, establishing training funds and providing fiscal incentives such as tax rebates, training credits and training awards. Policies also promote collective training agreements and promote the establishment of apprenticeship schemes.[5] Empirical evidence on the effectiveness of training policy reforms, however, demonstrates at best a mixed record in motivating firms to invest in transferable skills.[6]

In the informal economy, training is provided mainly on the job and informal training systems remain the dominant form of learning skills in developing countries.[7] Apprentices acquire the relevant skills of a trade, many of which are general and transferable in nature. Training is almost exclusively financed by the private sector. In traditional apprenticeship systems, the employers and workers share the training costs, and firms finance training in general and transferable skills in the absence of training policies and government interventions providing extra incentives.[8] This implies, first, that firms and workers receive sufficiently high rates of return to their investment in training and secondly, that apprenticeship provides a safeguarding mechanism by which firms can protect their investment in general skills training. According to Castro *et al.*, 'One of the reasons that traditional, informal apprentices enroll by the millions in Africa and that formal apprenticeship accounts for only a few hundred is that the traditional system makes economic sense. Protecting this incentive should be the most sacrosanct policy.'[9]

This chapter analyses the mechanism by which firms safeguard their investment in general skills training in traditional apprenticeship arrangements. It argues that institutions create strong incentives for apprentices to stay with the training firm until it has recovered its training costs. This provides motivation to firms to finance training in general skills even in competitive markets.

The chapter proceeds as follows. First, a model is presented which describes the strategic nature of the training decision a firm and a worker face in financing general skills. Secondly, institutions are discussed as a way to provide incentives to apprentices to stay with the training firm and to motivate the firm to finance general skills training. Thirdly, the chapter introduces institutional arrangements into the training model. Fourthly, cases and examples from East and West Africa are provided to illustrate the role of institutions and the implications for investment in training. Finally, conclusions are drawn.

4.2 Strategic decision of firm and worker: a trust game

This chapter models the strategic decision the firm and the worker face in financing workplace training in general skills. The training arrangement is considered as a contract between the firm and the apprentice where the firm promises to train the worker in transferable skills and to finance part of it. Training increases the worker's productivity in subsequent periods, and the worker agrees to share with the firm the returns from training by accepting a wage below his or her productivity level. The worker promises to stay with the firm for a certain period of time to allow full recovery of training costs. Obviously, the worker will receive a wage below the market wage during this cost-recovery period.

Such a training contract is non-simultaneous since the fulfilment of the promises occurs at subsequent points in time and 'one party makes an investment, the profitability of which depends on the other party's future behaviour'.[10] The firm which finances general training faces uncertainty in terms of the trained worker's future behaviour as the worker may break the promise. Financing general skills training therefore makes the firm vulnerable to a 'hold-up' on its investment, that is, general training has increased the worker's bargaining power and they therefore may demand a larger share of the returns to training or threaten to leave the training firm.

The training trust game

The decisions of the firm and the apprentice are represented by a two-move trust game.[11] The firm and the worker move sequentially, reflecting the strategic aspect of the decision to invest in training. The game is not repeated since a particular firm and the apprentice only play the training game once. Each strategy results in a particular outcome or pay-off to the firm and to the worker.

The model is presented in an extensive form. The tree describing the two-move game is depicted in Figure 4.1.

The firm moves first and has to choose between two strategies: 'investing in training', Y1, and 'not investing in training', N1. We assume that the worker is unable to finance extensive apprenticeship training. If the firm decides not to invest (N1) the game ends and the pay-off to each player is nil (0,0).

However, if the firm has chosen the strategy 'investing in training' (Y1), it finances the training of the worker. Once the firm has invested and the worker has acquired the general skills, it is the trained worker's turn to move. The worker also has the choice between two strategies: 'keep promise' (Y2), (i.e. allowing the firm to collect returns from its investment), and 'break promise' (N2) (i.e. to defect and to hold up the firm's investment). The game ends once the apprentice's choice is made.

The pay-off structure is asymmetric, that is to say the firm's pay-off differs from the worker's pay-off. If the firm chooses to invest in training and the apprentice chooses to cooperate (strategy Y1, Y2), the firm and the worker will share the benefits from increased productivity during the cost-recovery period. The pay-off to the firm is $\beta > 0$, the worker's pay-off is $\alpha > 0$. Upon completion of the apprenticeship contract, the apprentice will receive

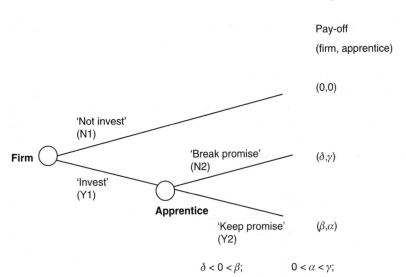

Pay-off

(firm, apprentice)

$\delta < 0 < \beta;$ $0 < \alpha < \gamma;$

Figure 4.1 Trust game in training

a skilled worker's income (see Annex for a detailed analysis of the pay-off structure).

Should the worker decide to break the promise and leave the training firm before the termination of the apprenticeship contract, the worker will receive the higher market wage immediately after training; the pay-off is $\gamma > \alpha$. The firm cannot recover its costs and its net benefit is negative $\delta < 0$.

The structure of the pay-off has two important implications. Firstly, from $\alpha < \gamma$ it follows that the apprentice has incentives to break the contract once the firm has invested. The firm faces strategic uncertainty because the trained apprentice may leave the firm before it has fully recovered training costs.[12] Rational firms therefore will not invest in general skills. Since we are assuming that the worker is unable to finance apprenticeship training, the market fails to provide general skills training. Training models developed in the neoclassical tradition are based on this line of argument.

Secondly, the strategy (N1) represents a unique equilibrium of the game which does not represent the most efficient outcome.[13] From $0 < \beta$ and $0 < \alpha$[14] follows that the firm and the apprentice would be better off had they chosen to play the cooperative strategy (Y1, Y2). The firm would prefer to invest in the general skills of its workers since it could benefit from higher productivity and adoption of new technologies. The worker who cannot afford to finance long-term apprenticeship training would prefer a strategy where the firm finances her training and she cooperates. In this situation, the apprentice would love to persuade the firm of her intentions to fulfil the contract, 'but mere words would not ... be sufficient'.[15]

Credible commitment through institutions and hostages

The challenge in the strategic training game is for the apprentices to provide credible commitment to the firm that they will fulfil the training agreement and choose the cooperative strategy. Obviously, markets are unable to solve the commitment problem.[16] This chapter argues that institutions play a central role in providing credible commitment to firms in apprenticeship arrangements. Institutions create commitment devices which change the apprentice's *pay-off and incentive* structure such that cooperation becomes rational *ex-post*. Institutions can be defined as rules which guide human behaviour and shape human interaction.[17] Informal institutions such as traditions, customs and norms, and formal institutions such as laws and regulations constrain human behaviour, increasing behavioural predictability and thereby reducing strategic uncertainty.[18] Institutions therefore create incentives to economic players to enter non-simultaneous agreements.

This chapter argues that traditional apprenticeship arrangements in West African countries are based on informal institutions which guide the decisions and behaviour of firms and apprentices. By following the rules provided by apprenticeship arrangements, credible commitment devices are created which persuade the firms to invest in general skills.

Furthermore, the chapter identifies 'economic hostages' as the commitment device in apprenticeship arrangements.[19] The issue of a final apprenticeship certificate represents an important economic hostage. Apprentices receive a certificate or a letter at the end of the apprenticeship period if the apprentice had respected the apprenticeship agreement and had played the cooperative strategy. If the apprentice breaks the contract, the firm will not issue the final certificate to the apprentice. In other words, the firm will destroy the economic hostage which has no value for the firm, but high value for the worker.

The certificate has high value for the apprentice since it gives privileged or exclusive access to employment or self-employment in the trained occupation, craft or trade. The final apprentice certificate therefore becomes an entry requirement to the skilled labour market or to self-employment in the trained trade. As a consequence, only those apprentices who have received the certificate can derive the full returns from the skills and human capital they have acquired in apprenticeship training.

The hostage training game

Let us introduce economic hostages into the training game and view how they change the strategic decision of firms and apprentices. The tree describing the hostage training game is depicted in Figure 4.2.

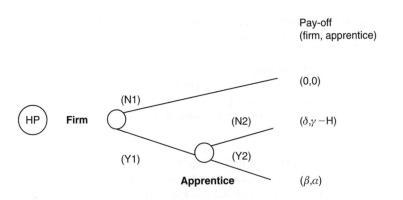

$\delta < 0 < \beta; 0 < \alpha < \gamma; H > 0$

Figure 4.2 Hostage training game

Economic hostages are available to the firm *prior* to the firm's decision whether or not to invest in training. We may consider hostage posting (HP) as a strategic move in the training game. The value of the hostage H to the apprentice is $H > 0$ and represents the value of future benefits the trained worker can derive once the hostage is given to them.

Since the hostage has no value to the firm, its pay-off structure will not be affected. Hostage posting, however, changes the apprentice's pay-off structure. By breaking the contract and leaving the firm once trained, the worker can avoid the low apprenticeship wage during the cost-recovery period. However, in contrast to the training game without hostages, the worker cannot gain an income that fully reflects the increased productivity. Without the certificate, the worker is denied access to self-employment or employment in the trained occupation. As a consequence, throughout their working life, the defecting apprentice will receive an income which is below the income they could have received had they obtained the certificate. The pay-off to the defecting apprentice is $\gamma - H$.

This hostage training model provides the conditions under which firms finance general skills training. First, the firm and the worker have incentives to engage in general skills training if the rate of return to their investment is positive, that is $\beta > 0$ and $\alpha > 0$.

Secondly, the firm will be willing to finance general skills if it can trust that the worker will cooperate and allow the firm to recover its training costs. The hostage arrangement needs to provide a credible commitment to the firm that the apprentice will play the cooperative strategy. This requires that the changes in the apprentice's pay-off structure result in an *incentive* structure which makes cooperation rational *ex-post*, that is,

- the value of the hostage is sufficiently high that the outcome of the cooperative strategy (Y1, Y2) exceeds the outcome of the defective strategy (Y1, N2), that is $\alpha > \gamma - H$ or $H > \gamma - \alpha$[20];
- the hostage arrangement is irreversible and cannot be made void by the apprentice.[21]

Thirdly, the worker is willing to accept the hostage arrangement if she has trust in the firm and is confident that it will issue the certificate once she has kept her promise and respected the apprenticeship agreement. Dasgupta argues that people develop confidence in the ability of social institutions 'to function as is expected of it'.[22] This confidence in institutional functioning is based on reputation which is acquired through 'behavior over time in well-understood circumstances' and repeated experience and observation that institutions enforce the rules. In traditional apprenticeship, firms follow informal rules, workers observe that these rules are enforced and they therefore develop trust in the institution apprenticeship. This convinces apprentices to play the cooperative strategy in the training game.

Fourthly, hostage posting and the release or destruction of hostages incurs transaction costs to the apprentice and to the firm. These transaction costs need to be sufficiently low in order to motivate the firm and the worker to establish and use a hostage arrangement. The firm's transaction costs τ^F and the worker's transaction costs τ^W need to be below the pay-off to the investment in training, that is, $\tau^F < \beta$ and $\tau^W < \alpha$. If the transaction costs are prohibitively high, the hostage is not posted and, consequently, the firm will not invest in training. It is a major function of institutions to reduce transaction costs. By providing rules, the behaviour of people becomes, to a large extent, predictable and reduces the transaction cost of human interactions.[23] Rule-following behaviour of firms on the labour market or in a particular trade/sector establishes the certificate as an entry requirement to employment or self-employment. The final apprenticeship certificate can be issued at low costs and it costs even less to destroy the hostage, that is, to deny the issue of the certificate to the defecting apprentice. The institutionally provided hostage arrangement therefore involves low transaction costs for the individual firm and apprentice. As a consequence, many firms use the hostage arrangement and they finance a significant amount of general skills training.

4.3   Evidence from Africa

The hostage training game has highlighted the critical role institutions play in meeting the conditions under which firms and workers have an incentive to invest in training and are willing to finance general skills training during apprenticeships. The following examples from Africa provide illustrations of how firms secure their investment in transferable skills through hostages. A study of the traditional apprenticeship system in Togo demonstrates the role of institutionally-provided hostages in motivating many firms to finance general skills training in apprenticeship. An example of a private hostage arrangement between a firm and a worker is provided by the case of a formal enterprise in Kenya. The case shows that such arrangements may involve substantial transaction costs and therefore will result in limited motivation of firms to invest in training. Finally, a study of the informal apprenticeship in Kenya provides a good example where the lack of both institutional and private hostage arrangements largely prevents firms from financing general training. The study indicates that training in this context is largely financed by the apprentices.[24]

Traditional apprenticeship in Togo

In a study of traditional apprenticeship in Lomé, Togo, Fluitman and Oudin estimated that in 1989 about 25,000 young people worked as apprentices in the informal economy and that each year as many as half of the new entrants to the Lomé labour force found places as apprentices.[25] Apprenticeship remains well established in the informal economy in West African cities, in almost all artisan trades and repair services. Training incidence in apprenticeship systems is high and many firms provide apprenticeship training.

Apprenticeship lasts for several years in Togo. This provides the opportunity to teach a broad range of transferable skills. Apprentices learn trade-specific technical skills and how to use the tools and equipment of their trade and 'it is not uncommon to find that masters follow a plan, even if unwritten'.[26] In addition, apprentices acquire skills which apply to many trades such as negotiating with customers and suppliers or repairing equipment.

The conditions under which an apprentice enters into training with a master craftsperson are clearly specified for both parties.[27] The master negotiates and concludes a contract with the parents. The contract stipulates the conditions such as the duration of the apprenticeship, entry payments and gifts to be made, probation period, the obligation of the master and those of the apprentice, and are usually written and signed in the presence of witnesses.[28] Apprentices stay with their master craftsperson for several years. The length of the cost-recovery period is determined in advance and the apprentice continues to stay even having acquired all relevant skills.

Costs are shared between the worker and the master. Most apprentices in the study, for example, paid their master an initial fee equivalent to the monthly wage of an unskilled worker and many apprentices offer a gift to the master. The apprentice is not paid a wage but receives pocket money at the master's discretion, the frequency and amount tending to increase as the

Table 4.1   Apprenticeship fee in Togo

Duration of apprenticeship (in years)	2	3	4	5
Payment (in FCFA)	45,000	25,000	20,000	18,000

apprentice becomes more productive, and some are offered free lodging and meals.[29]

Although there are no data available on the magnitude of investment of informal enterprises in apprenticeship training, an interesting indicator of a firm's investment can be found in a training contract which has been used by firms in Lomé since 1982.[30] The fee an apprentice has to pay depends on the length of his or her cost-recovery period. Table 4.1 shows that the fee decreases as the apprenticeship period is extended.

The structure of fees suggests that the firm bears net costs mainly during the first two years of training. Studies of traditional apprenticeship training in West African countries confirm that a large part of training and learning takes place during the first two years of apprenticeship.[31] Should an apprenticeship be terminated after this period, the firm would have only a limited period of time to recover some returns from increased productivity. The worker therefore has to pay a fee which covers net costs. However, if the firm has negotiated a longer training period it can recover costs from increased productivity during subsequent periods. The large difference in fees between an apprentice who stays for two years and one staying for three years indicates that the firm recovers costs of up to 20,000 FCFA during the third year. The comparatively small reduction in fees for apprentices staying for four or five years is explained by increases in pocket money. The firm recovers costs from improved productivity but passes on an increasing share of the marginal product to the worker during the fourth and fifth years.

At the end of the agreed apprenticeship period most apprentices are expected to pass a test or produce a 'master piece'. Apprentices 'gain their freedom' and receive a certificate, 'le free', showing that they have successfully completed their apprenticeship.[32]

'Le free' functions as a hostage which the entrepreneur keeps to enforce the training contract. It gives privileged access to self-employment in the informal economy in an apprenticeable trade since 'many [artisans] insist that whoever wants to get started in their trade should have demonstrated, through a traditional apprenticeship, to be a worthy newcomer'.[33] Without the certificate, aspiring entrepreneurs are likely to encounter harassment or worse from others in the trade. Established firms discourage a defecting apprentice from establishing a competing enterprise by threats and may beat him or her and eventually destroy the enterprise. Available data confirm that a successful apprenticeship is the major entry requirement into a craft or trade; almost all male entrepreneurs in apprenticeable trades (car repair, dressmaking, metalwork, carpentry, radio/TV repair and masonry) and female dressmakers have been apprentices in the trade in which they now practice as self-employed workers.[34]

Formal apprenticeship in Kenya: individual hostage arrangement

In the 1980s, training policy in Kenya aimed to encourage firms in the formal economy to finance skills development of their workers and to overcome the market failure in general skills training. The government established a training levy-grant system to redistribute training costs between training and non-training firms. A levy was raised as a percentage of the payroll tax of formal enterprises and a training grant was given to firms which had financed approved vocational and technical training. The levy grant reimbursed to the firm makes up part of its training costs.

In Kenya, the textile industry was among the earliest modern manufacturing activities, and in the early 1980s, it was the leading manufacturing activity in Kenya. Demand for skilled textile workers was high and the poaching of skilled workers a serious problem. The town of Eldoret, about 300 kilometres north-west of Nairobi, hosted three large textile companies. The companies faced a serious shortage of skilled textile workers and the firms blamed each other for poaching the other firm's skilled workers.

During an interview conducted with the manager of a privately owned textile company in 1986, the manager explained the mechanism his firm used to safeguard its investment in formal skills training of some of the workers.[35] The firm faced a serious shortage of skilled workers and it could not recruit them from the labour market. In addition, the company wanted to recover its contribution to the training levy fund. The firm financed approved apprenticeship training for some selected workers and recovered part of these costs from the training fund. Since the training was in general and transferable skills the trained worker had the opportunity to leave the firm after training. This made the firm vulnerable to losing out on its investment and it needed to safeguard that part of the training costs which was not covered by the training fund.

The training scheme was not supported by institutions which could give credible commitment to the firm. The commitment problem was solved by a private hostage arrangement between the firm and the worker. According to the manager's statement, the firm proposed formal apprenticeship training to those workers whose family members worked in the company as unskilled workers. In addition, it recruited even more family members as unskilled workers while the worker was trained. By employing a critical number of relatives, the firm created an economic hostage which it could destroy if the trained worker attempted a hold-up on the firm's training investment. The firm would simply dismiss all his relatives. The worker was aware of the hostage posting and the threat of the firm to destroy the hostage in case of opportunistic behaviour.

In this example, the economic hostage had a high value to the trained worker. Unemployment for unskilled labour was high, and the family members would have had serious difficulties in finding employment elsewhere. Hence, the worker's family would experience a loss in future income and the worker would have to increase his support to the extended family. The economic hostage provided incentives to the worker to stay with the firm during the cost-recovery period and it motivated the firm to finance his general skills training. Such private hostage arrangements, however, can only be applied to a limited number of apprentices and therefore, the incidence of training tends to remain low.

Informal apprenticeship in Kenya: A lack of hostages

In their studies of informal apprenticeship in the late 1970s, King and McLaughlin both argue that arrangements in East Africa differ from the West African apprenticeship system in that they are less institutionalized.[36] The training agreement in East African apprenticeship does not stipulate an apprenticeship period. Apprentices stay between a few months and not much above a year and they leave when they master the skills. There is none of the codification and informal rules of the West African system and no ritual of freeing the apprentice at the end of his apprenticeship period.[37]

This 'open' apprenticeship system does not provide hostages to firms. King reports from the indigenous apprenticeship in Kenya that 'there seem to be no sanctions that the master can use to hold on to his trainees beyond the time they wish to stay'.[38] The most obvious feature of the system is the determination of trainees to establish their own business as soon as possible. As a consequence, firms are not motivated to finance general skills training. King reports that trainees (or their parents) paid the entrepreneur for the particular skills that they wanted to learn.[39] Depending upon the skill, they paid between 100 KSh and 600 KSh, with auto repair costing 450 KSh, the equivalent of one year's fees in a government boarding school.

Furthermore, the duration of training is limited by the ability of young workers to finance training. McLaughlin finds that training in Kenya, even in the more established trades like automotive repair, seems to be far shorter in duration than in the same trades in West Africa. In Kenya, apprentices develop a narrow specialty and quickly progress to master status as compared 'with the more comprehensively trained and financially prosperous craftsmen in West Africa'.[40]

In addition, while a high percentage of young people have access to training in West African countries, in East Africa fewer young people receive training, partly because those from poor families are unable to afford the training fees. In contrast, in Togo institutionally provided hostages allow many firms to finance and create relevant skills in significant quantities.

4.4 Conclusions

Institutions play a critical role in providing incentives to firms to finance apprenticeship training. They help to overcome market failure in general skills training by changing the apprentice's pay-off and incentive structure. This provides credible commitment to firms that the apprentice will stay until the firm has recovered its training costs.

Training contracts which are not supported by institutional arrangements provide limited incentives to firms to finance general skills. These contracts require firms to protect their investment in general skills by measures such as private hostage arrangements, levy grant, tax refund or public subsidies. Also, labour market imperfections resulting in limited outside options to trained workers provide some incentives for firms to finance general skills training.

Furthermore, the institutionally provided hostage arrangement in traditional apprenticeship opens training opportunities for poor young people. They lack the means to finance long-term training themselves and they cannot receive credit due to a lack of collateral and imperfect capital markets. By accepting the final certificate as a hostage, poor apprentices can offer their *future* income from increased human capital to persuade the firm to finance their general skills training.

Finally, traditional apprenticeship training often suffers from serious shortcomings such as the low quality of training, the provision of traditional skills, lack of theoretical knowledge, poor working conditions and missing links to the formal training system. Training policies therefore may aim to upgrade the traditional apprenticeship system and link it with the formal training system and labour market. In order to protect the incentives for firms to finance general skills training, such policy interventions need to be carefully designed and they need to be sensitive to the role of informal institutions, traditional rules and customary laws. In particular, care must be taken not to destroy the mechanism which safeguards the firm's investment. In some countries efforts are made to recognize prior learning of workers in the informal economy in order to increase their employability in the formal economy. The assessment and certification of workers' skills and competencies by formal institutions become problematic for traditional apprenticeship if an apprentice's skills can be recognized before the end of the apprenticeship period. The final apprenticeship certificate would lose its function as a hostage and firms may be less motivated to finance apprenticeship training.

ANNEX: The training game

The worker and the firm conclude an apprenticeship contract

$t = 0, \ldots, g$:   agreed apprenticeship period

$t = 0$:	the firm invests in training I(0)
$W(0)$:	wage of apprentice without training
$MP(0)$:	marginal productivity without training

$t = 1$:	the apprentice decides whether to fulfil the contract or to break it.
$t = 1, \ldots, n$:	the worker's productivity is enhanced due to general skills training

$W(t)$:	wage of trained apprentice
$MP(t)$:	marginal productivity of trained apprentice

Assumption: the firm covers all training costs

Playing strategy (Y1, Y2): the firm invests, the worker respects the contract

$t = 1, \ldots, g$:	the apprentice receives the apprentice wage $W(t) < MP(t)$ which is below the market wage of skilled workers the firm recovers costs from $MP(t) - W(t)$
$t = g$:	the firm has fully recovered training costs
$t = g + 1, \ldots, n$:	the skilled worker receives the higher market wage

α:	net present value of the worker's finite sequence of pay-offs
$1/(1+q)$:	the worker's discount factor

$$\alpha = \sum_{t=1}^{n} \frac{W(t) - W(0)}{(1+q)^t}$$

β:	net present value of the firm's finite sequence of pay-off
$1/(1+r)$:	firm's discount factor

$$\beta = \sum_{t=1}^{g} \frac{MP(t) - W(t)}{(1+r)^t} - I(0)$$

Playing strategy (Y1, N2): the firm invests, the worker leaves the firm after training

$t = 1, \ldots, n$:	the apprentice receives the market wage $W(t)$ and avoids the low apprenticeship wage during $t = 1, \ldots, g$; the firm cannot collect returns to its investment
γ:	net present value of the worker's infinite sequence of pay-offs

$$\gamma = \sum_{t=1}^{n} \frac{W(t) - W(0)}{(1+q)^t}$$

δ:	firm's net pay-off to training

$$\delta = -I(0)$$

Notes

1 ILO (2003) *Learning and Training for Work in the Knowledge Society*, Report IV(1), International Labour Conference, 91st Session, p. 104; Human Resources Development Recommendation, 2004 (No. 195).

2 G.S. Becker (1975) *Human Capital* (Chicago: The University of Chicago Press).

3 This is due to low family income, lack of savings and a failure of the capital market to provide credit for investment in human capital.

4 A.G. Mitchell (1998) 'Strategic Training Partnerships Between the State and Enterprises', *Employment and Training Paper 19*, Training Policies and Systems Branch (Geneva: ILO), p. 33, and ILO (1999b) *World Employment Report: 1998–99* (Geneva: ILO), p. 93.

5 ILO (1999b).

6 I.S. Gill, F. Fluitman and A. Dar (2000) *Vocational Education and Training Reform: Matching Skills to Markets and Budgets* (Washington, DC: World Bank and Oxford University Press), p. 33.

7 ILO (1999b), p. 60.

8 Mainstream economic models cannot explain this phenomenon. The economic literature refers to tradition, culture and positive attitudes towards training, and a 'common vision' of firms as possible factors contributing to a firm's incentive to finance training (A.G. Mitchell, op. cit., p. 18). See also F. Fluitman and A.K. Sangré (1989) 'Some Recent Evidence of Informal Sector Apprenticeship in Abidjan, Cote d'Ivoire', in *Training for Work in the Informal Sector* (Geneva: ILO), and K. King (1977) *The African Artisan: Education and the Informal Sector in Kenya* (London: Heinemann).

9 C. de Moura Castro, K. Kempner and D. Bas (2000) 'Apprenticeship: The Perilous Journey from Germany to Togo', in C. de Maura Castro, K. Schaack and R. Tippelt (eds), *Vocational Training at the Turn of the Century* (Frankfurt am Main: Peter Lang), p. 146.

10 A.A. Alchian and S. Woodward (1988) 'The Firm is Dead; Long Live the Firm. A Review of O.E. Williamson's *The Economic Institutions of Capitalism*', *Journal of Economic Literature*, 26(1), p. 66.

11 The training game adopts the trust game suggested by P. Dasgupta (1988) 'Trust as a Commodity', in D. Gambetta (ed.), *Trust: Making and Breaking Cooperative Relations* (New York: Basil Blackwell) and D.M. Kreps (1990) 'Corporate Culture and Economic Theory', in J.E Alt and K.A. Shepsle (eds), *Perspectives on Positive Political Economy* (Cambridge: Cambridge University Press). It represents a one-sided Prisoner's dilemma game in the sense that players' strategy set and pay-offs are asymmetric (E. Rasmusen (1995) *Game and Information* (Cambridge, MA: Blackwell), p. 139). The game is assumed to be played non-cooperatively, that is, individuals are motivated only by the monetary pay-offs involved, and that they have no opportunity to sign a binding and enforceable contract. Further, it is assumed that the players have complete information on the structure of the game and the pay-off.

12 In the training game, the firm makes its training decision by reasoning *backwards* (Dasgupta (1988), p. 61). Backward induction can be applied to any two-stage game of perfect information. See D. Fudenberg and J. Tirole (1993) *Game Theory* (Cambridge, MA: MIT Press), p. 73.

13 The equilibria is pareto sub-optimal.

14 The firm has preferences of strategies (Y1, Y2) > (N1) > (Y1, N2), The trainee has preferences of strategies (Y1, N2) > (Y1, Y2) > (N1).

15 Dasgupta (1988).
16 Training models in the neoclassical economics tradition therefore have a hard time explaining firms' investment in general skills. More recent training models introduce market imperfections in order to explain investment of firms in general training. Imperfect product markets (H. Gersbach and A. Schmutzer (2001) 'A Product Market Theory of Training and Turnover in Firms', Discussion Paper No. 327 (Bonn: IZA (Institute for the Study of Labour)) and imperfection in labour markets, such as compressed wage structures and mobility costs (D. Harhoff and T.J. Kane (1997) 'Is the German Apprenticeship System a Panacea for the U.S. Labor Market?', *Journal of Population Economics*, 10), as well as asymmetric information (D. Acemoglu and J.-S. Pischke (1998) 'Why do Firms Train? Theory and Evidence', *The Quarterly Journal of Economics*, 113(1)), provide some incentives to firms to invest in general skills training.
17 D. North (1990) *Institutions, Institutional Change and Economic Performance* (Cambridge, MA: Cambridge University Press), p. 182.
18 O. Williamson (1985) *The Economic Institutions of Capitalism: Firms, Market and Relational Contracting* (New York: Free Press), pp. 17 and 29.
19 T. Schelling (1960) *The Strategy of Conflict* (Cambridge, MA: Harvard University Press) and Williamson (1985) introduce the concept of 'economic hostages' as a commitment device.
20 The game has a sub-game perfect equilibrium such that a valuable hostage is posted, the firm chooses to invest in general training, and the apprentice chooses to fulfil the contract. Cooperation has become an individually rational strategy in the sub-game played after hostage posting. The apprentice has the opportunity to make a hold-up, but no longer has incentives to do so.
21 Schelling (1960), p. 127.
22 Dasgupta (1988), p. 52.
23 Williamson (1985), p. 29.
24 It should be noted that the term 'apprenticeship' is used for many different arrangements between an employer and a young worker. Often, these arrangements lack a training agreement and they have to be considered as disguised child labour where little training takes place or where workers only acquire some skills as a side effect of their work.

    In addition, it is often argued that long indenture periods are a means of exploitation. Further empirical research is required to determine whether the indenture period of apprenticeships exceeds the length of the cost-recovery period, given the firm's costs and returns to training.
25 F. Fluitman and X. Oudin (1992) 'Skill Acquisition and Work in Micro-enterprises: Evidence from Lomé, Togo', Discussion Paper, Vocational Training Branch (Geneva: ILO), p. 8.
26 Ibid., p. 42.
27 S.D. McLaughlin (1979) *The Wayside Mechanic: An Analysis of Skill Acquisition in Ghana* (Amherst, MA: Centre for International Education), p. 77.
28 Fluitman and Oudin (1992), p. 41.
29 Ibid., p. 42. In the study, 25 per cent of apprentices in the sample received free food and lodging.
30 C. Maldonado and G. Le Boterf (1985) 'L'Apprentissage et les apprentis dans les petits métiers urbains. Le cas de l'Afrique francophone', Working Paper, WEP (Geneva: ILO), p. 110.
31 Fluitman and Sangré (1989).

32 Fluitman and Oudin (1992), p. 43.
33 Ibid., p. 39.
34 Ibid., p. 19.
35 The interview was conducted by the author in the context of a research project to study the implementation and effectiveness of the industrial training funds in Kenya.
36 King (1977); McLaughlin (1979).
37 King (1977).
38 Ibid., p. 51.
39 Ibid., p. 50.
40 McLaughlin (1979), p. 57.

5

The Origins of Unemployment Insurance: Lessons for Developing Countries

Janine Berg and Matthew Salerno[1]

5.1 Introduction

Since the beginning of the twentieth century, programmes to aid workers who have lost their jobs have become a predominant feature of labour markets, but the controversy surrounding these programmes – severance pay, unemployment insurance and unemployment assistance – is as great today as it was when the programmes were first established. Though most industrialized countries established unemployment insurance programmes nearly a century ago, many countries in the developing world have no unemployment insurance systems in place and only limited programmes of unemployment compensation.

While there is much agreement that the severance pay systems that exist in the developing world should be revised in order to allow businesses to adjust their workforce to the demands of international competition, there is considerable debate about what programmes, if any, should replace these systems. Many critics argue that unemployment insurance is inappropriate for developing countries because they cannot afford them and worse, that the benefits would only privilege the already better-off.

On the other hand, it is recognized that unemployment is a significant problem in many developing countries and that high levels of economic insecurity pose both political and economic problems. Moreover, workers alone should not be forced to bear the adjustment costs associated with globalization. What is proposed instead is a 'flexicurity' system whereby workers receive some sort of income protection as they make the transition between jobs. This chapter gives a history of the development of unemployment insurance in Europe since the late nineteenth century in order to draw lessons on the appropriateness of such a system for developing countries. The purpose is not to promote unemployment insurance as the only viable programme, but as one of several programmes available that developing countries can institute in response to the varying needs of its workforce.

5.2 The different ways of compensating unemployment

Compensation to the unemployed can take a variety of forms – severance pay, unemployment insurance, unemployment assistance, work programmes as well as traditional poor relief – each of which responds to different policy objectives with concomitant benefits and drawbacks for workers, employers and governments. In general, all of the different programmes cushion workers from the financial costs of job loss and in doing so mitigate the economic effects of a recession.

Severance pay is a benefit paid by the employer to the employee upon termination of the employment contract. Severance is essentially a lay-off tax paid by employers that discourages dismissal, potentially increasing labour force attachment. If, however, termination of contract is due to employee fault, such as misconduct, or is the employee's choice, then no severance is paid. Firms subject to severance pay laws are presumed to invest more in their workforce, because of their greater labour force attachment, though critics contend that the policy infringes mobility. Moreover, severance pay can worsen a firm's financial condition if it is forced to pay benefits during an economic recession. Workers also risk losing their benefits if a firm declares bankruptcy.

Unemployment insurance seeks to improve labour force matching by ensuring that workers have sufficient time to find a job that better matches their skill level, potentially improving the overall productivity of the economy. By providing security to workers, unemployment insurance can facilitate the restructuring associated with economic opening. It can also allow enterprises to adjust to changes in the market or the economy as a whole by laying off workers in difficult times and then re-hiring them when the business conditions improve. Unemployment insurance, however, is criticized for increasing unemployment if benefits are so high that workers prefer idleness to working (the so-called moral hazard problem).

Unemployment insurance savings accounts (UISA) are private savings accounts that workers can draw on in the case of job losses, retirement or death (in which case the heirs receive the funds). Because the accounts are individual, the worker internalizes the cost of the benefits and thus does not have the incentive to prolong unemployment.[2] But UISAs are also associated with their own form of negative incentives, such as encouraging workers to quit their jobs in order to access the funds. Also, as UISAs are forced savings rather than insurance, risk is not pooled. As such, they can only play a limited role in protecting against contingency as unemployment can occur before sufficient funds have been accumulated – particularly in developing countries where job tenure is much lower and turnover much greater. Unemployment may also simply outlast the funds.

Unemployment assistance is a means-tested benefit programme that seeks to help those workers with the greatest needs. Some countries combine unemployment insurance with unemployment assistance programmes that allow the long-term unemployed to shift to an assistance programme after their unemployment insurance benefits are exhausted. Traditional poor relief programmes, also known as social assistance or welfare programmes, similarly target the neediest segments of the population through self-selection. Historically, poor relief was aimed at women and children and discouraged 'able-bodied' men from receiving benefits, oftentimes by requiring that beneficiaries live in poor houses.

Work programmes also self-select from the neediest groups by paying wages that are at or below the minimum wage, and sometimes in kind, in exchange for work. Some programmes are well organized and include projects to build roads, schools and clinics, thus improving a country's infrastructure while simultaneously teaching skills to participants. Other programmes are less well run and unable to organize productive work projects, and are sometimes accused of profligacy.

Depending upon the profile of the employer, worker, employer or government, there are distinct advantages and disadvantages to each of the policies. Employers will have different preferences towards one system or another depending upon how affected the firm is by fluctuations in market demand as well as the skill level of its workforce. According to Mares, firms in industries that are subject to large fluctuations in market demand will prefer a universal programme that low-risk firms will oppose as they do not want to subsidize high-risk industries. If the high-risk firm employs highly skilled workers it is likely to support a universal, contributory insurance programme that pools risks but preserves existing wage and skill hierarchies; by contrast, a low-risk industry employing mostly low-skilled workers will prefer not to have any programme, or, as a second-best option, will prefer a universal, tax-financed programme that pays a low level of benefits.[3]

Workers will be guided by similar preferences, according to their earnings. Thus, better-paid workers with strong labour force attachments will prefer severance or contributory unemployment insurance programmes with benefits determined by the level of earnings whereas low-wage workers will prefer universal programmes, including social assistance. For this reason, some European trade unions opposed the introduction of universal programmes on the grounds that their higher-skilled workers would be subsidizing the benefits of low-skilled workers; they were also reluctant to surrender control of union-run programmes.

For governments, the main considerations are the policy objectives as well as the costs of the programme, both financial and administrative. Severance pay, for example, imposes no costs on governments and is thus attractive to countries with low administrative capacity. There is no enrolment by workers or employers and governments are not obliged to monitor the actions of beneficiaries.[4] If, however, governments would like to ensure that beneficiaries are indeed unemployed and actively looking for work, then they are more likely to adopt programmes that have controls on the beneficiaries. These are more costly to run, but help to ensure that the programme meets its social policy objectives. For example, in an attempt to decrease long-term unemployment in Europe, the European Commission has mandated that unemployed workers, after a certain time, participate in training or other active labour market policies or else risk losing benefits. These programmes are considerably more expensive than simply issuing a cheque, as they require governments to organize or monitor different types of work and training programmes. Nevertheless these policies improve the labour force integration of workers.[5] Similarly, experience rating on employers is a form of control placed on employers by government to deter lay-offs. Under experience rating, companies' contributions to unemployment insurance funds are higher if they lay off workers more frequently. Because companies' termination payments increase the more they lay off, there is an additional incentive to limit lay-offs. Moreover, the policy helps to limit firms with a stable workforce from subsidizing firms with an unstable workforce.

Depending upon the policy objectives, unemployment benefit programmes differ with respect to their generosity (the level and duration of benefits), their coverage and the degree of controls – specifically, the monitoring, means testing, job search and work requirements associated with the programme. Conditions for receipt of benefits include waiting periods, qualification period (contingent on time in job and contributions into the system), qualifying conditions (must be actively looking for work) and disqualifications (dismissal for misconduct or voluntary leaving), as well as different types of financing and calculation of contributions (flat or earnings related).[6] Moreover, benefit schemes can be voluntary or compulsory; local or national, and either publicly or privately run, including by trade unions, mutual aid societies or private firms.

Developing countries have generally favoured severance pay, work programmes and poor relief over unemployment insurance and unemployment assistance programmes. On the other hand, most industrialized countries use unemployment insurance to compensate the unemployed, with a smaller number favouring unemployment assistance programmes. Nevertheless, as mentioned earlier, activation policies – specifically training requirements – have become a prominent feature of insurance programmes. Still, the preferences of countries have evolved over time, as we will see in the next section.

5.3 The origins of unemployment insurance

It took many years for the concept of aid to the unemployed to become widely accepted. One of the first forms of government-sponsored social assistance was the English Poor Laws, established in 1598 to provide financial support to women, children and the elderly poor. When the laws began to provide for unemployed able-bodied males at the beginning of the Industrial Revolution, the legislation was heavily criticized for encouraging idleness and perpetuating rather than alleviating unemployment. As a result, a stigma was placed on any able-bodied, unemployed workers who sought relief. To further discourage the unemployed, unpleasant 'workhouses' were created, where poor working conditions and limited aid repelled all but the most desperate from collecting aid.[7] But with the Industrial Revolution and the development of a mass of urban labourers, came the vicissitudes of market capitalism – fluctuations in the demand for labour and, as a result, spells of high unemployment. The need for some sort of safety net to protect displaced workers from the vagaries of the labour market was apparent, but it would nevertheless take more than a century for the first national unemployment insurance systems to be established.

Most of the early aid given to the jobless came from trade unions, labour federations and other collective groups unaffiliated with the national government. These groups sought to establish a basic form of protection against the instability of the labour market. After the foundation of the English Foundrymen's Union in 1831, the first trade union fund for the unemployed, other trade union funds quickly developed. By 1900, well over one hundred different trade union funds were established across England, covering some 1.2 million workers.[8]

A distinctive characteristic of these unions, however, was their exclusivity. Because membership was limited to the more skilled trades and the payment of dues, less-skilled workers, who were more vulnerable to the loss of their jobs, were almost always excluded. In 1892, for instance, fewer than 10 per cent of workers in England were members of trade unions, and of those, only six out of ten received any form of unemployment insurance. In other words, despite hundreds of trade unions in existence servicing over a million workers across the United Kingdom, 94 per cent of workers had no protection against unemployment. Yet despite their low coverage levels, trade unions did provide a level of protection for those fortunate enough to be members. And, more importantly, these unions blazed a trail for the enactment of national systems of unemployment protection by ameliorating some of the stigma associated with collecting unemployment benefits, as well as by establishing financing systems based on contributions by members, independent of individual risk.

Between 1880 and 1890, Europe was ravaged by widespread unemployment. As the unemployed became more of a strain on parishes and poor relief systems, local unemployment funds began to appear across Europe. The first local unemployment scheme was put in place in Bern, Switzerland in 1893, and this was mimicked quickly by Cologne, Germany in 1896.[9] Both schemes were financed by voluntary worker contributions, but were limited in scope: Bern's local system only had 597 members; Cologne's, 536. In 1895,

St Gallen, in Switzerland, became the first city to implement an unemployment insurance system financed by compulsory contributions from workers. Unfortunately, the programme lacked measures to prevent abuse and went bankrupt after only two years. The unemployment scheme developed in Ghent, Belgium in 1901 was financed by member contributions as well as public subsidies (accounting for between 50 and 75 per cent of fund benefits). In 1902, the Ghent system had 12,239 members and provided benefits to 27 per cent of them; by 1908, the system had grown to include 17,600 members, providing 43 per cent with benefits in the same year. Together, these local unemployment schemes, based on voluntary and compulsory workers' contributions and government subsidies, became the basis from which the first national unemployment schemes would soon emerge.

In 1905, France instituted the first national unemployment insurance scheme, modelled on the Ghent system in Belgium. The scheme provided government subsidies to locally organized programmes. By the end of 1906, 47 associations had been formed, providing coverage to over 33,000 members. Each association that met certain criteria would receive government funds, which along with the individual contributions, were distributed to unemployed members. Within two years of development, Ghent (or voluntary) systems were established in Norway and Denmark, and by 1934, the Netherlands, Finland, Belgium, Switzerland, and Sweden had developed similar schemes.

Governments were more reluctant to implement compulsory unemployment insurance, and it was not until 1911 that the first national compulsory system of unemployment insurance was established. Ironically, the movement came from the pioneers of both the Poor Laws and the workhouse – England. The English system was revolutionary for a number of reasons. First, the legislation marked a dramatic shift from the Poor Laws that had been in place for hundreds of years, thus signalling a slow but pervasive change in the mentality of countries towards the unemployed. And secondly, the English system used a tripartite system of unemployment insurance financing (paid for by workers, employers and the government) based on flat contributions.

Over the course of the next 20 years, Austria, Germany, Ireland and Italy all adopted unemployment compensation schemes. By 1949, 22 countries had developed some form of insurance to protect the unemployed, 19 of them OECD countries, and 50 years after the passage of the first compulsory unemployment compensation scheme, all European countries had some form of unemployment insurance in place.[10] In the postwar period, approximately 50 more countries adopted plans, so that by 2005, roughly 80 unemployment benefit programmes existed in the world.[11]

Considering the reluctance of countries to implement any types of protection for the unemployed from 1596 to 1905, it was remarkable that such a revolutionary system gained wide acceptance in such a narrow frame of time. Unemployment insurance was quite distinct from poor relief in that its main intention 'was not to help destitute people in cases of emergency, but to prevent destitution through routine measures'.[12] It focused on the maintenance of earned income by providing benefits to the (male) breadwinner as opposed to women and children, who had been the primary beneficiaries under poor relief. Moreover, by requiring beneficiaries to contribute to the financing of the programmes, it strengthened their legal claim to benefits.[13] But unemployment insurance was generally the last of the social insurances to be adopted. Typically, the first was insurance for industrial accidents, followed by sickness, old age and, then, unemployment. It was usually introduced last 'because the notion of state support for undeserving poor required the most radical break with liberal and patrimonial principles'.[14]

As part of a string of social insurance programmes, unemployment insurance may have been anticipated, but there is no one condition that prompted its establishment. High levels of unemployment and strengthened social movements propelled some countries into passing unemployment insurance programmes, but differences prevailed in the social and political contexts of the countries that limit the drawing of general conclusions. In the case of Germany, for example, the 1881 decision by Bismarck to institute the world's first welfare state was less a gesture of goodwill and more part of 'a campaign to destroy the growing social democratic movement'.[15] Bismarck reasoned that by creating contented workers, there would be less of a reason for them to join the newly developed socialist party.[16] Germany was not the only country where this strategy was employed. In Denmark, 'the appearance of a fairly strong trade union movement ... [in conjunction with] the Social Democratic Party convinced the conservatives and liberals of the necessity to reform the Poor Law system'.[17] In other instances, however, such as in Norway and France, union leaders originally opposed state-sponsored insurance 'for fear that state participation would threaten union autonomy'.[18] Alber, studying the political parties in place when unemployment insurance was established in 11 European countries, finds that liberal and labour governments had a greater propensity to establish programmes than conservative governments. Liberal governments favoured voluntary schemes whereas labour governments had the highest propensity to adopt compulsory programmes.[19]

In the United States, the destitution created by the Great Depression, which poor relief and private charities were unable to ameliorate, prompted the government to introduce a national unemployment insurance system in 1935, despite their having initially distanced themselves from European trends. Similarly, Australia's decision to introduce a national insurance programme in 1945 stemmed in part from the high level of unemployment experienced in the early 1930s.[20] The Recommendations and Conventions of the International Labour Conference (ILC) of the ILO also influenced countries' decision to set up unemployment insurance programmes.[21] Indeed, the first Recommendation adopted by the ILC was the Unemployment Recommendation of 1919, which stated:

> The General Conference recommends that each Member of the International Labour Organisation establish an effective system of unemployment insurance, either through a Government system or through a system of Government subventions to associations whose rules provide for the payment of benefits to their unemployed members.

In 1934, in the midst of the Great Depression, the ILC adopted the Unemployment Provision Convention (No. 44) which mandated that countries establish and maintain benefits and allowances to unemployed workers.[22] The Convention, however, included a number of important exceptions, including domestic servants, employees in public services, youths, agricultural workers and fishermen.[23]

The Convention reflected the practice in national law of excluding certain workers. Many countries excluded agricultural workers because of the difficulties involved in levying contributions as well as the 'special nature of their employment' given that it was 'difficult to distinguish between wage-earning agricultural workers, and those that cultivate a certain amount of land on their own behalf, and are consequently able to work for themselves, even if they are unable to obtain paid employment'.[24] Italy, for example, originally included agricultural workers in the Decree of 19 October 1919, but it was 'found impossible to apply the principle of compulsory insurance' to agricultural workers, prompting the government to exclude them in the Decree of 30 December 1923.[25] Similarly, most countries excluded domestic servants. In Germany, the motive given was 'the favourable state of the labour market for domestic servants and also the fact that contributions impose too heavy a financial burden on them'.[26] Nevertheless, in countries that had voluntary systems, such as Denmark and Finland, domestic servants could become insured through membership in the trade union fund.

Coverage was an important concern for governments because of the challenge it posed to the financing of any scheme. The German system of unemployment insurance was implemented just before the Great Depression, before sufficient reserves could be accumulated. This prompted the government to severely limit the coverage of the scheme until sufficient funds were accumulated to broaden the programme. Similarly, the British system ran into massive deficits upon its inception, as it tried to create too broad a coverage. In Australia, poor records of unemployment leading up to the programme's development made it impossible to estimate potential costs, and some states refused to fund the programme if it meant subsidizing other states. In the United States, high contribution rates were temporarily established across all states to make sure the programme would not collapse from insufficient funding. Furthermore, there was a two-year gap between the establishment of the insurance system and the first benefit payouts in order to ensure enough funds to support the massive number of unemployed.[27] Even the Polish system, which was established in 1989 during its transition to capitalism, ran into severe deficits three years into the programme, forcing the government to impose work tests, tighten eligibility and switch to flat benefits.[28] Thus, although many countries experienced challenges with financing, all took measures to solve the problems without terminating their programmes and many programmes are continuously being adjusted to ensure proper financing.

Many of the European unemployment insurance programmes began as voluntary (also known as Ghent) systems and then were made compulsory, though Denmark, Finland and Sweden retained voluntary systems (see Table 5.1). 'Voluntary' systems received dedicated funds from the state, were protected by law, and mandated affiliation and contributions by its members. What classified them as voluntary is that they were voluntarily established and administered by trade unions, tripartite boards or mutual aid societies, rather than by governments. In common with other insurance programmes, risk was pooled; thus they should not be confused with self-insurance programmes.

The adoption of voluntary systems versus compulsory programmes depended on economic and political interests in the countries. For example, France originally chose a voluntary system because of resistance on the part of French employers to the more costly compulsory system advocated by trade unions.[29] The French economy was dominated by small businesses, most of which were not unionized, thus 'a Ghent system was not a concern nor was a means-tested policy of unemployment assistance'.[30] In Germany, on the other hand, the economy was dominated by large firms who preferred a compulsory, contributory system to unemployment assistance or to union-run voluntary programmes, as this would allow them to retain some control by defining eligibility conditions and benefits. In the employers' view, a voluntary system 'was a subsidy to the strike fund of unions'.[31] It was only after the German trade unions dropped their demands for a voluntary system, and there was a time of discontent among employers and unions alike with the assistance programme, that the government, along with the social partners, was able to introduce a compulsory insurance programme.

As Table 5.1 indicates, European governments typically opted for unemployment insurance, both voluntary and compulsory, before adopting assistance programmes. Only in Germany and Sweden did assistance programmes precede insurance programmes, and, as explained in the case of Germany, discontent with this system spurred the establishment of a compulsory insurance programme in 1927. Unemployment assistance programmes were transitional measures instituted to mitigate destitution during economic crises as well as to alleviate some of the strain placed on insurance programmes, particularly from the long-term unemployed.

Table 5.1 Dates of legislative enactment of unemployment compensation

Country	Voluntary insurance	Compulsory insurance	Extension to agriculture	Unemployment assistance
Austria	—	1920	1949	1926 (1918, 1922)
Belgium	1920	1944	1944	—
Denmark	1907	—	1907	1921
Finland	1917	—	1917	1960
France	1905	1967	—	1914
Germany	—	1927	1927	1918
Ireland	—	1923	1953	1933
Italy	—	1919	1949	1946 (1917–19)
Netherlands	1916	1949	1949	1964
Norway	1906	1938	1949	—
Sweden	1934	—	1934	1916
Switzerland	1924	1976	n.a.	(1917, 1924, 1942)
UK	—	1911	1936	1934

Notes: () Indicates temporary measures.
— not applicable.
n.a. not available.
Source: Alber (1981).

Another characteristic of the programmes is that most countries, with the exception of Denmark, Finland, Germany and Sweden, adopted limited programmes that were only later – usually in the 1940s – extended to agricultural workers. Because the right to insurance in Denmark, Finland and Sweden was based on joining the trade union fund, including agricultural workers imposed little administrative difficulty.

Benefits provided by the programmes varied from scheme to scheme (see Table 5.2). In the United Kingdom and Ireland, which had flat-rate systems, benefits equalled 20 per cent of average weekly earnings in the United Kingdom and 25 per cent in Ireland. For the other compulsory systems, benefits were calculated as a percentage of the worker's average earnings, usually at about one-third of the wage. In the voluntary systems, benefits varied both within and across countries, depending upon the programme, but were typically set at between 50 per cent (Norway) and 66 per cent (Denmark) of earnings, though programmes included statutory maximums. Many programmes also distinguished civil status, paying higher benefits to married workers with children. Benefit duration in the original European programmes was shorter than that which exists today. Benefits ranged from 12 weeks in Austria to 26 weeks in Germany. All programmes included qualifying periods, ranging from 26 to 52 weeks in the voluntary programmes, and from 20 to 45 weeks in the compulsory systems. In the compulsory systems, financing was tripartite – with the exception of Germany, where funding was from

Table 5.2 Characteristics of original unemployment insurance systems

Country	Type of system	Level of benefits	Benefit duration	Financing	Qualifying period
Austria	Compulsory	36%	12 weeks	Tripartite and earnings-related contributions	20 weeks
Belgium	Voluntary	Variable, according to fund	Variable, according to fund	One-half worker, one-half state	Variable, according to fund
Denmark	Voluntary	Variable with a max. of two-thirds of wage	Variable, with min. of 70 days	State subsidy equalled 35% of contributions	52 weeks
Finland	Voluntary	Variable	90 days	State subsidy from one-third to one-half of contributions	26 weeks
France	Voluntary	Variable	10 weeks	State subsidy about 20–30%	26 weeks
Germany	Compulsory	Earnings-related, progressive, 35%	26 weeks	One-half worker, one-half employer	26 weeks
Ireland	Compulsory	Flat-rate, 25% of avg. weekly earnings	15 weeks	35% worker, 39% employer, 26% state	20 weeks
Italy	Compulsory	Earnings-related, progressive, 36%	20 weeks	One-half worker, one-half employer	48 weeks
Netherlands	Voluntary	Earnings-related with maximum	60 days	State and commune-funded	n.a.
Norway	Voluntary	Earnings-related with maximum	15 weeks	Three-quarters worker, one-quarter state	26 weeks
Sweden	Voluntary	Earnings-related with maximum	20 weeks	State subsidy about 35%	52 weeks
Switzerland	Voluntary	50–60% of earnings	90 days	State subsidy about 40%	30 weeks
United Kingdom	Compulsory	Flat-rate, 20% of avg. weekly earnings	15 weeks	37.5% worker, 37.5% employer, 25% state	26 weeks

Source: ILO (1925) and Alber (1981).

the employer and the worker unless there was a deficit. Employers did not participate in the voluntary systems, though contributions from the state ranged from 25 per cent (France, Norway) to 50 per cent (Belgium).

Over time, the programmes were made more generous through increases in the replacement rate and the duration of benefits – sometimes in connection with the replacement of voluntary with compulsory systems. For example, the French compulsory system, established in 1967, provided up to 52 weeks in benefits. Nevertheless, in the 1990s, many of the programmes added conditions to benefit receipt after a specific length of time, such as six months or a year, in an effort to improve labour market reintegration and reduce the level of long-term unemployment.

5.4   Is unemployment insurance suitable for developing countries?

What do the origins of unemployment insurance in Europe teach us about its applicability for developing countries? Many of the first unemployment insurance programmes were worker-initiated, collective efforts designed to provide protection from the loss of income. After some delay, governments recognized the importance of some sort of protection for workers and, in doing so, acknowledged that unemployment was not always the fault of the worker and thus was not a loss that the worker alone should bear. Often this acknowledgement came at the peak of economic crises. Governments chose either to support voluntary, often union-run schemes, by subsidizing the programmes, or to create a state-run system, often with tripartite contributions. In addition, the governments sometimes created unemployment assistance programmes during crisis periods, aimed at the more impoverished. Over time, programmes were adapted – and continue to be so – by improving financing and monitoring, including establishing work and training requirements on the long-term unemployed.

Most of the European programmes were adopted in the first three decades of the twentieth century, a time of great economic and political uncertainty and also a time when much of the labour force was still employed in agriculture. Figure 5.1 shows the percentage of the labour force employed in agriculture at the time that unemployment insurance, either voluntary or compulsory, was enacted. As the figure indicates, the 33 countries and territories listed show a wide variation in the employment share in agriculture. Finland, for example, had 69 per cent of its labour force employed in agriculture when it adopted its Ghent system in 1917, compared with just 8.8 per cent in the United Kingdom in 1911. The average for the countries is 33 per cent, whereas the average for the 13 European countries listed in Table 5.1 is 35.7 per cent. If we compare with developing countries that have insurance schemes in place, the pattern is again mixed, though most had an agricultural employment share of around 20–30 per cent. An important exception

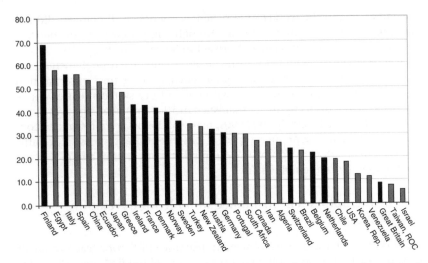

Figure 5.1   Percentage of labour force employed in agriculture at year of enactment, select countries and territories
Source: Enactment data from Alber (1981). Percentage of labour force in agriculture from B.R Mitchell (1982), *International Historical Statistics: Africa and Asia* (London and Basingstoke: Macmillan) and B.R. Mitchell (1982), *European Historical Statistics 1750–1975* (London and Basingstoke: Macmillan).

is China, where 54 per cent of the labour force was employed in agriculture when it adopted its scheme in 1986. Its scheme, like many others, excludes agricultural workers. In Brazil in 1986, 23 per cent of the labour force was employed in agriculture, whereas only 12.4 per cent were when the Republic of Korea adopted its scheme in 1995, just before the 1997 Asian crisis.

One of the main criticisms concerning the suitability of unemployment insurance for developing countries is that far too many workers do not benefit from the system as they are employed informally, either in agriculture or in urban services. Though this criticism may be true, what Figure 5.1 shows is that in many of today's industrialized countries, a large part of the labour force was employed in agriculture, and because of frequent exemptions in the legislation, also did not benefit from the newly founded programmes.

A similar criticism is that those who do benefit are 'privileged insiders' that are less in need of assistance than the informal, more impoverished members of the labour force. While it is true that only those workers that are in formal jobs benefit from the insurance, what is debatable is whether this benefit causes hardship to other non-insured members of the labour force, particularly if most of the financing comes from workers and employers. Moreover, as explained earlier, the purpose of unemployment insurance is quite distinct from poor relief and thus its appropriateness should be analysed with its objectives in mind. If a country is more concerned with providing short-term relief measures during crisis, then a means-tested assistance programme or self-selecting works programme is more appropriate. If, however, the goal is to discourage skilled workers from accepting a job that is below their skill profile out of necessity, including in the informal economy, then a contributory unemployment scheme is more appropriate. Furthermore, it is also not always apparent that only the 'rich' are benefiting. In Brazil, for example, the majority of unemployment insurance beneficiaries are low-wage earners: 54 per cent earn less than two minimum wages per month and 80 per cent earn fewer than three minimum wages.[32] Furthermore, as is typically the case in other countries, low-income, less-educated workers are more likely to become unemployed.[33]

A further criticism is that an unemployment insurance programme raises the cost of labour and thus dampens the creation of formal jobs, negatively affecting informal workers. Labour costs can rise either because of the additional cost of the programme (though there are also debates about whether workers already bear this cost in the form of lower pay) or because unemployment insurance increases the bargaining power of workers since it makes them less fearful of unemployment. On the flip side, unemployment insurance can act as an automatic stabilizer by mitigating the drop in consumption during an economic downturn, thus boosting aggregate demand and therefore employment.[34] How these competing effects play out in practice is an empirical question that is both time and place specific, limiting our ability to make generalizations. Ultimately, what Figure 5.1 endeavours to show is that many workers were originally excluded from the programmes when they were first adopted in Europe without any significantly notable impact on the economic development of the countries or on the expansion of the systems over time.

Another common criticism surrounding the suitability of unemployment insurance for developing countries is their perceived inability to afford the programme. Yet the GDP per capita of today's industrialized countries at the time unemployment insurance was enacted, is similar to the GDP of many of today's middle-income developing countries. Figure 5.2 gives information on the level of GDP per capita, measured in 2001 dollars, for 35 countries.[35] The median level of GDP per capita at the time of adoption was US$3,941. Seventeen countries had a lower level of GDP per capita, including Japan (US$1,541 in 1947), Finland (US$1,581 in 1917), Greece (US$2,358 in 1954), Italy (US$2,845 in 1919), France (US$2,894 in 1905) and South Africa (US$3,615 in 1966). Great Britain had a GDP of US$4,709 in 1911, whereas Brazil was slightly richer, with a GDP of US$5,205 in 1986, just under the USA at US$5,467 in 1935. On the high end, Australia, ranking at the 90th percentile for this group, had a GDP of US$7,362 in 1944. The richest territory was Taiwan, China, with a GDP of US$16,214 in 1999, when it adopted unemployment insurance.

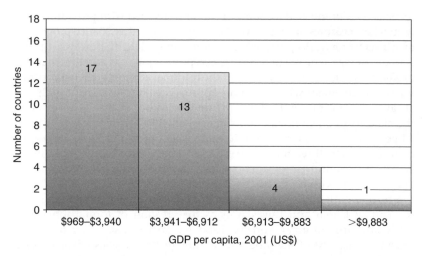

Figure 5.2 GDP per capita when unemployment insurance was enacted, 2001 (US$).
Source: Data of enactment from US Social Security Administration (1999) 'Social Security Programs Throughout the World, 1999' (Washington DC). Historical GDP data from A. Maddison (2003) *The World Economy: Historical Statistics* (Paris: OECD).

In comparison, many developing countries have no system of unemployment insurance, even though they are richer than some of the industrialized countries were at the time of adoption. Figure 5.3 shows the GDP per capita in 2001 of select countries without unemployment insurance. The line marks the median level of GDP per capita at the time of adoption for the 35 countries listed in Figure 5.2, which was US$3,941 – or middle income, according to the World Bank classification.[36] As the figure clearly shows, there are many countries that are above this level, including Tunisia (US$4,710 in 2001), which is at approximately the same level that Great Britain was in 1911; Lebanon (US$5,069) – above Switzerland's level of US$5,039 in 1924 – and Mexico (US$7,089), which is higher than the United States ($5,467 in 1935) and also above Argentina (US$6,980 in 1991). This comparison, although somewhat crude,[37] nevertheless demonstrates that many middle-income developing countries have a level of economic development that is sufficiently high to permit the institution of a programme.

Another criticism often raised is that developing countries do not have the capacity to administer an unemployment insurance programme. While it may be true that there are administrative bottlenecks that must be overcome in developing (as well as some developed) countries, this allegation is often asserted without any supporting evidence, sometimes based on theoretical models that merely 'assume' weak capacity.[38] Was the capacity of Great Britain in 1911 or Italy in 1919, when they instituted national compulsory

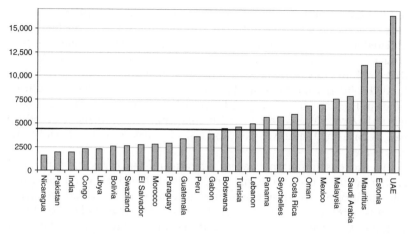

Figure 5.3 GDP per capita in 2001 of selected countries without unemployment insurance

systems, better than that of today's middle-income developing countries? It is hard to say, and certainly country specific. But there are many middle-income developing countries that already administer pension systems, training programmes, accident insurance and which have some, even if weak, system of labour offices in place. With technical assistance, these countries can develop their administrative capacities for administering either an unemployment insurance programme, or some other form of benefit programme deemed appropriate for the needs of the country.

5.5 Is unemployment insurance the right approach?

To date we have argued that the conditions that existed in today's industrialized countries are not very far removed from the conditions in today's middle-income developing countries that would prevent them from adopting some sort of benefit programme. Nevertheless, there are still some important considerations to keep in mind when adopting an unemployment benefit programme, either unemployment insurance or some other form of assistance.

One important consideration is informality. Although industrialized countries also had many workers that were ineligible for assistance because they were employed in agriculture, the presence of urban informal opportunities in developing countries makes monitoring difficult. As some critics have argued, it is possible for beneficiaries to work informally as they receive unemployment payments, or worse, to only search for informal work, so that they can continue receiving benefits.[39] For this reason, some analysts propose the adoption of unemployment insurance savings accounts (UISAs), since in a self-funded account, the worker pays the benefits. But, as mentioned earlier, a pure UISA may not provide sufficient insurance for workers if the funds accumulated are too low to sustain the worker during unemployment. A more attractive option is a hybrid system, such as that recently created in Chile that combines private savings accounts with an employer- and government-funded solidarity fund that workers can draw from if they have insufficient funds in their account. A hybrid design has the advantage of mitigating the moral hazard effects associated with collecting unemployment benefits as well as ensuring that lower-paid workers, who may have insufficient funds, are covered.

Still, the most important concern regarding informality is that many workers are excluded from receiving benefits, even though they too suffer from job and income loss during economic recessions. UISAs could be open to informal workers, but it is unlikely that many informal workers would join voluntarily. What is needed is a portfolio of programmes to address the competing needs of their labour force. Thus governments could combine some sort of insurance system, financed with tripartite contributions, with government-financed active labour market policies (ALMPs). ALMPs include a range of supply and demand measures that seek to engender labour market integration, including training programmes, work programmes, employment subsidies to enterprises, and labour market services. Work programmes, which provide a benefit in exchange for work, are commonly found in developing countries and also have a long history in industrialized countries. The programmes self-target the neediest groups through the low wage that is offered, and if they are well administered they have the benefit of creating or improving public infrastructure. Training programmes can also improve labour market integration if they teach necessary skills. Labour market services are an important anchor for coordinating the different benefit programmes as well as monitoring insurance beneficiaries. If insurance beneficiaries are still out of work after a specified time, the labour market services can then integrate the person into a work or training programme.

Since organizing work requires experience, policy-makers cannot expect to institute these programmes for a one-time crisis. Rather, the programmes should be a permanent feature of economic policy, since even though extreme economic crises may be rare, business cycle fluctuations and partial adjustment shocks are recurrent. Thus, ALMPs should not be considered a short-term solution. They can be designed and used effectively during different stages of the economic cycle (for example, public works programmes in times of job destruction or stagnation, or in response to natural catastrophes; emphasis on training during recovery periods for those workers finding it difficult to integrate in the expanding labour market). Making labour market policies, both passive and active, a permanent government policy will not only improve effectiveness at the micro level, but will also help to stabilize economic cycles.

5.6 Conclusions

Since the 1990s there has been much debate about the need for labour market flexibility. This debate, however, has become more circumspect, arguing instead that flexibility should be accompanied by some sort of security for workers. 'Flexicurity' has become the latest buzzword and while the concept is certainly appealing, particularly under conditions of globalization, there are many different views about how to ensure security. Many of the security proposals are indeed quite limited, often based on providing mechanisms for self-insurance, at times augmented with employers' contributions. This view stems from the belief that developing countries lack the resources or capacity to have programmes or that the programmes are not appropriate as they help the already privileged members of the labour force.

This chapter has tried to address some of these concerns. We have seen that many of today's middle-income developing countries are as rich and as industrialized as the industrialized countries were when they first enacted unemployment insurance. These programmes did not cover large segments of the workforce and were only extended later. Financing was at times difficult, but solutions were found to make the programmes sustainable. Benefits were modest, but nevertheless provided an important source of income during job loss. The historical analysis also highlighted the role of competing political interests in establishing programmes, making apparent the importance of tripartite dialogue when designing and implementing a new system.

If middle-income developing countries decide to adopt an unemployment insurance programme, they may also need to adopt other programmes, such as public works or training programmes, in order to ensure that informal workers also have access to income protection during difficult times. The choice of programmes will depend upon the different policy objectives. Unemployment insurance, unemployment assistance and public works or training programmes seek different outcomes and should therefore be evaluated accordingly. Where the goal is to provide relief to the neediest, a social assistance or works programme is preferable. If, however, the objective is to give firms flexibility in adjusting their labour force while ensuring that workers have income protection, improving their ability to search for a job or sustaining them during a temporary lay-off, then an insurance programme is more appropriate. Because labour markets include many different types of workers, countries are better off offering a portfolio of programmes to meet these competing but important objectives.

Notes

1   We would like to thank Zafiris Tzannatos and Maria Sabrina de Gobbi for helpful comments on earlier drafts of this chapter.

2 M. Feldstein and D. Altman (1998) 'Unemployment Insurance Savings Accounts', NBER Working paper 6860.

3 I. Mares (2001) 'Firms and the Welfare State: When, Why and How Does Social Policy Matter to Employers?', in P.A. Hall and D. Soskice (eds), *Varieties of Capitalism: The Institutional Foundations of Comparative Advantage* (Oxford: Oxford University Press).

4 D. MacIsaac and M. Rama (2001) 'Mandatory Severance Pay: Its Coverage and Effects in Peru', mimeo, World Bank.

5 ILO (2003) 'Active Labour Market Policies', Paper prepared for the 288th session of the Governing Body, GB.288/ESP/2.

6 J. Alber (1981) 'Government Responses to the Challenge of Unemployment: The Development of Unemployment Insurance in Western Europe', in P. Flora and A. Heidenheimer (eds), *The Development of Welfare States in Europe and America* (New Brunswick: Transaction Books).

7 P. Lindert (2004) *Growing Public: Social Spending and Economic Growth since the Eighteenth Century*, vol. 1 (New York: Cambridge University Press).

8 Alber (1981) and I. Gibbon (1911) *Unemployment Insurance: A Study of Schemes of Assisted Insurance* (Westminster: P.S. King and Son).

9 This paragraph and the next one draw on Gibbon (1911) and Alber (1981).

10 W. Vroman (2004) 'International Evidence on Unemployment Compensation Prevalence and Costs', Paper prepared for the International Social Security Association meeting, Beijing.

11 Tzannatos and Roddis (1998) counted 77 unemployment benefit programmes in the world. See their paper for a list of the programmes, including information on the type of programme, its coverage and sources of financing. Since their survey, the Republic of Korea, Kuwait and Taiwan (China) have established programmes. (Z. Tzannatos and S. Roddis (1998) 'Unemployment Benefits', *Social Protection Discussion Paper Series*, No. 9813, World Bank).

12 Flora and Heidenheimer (1981) 'The Historical Core and Changing Boundaries of the Welfare State', in Flora and Heidenheimer (eds), op. cit., p. 279.

13 Ibid.

14 Flora and Alber (1981) 'Modernization, Democratization and the Development of Welfare States in Western Europe', in Flora and Heidenheimer (eds), op. cit., pp. 51–52.

15 Flora and Heidenheimer, op. cit., p. 17.

16 US Library of Congress, 'Social Welfare, Health Care, and Education', *Country Studies* [Online Available] 2003. http://countrystudies.us/germany/111.htm.

17 As quoted in Korpi (2004) citing N.F. Christiansen and K. Petersen (2001) 'The Dynamics of Social Solidarity: The Danish Welfare State, 1900–2000', *Scandinavian Journal of History* 26(3): 179.

18 Alber (1981), p. 154.

19 Ibid.

20 G.H. Ince (1937) *Report of Unemployment Insurance in Australia*, The Parliament of the Commonwealth of Australia, 22 February.

21 Ibid.

22 Since 1934, the ILC has promulgated two more Conventions concerning benefits to the unemployed: the Social Security (Minimum Standards),1952 (No. 102), and the Employment Promotion and Protection against Unemployment Convention, 1988 (No. 168). Convention No. 102 set forth specific standards on eligibility and benefits. Convention No. 168, passed in 1988 and considered up to date by the

ILO's Governing Body, highlights the contribution that social security can make to employment promotion and strengthens the recommendation on unemployment benefits given in Convention No. 102, as this level had been surpassed by most industrialized countries.

23 A. Alcock (1971) *History of the International Labour Organisation* (London: Macmillan), p. 108.

24 ILO (1925) 'Unemployment Insurance: Study of Comparative Legislation', *Studies and Reports Series C* No. 10, Geneva, pp. 12–13.

25 Ibid., p. 13.

26 Ibid., p. 15.

27 S. Blaustein (1993) *Unemployment Insurance in the United States: The First Half Century* (Kalamazoo, MI: W.E. Upjohn Institute for Employment Research).

28 J. Mazza (1999) 'Unemployment Insurance: Case Studies and Lessons for Latin America and the Caribbean', Inter-American Development Bank, Working paper, May.

29 I. Mares (2000) 'Strategic Alliances and Social Policy Reform: Unemployment Insurance in Comparative Perspective', *Politics and Society* 28(2).

30 Ibid., p. 228.

31 Ibid.

32 The Brazilian minimum wage was 260 reais per month in 2003 or approximately US$84 per month.

33 Based on probit analysis by author using the Brazilian household survey (PNAD) for 2002 and 2003.

34 For example, a study of the effects of unemployment insurance in the United States estimated that the programme mitigated the loss in real GDP by approximately 15 per cent during the five recessions that occurred between 1969 and the early 1990s, resulting in an average peak saving of 131,000 jobs. See L. Chimerine, T. Black and L. Coffey (1999) 'Unemployment Insurance as an Automatic Stabilizer: Evidence of Effectiveness Over Three Decades', Occasional Paper 99–8 (Washington, DC: US Department of Labor).

35 Figure 5.2 excludes countries from Central and Eastern Europe as they adopted unemployment insurance programmes during atypical circumstances – namely their transition to capitalism in the early 1990s. Some of them, for example Poland in 1924, had adopted programmes in the first part of the twentieth century, but these were later discontinued. The remaining countries were chosen based on availability of information.

36 The World Bank classifies countries as low income if their GNP per capita is US$477 or less; lower middle income as US$1,612; middle income as US$2,170; and upper middle income as US$4,482. Based on 2005 data from *World Development Indicators* online.

37 A preferable comparison would be to use purchasing power parity (PPP), but such historical PPP data do not exist.

38 See, for example, M. Vodopivec (2006) 'Choosing a System of Unemployment Income Support: Guidelines for Developing and Transition Countries', *World Bank Research Observer* 21, and I. Gill and N. Ilahi (2000) 'Economic Insecurity, Individual Behavior and Social Policy', paper prepared for the regional study, *Managing Economic Insecurity in Latin America and the Caribbean* (Washington, DC: World Bank).

39 Vodopivec (2006).

6
The Revival of Minimum Wage Setting Institutions

François Eyraud and Catherine Saget

6.1 Introduction

The minimum wage is a labour market institution used in the majority of countries throughout the world. This is illustrated by the fact that a large number of countries, 116 in total, have ratified one or both of the two ILO minimum wage fixing Conventions.[1] In addition, many more countries have established minimum wage fixing procedures, even though they have not ratified these Conventions.[2] The minimum wage has had a long and turbulent history. Today, after decades of being dismissed as a social and economic policy tool, the minimum wage is now back in favour, in part thanks to the many impact studies which have adopted a more objective approach in dealing with the issue. This chapter will show that, contrary to widespread belief, the minimum wage is commonly used by governments and social partners in developing countries. Amongst the most noticeable and promising changes in recent legislation are the attempt to extend coverage and also the more careful use of economic and social criteria for adjusting the minimum wage.

At first glance, it seems all too easy simply to define the minimum wage as the wage floor applying to all wage-earners in order to ensure that they receive at least a minimum of protection when it comes to their pay. In reality, things are a lot more complicated, as may be seen by the amazing variety of legislative texts and practices existing in this area. The first section will give an overview of the complexity and the variety of institutional arrangements put in place to set the minimum wage. However, a careful analysis of the way minimum wages are set shows the very close link between minimum wages institutions and the development of collective bargaining. This will be addressed in the second section. We will then see how the minimum wage has become a major instrument of economic and social policy that makes its analysis quite complex. First, it is often considered as a useful tool for the reduction of poverty. This will be considered in section 6.4, while we will address the more specific issue of workers without any form of wage protection in section 6.5. Linked to the question of poverty, the minimum wage is seen as having a significant impact on wage inequality. This relationship will be detailed in section 6.6. Finally, its effects on employment have also been studied at length. We will consider in section 6.7 where we stand on this issue.

6.2 Minimum wage setting institutions

International labour standards on minimum wages have both been influenced by and have, in turn, influenced national mechanisms. The first relevant Convention (No. 26) was adopted in 1928; the second (No. 131), which makes a special reference to developing countries, in 1970. They are very similar in the principles they set out. Convention No. 26 asks the members who ratify it to create minimum wages in trades 'in which no arrangement exists for the effective regulation of wages by collective agreement or otherwise and rates are exceptionally low'. Convention No. 131 is less specific by referring to 'all groups of wage earners whose terms of employment are such that coverage would be appropriate'. In terms of the coverage of both cases, however, neither one imposes (though does not exclude) a national statutory minimum wage. Nonetheless, minimum wages set should be binding to the employers to which they apply. The other main common principle is that both Conventions require, as a minimum, the full consultation of the social partners. However, only Convention No. 131 is specific about the criteria, by explicitly referring to two sets of factors to take into account when fixing minimum wages: the needs of the workers and economic factors.[3]

Indeed, these basic principles are embedded in the national mechanisms that countries have established. However, the range of possible devices is endless, depending upon the number of parties involved in the wage-fixing process and the characteristics of the work or the types of employee in question (the kind of activity, where it is carried out, the worker's qualifications, and so on). To better understand these mechanisms, it is useful to distinguish them on the basis of two axes: the type of social dialogue procedures and the categories covered.

In the context of social dialogue, minimum wage fixing procedures vary from governmental statutory decisions to the negotiation of wages through joint agreements. In the Lao People's Democratic Republic and Nigeria, it is the government that sets the minimum wage, while in Greece it is fixed through an agreement between the social partners. In Poland, a tripartite commission establishes the minimum wage. Nevertheless, in most cases, it is the government that decides, usually after consultation or bargaining with trade unions and employers' organizations.

With regard to the categories covered, these methods fall within a range stretching from the setting of a single minimum rate, to the fixing of wages covering a large section of the wage hierarchy used in companies: Madagascar has a single rate; India, 1,230 rates. No universal system exists that would, for example, limit the role of the minimum wage to the protection of the most at-risk workers regardless of economic activity whilst playing a clearly defined role within the national system of minimum social protection. Table 6.1 summarizes the main systems.

Finally, it should be stressed that a wide range of criteria are employed for deciding on minimum wages that vary according to the country and the period in time.[4] The reason for this is that each of these criteria is linked to different objectives. In one country, the minimum wage may be perceived as a way of ensuring a decent standard of living; in this case, the criterion of purchasing power will take precedence over other considerations. However, the fight against inflation may well be a priority in another country – or might become so in the same country at a later date. Here, it is the inflation rate that will be the main factor. Yet again, there is an aspect common to all these different situations: the minimum wage is an economic and social policy instrument which makes it possible to achieve varied objectives – from income distribution to economic competitiveness. In each country, it is adjusted in many ways, reflecting national characteristics and models – a process that is not devoid of contradictions, as we will see in the following sections. But first let us consider the question of the link between minimum wage fixing machinery and the development of collective bargaining.

6.3   The minimum wage and collective bargaining

Despite the variety of procedures, there is one basic issue that is common: collective bargaining, or, rather, the 'choice' that is made between state intervention and collective bargaining. The latter is always a factor in the minimum wage fixing process: through attempts to make up for its absence or to curtail, establish or develop it. In many cases, the minimum wage is a starting point, from which – once it has been established – the collective bargaining process branches out to cover other aspects of working conditions.

If this is the case, it is because from the outset minimum wage fixing has been linked intrinsically to the level of development of collective bargaining and the role of the state in wage policy. Indeed, wages have always been the primary concern for wage-earners. More often than not, in the absence of a structured collective organization, requests for pay increases have led to disputes and strikes. To make up for the lack of a collective bargaining structure that would have provided the means to settle disagreements amicably, governments have often had to intervene directly to resolve wage disputes. With time, in certain states, collective bargaining has gradually been developed to such an extent that, in the end, it has been capable of dealing with wage disputes. In other countries, the state has continued to play the main role in wage-setting.

Table 6.1 Minimum wage-fixing procedures

National or regional minimum wage rate set by government or tripartite body	Sectoral and/or occupational minimum wage rate set by government or tripartite body	National or regional minimum wage rate set through collective agreement	Sectoral and/or occupational minimum wage rate set through collective agreement[1]
ASIA			
Australia, China, India,[2] Indonesia, Japan, Republic of Korea, Lao People's Democratic Republic, Nepal, New Zealand, Pakistan, Papua New Guinea, Philippines, Thailand, Viet Nam[3]	Bangladesh, Cambodia, Fiji,[4] India,[5] Japan, Malaysia,[5] Nepal, Pakistan,[5] Philippines, Solomon Islands, Sri Lanka		Fiji, India, Malaysia, Pakistan
AFRICA			
Algeria, Angola, Burkina Faso, Chad,[6] Gabon, Ghana, Guinea-Bissau, Madagascar, Morocco, Mozambique, Nigeria, Sao Tome and Principe, Senegal, Tunisia	Botswana, Lesotho, Mauritius, South Africa		Botswana, Namibia, South Africa
AMERICAS			
Argentina, Bahamas, Bolivia, Brazil, Canada,[7] Chile, Colombia, Haiti, Mexico, Panama, Paraguay, Peru, Trinidad and Tobago, United States, Uruguay, Venezuela	Belize, Costa Rica, Cuba, Dominican Republic, El Salvador, Ecuador, Guatemala, Honduras, Mexico, Nicaragua, Panama, Paraguay		

(Continued)

Table 6.1 (Continued)

National or regional minimum wage rate set by government or tripartite body	Sectoral and/or occupational minimum wage rate set by government or tripartite body	National or regional minimum wage rate set through collective agreement	Sectoral and/or occupational minimum wage rate set through collective agreement[1]
ARAB STATES Lebanon, Syria			
EUROPE Albania, Bulgaria, Czech Republic, Estonia, France, Hungary, Ireland, Israel, Latvia, Lithuania, Luxembourg, Malta, Netherlands, Poland, Portugal, Romania, Russian Federation, Slovenia, Slovakia, Spain, Turkey, United Kingdom	Cyprus, Czech Republic,[8] Malta	Belgium, Greece	Austria, Finland, Germany Island, Italy, Switzerland, Sweden

Notes:
1. In many countries, collective bargaining determines wage rates for certain sectors that are higher than the minimum rates set by an authority. These are not included in the table, as rates thus set are an addition to the basic statutory minimum. Note has only been made of examples where collective bargaining is the only means used to establish minimum wage rates, either for sectors that do not have minimum wage rates set by an authority (e.g. India) or those countries in which all minimum wage rates are determined by collective bargaining (e.g. Germany).
2. Reference is made here to one of the three procedures used in India: the recommended federal floor.
3. In Viet Nam, minimum wage rates vary depending on whether a company is foreign or locally owned.
4. The Minister of Labour establishes minimum wage rates for workers in sectors where there is no effective collective bargaining mechanism in place.
5. Minimum wage rates established for sectors or occupations in which there is no effective collective bargaining mechanisms in place.
6. The Labour Code, 1996, states that minimum wages should be determined by collective agreement, but in fact minimum wages fixed by the government at that date have not been adjusted since this new method was introduced.
7. Two states have been provided as an example: Ontario and Manitoba.
8. In addition to the national minimum wage, the government sets minimum tariffs. These minimum tariffs only apply if an employer chooses not to conclude a collective agreement.

New Zealand is thus held to be the first country to have implemented a modern system to regulate minimum wages with the principal aim of avoiding labour disputes. This system was introduced at the end of the nineteenth century. Much later on, in Uganda in 1957, the colonial authority at the time published a report recommending an increase in the minimum wage, which had been frozen for around ten years, on the grounds that the absence of an appropriate wage-fixing system could lead to unrest and strikes.[5] It is also very revealing that the first example of state intervention regarding minimum wages in European countries, at the beginning of the last century, was an attempt to protect domestic workers. Indeed, the fact that this group was fragmented and covered very many distinctive employment relationships, made it extremely difficult for its members to have even a minimum organization to enable them to defend their rights through collective bargaining. Other categories of workers were supposedly able to organize themselves to defend their interests through collective bargaining. In the United Kingdom, wages councils were therefore set up for these very reasons in the sectors where organization was at its weakest; in others, the social partners fixed wages through collective bargaining. A pattern was then designed that is still present in many former British colonies.[6] This clearly shows that minimum wage systems are closely linked to the ability – or lack of it – of collective bargaining to deal with wage fixing. From the outset, therefore, state regulation and intervention, on the one hand, and collective bargaining, on the other, have, on this issue, been interchangeable; the context is the determining factor.

This relationship between minimum wage fixing, state intervention and the development of collective bargaining is still present in countries which have recently moved to introduce such systems. The system in Lesotho, which fixes wages for 21 manual occupations, is under the control of the government. Taking into account the details involved, this is not just a straightforward minimum wage system; it is much more a regulation of actual wage policies. Nowadays, trade unions disapprove of this type of rigid mechanism that does not take into account the ability of companies and sectors to pay. Trade unions now feel strong enough to replace this system with true sectoral collective bargaining. Should this trend continue, the minimum wage will have served as a catalyst in the development of collective bargaining. Once established, negotiation procedures might deal with a wider range of issues than just wages (working time, working environment, and so on).

One basic conclusion may be drawn from this analysis: historically, the minimum wage has, more often than not, triggered the development of collective bargaining. But that does not mean that the passage has always been smooth or that there have been no exceptions to the rule. For instance, British trade unions were long opposed to the establishment of a minimum wage, based on the very practical concern that wage-earners guaranteed a minimum wage would have less reason to join a trade union in order to defend their interests.[7] The basic problem lies in the definition of the aim of having a minimum wage: fixing a wage floor or regulating the entire wage-fixing process. The political will of the actors concerned and their efforts to organize are linked to this problem.

Experience has shown that, when social dialogue deals only with the fixing of a minimum wage at the national level, considerable pressure is exercised at this level, leading to demands for increases that may seem excessive. This is the case because it is the only forum in which trade unions can show clearly what they are doing to defend the workers. Minimum wage fixing therefore becomes a serious source of conflict. Adjusting bargaining levels to the stated objectives reduces the social pressure involved in minimum wage fixing. Associating this process with sectoral or enterprise-level negotiations that set out to establish wage levels adapted to their economic situation, as well as their internal job market, means that possibilities and constraints can be better taken into account, thus introducing increased objectivity and rationality into social dialogue.

Once it has been set up, a statutory minimum wage fixing system can still carry out functions other than those that fall under collective bargaining. This is especially true when it comes to issues within the field of economic policy – be they poverty, wage inequality or employment.[8] The system acquires another dimension which explains, if not justifies, why, once established, the state wishes to retain control over it rather than placing it back in the hands of collective bargaining. That is what this chapter seeks to explore.

6.4   The minimum wage and poverty

The main aim of the minimum wage is to protect the lowest wage-earners in order to guarantee them a decent standard of living. This aim represents what is both laudable and ambiguous about the minimum wage. On the positive side, it is an instrument used in the defence of the poorest wage-earners. It is, however, ambiguous because of this very virtue, in that it is often seen as the perfect instrument in the fight against poverty in general, a role that it cannot possibly fulfil in isolation.

From the very beginning, the principle of the minimum wage has been that it is an income unconnected with the act of production; it is a sum owed to the worker and essentially linked to the status of the wage-earner. The earliest methods of minimum wage fixing clearly demonstrate this approach. It is irrelevant whether or not an enterprise can pay or if the wage-earner's output is sufficient; the minimum wage is primarily concerned with how much the worker needs to live on – and not only the worker, but his or her family. No reference is made to the worker's contribution to the enterprise in terms of production; what counts is whether a worker can provide for himself and his family. When the minimum wage was first introduced in industrialized countries, wage-earner productivity was not even an issue. Wages were so low that workers were not properly paid, no matter how much they produced. Of course, things are very different today in a number of countries. Could the minimum wage now be used as a tool in the fight against poverty?

A common criticism levelled against the minimum wage as an anti-poverty instrument is that it benefits only wage-earners and, furthermore, only those working in the formal economy, provided it is applied. Of course, this is a particularly serious restriction in developing countries but, all too often, the level of restriction has been exaggerated. The wage paid to a worker in the formal economy goes towards ensuring, in part, the survival of an extended family, whatever the country's level of development. What is more, the minimum wage has an impact on wages in the informal economy, in that it provides a benchmark. It has been demonstrated that an increase in the minimum wage has led to a rise in wages in the informal economy. This has been the case in certain Latin American middle-income countries, such as Argentina, Brazil, Mexico and Uruguay, where the minimum wage was relatively low during the 1980s, at between 20 and 25 per cent of the average wage. In those countries, almost all workers in the formal economy received wages that were higher than the minimum wage, while many workers in the informal economy received exactly the minimum wage. Many saw their wages rise with each readjustment of the minimum wage, including during periods of low inflation.[9] Finally, the minimum wage is a powerful means of increasing the wages of individuals at the bottom of the pay scale. For example, when the minimum wage in the United States was raised by 13 per cent in 1990, workers whose wages were lower than the new rate, received, on average, a 10 per cent increase.[10]

The fact that, in many countries, certain social benefits are linked to the level of and variations in the minimum wage is often overlooked. Most commonly, the relationship is with retirement benefit and disability payments. It is less often linked to unemployment and maternity benefits. In many West African, North African and Latin American countries, a fixed percentage of the minimum wage (between 60 and 100 per cent) makes up the minimum retirement benefit of beneficiaries. In the Netherlands, the threshold for unemployment benefits, as well as that for disability payments, is 70 per cent of the minimum wage.

In this way, the minimum wage is being used as a 'social floor'. For example, in such a system, the adjustment of retirement benefits with each increase in the minimum wage should, in principle, maintain the purchasing power of the very poorest pensioners. In addition, society as a whole is able to benefit from the progress brought about by economic development and the fruits of growth when minimum wage adjustments are linked accordingly.

When the minimum wage has this basic role, it is both fair (the most vulnerable pensioners need a guarantee that the purchasing power of their retirement benefits will not be eroded) and straightforward (a single instrument adjusts an entire section of the social protection system). However, there is clearly a risk that any rise in the minimum wage may lead to a huge increase in social security costs – and a certain lack of flexibility ensues. An interesting case in point is Brazil. Since the mid-1990s, the minimum wage in this country has risen in real terms and the government increased it by 8.33 per cent in May 2004 – i.e. at a rate higher than that of inflation. But this policy change did not satisfy the trade unions because, in terms of purchasing power, as the minimum wage had lost ground after years of increases at rates which did not keep up with rises in the cost of living, this latest increase could not make up the difference. The government's basic objection to a massive increase in the minimum wage lay in its link to numerous social security benefits. Such a move would have threatened the stability of the public budget.

In conclusion, it is fair to say that the minimum wage plays – or can play – a role in the fight against poverty. However, in order for this to be meaningful, the minimum wage should be part of a battery of measures forming a coherent policy in the fight against poverty amongst workers. This is also the position adopted in the Minimum Wage Fixing Recommendation, 1970 (No. 135). There should be no contradiction between the level of the minimum wage and the system that provides the subsidies enabling the most destitute to live, whether or not they be wage-earners.[11] Looking at things from this angle, an assessment of earnings of workers paid the minimum wage should be one of the criteria for judging the success or failure of this policy – alongside its impact on employment, for example. In addition, the impact of a minimum wage policy on poverty cannot be studied seriously without discussing legislation that applies to the poorest groups of workers.

6.5   Workers with no form of wage protection

Workers lacking any form of wage protection include domestic, agricultural and casual workers, as well as those who work from home (homeworkers). Table 6.2 lists the countries in which these groups are not covered by the minimum wage or receive a lower minimum wage.[12]

Most common among the excluded groups are domestic workers. In a number of Asian countries, they are not covered by minimum wage legislation. As mentioned above, these countries define only the categories of employment where the minimum wage applies, and the excluded groups are not listed. In Nepal, for example, the minimum wage is defined as being applicable only in firms, and in a given subset of firms at that. By default then, domestic workers are not covered in this country, nor do they benefit from minimum wage protection in Cambodia, the Republic of Korea, the Lao People's Democratic Republic, the Solomon Islands, Sri Lanka and Thailand.[14] In India, there is a minimum wage system targeted at the informal economy which covers most unskilled occupations and sectors. However, domestic workers are not among those covered. In several other countries (e.g. Bangladesh, Cyprus,

Table 6.2 Categories of workers excluded from the principal legislation on the minimum wage

	Excluded from coverage by the primary legislation on minimum wage	Receive a minimum wage below the standard minimum wage
Domestic workers	Bangladesh,[1] Cambodia, Indonesia, India,[2] Republic of Korea, Lao People's Democratic Republic,[2] Malaysia, Nepal, Solomon Islands, Sri Lanka,[2] Thailand, Guinea-Bissau, Tunisia,[2] Morocco, Lebanon, Manitoba (Canada),[3] Haiti, United States,[4] Cyprus, Netherlands[5]	Chile, Ecuador, Paraguay, Philippines
Agricultural workers	Cambodia, Lao People's Democratic Republic,[6] Malaysia, Pakistan, Thailand, Sri Lanka,[7] Botswana, Nigeria,[8] Bolivia, Manitoba and Ontario (Canada),[9] United States,[9] Cyprus	Burkina Faso, Chad, Guinea-Bissau, Madagascar, Morocco, Mozambique, Senegal, Tunisia Solomon Islands El Salvador, Guatemala, Nicaragua, Panama
Casual workers	Belgium, Belize, Malaysia	Republic of Korea[10]
Homeworkers	Philippines (homeworkers sewing), Thailand, United States (homeworkers making wreaths)	

Notes:
    The table cites only the most common breakdown of employment by category of worker. Other categories include part-time workers, who are covered in most countries by minimum wage legislation on a pro-rata basis according to the number of hours worked, but who are excluded from minimum wage coverage in Ghana and Nigeria. Although specifically excluded in the same two countries, piece-rate workers are covered in a number of others where, for example, the legislation sets their wage to correspond to the minimum wage of a worker of average productivity.
1. Domestic workers are specifically included within the scope of the minimum wage. In practice, however, minimum wage rates have been established only for export processing zones, agricultural and textile workers.
2. Regarding the definition of 'worker' or 'entrepreneur', in Indonesia, the Lao People's Democratic Republic, Nepal and Tunisia, the law applies only to workers employed by firms. Domestic workers are therefore excluded because they do not work in or for a firm.
3. In Manitoba, Canada, the exception concerns workers who work less than 24 hours per week for the same employer.
4. The exception concerns domestic workers hired on a casual basis (such as babysitters).
5. According to our information, most workers in the Netherlands are covered by minimum wage provisions, except apprentices and domestic workers.[13]
6. The minimum wage applies only to the formal economy.
7. The minimum wage applies in plantations, not in the rest of the agriculture sector.
8. The exception applies to seasonal agricultural workers and to all workers who work for firms with less than 50 employees.
9. Even though the majority of agricultural workers in Canada and the United States are covered by minimum wage legislation, some are excluded due to the nature of their worker or the size of the farm. Harvesting by hand, seasonal work and livestock shepherding are some of the notable exceptions.
10. Submitted for approval to the Ministry of Labour and Employment.

Malaysia), minimum wages are fixed for a small number of occupations and sectors which do not include domestic work. Domestic workers also lack minimum wage protection in Guinea-Bissau, Haiti, Lebanon, Morocco, the Netherlands, Tunisia and, in certain cases, Canada and the United States. Only four countries provide domestic workers with a minimum wage that is lower than the standard one – namely Chile, Ecuador, Paraguay and the Philippines. By reading Table 6.2 'backwards,' that is, by sorting the data by country where domestic workers are covered, one can see that many developing countries apply such a provision. In most Latin American countries and in Lesotho, domestic workers are explicitly included in legislative coverage.

Agricultural workers constitute the second broad category of workers most often excluded from minimum wage legislation. They do not benefit from the protection afforded by a minimum wage threshold in Botswana, Bolivia, Cambodia, Cyprus, Malaysia, the Lao People's Democratic Republic (except for the formal economy), Nigeria (seasonal workers are not covered, nor are those working in firms with less than 50 employees), Pakistan, Sri Lanka (only workers in plantations are covered), Thailand and, for certain types of agricultural labour, Canada and the United States. However, in two of these countries, there are developments towards extending the scope of application of minimum wage legislation to agricultural workers. In Bolivia, a Supreme Decree is currently in the process of adopting a law while in Pakistan there is ongoing discussion on the need to include agricultural workers in minimum wage coverage.

Other countries, particularly in Africa, offer a threshold of protection below the standard minimum wage. Several reasons can be advanced to explain why agricultural workers are afforded a lower standard of protection. First and foremost, they are often partially paid in kind, and in rural areas the cost of living is lower. Other reasons include the difficulty of enforcing the minimum wage in isolated rural areas, the policy objective of maintaining a high employment rate in areas where there are few alternatives to employment in the agricultural sector, and perhaps even a bias against agricultural labour. Several African countries (Burkina Faso, Chad, Guinea-Bissau, Madagascar, Morocco, Mozambique, Senegal and Tunisia), as well as El Salvador, Guatemala, Nicaragua, Panama and the Solomon Islands, have enacted a minimum wage for agricultural workers, although it is lower than the prevailing standard minimum wage.

Casual workers are not covered in Belgium, Belize and Malaysia. As for homeworkers, they are excluded from minimum wage legislation in Thailand and, in certain cases, in the Philippines and the United States.

Table 6.2 represents a qualitative approach, as precise figures on the number of workers not covered by minimum wage legislation are difficult to obtain. However, a rough estimation can be made for the United States, where casual agricultural workers and homeworkers represent the largest components of the group excluded from coverage by the minimum wage, equivalent to 4.5 per cent of wage-earners in 1981.[15]

In conclusion, Table 6.2 clearly shows that the two most vulnerable categories of workers are agricultural workers and, even more so, domestic workers, who most often do not fall within the scope of application of the minimum wage in a small number of developing countries. Paradoxically, it is not uncommon to observe that the minimum wage applies to sectors where workers are well organized, whereas the initial and primary objective of a minimum wage policy is to protect the most vulnerable. Identifying universal factors to explain this conclusion is not an easy task, particularly as geographic location, culture and the level of development do not suffice to explain this phenomenon. Domestic workers and, to a lesser extent, agricultural workers are excluded from minimum wage provisions in a number of Asian countries, but are covered in most of Latin America and in some African countries. The legislative treatment of vulnerable workers often exhibits strong cross-country differences, even in countries with similar levels of development. For example, agricultural workers are not included in the minimum wage coverage of six Asian countries, but are included in all others. On the other hand, domestic workers are covered in Brazil and Colombia but not in Thailand, although these three countries are similar in terms of socioeconomic development. The disparity of these exclusions warrants a country-by-country analysis.

6.6 The minimum wage and wage inequality

The minimum wage affects the level of inequality under certain conditions. In fact, the adjustment of the minimum wage may contribute to reducing the general level of inequality, but only if it is received by the lowest-paid workers. Depending on who belongs to the lowest-paid categories of workers, the minimum wage may increase wages earned by women, migrant workers and ethnic minorities with respect to more established workers. Hence, the minimum wage may be used to promote pay equity by levelling out differences in wages – particularly in reducing the gap between the average wage of men and women. There are two ideas involved here: first, the minimum wage introduces the same pay threshold for both sexes, which immediately cuts down on discrimination; and secondly, those wage-earners at the bottom of the pay scale, the majority of whom are usually women, benefit from the minimum wage.

It is often believed that minimum wage-earners in developing countries do not belong to the bottom scale of the wage distribution. If this is the case, the minimum wage as a tool of reducing wage inequality would not be of any interest for those countries. In fact, a close examination of figures reveals that, in a sizeable minority of countries, the minimum wage is relatively low in the wage distribution. This is obvious from comparing minimum wage rates available from the ILO database[16] with various indicators such as average wage or GDP per worker.

Furthermore, empirical evidence had shown that the minimum wage has an impact on wage inequality in several middle-income countries.[17] In Latin America in general, higher minimum wages reduce wage inequality. However, they do not necessarily reduce the gender pay gap: female wage-earners are not necessarily at the bottom of the pay scale.[18] On the other hand, however, a static minimum wage will most often have the opposite effect: a rise in wage inequality. In Brazil, for example, the fall in the actual value of the minimum wage over the 1963 to 1979 period went hand-in-hand with a drop in the earnings of 'blue-collar' workers compared with those of 'white-collar' workers.[19] In a similar fashion, in the United States, the drop in the minimum wage between 1970 and 1990 was largely responsible for the increase in the pay gap between native-born wage-earners and immigrants.[20]

It should be noted here that, in a small number of countries, the government seeks to limit the pay gap by using the minimum wage as a 'benchmark': a figure to be referred to when fixing other wages. Such is the case in Algeria, where basic pay rates for state managerial staff or particular categories of civil servants are set at x times the minimum wage – thus, in part, limiting the pay gap.

6.7   The minimum wage and employment

The relationship between minimum wages and employment has been considered more deeply than any other and is also the most controversial. Admittedly, when employers apply the minimum wage, increases in that wage definitely represent an extra production cost for businesses.[21] This rise may lead employers to replace labour with capital, or unskilled workers with skilled workers, since unskilled workers are those most likely to receive the minimum wage, thus contributing to the growth in unemployment. What do the empirical studies show? The first studies, carried out in the 1970s and 1980s, were based on time series analysis. The principle is to estimate the following type of equation:

$$\text{Ln(EMP/POP)}_{-t} = \text{ß1ln(MINWAGE/AVERAGEWAGE)}_{-t}$$
$$+\text{ß2ln(REALGNP)}_{-t} + \text{ß3TREND} + e$$

Where EMP/POP represents the ratio of the employment rate to the working age population at time t, MINWAGE and AVERAGEWAGE are, respectively, the legal minimum wage and the average wage in national currency, REALGNP is real GNP at time t, and TREND captures technological progress, which can have an impact on manufacturing hires. Both REALGNP

Table 6.3 Impact of a 10 per cent minimum wage increase on employment amongst young people in the United States, 1954–1979 (percentages)

Method	Results
D. Brown, C. Gilroy and A. Kohen (1982): Analysis of classic time series	−0.95
J. Bernstein and J. Schmitt (1998): Analysis of time series taking into account the volatility of seasonal employment and respecting the statistical conditions of stationarity	−0.5 (not significant)

and TREND act as an indicator of economic activity. ß are the coefficients to be estimated.

Brown, Gilroy and Kohen (1982) take as an example the results from such classic time series analysis, which can be found in Table 6.3 (first line).[22] The analysis shows that, between 1954 and 1979, a 10 per cent minimum wage increase in the United States reduced employment amongst young people by almost 1 per cent. The coefficient was found to be statistically significant at 1 per cent confidence interval.

Such analyses became very popular and have been replicated for almost every country with published longitudinal data on employment and wages. They have enshrined in people's minds the idea that increases in the minimum wage destroy numerous jobs. It is to the great merit of Card and Krueger (1995) that they used innovative methods of estimation which led to opposite results.[23] One chapter of this book relies on a specificity of minimum wage legislation in the United States – namely, the provision that states may fix the minimum wage at a rate higher than the federal threshold. Comparing employment in low-paying industry between a state that had increased the minimum wage above the federal minimum and a state that had not was extremely revealing. It showed that employment in the latter state, far from decreasing, had in fact slightly increased in response to the increase in the minimum wage.

Later studies showed the weakness of classic time series analysis of minimum wage impact. In particular, it showed that statistical hypotheses which ensure the robustness of the analysis were not respected. In many cases, the statistical series were not stationary as they ought to be. The simple fact of ensuring stationarity of the series can have a huge impact on the result.

For example, Bernstein and Schmitt's study uses two different methods based on identical data covering the same period to estimate the impact of a minimum wage increase on employment in the United States.[24] The first analysis, based on classic time series, replicates that from Brown, Gilroy and Kohen (1982). The second analysis, which takes into account the volatility of seasonal employment and respects the conditions of stationarity, shows that

Table 6.4   Effect of the minimum wage on employment in certain developing countries

Rama[1]	Indonesia, 1990–95	The doubling of the minimum wage in real terms had a negative but slight effect on employment (−2 per cent). Employment apparently decreased in small enterprises and increased in large ones.
Lemos[2]	Brazil, 1982–2000	A 10 per cent increase in the minimum wage was linked to a total employment effect ranging between −0.9 and +1.4 per cent.

Notes:
1. M. Rama: *The consequences of doubling the minimum wage: The case of Indonesia*, Policy Research Working Paper No. 1643 (Washington, DC: World Bank, 1996).
2. S. Lemos: *A menu of minimum wage variables for evaluating employment effects: Evidence from Brazil*, University College London Working Paper 03-02 (London, 2003).

although the effect of the minimum wage on employment among young people in the United States remains negative, it is clearly less marked. In this case, a 10 per cent minimum wage increase only reduces employment by 0.5 per cent, which is not a statistically significant coefficient (Table 6.3, second line).

It is apparent from Table 6.3 that classical time series analysis overestimates the negative impact of the minimum wage on employment. There is no doubt that economists have been very slow in recognizing the weakness of this type of analysis. This is not surprising. As shown in the analysis of Jesus Felipe and J.S.L. McCombie in this volume, neoclassical labour demand functions systematically find a negative relationship between employment and wages for reasons of accounting identity and not for economic reasons.

Classical time series analysis is still a popular method of estimating the minimum wage impact in middle-income developing countries, such as Brazil or Indonesia. Examples are provided in Table 6.4. The available studies show that the negative effect of the minimum salary on employment is small and, in some cases, positive.

Therefore, readjustments of the minimum wage do not always have a significant effect on the level of employment. They may, nonetheless, lead to a drop in employment within certain categories of the population and a parallel rise within others. This may be attributed to the fact that the group of low-paid workers affected by changes in the minimum wage is very mixed (students, people with few skills, people waiting to find a better job in certain countries, skilled workers in other countries).

This has been observed in the case of industrialized countries. Yuen shows that, in Canada, increases in the minimum wage reduce employment among those workers at the bottom of the pay scale, whose productivity is low and who have few skills and little chance of finding a better paid job.[25] However, they give a boost to employment among other categories of workers receiving the same wage, such as students or workers temporarily 'trapped' in a low-paid job but whose skills mean that they have every prospect of finding a better job in the future.[26]

The fact remains that during periods when unemployment levels are high, especially among low-skilled workers and young people – two categories often over-represented when it comes to those earning the minimum wage – it is very tempting to play around with the level of the minimum wage in the hope that the level of employment will rise. This means taking the risk of weakening the role that the minimum wage might be able to play in poverty-reduction strategies.

Nonetheless, proposed minimum wage increases should not be out of proportion with the prevailing economic and social conditions – for fear of producing a negative effect on competitiveness, or, more simply, of not respecting adjustments. In Chile, the adjustment to the minimum wage, which was 17.1 per cent higher than that of productivity between 1998 and 2000, led to a growth in the proportion of workers paid less than the minimum wage and the proportion of workers without written contracts, without affecting unemployment in the short term.[27]

However, suggesting to trade unions that any increase in the minimum wage must be curbed in order to avoid increased unemployment is rather a spurious argument. It may well come across as an excuse to fix the minimum wage at a level which would make it meaningless. Slovenian trade unions thus refute the argument whereby a minimum wage, even a low one, would run the risk of seriously affecting the country's textiles sector. They note that a number of businesses in this sector are, in any case, certain to fail due to competition from developing countries and that the argument about the textiles sector cannot be used continually to block the fixing of a decent minimum wage. This is similar to the idea advanced by the Low Pay Commission, the body that deals with minimum wage fixing in the United Kingdom, when it notes that the use of low wages as a tool for competitiveness is common amongst companies, especially the smallest companies, where personnel management is particularly poor. The question that then arises is not that of the survival of marginal businesses, but of whether successful companies can recover the markets lost by these businesses following the increase in the minimum wage, alongside the workforce consequently made redundant.[28]

Nonetheless, the government of the United Kingdom was keen to ensure that the establishment of a minimum wage should not affect its youth unemployment reduction policy. That is why a reduced rate for young people aged 18 to 22 years was put into place. It should be stressed that only a minority of countries have introduced lower rates for young people. This decision was doubtlessly justified on the grounds of professional experience – but the basic reason was that unemployment was particularly high among young workers and it was reasoned that employers would be more likely to recruit them if the hiring costs were reduced.

In conclusion, in middle-income developing countries, the perception that the minimum wage creates unemployment is still widespread, even though available studies show that such conclusions have to be qualified. The striking result of the recent and more reliable studies makes it legitimate to look for the factors behind this weak effect. On the supply side, the possibility that most employers have to compensate for higher labour costs by slight changes in work organization leading to productivity gains is crucial. On the demand side, raising the income of those workers with a low propensity to save has a positive effect on consumption levels. Other elements can be evoked to explain the weak impact of the minimum wage on employment, such as the weak wage effects higher in the wage structure, as well as the fact that in countries like Brazil, workers paid the minimum wage often work in the service sector rather than in manufacturing, insulated from international competition.

6.8   Conclusion

The information collected to date makes it possible to draw some fairly reliable conclusion about the minimum wage.

- First, the minimum wage could be, under certain conditions, a good instrument for protecting poor workers, as well as other vulnerable categories.
- Second, the minimum wage has an effect on the wage hierarchy and can be used to combat inequality and improve the standard of life of workers at the bottom of the pay scale.
- Third, during periods of growth, appropriate increases in the minimum wage have no real significant effect on unemployment.

Given all of this, we believe it advisable to refocus on the primary function of the minimum wage – that is, the defence of the lowest-paid wage-earners and the fight against wage inequality.

When governments keep minimum wage increases in check in order to curb unemployment or better control inflation – or for other reasons, such as the search for competitive wage costs – they run the risk of eventually losing an effective social policy instrument. The same is true if too many social security benefits are automatically linked to minimum wage adjustments. This, for example, is what happened in Uruguay from 1976 onwards, or in the Russian Federation in 1992, when the minimum wage accounted for only 5.6 per cent of the average wage (as opposed to 14 per cent in 1991 and 23.6 per cent in 1989), showing how meaningless it was within the wage hierarchy.[29] It is worth recalling a number of countries where the level of the minimum wage remained unchanged over a period of several years: Côte d'Ivoire between 1982 and 1993 (the purchasing power of the minimum wage fell by three-quarters); El Salvador between 1980 and 1985 (the purchasing power of the minimum wage was halved); and the United States on numerous occasions, for example between 1950 and 1955 (−10.1 per cent), and between 1981 and 1989 (−26.7 per cent). Another risk that governments run in allowing the minimum wage to fall in value is that they may be faced with demands that would be difficult to meet.

Finally, the use by governments of the minimum wage as a tool for economic policy is closely linked to its use in relation to collective bargaining. Basic, undeveloped collective bargaining can leave the field open to extending the influence of a statutory minimum wage, increasing the number of rates and categories covered. In turn, the intensive use of the minimum wage by a government with a view to achieving various economic policy objectives will lead it, willingly or not, to reducing the role of collective bargaining in the field of wages in order to better control its development. Conversely, a well-established collective bargaining process will be more likely to have the effect of excluding government intervention or restricting its role to the protection of the most poorly paid wage-earners.

It is vital to take into account these different relationships when creating or adjusting a minimum wage system. Finally, the desired objectives must be carefully identified, while bearing in mind the fact that the primary aim remains the protection of the lowest-paid wage-earners.

Notes

1 Minimum Wage-Fixing Machinery Convention, 1928 (No. 26), and Minimum Wage Fixing Convention, 1970 (No. 131), available at www.ilo.org/ilolex/.
2 The International Labour Office has created a database summarizing the principal legal provisions and minimum wage-fixing mechanisms in about 100 countries. It is available at www.ilo.org/travail/database.
3 The Minimum Wage Fixing Recommendation, 1970 (No. 135), which is the accompanying text to Convention No. 131, establishes a detailed list of criteria.
4 The criteria most often referred to are the average level of wages, social security benefits, the needs of workers and their families, the inflation rate and/or the cost of living, the employment level, the economic situation and/or the development productivity, and the capacity of enterprises to pay.
5 J. Weeks (1971) 'Wage Policy and the Colonial Legacy: A Comparative Study', *The Journal of Modern African Studies*, 9(3).
6 The United Kingdom itself abandoned this system in 1991 to recreate a minimum wage mechanism based on the national statutory minimum wage principle.
7 The Trades Union Congress (TUC) came round to the idea of a minimum wage in 1985, followed by the Labour Party in 1986. See D. Metcalf (1999) 'The British National Minimum Wage', *British Journal of Industrial Relations*, 37(2).
8 Another major link is between minimum wage and inflation, which is not addressed in this chapter.

9   M. Neri, G. Gonzaga and J.M. Camargo (2001) 'Salário mínimo, "efeito-farol" e pobreza', *Revista de Economia Política*, 21(2).

10 D. Card and A.B. Krueger (1995) *Myth and Measurement: The New Economics of the Minimum Wage* (Princeton, NJ: Princeton University Press).

11 R. Burkhauser and A. Finegan (1993) 'The Economics of Minimum Wage Legislation Revisited', *Cato Journal*, 13(1).

12 F. Eyraud and C. Saget (2005) *The Fundamentals of Minimum Wage Fixing* (Geneva: ILO).

13 Direct request from the Committee of Experts on the Application of Conventions and Recommendations, 2003. Available at http://webfusion.ilo.org/public/db/standards/normes/appl.

14 Until 2003, they were also excluded from minimum wage protection in China.

15 Calculated from J.M. Abowd, F. Kramarz and D.N. Margolis (1999) *Minimum Wages and Employment in France and the United States*, NBER Working Paper No. 6996 (Washington, DC: National Bureau of Economic Research).

16 See endnote 2.

17 The impact of a minimum wage upon the wage distribution within a neighbourhood has been shown in the case of Columbia by W.F. Maloney and J. Nuñez Mendez, 'Measuring the Impact of Minimum Wages', in J.J. Heckman and C. Pagés (eds), (2004) *Law and Employment Lessons from Latin America and the Caribbean* (Chicago: University of Chicago Press), pp. 109–30.

18 D. Grimshaw and M. Miozzo (2003) *Minimum Wages and Pay Equity in Latin America: Identifying the Employment and Pay Equity Effects*, DECLARATION Working Paper 12/2003 (Geneva: ILO).

19 J.M. Camargo (1998) 'Minimum Wages in Brazil: Theory, Policy and Empirical Evidence', *Labour Management Relations Series*, No. 67 (Geneva: ILO).

20 K. Butcher and J. DiNardo (2002) 'The Immigrant and Native-born Wage Distributions: Evidence from United States Censuses', *Industrial and Labor Relations Review*, 56(1).

21 Omitting situations where the minimum wage is so low that it plays no role whatsoever in the wage hierarchy.

22 C. Brown, C. Gilroy and A. Kohen (1982) 'Time-series Evidence of the Effect of the Minimum Wage on Youth Employment and Unemployment', *Journal of Human Resources*, 18(1).

23 D. Card and A.B. Krueger (1995) *Myth and Measurement: The New Economics of the Minimum Wage* (Princeton, NJ: Princeton University Press).

24 J. Bernstein and J. Schmitt (1998) *Making Work Pay: The Impact of the 1996–97 Minimum Wage Increase* (Washington, DC: Economic Policy Institute).

25 T. Yuen (2003) 'The Effect of Minimum Wages on Youth Employment in Canada: A Panel Study', *The Journal of Human Resources*, 38(3).

26 A study conducted in Chile between 1960 and 1998 shows a negative impact on unskilled workers (particularly unskilled youth), but a positive impact on skilled workers, C.E. Montenegro and C. Pagés, 'Who Benefits from Labour Market Regulations? Chile 1960–98', in J.J. Heckman and C. Pagés (eds) (2004).

27 R. Infante, A. Marinakis and J. Velasco (2003) *Minimum Wage in Chile: An Example of the Potential and Limitations of this Policy Instrument*, Employment Paper 2003/52 (ILO: Geneva).

28 Brown *et al.* (1982).

29 G. Standing and D. Vaughan-Whitehead (eds) (1995) *Minimum Wages in Central and Eastern Europe: From Protection to Destitution* (Budapest: Central European University Press).

7
What Can the Labour Demand Function Tell Us About Wages and Employment? The Case of the Philippines

Jesus Felipe and J.S.L. McCombie[1]

> ...what is not so easy to explain is the fact that the marginal product of labor in such an estimated relationship [aggregate production function] appears to give a reasonably good explanation of wages as well.
>
> F.M. Fisher[2]

> ...not everyone is convinced about how much we really know on even the simplest question – the constant-output own-price elasticity of demand for aggregate labor. ...Because this parameter is fundamentally important for understanding the impacts of such diverse policies as payroll taxation, subsidies for employment growth, and others, one wonders whether there is any hope of convincing skeptics that something can be known. Part of the reason for the skepticism may be the fact that most empirical research is based on labor markets in industrialized countries.
>
> D.S. Hamermesh[3]

7.1 Introduction

Since the 1980s, when discussions about the meaning and implications of the term *globalization* started to appear in the press and academic journals,[4] policy-making in many countries has been dominated by the objective of increasing *competitiveness*. Unfortunately, the ambiguity with which this term is often used (in particular, its meaning at the national level) has led to a great deal of confusion in terms of policy recommendations.[5] Most often, however, concerns about the need to be competitive are translated into recommendations for wage restraint. Indeed, the heralded normative goal of competitiveness, at times being pursued with an ideological zeal, has put enormous pressure on workers. The consequence is that a great deal of

119

anxiety is being felt all over the world because the situation is possibly lead-ing to a 'race to the bottom', according to which globalization is forcing workers to compete to attract capital by accepting lower wages.[6] This means that the concept of competitiveness seems to be driving economic policy in many countries, hence the emphasis on costs, productivity and labour market reform in order to achieve greater 'flexibility' in the labour market. Wage restraint and limitations on social expenditures (such as reduction and even elimination of workers' benefits, such as unemployment subsidies or minimum wages) are seen as necessary conditions for improved economic performance.

In this context, one of the most enduring controversies in macroeconomics has been, and remains, the question of whether or not unemployment can be largely attributed to real wages being too high. The classical (and neoclassical) argument is that unemployment arises as a result of wages being set above the market-clearing level for reasons such as efficiency wages, collusion among workers, or due to the juxtaposition of institutional forces different from supply and demand. These institutional forces are minimum wages, labour unions, public sector pay policies, multinational corporations and labour codes. These forces create inflexible labour markets.[7] In this model, increases in real wages will cause employment to decline for two reasons: (i) higher wages will induce firms to substitute other inputs for labour; and (ii) higher wages will entail cost increases, which induce buyers to shift suppliers. From a policy perspective, adherents to this view contend that a competitive mar-ket has an internal mechanism that allows it to eliminate unemployment; in particular, that a competitive economy has a long-run tendency to full employment. This mechanism is the speedy adjustment of wages to their equilibrium level, at which labour demand equals supply. Thus, existing unemployment is the result of workers refusing to accept the equilibrium wage rate as determined by labour demand and supply. The policy impli-cation, and the solution to the unemployment problem, is seen as more competition and less government intervention in the market through, for example, the setting of minimum wages or through ensuring job security. In competitive markets, the law of demand and supply ensures that eventually the demand for labour will equal the supply of labour – so that the labour mar-ket will clear and there will be no unemployment. The most important policy prescription of this paradigm is that, in order to eliminate unemployment, it is necessary to reduce real wages by cutting the money wage rate.

The theoretical refutation of the simplistic conclusion that a reduction in money wages increases employment was seen initially as one of the cen-tral achievements of Keynes' *General Theory*.[8] The standard argument is that the reduction in wages reduces the cost of production. Under these circum-stances, firms believe that they can sell at higher profit. This would stimulate business and, as a consequence, employment would increase. But is this true? Keynes argued that profits would increase only if 'the community's marginal propensity to consume is equal to unity ... or if there is an increase in investment, corresponding to the gap between the increment in income and the increment in consumption'. Unless one of these two conditions is fulfilled, the revenue from increased output will be less than what entrepreneurs expected and thus employment will not change. If entrepreneurs offered employment on such a scale that provided the public with incomes out of which they would save more than the amount of current investment, firms would make a loss equal to the difference. This will be so irrespective of the level of money wages. Thus, increased flexibility (i.e., the possibility of reducing the cost of production) need not lead to higher employment.[9]

Subsequently, however, the question has been interpreted as being essentially an empirical issue. Hamermesh has provided a comprehensive survey of the literature and although the estimates of the elasticity vary often quite considerably between studies, they are nearly always statistically significant and negative: 'If one were to choose a point estimate for this parameter [the elasticity of labour demand], 0.30 would not be far wrong.'[10] This is roughly the same figure Cobb and Douglas[11] found and is consistent with a labour share of 0.7.[12] As Hamermesh further remarks, 'the immense literature that estimates the constant-output demand elasticity for labor in the aggregate has truly led us "to arrive where we started and know the place for the first time" '.[13]

Today's mainstream explanation for unemployment is that labour market institutions are 'too rigid' and wages are 'too high'. Often, the theoretical models used to support these conclusions tend to be variants of the non-accelerating inflation rate of unemployment (NAIRU). The OECD[14] and IMF,[15] for example, have insisted for several years that, in order to accelerate growth, Europe has to reform its labour markets so as to make them more flexible, following the American approach.[16] But the argument over the need to reform labour markets is also sweeping across developing countries. This is the case advanced, for example, by Heckman and Pagés in the case of Latin America.[17] The conclusions of the country studies contained in their volume lead them to advocate labour market reforms with a view to making labour markets more flexible. Heckman and Pagés summarize estimates of constant-output labour demand elasticities for Latin America from 11 studies. The estimates range between 0 and −1.5 and most of them are between −0.2 and −0.6.[18] In the authors' words: 'This range of estimates implies that a 10 per cent increase in labour costs will result in a sizeable decline in employment, between 2 per cent and 6 per cent.'[19] Likewise, Hamermesh shows estimates of constant-output own-wage labour demand elasticities from seven studies, also for Latin American countries.[20] He concludes, 'Despite the obvious differences, the results are remarkable for their apparent consistency ... the average constant-output own-wage elasticity is −0.30 ... taking all the elasticities together, one must infer that they reinforce the consensus estimate, −0.30, that I identified'.[21] Hence, Hamermesh seems to imply that it is reassuring that the same result appears in estimations of labour demand functions for developed and developing countries. Finally, Cárdenas and Bernal also find negative wage elasticities of labour demand at the firm level (a sample of 2,570 Colombian manufacturing firms) and at the industrial sector (a panel of 92 industrial sectors for 1978–95).[22] These results, taken as a whole, have been seen by some as confirming the neoclassical view that an increase in the real wage, *ceteris paribus*, will increase unemployment by lowering the demand for labour.[23]

In this chapter we contend, however, that this alleged empirical evidence does not necessarily validate the theoretical claims. Hence we are sceptical about how much can be learnt from these exercises. The problem is that the neoclassical labour demand function is derived from an aggregate production function. It has been well established for some time now that the use of value data (either value added or gross output) poses intractable problems for the interpretation of any statistical estimate derived from aggregate production functions.[24] In this chapter, we show that because of an underlying accounting identity, it is possible to obtain a negative value of the elasticity of labour demand with respect to the wage rate, although there may be no underlying behavioural relationship. Indeed, it is very difficult to obtain anything other than a statistically negative 'elasticity'. In fact, with real data, it is practically impossible. The reason is that all that is being estimated is an approximation of an identity, that is, of course, true by definition. This result questions the validity of many empirical estimations of labour demand functions and the policy implications often derived from them.

The rest of the chapter is structured as follows. In section 7.2 we summarize the standard derivation of the wage elasticity of demand for labour and the negative relationship between employment and the wage rate. In section 7.3 it is argued that there is a more parsimonious interpretation for the observed negative relationship between these two variables that is observed in estimating neoclassical labour demand functions. This is that the results are driven by the accounting identity according to which output is the sum of the wage bill plus total profits. Sections 7.4 and 7.5 illustrate the argument in the context of the Philippines. We must make it clear that the empirical analysis we provide is for illustrative purposes only. The theoretical argument shows, *per se*, the insurmountable problems involved in the econometric estimation of aggregate labour demand functions.

What we provide here, step by step, is a more parsimonious interpretation of the results. The purpose of these two sections is also to address and question Hamermesh's view, quoted at the start of this chapter, that there may be scepticism about how much can be known about the constant-output own-price elasticity of demand for aggregate labour due to the fact that most empirical research refers to the developed countries. In section 7.4 we analyse the relationship between minimum wages and employment in the context of the marginal revenue product curve. As noted above, for all practical purposes, virtually all data sets will yield a negative relationship between these two variables. This section explains the unusual circumstances under which this could occur. In section 7.5 we review the problems interpreting the estimates of the labour demand function. Section 7.6 evaluates the impact of changes in the minimum wage rate on the average wage rate of the Philippines. The results of the empirical analysis indicate that the effect of increases in the minimum wage is insignificant. Section 7.7 concludes. Annex 7.1 summarizes Lavoie's arguments[25] about the problems estimating the NAIRU model as specified by Layard, Nickell and Jackman.[26] The argument is also that what drives the empirical results is the accounting identity according to which output equals the sum of the wage bill plus total profits. Lavoie's (2000) paper was published in French and hence is not known to many scholars of labour economics.

7.2 Derivation of the elasticity of demand for labour[27]

The theoretical foundations of the labour demand function are based on standard neoclassical assumptions. A well-behaved aggregate production function $Q = F(K, L)$ is assumed to exist, where Q denotes the constant-price value of output and K denotes the constant-price value of the capital stock. Perfect competition is usually, but not always, assumed to prevail and factors are paid their marginal products, i.e., $w = F_L$ and $v = F_K$, where w and v are the real wage rate and the real user cost of capital, respectively.[28] In order to derive the elasticity of demand for labour, two different assumptions are made – the first holding output constant, the second holding capital constant – which lead to different functional forms.

(i) Holding output constant: In this first case, output and the user cost of capital are held constant. On the other hand, capital and labour vary as the relative price of inputs changes. The elasticity of demand for labour is obtained by solving the three-equation system given by differentiating the production function and the two first-order conditions. This yields $\eta_{LL/Q} = -(1 - a)\sigma$, where $(1 - a)$ is the share of capital in total output (assumed to be equal to capital's output elasticity) and σ is the elasticity of substitution.

Assuming the production function is the Cobb–Douglas $Q = A_0 e^{\lambda t} L^\alpha K^{(1-\alpha)}$, the three-equation system leads to the equation:

$$\ln L = -\{(1 - \alpha)\ln[(1 - \alpha)/\alpha]\} - \lambda t + \ln Q - (1 - \alpha)\ln w + (1 - \alpha)\ln v \quad (7.1)$$

where the estimate of $\ln w$ is the elasticity of demand for labour, given that $\sigma = 1$ (Cobb–Douglas). In this case, if the firm is in equilibrium and there is perfect foresight, given $a = \alpha = 0.75$, if we were to estimate $\ln L = c + b_1 t + b_2 \ln Q + b_3 \ln w + b_4 \ln v$, we should expect that $\hat{b}_2 = 1.0$, $\hat{b}_3 = -0.25$ (the elasticity of demand for labour) and $\hat{b}_4 = 0.25$.

A second procedure uses the Cobb–Douglas cost function and Shepard's lemma ($\partial C / \partial w = L$). The cost function is given by $C = Bw^\alpha v^{(1-\alpha)} Q e^{-\lambda t}$.

Differentiating with respect to the real wage rate and expressing the result in logarithmic form leads to expression (7.1).

Alternatively, one can use the marginal revenue product of labour curve to obtain an estimate of the elasticity of demand for labour. This can be obtained by differentiating the total revenue function with respect to labour. In the case of the Cobb–Douglas, this yields:

$$\ln L = \ln \alpha + \ln Q - \ln w \qquad (7.2)$$

In this case, the elasticity of demand for labour can be obtained from the estimate of the intercept as $\hat{\eta}_{LL/Q} = -[1 - exp(\ln \hat{\alpha})] = \hat{\alpha} - 1$, and it is important to emphasize that it is not given by the coefficient of $\ln w$ A negative elasticity implies that the estimated intercept must be negative.

Given that the Cobb–Douglas production function implies $\sigma = 1$, researchers often work with a CES production function $Q = A(t)[\delta L^{-\rho} + (1 - \delta)K^{-\rho}]^{-1/\rho}$ where δ is a distribution parameter and $\sigma = \frac{1}{1+\rho}$ is the elasticity of substitution, to derive estimates of the elasticity of demand for labour. Following a procedure similar to that above leads to $\ln L = \ln A_0 \delta + \frac{\sigma}{1-\sigma} \left[1 + \left(\frac{1-\delta}{\delta} \right)^{\sigma} \left(\frac{v}{w} \right)^{(1-\sigma)} \right] + \ln Q - \lambda t$. However, given the nonlinear nature of this form, it is rarely, if ever, used. Instead, what is used is the marginal revenue product curve, obtained by differentiating the total revenue function with respect to labour. This yields:

$$\ln L = (1 - \sigma) \ln A_0 + \sigma \ln \delta + \sigma \ln w + \ln Q - (1 - \sigma)\lambda t \qquad (7.3)$$

As in the Cobb–Douglas case, this form avoids the need to use the user cost of capital, and it has the advantage that it is more flexible. The elasticity of demand for labour is obtained by multiplying the estimated elasticity of substitution ($\hat{\sigma}$) times the capital share in total output from the national accounts. It can be seen that as $\sigma \to 1$, equation (7.3) tends to $\ln L = \ln \alpha + \ln Q - \ln w$, that is, equation (7.2).

(ii) Holding capital constant: In this case, it is assumed that the capital stock is constant, in which case output varies. If the capital stock remains constant, then as employment falls, with a rise in the real wage rate, output will decrease. In this case, the elasticity of demand for labour is given by $\eta_{LL/K} = -\sigma/(1 - a)$, where, as before, the capital share in output is assumed to be equal to the elasticity of output with respect to the capital stock.

In the case of the Cobb–Douglas function $Q = A_0 e^{\lambda t} L^{\alpha} K^{(1-\alpha)}$, one can estimate the change in output as labour changes with the capital stock held constant, directly from the expression for the marginal productivity of labour $\frac{\partial Q}{\partial L} = w = \alpha A_0 e^{\lambda t} \left(\frac{K}{L} \right)^{1-\alpha}$. Rearranging this expression and writing it in logarithms leads to:

$$\ln L = c + \left(\frac{\lambda}{1-\alpha}\right)t - \left(\frac{1}{1-\alpha}\right)\ln w + \ln K \qquad (7.4)$$

where since the elasticity of demand for labour equals in this case $\eta_{LL/K} = -1/(1-\alpha)$, it is directly given by the estimate of $\ln w$.

For estimation purposes, equations (7.1) to (7.4) are estimated today using modern econometric methods. For example, with time-series data, researchers would test for unit roots and the possibility of co-integration among the series.

7.3   A more parsimonious interpretation

In this section we propose a more parsimonious interpretation of the equations used to derive estimates of labour demand. In doing so, there are two issues that must be taken into consideration. The first issue is theoretical in nature. It refers to the fact that the labour demand function, as discussed above, is a concept without a satisfactory theoretical foundation. The reason is that in order to derive it, one needs to assume the existence of the aggregate production function. This means that the implications of the Cambridge Capital Theory Controversies are either ignored or assumed unimportant.[29] Likewise, the serious aggregation problems in production functions are sidestepped.[30] These are not innocuous issues, for both the Cambridge Capital Controversies and the aggregation literature proved conclusively that aggregate production functions, as well as the notion of an aggregate stock of capital, have no theoretical foundations, except under extremely restrictive and implausible assumptions. It can be said therefore that the aggregate production function does not exist. By this, it is meant that the aggregate production function cannot be derived in an internally consistent manner and, therefore, it is a problematic concept. This implies that the concepts of a labour demand curve and the wage elasticity of demand for labour must be seriously questioned.

The second consideration is that given the previous point, the relevant question must be one of how to interpret empirical estimates of equations (7.1) to (7.4), given that they are not estimates of aggregate labour demand functions or of marginal revenue curves (this is because they do not exist, in the sense explained in the previous paragraph). To answer this question it should be noted that, in practice, data used in the estimation of these equations are not physical quantities but value data, constant dollars of output and capital stock.[31] This has very important implications, as we shall see. The reason is that we are bound to obtain a close statistical fit to the above equations, purely because of the existence of an underlying accounting identity. For example, an alternative interpretation of these equations is that all that is being estimated is a pricing equation and the negative coefficient of ln w is simply a consequence of this. In these circumstances, the inverse relationship between ln L and ln$w$, *ceteris paribus*, has no causal significance whatever. To see this, let us assume that the i'th firm pursues a constant mark-up pricing policy on unit labour costs:

$$p_i = (1 + \pi_i)w_i^n L_i / q_i \tag{7.5}$$

Where p_i is the price in, say, dollars per unit output, π_i is the mark-up, w_i^n is the nominal money wage and q_i is the output measured in homogeneous units. Let us, for illustrative purposes, further assume that the underlying micro production function is one of fixed coefficients, so that relative prices have no effect on the choice of the ratio of factor inputs. Total value added is given by $PQ = \sum p_i q_i = \sum (1 + \pi_i)w_i^n L_i$, where P is the value-added deflator and Q denotes real value added.[32] For expositional ease, let us further assume that this equation may be approximated by $PQ = (1 + \pi)w^n L$, where w^n is the average nominal wage rate. If $(1 + \pi)$, the average mark up, is, say, 1.33, this implies that labour's share will be constant and will take a value of 0.75.

For every firm (and every industry) there is an associated identity for real value added:

$$Q_i \equiv w_i L_i + r_i K_i \tag{7.6}$$

where Q_i is real value added, K_i is a constant-price *value* measure of the capital stock, w_i is the real wage rate and r_i is the *ex-post* real profit rate. Aggregating gives the accounting identity:

$$Q \equiv wL + rK \tag{7.7}$$

where w and r are the average real wage and profit rates.[33] This may be expressed in growth rates as:

$$\hat{Q}_t \equiv a_t \hat{w}_t + (1 - a_t)\hat{r}_t + a_t \hat{L}_t + (1 - a_t)\hat{K}_t \tag{7.8}$$

where the circumflex denotes growth rates. The shares have time subscripts as they vary over time. If they are constant, equation (7.8) may be integrated to give:

$$Q_t \equiv B w_t^a r_t^{1-a} L_t^a K_t^{1-a} \tag{7.9}$$

If, as is often empirically the case, w is strongly trended and r is roughly constant, then equation (7.9) may be expressed as:

$$Q_t \equiv A(t) L_t^a K_t^{1-a} \tag{7.10}$$

where $A(t) = A_0 \exp(\lambda t)$ and $\lambda = a\hat{w}$ (as $\hat{r} \cong 0$). Hence, if we were to estimate $\ln Q_t = c + b_5 t + b_6 \ln L_t + b_7 \ln K_t + \varepsilon_t$ then simply by virtue of the identity, the estimate of $b_6 = a$ and $b_7 = 1 - a$.

The key issue here is to understand what equation (7.10) is. Clearly it is not a Cobb–Douglas aggregate production function. This is because we know that it does not exist; and secondly, because of how equation (7.10) has been derived: it is simply the accounting identity equation (7.7), rewritten under the assumptions that factor shares are constant and that $a\hat{w}_t + (1-a)\hat{r}_t$ is also constant, equal to λ. Provided these assumptions are more or less correct empirically, equation (7.10) will provide an excellent fit to the data, even though the aggregate production function does not even exist (again, in the sense explained at the beginning of this section).[34] This argument may be easily generalized. Suppose factor shares are not constant over time, but vary, then equation (7.10) will not give the best fit to equation (7.7). What we require is a more flexible approximation, such as the CES or translog.[35] However, we insist that these should not be regarded as 'production functions', *per se*, but simply as mathematical transformations that give a good approximation to equation (7.7).

The second important implication of this result, crucial for the purposes of this chapter, is as follows. Rearranging the identity equation (7.9) and taking logarithms, we may express it as:

$$\ln L \equiv -\ln B + (1/a)\ln Q - \ln w - [(1-a)/a]\ln r - [(1-a)/a]\ln K \quad (7.11)$$

What does this result mean? It should be re-emphasized that as this equation is an identity (as long as factor shares are constant), it is compatible both with *any* state of competition and with *any* functional form for the production function, if, indeed, one actually exists. The main point of this argument is the obvious similarities between the identity equation (7.11) and the labour demand function equation (7.1), in particular the negative sign of $\ln w$. Our argument is that the negative sign of this variable in equation (7.1) is determined by the identity equation (7.11). Stated in different terms, the latter is no more than an approximation to the former.[36]

We start the empirical analysis in section 7.4 with a discussion of minimum wages in the Philippines in the context of the estimation of the marginal revenue product curve. Then in section 7.5 we discuss the estimation of the labour demand function. It should be noted that there are two differences between equations (7.1) and (7.11). The first is that the identity (7.11) contains the constant price value of the stock of capital, while the labour demand function does not; the latter, on the other hand, contains a time trend that the former does not have. Secondly, equation (7.11) uses the profit rate (r), which theoretically has a negative sign; while equation (7.1) uses the real user cost of capital (v), whose expected sign is positive. Section 7.5 discusses the implications of these two differences.

It must be stressed that the purpose of the next two sections is to support our theoretical arguments discussed above, which question both the usefulness and the conclusions of the neoclassical apparatus. To this purpose, we start by corroborating that the identities yield the expected results in terms of size and sign of the coefficients; then we show how the results vary as the equations estimated deviate from the identities. In general, the sizes of the coefficients vary, but the signs remain.

7.4   Do minimum wages cause unemployment in the Philippines?[37]

> For most economists, the idea of increasing the minimum wage is taboo. Raise the idea and one instantly gets tagged for being leftist. Mention the thought and everybody jumps on one for defying the law of supply and demand. Tinker with it and one supposedly endangers the health of the economy by increasing the rate of unemployment.

> L. Dumlao[38]

Minimum wage setting is highly contested all over the world. Freeman argues that:

> The minimum wage is a *bête noire* to distortions because it is the textbook case of an intervention that misallocates resources: an effective minimum wage reduces employment. The major question is whether the introduced increase is worth the job loss. If it does raise the wages of the most poverty-stricken at little cost to employment, many would find this an appealing way to redistribute income. If, by contrast, the cost is many jobs, and only a few highly paid formal sector workers benefit at the expense of lower-paid informal or rural sector workers, few would favour minimum wage policies.[39]

The theoretical effects of a minimum wage rate in a perfectly competitive market are very clear. In this model, by making labour more expensive, a minimum wage pushes firms up along their labour demand curve. This is because the minimum wage causes the firm to reduce labour usage as it will both substitute capital and other inputs for labour and cut back output. When labour markets are imperfectly competitive, however, the predictions are not so clear-cut, as, depending on the shifts of the supply and the marginal expense curves as a result of the implementation of a minimum wage, firms may even increase their profit-maximizing choice of labour input.

Using aggregate data, the profession has reached a consensus around the conclusion that minimum wages reduce employment.[40] In a recent study of unemployment in the Philippines, Brooks concluded, despite acknowledging that the correlation between employment and the minimum wage was not a very robust finding, 'that higher economic growth and *moderate increases* in the real minimum wage are required to reduce unemployment'.[41]

This conclusion was derived from the results of a regression with aggregate data of the logarithm of employment ($\ln L$) on the logarithms of real GDP ($\ln Q$) and the real minimum wage ($\ln w^*$), i.e.:

$$\ln L_t = c + \delta_1 \ln Q_t + \delta_2 \ln w_t^* + u_t \tag{7.12}$$

where u_t is the disturbance term. This expression is almost identical to the marginal revenue curve specification, discussed above, i.e. equation (7.2). Brooks's regressions (Table 2 in his paper) show invariably that δ_1 is positive and statistically significant, in most cases around unity.[42] On the other hand, δ_2 is negative (in some of the regressions it is not significant). In the two regressions where the variable was significant, it took the values of -0.55 and -0.63. The difference between this specification and the one in equation (7.2) is that while the former uses the minimum wage rate (w^*), the latter uses the average wage rate (w). There are two problems with equation (7.12). First, its theoretical underpinnings are not clear, although in footnote 7 of the paper, Brooks indicates that this 'approach assumes that the underlying technology is a CES production function'. Brooks seems to interpret the coefficient δ_2 as that of the elasticity of demand for labour. However, as noted above, and assuming equation (7.12) has been derived from a CES production function, the elasticity of demand for labour is $\eta_{LL/Q} = -(1 - \alpha)\delta_2$ (see equation 7.3).[43]

The second problem is that the policy conclusions Brooks derived from this type of work are problematic because there is no way in which he could have obtained different results, i.e. the regression specified above must yield a positive δ_1 and a negative δ_2 without implying any causality from the two right-hand-side variables to employment. In other words, no data set can reject statistically the relationship embedded in this regression. Hence, as a potentially refutable theory, it is of little use. Too see this, note that, by definition, one can write the identity for the labour share in output (a_t) as $a_t \equiv (w_t L_t)/Q_t$, where w_t is the average wage rate. We use the symbol $\equiv$ to denote that this expression is an accounting identity, not a behavioural equation. This identity can be rewritten as $L_t \equiv a_t(Q_t/w_t)$, which in logarithms can be written as:

$$\ln L_t \equiv c + \gamma_2 \ln Q_t + \gamma_3 \ln w_t \tag{7.13}$$

where $c \equiv \ln a_t$, provided the labour share is constant. It is obvious that this regression must provide suspiciously good results, with $\gamma_2 \cong 1$, $\gamma_3 \cong -1$ and a very high statistical fit (potentially $R^2 = 1$). It is an identity and hence it does not *explain* anything, except that, for some reason, factor shares are constant. The negative relationship between employment and wage rate is embedded in the identity. Using this framework, it is impossible to refute statistically the null hypothesis that employment and wage rate are negatively related.

Note that the econometric argument about the identity

$$\ln L_t \equiv \gamma_1 \ln a_t + \gamma_2 \ln Q_t + \gamma_3 \ln w_t \tag{7.14}$$

where $\gamma_1 = 1$, $\gamma_2 = 1$ and $\gamma_3 = -1$, holds whether the labour share (a_t) is constant or not. What the argument says is that *if* the labour share is perfectly constant, and thus it is well approximated by the constant term c in regression (7.13), then the identity explains parsimoniously the results in this regression. What if the labour share is not perfectly constant (as it is in real data)? The argument still applies. Suppose the labour share shows some slight variation. In this case, nothing changes for practical purposes. If, on the other hand, the variation from year to year is very large, it is true that results will deviate substantially from the identity. But this will simply indicate that the labour share varies too much to be approximated by a constant. Hence, one will need to approximate the labour share through a different form, for example, a trend if it is increasing. It does not imply, however, that employment, output and wages are statistically unrelated (that is, rejection of the labour demand curve) or that our argument does not apply. For all practical purposes, the variation from one year to the next displayed by the actual labour shares of most countries is not large enough to induce a severely large bias so as to turn the (theoretically) negative sign of the wage rate into a positive sign.

The difference between regression (7.13) and Brooks's regression (7.12) is that he used the minimum wage rate (w^*) instead of the average wage rate (w). This is what induces in his results the deviation from the (perfect) results embedded in the labour share identity specification. However, the negative sign of the wage rate variable and the positive sign of output remain. This must be indeed the case. In the extreme, suppose the minimum wage rate is a constant fraction of the average wage rate. Then the two regressions (variables) are identical. But this is not the case in general, i.e., the minimum wage rate is not a constant fraction of the average wage rate. To see this, note that the labour share $a_t \equiv (w_t L_t)/Q_t$ can be written in terms of the minimum wage as $a_t \equiv [(w_t^*/\theta_t)L_t]/Q_t$, where $w_t^* = \theta_t w_t$. Hence, it follows that $L_t \equiv a_t Q_t [1/(w_t^*/\theta_t)]$. And in logarithms, this identity becomes:

$$\ln L_t \equiv \delta_0 \ln a_t + \delta_1 \ln Q_t + \delta_2 \ln w_t^* + \delta_3 \ln \theta_t \tag{7.15}$$

where $\delta_0 = 1$, $\delta_1 = 1$, $\delta_2 = -1$ and $\delta_3 = -1$. This expression is parallel to equation (7.14), and it is the identity that serves as a reference point to understand equation (7.12). In practice, it is estimated with a constant term and without the variables $\ln a_t$ and $\ln \theta_t$, that is, $\ln L_t \equiv c + \delta_1 \ln Q_t + \delta_2 \ln w_t^* + u_t$, in other words, equation (7.12).

In order to understand the results obtained in the estimation of equation (7.12), one must analyse the two variables a_t and θ_t in equation (7.15). There are two cases: (i) $a_t = a$ and $\theta_t = \theta$. In this case, a and θ become part of the

Table 7.1 Marginal revenue product of labour function, the minimum wage rate and the accounting identity, the Philippines, 1980–2003

Average wage rate

	$\ln a_t$	c	$\ln Q$	$\ln w$	R^2, DW
(a)	1.00		1.00	−1.00		1.00, 0
(b)		−4.78	0.82	−0.68		0.99, 1.47
		(−11.20)	(47.86)	(−26.77)		
(c)		−4.60	0.81	−0.66		0.99, 1.50
		(−10.61)	(46.29)	(−24.92)		

Minimum wage rate

	$\ln a_t$	c	$\ln Q$	$\ln w^*$	$\ln \theta_t$	R^2, DW
(d)	1.00		1.00	1.00	1.00	1.00, 0
(e)		−12.74	1.15	−0.50		0.90, 0.59
		(−7.64)	(13.13)	(−3.30)		
(f)		−9.51	1.03	−0.64		0.98, 2.44
		(−1.81)	(3.82)	(−1.36)		

Notes: t-statistics in parenthesis. *DW* is the Durbin–Watson statistic. Equations (b) and (e) are static regressions estimated using OLS; regressions (c) and (f) were also estimated with OLS but including the lag of the dependent variable. Results shown for these two regressions are already the derived long-run elasticities. Regressions (a) and (d) included the constant term.

constant term in the regression and estimation of equation (7.12) is identical to that of equation (7.15), the complete identity; (ii) $a_t \neq a$ and $\theta_t \neq \theta$. This is the general case. Regression (7.12) suffers now from a problem akin to that of omitted variable bias if a_t and θ_t are correlated with the included regressors, output and minimum wage rate. As this is usually the case, the omission of these two variables will induce a bias in the coefficients of the estimated regression, that is, in δ_1 and δ_2.

The conclusion is that if Brooks ran his regression to 'test' a behavioural model, the problem is that such a regression will not be able to reject the alleged model: the signs of the two variables are a forgone conclusion and the magnitudes of the coefficients will be relatively close to what the identity predicts. The conclusion is that this type of empirical analysis has no policy implications whatsoever.[44]

Table 7.1 shows the results of the estimation of equations (7.12) as well as the identities (7.13)–(7.14) and (7.15).

The most salient results of this exercise are as follows:

(i) Regression (a) is the full accounting identity, equation (7.14). All this regression does is to confirm that the data set is consistent in the sense

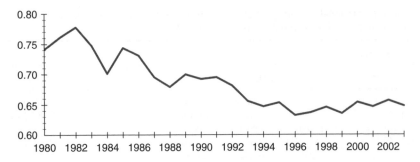

Figure 7.1   Labour share, the Philippines 1980–2003

that it satisfies the said identity. Certainly this regression has no other implications whatsoever.

(ii) Regressions (b) and (c) can be interpreted in two different ways. First, as the identity estimated in regression (a) assuming that the labour share is a constant, i.e. equation (7.13). The second interpretation is in terms of the marginal revenue product of labour function, equation (7.2). Regression (b) is the static equation and regression (c) is estimated including the lagged dependent variable. Under the first interpretation, the different estimates obtained in regressions (a) and (b) are the result of, as noted above, what could be attributed to omitted variable bias, as the labour share a_t is subsumed into the constant term in regression (b). The results are very good econometrically, despite the fact that the labour share is clearly not constant, as shown in Figure 7.1. The important aspects to note are the negative sign of the average wage rate, and the positive sign of output, both variables with values that would be interpreted as plausible (also note the extremely high t-statistics). Under this interpretation, as argued above, regression (b) is simply an accounting identity with no behavioural content. Under the second interpretation, the elasticity of employment with respect to the wage rate must be derived from the constant term, i.e. $c = \ln \alpha$ (see equation (7.2)), which in this case implies an elasticity of demand for labour of $\hat{\eta}_{LL/Q} = -[1 - exp(\hat{c})] = -0.99$ (t-statistic of -278.32).

(iii) Regression (d) is the full accounting identity with the minimum wage rate, equation (7.15).[45] Figure 7.2 shows both the real average and minimum wage rates for the Philippines for 1980–2003.[46] And Figure 7.3 shows θ_t, the ratio between both variables. All this regression does is confirm that the data set is consistent in the sense that it satisfies the said identity.

(iv) Regression (e) is the equation Brooks estimated, equation (7.12).[47] Given our arguments, we know that the coefficients of this regression suffer

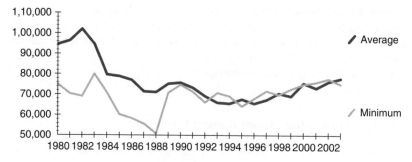

Figure 7.2 Real average and minimum wage rates. Philippines 1980–2003

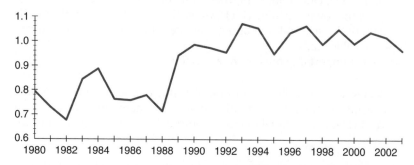

Figure 7.3 Ratio minimum to average wage rates. Philippines 1980–2003

from two types of omitted-variable bias, namely the omissions of the labour share (a_t) and of the relationship between minimum and average wage rates (θ_t). Both variables are subsumed into the constant term. Despite this, results are very good, as the positive sign of output, with a value around one, remains. The negative sign of the minimum wage rate also remains, with a value of −0.50, similar to what Brooks obtained. As argued above, this estimate cannot be interpreted as an estimate of the elasticity of demand for labour. The latter, interpreted now as the elasticity with respect to the minimum wage rate, is given by $\hat{\eta}_{LL/Q} = -[1 - exp(\hat{c})] = -1.00$ (t-statistic of −205,181.1).

(v) The major objection to regression (e) is that it is most likely spurious (see the low Durbin–Watson statistic). Hence we re-estimated it introducing the dependent variable lagged one period (regression (f)). The conclusions remain unchanged.[48] In this case, the elasticity of the demand for labour with respect to the minimum wage rate is $\hat{\eta}_{LL/Q} = -[1 - exp(\hat{c})] = -0.70$ (t-statistic of −2.07).

Summing up, this section has shown that the conclusions derived by Brooks about the impact of minimum wages in the Philippines are not meaningful, in the sense that he could not have obtained anything other than a negative estimate of the coefficient of the minimum wage rate. His specification of the relationship between employment and the wage rate does not allow him to obtain any other result. Like all near tautologies, it can explain nothing; and as a consequence, it carries no policy implications whatsoever.

7.5   The Philippine labour demand function

We now discuss the estimation of the labour demand function, equation (7.1). As above, we start by estimating the accounting identity, in this case equation (7.11). Our argument is that estimation of equation (7.1) is simply an approximation to equation (7.11), where the latter determines the baseline estimates of the size and sign of the estimates of the former. The results are shown in Table 7.2.

The most important conclusions are as follows:

(i) Regression (a) is the accounting identity equation (7.11). Its validity depends on the sole assumption that factor shares are constant. As we saw in Figure 7.1, the labour share shows a downward trend. Despite this,

Table 7.2   The labour demand function and the accounting identity, the Philippines, 1980–2003

Accounting identity

	c	$\ln Q$	$\ln w$	$\ln r$	$\ln K$	R^2, DW
(a)	−7.23	1.35	−0.98	−0.39	−0.38	0.99, 0.93
	(−26.17)	(20.12)	(−25.83)	(−10.21)	(−6.85)	
(b)	0.002	1.21	−0.88	−0.32	−0.32	0.97, 2.43
	(0.94)	(17.38)	(−18.11)	(−10.43)	(−4.80)	

Labour demand function

	c	$\ln Q$	$\ln w$	$\ln v$	t	R^2, DW
(c)	−0.66	0.59	−0.53	0.016	0.008	0.99, 1.41
	(−0.45)	(7.75)	(−10.52)	(1.37)	(3.24)	

	c	$\ln Q$	$\ln w$	$\ln r$	t	R^2, DW
(d)	−13.54	1.23	−0.89	−0.35	−0.008	0.99, 2.49
	(−7.61)	(13.86)	(−16.31)	(−9.26)	(−3.12)	

Notes: t-statistics in parenthesis. *DW* is the Durbin–Watson statistic. Variables panel (b) are growth rates. Regression (d) was estimated using the Cochrane–Orcutt procedure with an AR(2) process.

the regression mimics the accounting identity rather well. The average labour share ($\bar{a}$) for the period in our data set is 0.68, with a standard deviation of 0.044. The theoretical estimate (equation (7.11)) of the coefficient of output (Y) is, therefore, $(1/\bar{a}) = (1/0.68) = 1.47$; the theoretical estimate of the wage rate (w) is -1; and the theoretical estimate of both the profit rate (r) and the capital stock (K) is $-(1 - \bar{a})/\bar{a} = -0.47$. Given the estimates of equation (a) all we can legitimately conclude from this regression is that indeed equation (7.11) is a very good approximation to the identity equation (7.7).

(ii) Since regression (a) displays a very low Durbin–Watson statistic together with very high t-statistics, the conclusion that some sceptics may draw is that the good fit of regression (a) may be spurious. To show that this is not the case and that, indeed, these results are driven by the fact that what is being estimated is an identity, the regression was run with all five variables expressed in growth rates. The results are displayed in panel (b). The similarity of the two sets of estimates can only be the result of the fact that what is being estimated is an accounting identity.

(iii) Regression (c) is the neoclassical labour demand function, given by equation (7.1). The signs are the expected ones. The estimates, though slightly different from the theoretical ones in equation (7.1), are nevertheless plausible. Overall, these results would be accepted by most researchers as representing the Philippine labour demand curve. The elasticity of demand for labour is given by the estimate of the coefficient of $\ln w$. The results indicate that a 1 per cent increase in the wage rate leads to a -0.53 per cent decline in employment.[49]

(iv) As noted at the end of section 7.3, there are two differences between the labour demand function, regression (7.1), estimated in equation (c), and the accounting identity, regression (7.11), estimated in equation (a). The first one is that is that the labour demand function includes a time trend (t) while the accounting identity includes the stock of capital (K). The second difference is that equation (7.1) uses the rental price of capital (v), which has a positive sign, while the identity (7.11) uses the profit rate (r), which has a negative sign. In what follows we discuss and reconcile the effect of these two issues.

The inclusion of the time trend as opposed to the stock of capital is the lesser of the two problems. Regression (d) in Table 7.2 reports the estimation of the accounting identity by replacing the stock of capital with the time trend, that is,

$$\ln L_t = c + (1/a)\ln Q_t - 1.0\ln w_t - [(1 - a)/a]\ln r_t - \lambda' t \qquad (7.16)$$

which looks very much like the labour demand function, equation (7.1), except for the sign of the coefficient of the profit rate. The results are, not

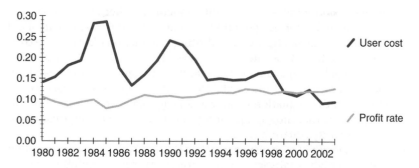

Figure 7.4   User cost of capital and profit rate. Philippines 1980–2003

surprisingly, very good and similar to those in regression (a) in Table 7.2. This is because the constant price value of the stock of capital is calculated through the perpetual inventory method. Hence, it is a smooth function of time. Consequently, when it is replaced into the identity with the linear time trend, the latter provides a good proxy and works well.

This result leads to the conclusion that the different values obtained in the estimation of the neoclassical labour demand function and the accounting identity are mostly due to the difference between the real profit rate (r) and the real user cost of capital (v). Here there are two related questions to consider. The first one is the difference in the signs of $\ln v$ (positive) in equation (7.1) and of $\ln r$ (negative) in equation (7.11). The second issue concerns the relationship between the real profit rate (r) and the real user cost of capital (v).

With respect to the first question, it can be shown that this is just a result of the way the two specifications are expressed and that, in fact, both equations are identical. To see this, assume for simplicity that $r = v$, then note that equation (7.1) can be rewritten as $\ln L = c - \ln w + \ln Q$. This is because, under neoclassical assumptions, λ, the rate of technical progress, is equal to $a\hat{w} + (1 - a)\hat{v}$, which means that $\lambda t = \alpha \ln w + (1 - \alpha) \ln v$. The capital share $1 - a = (rK/Q)$ can be written as $\ln Q = \frac{1}{1-a} \ln r + \frac{1}{1-a} \ln K$. Substituting the latter into the expression for $\ln L$ yields $\ln L = c - \ln w + \frac{1}{1-a} \ln r + \frac{1}{1-a} \ln K$, and noting that $\frac{1}{a} \ln Q = \frac{1}{a(1-a)} [\ln r + \ln K]$, then $\ln L = c - \ln w + (1/a) \ln Q - [(1 - a)/a] \ln r - [(1 - a)/a] \ln K$, which is, not surprisingly, the identity (7.11). The conclusion is that both specifications can be reconciled with each other and our argument is correct.

In order to see the effect of the second question, namely the fact that the two series used are different, we have plotted them in Figure 7.4.

While the profit rate is definitionally the ratio of total (residual) profits (Π) in the National Accounts to the stock of capital (K), i.e. $r_t = \frac{\Pi_t}{K_t}$, and it is, in general, a pro-cyclical variable, the user cost of capital is calculated following Jorgenson as $v_t = [q_t(i_t + \delta - \dot{q}_t)]/P_t$, where q_t is the price of the capital goods,

i_t is the nominal interest rate, $\dot{q}_t$ is the capital gain-loss, and P_t is the GDP deflator[50] and v_t is a countercyclical variable. In general, one should expect $v_t = [q_t(i_t + \delta - \dot{q}_t)]/P_t \neq \frac{\Pi_t}{K_t} = r_t$. How are the two variables related? The expost profit rate (r) is the sum of the user cost of capital (v) plus another return on monopolistic profits (v'), that is, $r = v + v'$. This is because the identity (7.7) can be written as $Q \equiv wL + vK + v'K \equiv wL + (v + v')K \equiv wL + rK$, where v' is the return on monopolistic profits.

In these circumstances, the closer r and v are to each other, the more estimation results of the neoclassical labour demand function will resemble those of the income accounting identity; and the more these two variables differ (due to the different cyclicality) the more the results will differ. In the case of the Philippines, the correlation coefficient between the two variables is -0.61.

7.6   Do increases in the minimum wage rate induce increases in the average wage rate in the Philippines?

The conclusion to be drawn from the previous sections is that the estimation of the labour demand function with a view to assessing the impact of wage rate (or of the minimum wage rate) increases on employment is a futile exercise. This does not mean that we cannot know anything about the impact of increases in the minimum wage rate on some other macroeconomic variables. In this section, we follow Rama's approach to assess the impact of increases in the minimum wage on the average wage rate.[51] As the approach uses a reduced form equation and is not trouble-free, some degree of caution must be exercised in drawing conclusions. The regression we estimate to analyse the impact of the minimum wage rate on the average wages rate is the same as Rama's but including lags, that is,

$$\hat{w}_t = a_1 + \sum_{i=1} b_i \hat{w}_{t-i} + \sum_{j=0} c_j \hat{w}^*_{t-j} + \sum_{k=0} d_k \Delta Z_{t-k} + a_2 D84 + u_t \qquad (7.17)$$

where $\hat{w}$ denotes the growth rate of the average real wage rate; $\hat{w}^*$ is the growth rate of the real minimum wage rate; ΔZ is a series of control variables, or determinants of the growth of the average wage rate; $D84$ is a dummy variables with value 1 for 1984 and 0 for the rest. This variable reflects the fact that the average real wage rate fell by 17 per cent in 1984. As the regression excluding the dummy variable does not pick up the influence of this year well, the inclusion of the dummy variable greatly helped to improve the goodness-of-fit of the estimated regressions. Finally, u_t is the disturbance term.[52] We used five control variables: the growth of real GDP, the growth of labour productivity, the growth of inflation, the growth rate of the share of employment in the industrial sector in total employment and the growth rate

Table 7.3   Impact of increases in the minimum wage rate on the average wage rate, the Philippines, 1980–2003

Variable	(A)	(B)	(C)	(D)	(E)	(F)
Constant	−0.001	−0.015	−0.005	0.002	−0.003	−0.003
	(−0.14)	(−1.33)	(−1.24)	(0.10)	(−0.42)	(−0.40)
D84	−0.163	−0.122	−0.03	−0.137	−0.173	−0.164
	(−3.42)	(−2.28)	(−1.28)	(−1.70)	(−3.72)	(−3.63)
ψ	0.064	0.095	0.010	0.19	0.21	0.18
	(0.65)	(0.58)	(0.20)	(1.46)	(1.78)	(1.48)
i, j, k in estimated regression	0, 0, 0	1, 1, 1	1, 0, 0	1, 1, 0	1, 1, 1	1, 1, 0
R^2	0.42	0.51	0.84	0.46	0.56	0.51
D.W.	2.21	1.98	1.69	2.05	2.02	2.02

Note: t-statistics in parentheses.
Regression *(A)* does not include any control variable. The control variable in regression *(B)* is the growth rate of real output; control variable in regression *(C)* is the growth rate of labour productivity; control variable in regression *(D)* is the inflation rate; control variable in regression *(E)* is the growth rate of the share of employment in the industrial sector in total employment; and control variable in regression *(F)* is the growth rate of the share of employment in the manufacturing sector in total employment.

of the share of employment in the manufacturing sector in total employment. The elasticity of the average wage with respect to the minimum wage rate is calculated as $\psi = \sum_{j=0} c_j / (1 - \sum_{i=1} b_i)$.

Table 7.3 summarizes the results of the estimation of equation (7.17). To simplify the table, we show the computed elasticity ψ instead of the coefficients of each variable. With the corresponding caveats mentioned above, the results are very clear: minimum wages in the Philippines do not appear to have a statistically significant impact on the average wage rate. Only in regression (E), where the control variable is the growth rate of the share of employment in the industrial sector in total employment, is the elasticity ψ statistically significant at the 10 per cent probability level. These results corroborate those of Rama for Indonesia, i.e., weak statistical significance.[53]

7.7   Conclusions

Constant references to the need to be competitive in order to survive in the global economy have put a tremendous burden on workers. This is because the main mechanism advocated to increase competitiveness is the reduction in labour costs. Indeed, in mainstream models, increases in real wages cause employment to decline as higher wages induce firms to substitute other inputs for labour, and as a result of the fact that higher wages entail cost increases, which induce buyers to shift suppliers. These arguments underlie the rationale for the neoclassical labour demand curve, i.e., the inverse relationship between employment and the wage rate, and calls for labour market reform in order to make it more flexible. This is the crux of the solution to the unemployment problem in mainstream analyses.

This chapter has argued that, contrary to what many economists believe, the theoretical foundations of the labour demand function are very shaky. The standard finding that there is a negative relationship between the level of employment and the wage rate underlies the neoclassical thesis that higher wages lead to lower employment and orthodox proposals for labour market reforms. It has been shown that this observed negative relationship is *determined* by the income accounting identity that relates the value of output to the wage bill plus puts profits. This accounting identity can be rewritten as a form that resembles the neoclassical labour demand function such that, when estimated econometrically, it yields the observed negative relationship between these two variables. As with all tautologies, this finding is consistent with any underlying structure and as such explains nothing; and as consequence, it carries no policy implications whatsoever. One important implication of our argument is that labour market reforms, with a view to making labour markets more flexible, advocated on the basis of this erroneous empirical evidence, should be viewed with caution.

The theoretical arguments have been corroborated with data for the Philippines, a developing country. It has been shown that claims about the need to contain minimum wages in this country based on analyses derived from neoclassical labour demand functions are not compelling. The empirical exercise has shown, step by step, why regressions of employment on the wage rate will indicate that there exists a negative relationship between both variables, although this result has no causal implications whatsoever. Hence, we remain sceptical about the standard interpretation of a negative elasticity of demand for aggregate labour and about the implication that higher labour costs have a negative impact on employment. For this reason, we disagree with Hamermesh's advice to policy-makers, 'that in developing economies, as in developed ones, polices that may be socially desirable, but that raise labour costs or increase labour market rigidity, have negative consequences for the level of employment'.[54] Clearly, the negative impact of wage increases has been based on fallacious empirical evidence.

Naturally, this disagreement does not mean that we believe that an increase in the average or in the minimum wage rates *does not* lead to a decrease in employment. This might be true, as Keynes remarked.[55] Our claim is simply that the empirical evidence often presented and derived from the estimation of neoclassical labour demand functions is not persuasive. On the other hand, it is not difficult to think of the potential positive effects of an increase in the minimum wage rate via an increase in the overall wage bill and, hence, in demand through the multiplier effect. This can lead to more jobs. Claims that increases in the minimum wage rate lead to decreases in investment and to an increase in the inflation rate have to be verified empirically.[56]

Annex 7.1   The NAIRU and the laws of algebra

Lavoie[57] has shown that a variant of a NAIRU model by Layard *et al.* (hereafter LNJ)[58] can be derived easily as a series of simple transformations of the variables that define the income side of the National Income and Product Accounts (NIPA). Hence, its econometric estimation has no policy implications whatsoever.[59]

LNJ argued that their model allowed them to explain the path of the rate of *equilibrium unemployment*, or NAIRU. They argued that 60 per cent of the increase in unemployment in France was due to increases in real interest rates and the rest was due to increases in the social security payments and other benefits.

The results seem to be very persuasive because the path of the equilibrium unemployment rate seems to match the evolution of observed unemployment. Lavoie (2000) argues that there seem to be a number of studies on the NAIRU highlighting the role of tax rates, as opposed to other traditional variables, such as the rate of unionization or the different measures of the costs of severance payment or of the generosity of social programmes. The model estimated consists of the following three equations:

$$\ln w = a_1 U + a_2 \ln wedge + \gamma t \tag{7.A1}$$

$$\ln w = b_1 U + b_2(\ln Q - \ln N) + b_3 t \tag{7.A2}$$

$$\ln w = \gamma t - \frac{(1-a)}{a} \ln i \tag{7.A3}$$

where (7.A1) is a behavioural equation that defines workers' target salary. In it w is the real wage rate, U is the rate of unemployment, *wedge* is the tax wedge, that is, the difference between workers' take-home pay and the costs of employing them, including income taxes and social security contributions; and t is a time trend. Equation (7.A2) represents the short-term labour demand curve. Here Q denotes real output and N is the level of active population. Finally, equation (7.A3) represents the long-term labour demand curve. i denotes the real interest rate. The coefficient γ represents the labour productivity gain, and $(1-a)/a$ is the ratio of the capital share to the labour share in output.

The intersection of equations (7.A1) and (7.A2) determines the mid-term *equilibrium* unemployment rate; while the intersection of equations (7.A1) and (7.A3) determines the long-term *equilibrium* unemployment rate, which in LNJ's model depends only on the tax wedge *wedge*, and on the real interest rate (plus a constant). These two relationships allow the authors to assert that the high long-term equilibrium unemployment rate is mainly due to the high real interest rates and due also partially to due to the high social security payments and other benefits.

The authors argue that theory implies that $b_1 = b_2 = 1$ in equation (7.A2). The only econometric result from this equation is $b_3 = -0.002$ (with quarterly data). The authors verify that $a_1 < 0$ and $a_2 > 0$ and around unity in equation (7.A1). This means that when the unemployment rate decreases, workers negotiate real salaries above what would be justifiable given the increases in productivity and also that increases in social security taxes and other benefits lead to increases in negotiated real salaries.

According to LNJ, equation (7.A2) indicates that for a given increase in *full employment productivity*, an increase in the real salary entails an increase in the unemployment rate, as a result of the maximization behaviour of firms.

However, Lavoie has argued that these equations can be easily derived from the income side of the NIPA, and thus that their econometric estimation does not imply anything in terms of testing a theory and policy implications. The NIPA allows the derivation of equations (7.A2) and (7.A3) in a few steps. Start from the definition of output (Q) as the sum of the total wage bill, itself the product of the average wage rate (w) and the level of employment (L); and total profits, the product of the profit rate (r) times the stock of capital (K):

$$Q \equiv wL + rK \qquad (7.A4)$$

In growth rates it becomes:

$$\hat{Q} \equiv a\hat{w} + (1-a)\hat{r} + a\hat{L} + (1-a)\hat{K} \qquad (7.A5)$$

where a and $(1-a)$ denote the labour and capital shares in output, respectively. Now rewrite it as:

$$\hat{w} \equiv (\hat{Q} - \hat{L}) - \frac{(1-a)}{a}(\hat{Q} - \hat{K}) - \frac{(1-a)}{a}\hat{r} \qquad (7.A6)$$

Note that $U = \frac{N-L}{L} = \frac{N}{L} - 1 \Rightarrow (1+U) = \frac{N}{L}$. Recall the approximation $\ln(1+U) \cong U \Rightarrow \ln(1+U) \cong \log(\frac{N}{L})$. Therefore, $U \cong \ln(\frac{N}{L}) \cong \ln(N) - \ln(L)$.

Taking the derivative with respect to time, the last expression becomes $\dot{U} \cong \hat{N} - \hat{L} \Rightarrow \hat{L} \cong \hat{N} - \dot{U}$. Substituting this expression for $\hat{L}$ into (7.A6) yields:

$$\hat{w} \cong (\hat{Q} - \hat{N}) + \dot{U} + \frac{a}{(1-a)}[\hat{Q} - \hat{K} - \hat{r}] \qquad (7.A7)$$

Integrating yields:

$$\ln w \cong (\ln Q - \ln N) + U + \frac{(1-a)}{a}ht \qquad (7.\text{A}8)$$

where $h = (\hat{Q} - \hat{K} - \hat{r})$. It is obvious that expressions (7.A8) and (7.A2) are the same for all practical purposes. No wonder econometric estimations lead to $b_1 = b_2 = 1$ and no wonder either that economists have succeeded at verifying empirically, based on equations like (7.A2) or (7.A8), that excessive increases in real salaries lead to increases in the unemployment rate. However, since this result is derived from an accounting identity, it does not have such an interpretation.

Let us now derive equation (7.A3). Returning to (7.A6), note that it can be written as:

$$\hat{w} = \frac{1}{a}[\hat{Q} - (a\hat{L} + (1-a)\hat{K})] - \frac{(1-a)}{a}\hat{r} \qquad (7.\text{A}9)$$

or,

$$\hat{w} = \frac{\lambda}{a} - \frac{(1-a)}{a}\hat{r} \qquad (7.\text{A}10)$$

where $\lambda = \hat{Q} - [a\hat{L} + (1-a)\hat{K}]$. Integrating yields:

$$\ln w = \frac{\lambda}{a}t - \frac{(1-a)}{a}\ln r \qquad (7.\text{A}11)$$

which can be approximated as:

$$\ln w = \gamma t - \frac{(1-a)}{a}\ln i \qquad (7.\text{A}12)$$

where $\gamma = \lambda/a$ and is the i interest rate. It can be seen that equations (7.A12) and (7.A3) are the same. But again, since (7.A12) is an accounting identity, its estimation does not have any economic implications.

Finally, Lavoie argues that the only behavioural equation in the system is (7.A1), even though he argues that the results are not convincing, but for reasons unrelated to those summarized above.[60]

Notes

1   We are grateful to the participants in the seminar on 'Labour Market Institutions and Employment in Developing Countries', organized by the International Labour Office, Geneva, Switzerland, 24–5 November 2005, for their comments. Janine Berg and David Kucera provided us with very valuable suggestions that greatly

improved the manuscript. Any remaining errors are ours. This chapter represents the views of the authors and does not represent those of the Asian Development Bank, its Executive Directors, or the countries that they represent.

2 F.M. Fisher (1971) 'Aggregate Production Functions and the Explanation of Wages: A Simulation Experiment', *Review of Economics and Statistics*, 53(4): 305.

3 D.S. Hamermesh (2004) 'Labor Demand in Latin America and the Caribbean: What Does it Tell Us?', in J. Heckman and C. Pagés (eds), *Law and Employment: Lessons from Latin American and the Caribbean* (Chicago: University of Chicago Press), p. 553.

4 For example, *Journal of Economic Perspectives* (1998) Symposium on Globalization in Perspective, 12(4).

5 See Asian Development Bank (ADB) (2003) and chapter on 'Competitiveness in Developing Asia', *Asian Development Outlook* (Manila: Asian Development Bank), pp. 203–72 for an in-depth analysis.

6 On this see H. Botwinick (1993) *Persistent Inequalities: Wage Disparity under Capitalist Competition* (Princeton, NJ: Princeton University Press) and D. Rodrik (1999) 'Globalization and Labour, or: If Globalization is a Bowl of Cherries, Why Are There So Many Glum Faces around the Table?', in R. Baldwin, D. Cohen, A. Sapir and A. Venables (eds), *Market Integration, Regionalism and the Global Economy* (New York: Cambridge University Press). The former offers an analysis of wage inequalities from a Marxian perspective, while the latter discusses the impact of globalization on labour, in particular: (i) how globalization affects unskilled labour as it becomes more substitutable; (ii) how labour standards (e.g., compliance with ILO standards) affect labour costs, comparative advantage and foreign direct investment; and (iii) the role of national governments in developed countries in sheltering domestic society from external risks.

7 J. Felipe and R. Hasan (eds) (2006) *Labour Markets in Asia: Issues and Perspectives* (Basingstoke: Palgrave).

8 J.M. Keynes (1936) *The General Theory of Employment, Interest and Money* (London: Macmillan).

9 Ibid., p. 261. Furthermore, see Chapter 19, in particular where Keynes argued that the classical argument that a reduction in money wages will stimulate demand by diminishing the price of the finished product is a fallacy. In particular, in the context of a closed economy, Keynes argued that while a reduction in money wages could indeed stimulate output, the reason for this result is not that of classical theory, that is, that a reduction in the wage rate would reduce the price of the finished product, and thus increase output and employment. Keynes argued that this line of reasoning necessarily assumed that aggregate effective demand is fixed. In his own words, 'the precise question at issue is whether the reduction in money-wages will or will not be accompanied by the same aggregate effective demand as before measured in money, or, at any rate, by an aggregate effective demand wish is not reduced in full proportion to the reduction in money-wages (i.e., which is somewhat greater measured in wage-units)' (ibid., p. 259). His key objection was that while the classical analysis might be possible for an individual product, it need not be true for the industry as a whole. It would be correct only under the assumption that aggregate demand is fixed (Keynes 1936, p. 259). S. Keen (2001) *Debunking Economics* (London: Pluto Press), Chapter 5, offers an accessible critique of the mainstream conceptualization of the labour market.

10 D. S. Hamermesh (1993) *Labor Demand* (Princeton, NJ: Princeton University Press), p. 92.

11   C. Cobb and P. Douglas (1928) 'A Theory of Production', *American Economic Review Papers and Proceedings of the Fortieth Annual Meeting of the American Economic Association*, 18(Supplement).

12   J. Felipe and F. Adams (2005) '"A Theory of Production": The Estimation of the Cobb–Douglas Function: A Retrospective View', *Eastern Economic Journal*, 31(3).

13   Hamermesh (2004), p. 92. G. J. Borjas (2005) *Labor Economics* (New York: Irwin McGraw-Hill), p.114, notes that there are criticisms of the marginal productivity theory of labour, but dismisses them. Some critics argue that the theory bears little relationship to the way that employers actually make hiring decisions. He dismisses it by arguing that if some employers did not behave the way that marginal productivity theory says they should behave; those employers would not last long in the marketplace. He also indicates that the value of this theory does not necessarily depend on the validity of the assumptions – or on whether it provides a 'realistic' depiction of the labour market. He argues that surely employers do not have any idea of what this theory says, but it must be true that employers in a competitive labour market must act as they know and obey the implications of this theory. In other words, the theory is infallible and the mere thought of it being refuted empirically seems to be something out of question.

14   Organization for Economic Co-Operation and Development (OECD) (1994) *The OECD Jobs Study: Facts, Analysis, Strategies* (Paris: OECD).

15   International Monetary Fund (IMF) (1999) 'Chronic Unemployment in the Euro Area: Causes and Cures', *World Economic Outlook*, May (Washington, DC), chapter IV; IMF (2003) 'Unemployment and Labor Market Institutions: Why Reforms Pay Off', *World Economic Outlook*, April (Washington, DC: IMF), chapter IV.

16   D. R. Howell (ed.) (2005) *Fighting Unemployment: The Limits of Free Market Orthodoxy* (Oxford: Oxford University Press) offers a collection of very critical papers of mainstream arguments for structural reforms of the labour market. It is particularly critical of the empirical work presented by the OECD (1994) and IMF (1999, 2003).

17   J. Heckman and C. Pagés (2004a) *Law and Employment: Lessons from Latin America and the Caribbean* (Chicago: The University of Chicago Press).

18   Heckman and Pagés (2004b) 'Introduction', in Heckman and Pagés (eds), *Law and Employment: Lessons from Latin American and the Caribbean* (Chicago: The University of Chicago Press), table 4, p. 38.

19   Ibid., p. 40.

20   Hamermesh (2004), table 11.1, p. 555.

21   Ibid. pp. 555–6.

22   M. Cárdenas and R. Bernal (2004) 'Determinants of Labor Demand in Colombia 1976–1996', in Heckman and Pagés (eds), *Law and Employment: Lessons from Latin American and the Caribbean* (Chicago: The University of Chicago Press), tables 4.7–4.8, pp. 264–5. With firm-level data, they find a short-run wage elasticity of -0.05 and a long-run elasticity of -2.27. With panel data, the estimated short-run real wage elasticity is -0.6 and the long run is -1.43.

23   Some Keynesians, while accepting the marginal productivity theory of factor pricing, would dispute this line of reasoning. They argue that while there is an inverse relationship between the wage rate and the level of employment (because of diminishing returns), the causation is not that of the neoclassicals. It is the level of demand that determines the demand for labour which in turn determines the real wage (e.g. A. P. Thirlwall (1993) 'The Renaissance of Keynesian Economics', *Banca Nazionale del Lavoro Quarterly Review*, 186). We shall not pursue this argument here.

T. Besley and R. Burgess (2004) 'Can Labor Relations Hinder Economic Performance? Evidence from India', *Quarterly Journal of Economics* (February), 91–134 is another well-known work for developing countries. These authors exploit state-level amendments to India's Industrial Disputes Act over the period 1958–92, and code legislative changes across major states as either pro-worker, neutral, or pro-employer. These legislative amendments are then used in a regression analysis of a variety of outcomes in the formal manufacturing sector, including employment outputs and investment. Consistent with expectations of reformers, Besley and Burgess find that pro-worker labour regulations have had a negative impact on employment, output and investment in formal manufacturing. Felipe and Hasan (eds) (2006), chapter 5, review this work and indicate that there might be some potential problems with the Besley and Burgess work. For example, reading off directly from legal statutes to measure rigidities could be highly misleading. Also, their coding of various states legislation seems to be puzzling. Felipe and Hasan also point out that Besley and Burgess's results indicate that pro-worker legislative amendments are not found to raise workers' wages. This is certainly puzzling.

24 See especially P. Brown (1957) 'The Meaning of the Fitted Cobb–Douglas Function', *Quarterly Journal of Economics*, 71, pp. 546–60; A. Shaikh (1974) 'Laws of Production and Laws of Algebra: The Humbug Production Function', *Review of Economics and Statistics*, 56; A. Shaikh (1980) 'Laws of Production and Laws of Algebra: Humbug II', in E. J. Nell (ed.), *Growth, Profits and Property: Essays in the Revival of Political Economy* (Cambridge: Cambridge University Press), pp. 80–95; H. A. Simon (1979) 'On Parsimonious Explanation of Production Relations', *Scandinavian Journal of Economics*, 81; Eastern Economic Journal (2005) *Symposium: Aggregate Production Functions*, 31(3); Felipe and Adams (2005); Felipe and J.S.L. McCombie (2001) 'The CES Production Function, the Accounting Identity and Occam's Razor', *Applied Economics*, 33; Felipe and McCombie (2002) 'A Problem with Some Recent Estimations and Interpretations of the Mark-up in Manufacturing Industry', *International Review of Applied Economics*, 16(2); Felipe and McCombie (2005) 'How Sound are the Foundations of the Aggregate Production Function?', *Eastern Economic Journal*, 31(3).

25 M. Lavoie (2000) 'Le Chômage d'équilibre: Réalité ou artefact statistique?', *Revue Economique*, 52(6).

26 R. Layard, S. Nickell and R. Jackman (1991) *Unemployment: Macroeconomic Performance and the Labour Market* (Oxford: Oxford University Press).

27 For an extension of these arguments see: J. Felipe and J.S.L. McCombie (2007) 'Are Estimates of Labor Demand Functions Mere Statistical Artefacts?', *International Review of Applied Economics*. Forthcoming.

28 See R.N. Waud (1968) 'Man-Hour Behavior in U.S. Manufacturing: A Neoclassical Interpretation', *Journal of Political Economy*, 76, for the case of a monopolist.

29 The so-called Cambridge Capital Theory Controversies took place between the 1950s and the 1970s. At stake was the question of the meaning of an aggregate stock of capital, especially for purposes of including it as a 'factor of production' in an aggregate production function. There are two related problems: (i) the first one is that the only way to express an aggregate stock of capital is in monetary terms. This is a problem because the production function is supposed to be a relationship among physical quantities; (ii) the second one is that there is a problem of circularity. So long as the capital stock is a collection of heterogeneous capitals (as it happens at the aggregate level), its measurement requires knowledge of the relative values of individual capital goods. This can only be achieved if the price vector

of the economy and the rate of profits are known *ex ante*. The consequence is that aggregate capital, the aggregate production function, and the marginal products of the factors can only be defined when the rate of profit is given, and this implies that they cannot be used to build a theory of the rate of profit or distribution. Indeed, capital goods are produced in a market economy where capitalists require profits. This implies that in order to provide a 'quantity of capital' one must know, first, its price. In fact, the price of any commodity cannot be determined independently of the technical conditions of production and of the rate of profits. In other words: the price of the aggregate factor capital is affected by the distribution of income among the factors. The value of capital changes as the profit and wage rates change so that the same physical capital can represent a different value, whereas different stocks of capital goods can have the same value. Some implications of the Cambridge–Cambridge debates for labour economics and in particular for the concept of a labour demand curve are discussed by I. Steedman (1985) 'On Input Demand Curves', *Cambridge Journal of Economics*, 9(2). He showed that labour need not be inversely related to the wage rate (i.e, the downward-sloping demand curve), as conventional models assume. For further information on the Cambridge Capital Theory Controversies see A. Cohen and G. Harcourt (2003) 'Whatever Happened to the Capital Controversies?', *Journal of Economic Perspectives*, 17(1).

30   See F.M. Fisher (1993) *Aggregation: Aggregate Production Functions and Related Topics* (London: Harvester Wheatsheaf); J. Felipe and F.M. Fisher (2003) 'Aggregation in Production Functions: What Applied Economists Should Know', *Metroeconomica*, 54(2–3). The aggregation problem refers to the search for the conditions under which macro aggregates (not only capital) exist. The question posed is as follows: what are the conditions under which micro production functions (with neoclassical properties) can be aggregated so as to yield an aggregate production function (also with neoclassical properties)?

31   Theoretically, one should use physical quantities in the production function. However, these do not exist at the aggregate level. Hence, constant-price values have to be used instead.

32   In practice, the mark-up will be on average direct costs (i.e. including the cost of materials). However, this does not affect the argument. Also, in practice, it is likely that mark ups will vary to the degree that the composition of firms with differing mark ups alter and there are changes in the individual mark ups, which may be temporary, as a result of the wage-bargaining process. Solow (1958) has shown that aggregation may well *decrease* the variability of the aggregate factor shares compared with the shares of the individual firms/industries. R. Solow (1958). 'A Skeptical Note on the Constancy of Relative Shares', *American Economic Review*, 618–31. On price theory see Lee (1999) for a detailed discussion. F. Lee (1999) *Post Keynesian Price Theory* (Cambridge: Cambridge University Press).

33   It should be noted that v, the user cost of capital, differs from r, the *ex post* profit rate. This does not affect the argument and is discussed below.

34   It could be argued that the argument depends on the constancy of the factor shares and that, therefore, it implies a Cobb–Douglas production function. This argument is invalid. We have already noted that the literature on aggregation proved that aggregate production functions cannot be derived theoretically (see Fisher 1971); hence the labour demand function cannot be derived. The constancy of the factor shares could be the result of firms applying a constant markup on unit labour costs, regardless of the form of the firms' individual production

functions. On the Cobb–Douglas and the identity see J.S.L. McCombie (1998) 'Are there Laws of Production?: An Assessment of the early criticisms of the Cobb–Douglas Production Function', *Review of Political Economy*, April; Felipe and Adams (2005).

35 See Felipe and McCombie (2001); Felipe and McCombie (2003) 'Methodological Problems with the Neoclassical Analyses of the East Asian Economic Miracle', *Cambridge Journal of Economics*, 27(5), 695–721, for the discussion of these two cases and the accounting identity.

36 It is worth noting that if we were to estimate this identity, assuming a relatively constant labour share of about $a = 0.75$, we should expect the estimates to be about $\ln L \equiv c + 1.33 \ln Q - 1.0 \ln w - 0.33 \ln r - 0.33 \ln K$ and a perfect fit. Certainly there is no reason to estimate this regression for its results are known *ex ante*.

37 For a comprehensive analysis of the Philippine minimum wage law, as well as of the country's labour market policies, see J. Felipe and L. Lanzona (2006) 'Unemployment, Labour Laws and Economic Policies in the Philippines', in J. Felipe and R. Hasan (eds) (2006). See Borjas (2005) for an introductory exposition of the neoclassical theory of the minimum wage rate.

38 L. Dumlao (2002) 'Lowering Unemployment by Hiking Minimum Wage', *Business World*, 7 May.

39 R. Freeman (1993a) 'Labor Market Institutions and Policies: Help or Hindrance to Economic Development?', *World Bank Annual Conference on Development Economics, 1992* (Washington, DC: World Bank), p. 126.

40 See the survey by C. Brown, C. Gilroy and A. Kohen (1982) 'The Effect of the Minimum Wage on Employment and Unemployment', *Journal of Economic Literature*, 20. This evidence was challenged in the 1990s by studies using data on net employment changes at the firm level. The studies of D. Card and A. B. Krueger (1994) 'Minimum Wages and Employment: A Case Study of the Fast-food Industry in New Jersey and Pennsylvania', *American Economic Review*, 84(4); Card, and Krueger (1995) *Myth and Measurement: The New Economics of the Minimum Wage*, (Princeton, NJ: Princeton University Press); L. F. Katz and A. B. Krueger (1992) 'The Effect of the Minimum Wage on the Fast-food Industry', *Industrial and Labor Relations Review*, 46(1) led to an important debate. See, for example, the symposium in the *Industrial and Labor Relations Review* (1995); or the articles by R. V Burkhauser, K. A. Couch, and D. C. Wittenburg (2000) 'A Reassessment of the New Economics of the Minimum Wage Literature with Monthly Data from the Current Population Survey', *Journal of Labor Economics*, 18, 653–701; Card and Krueger (2000) 'Minimum Wages and Employment: A Case Study of the Fast-food Industry in New Jersey and Pennsylvania: Reply', *American Economic Review*, 90: 1397–420; D. Deere, K. M. Murphy and F. Welch (1995) 'Employment and the 1990–1991 Minimum-wage Hike', *American Economic Review*, 85(2); J. Dolado, F. Kramarz, S. Machin, A. Manning, D. Margolis and C. Teulings (1996) 'The Economic Impact of Minimum Wages in Europe', *Economic Policy*, 23; J. Kennan (1995) 'The Elusive Effects of Minimum Wages', *Journal of Economic Literature*, 33; S. Machin and A. Manning (1996) 'Employment and the Introduction of a Minimum Wage in Britain', *Economic Journal*, 106; D. Neumark and W. Wascher (2000) 'Minimum Wages and Employment: A Case Study of the Fast-food Industry in New Jersey and Pennsylvania: Comment', *American Economic Review*, 90. See also the recent article by P. Portugal and A. Rute Cardoso (2006) 'Disentangling the Minimum Wage Puzzle: An Analysis of Worker Accessions and Separations', *Journal of the European Economic Association*, 4(5).

41   R. Brooks (2002) 'Why is Unemployment High in the Philippines?', IMF Working Paper 02/23 (Washington, DC: IMF), p. 21. It should be noted that we have italicized moderate increases in this quotation. This is because we believe the statement is somewhat inconsistent with the empirical evidence Brooks found. As he found that the minimum wage rate is inversely related to the employment level, the correct policy implication would be to recommend a decrease in the minimum wage rate, presumably to the market-clearing level. We believe that Brooks was trying to make a more politically acceptable statement. We are grateful to Janine Berg for bringing this issue to our attention. On the other hand, the argument could be that with a higher rate of output growth, a slower growth (rather than a decrease) of the minimum wage rate would lead to increased employment, under neoclassical assumptions.

42   Brooks estimated four regressions for different periods and using the GDP deflator and the consumer price index (CPI).

43   Brooks does not report the constant term.

44   G. Fields (2004) 'A Guideline to Multisector Labor Market Models', paper prepared for the World Bank Labor Market Conference, Washington DC, 18–19 November. Manuscript, p. 10 argues that the basic neoclassical model is often misused. He argues: 'One common misperception is that the wage "should" vary with labor productivity, commonly measured as value added per worker. Nothing could be further from the truth.' This is because the model's prediction is a relationship between the real wage rate and *marginal productivity*. However, Fields is not entirely correct on two grounds. First, what most economists do is to assume a Cobb–Douglas production function. In this case, the marginal productivity is equal to the average product of labour times the elasticity of output with respect to labour. The assumption of the Cobb–Douglas might be questionable, but once it is made, then it is true that the marginal product of labour is directly related to the average product. The doubt here is whether the statement that the wage rate *should* vary with labour productivity is a normative or a positive one. The second argument why Fields' statement is not entirely correct is that, in general, wage rates and labour productivity do move together. But this is true simply due to the labour share identity, which can be rewritten as $w_t \equiv a_t(Q_t/L_t)$. Since the labour share does not vary that much, any regression of the wage rate on the average product of labour will *work*. Unfortunately, many economists take this as evidence of the marginal theory of factor pricing because a similar relationship follows by assuming a Cobb–Douglas production function, which, as argued above, is what many economists do. (It works!).

45   The Philippines does not have a unique minimum wage rate. The Regional Tripartite Wage and Productivity Boards (RTWPB) and the National Wages and Productivity Commission set different minimum wage rates for 16 regions. These are daily wage rates. We converted the one for the National Capital Region (the highest) into an annual wage by assuming 300 days of work per year. Then this annual nominal wage rate was deflated using the GDP deflator.

46   Regarding Figure 7.2, Felipe and Lanzona (2006) argue that the data indicate that the average real annual minimum wage caught up with the average real wage rate in 1989. This suggests two things. First, that a significant number of employers have violated the minimum wage law. If the legally imposed minimum wage rate had been followed strictly, the average wage rate should have been higher. Secondly, the late 1980s saw the formation of new tripartite institutions that paved the way for the greater enfranchisement of both labour and employer groups in the

determination of minimum wages. The formation of tripartite channels of cooperation subsequently insured that minimum wages would not conflict with economic and industrial policies and programmes in response to the requirements of economic restructuring. The equal consideration of labour and management interests meant that minimum wages follow the general trend of average market wages.

47 Brooks (2002).
48 The reader could still argue that in modern time series econometrics this would not be the correct way to solve the problem of spuriousness. For example, an error correction model would be more appropriate. Felipe and McCombie (2007) discuss the issue and show that the argument is not affected.
49 Equation (7.1) indicates that the sign of the time trend should be negative. We do not have an explanation for why we obtain a positive sign. This finding does not undermine our arguments.
50 D.W. Jorgenson (1963) 'Capital Theory and Investment Behavior', *American Economic Review Papers and Proceedings*, (May).
51 M. Rama (2001) 'The Consequences of Doubling the Minimum Wage: The Case of Indonesia', *Industrial and Labor Relations Review*, 54(4). Rama also estimates the impact of the minimum wage rate on employment. However, we believe that the regression he estimates is subject to the critique advanced in previous sections.
52 Rama's (2001) starting regression is in levels and since it is estimated pooling time-series and cross-sectional data, it includes province and year-specific effects. In our case, we have pure time-series data. We will not discuss here the econometric details. Suffice to say that we tested the series for unit roots and for cointegration and estimated the equations in error-correction form. We settled for the simple specification in growth rates as it yielded the best results.
53 Ibid.
54 Hamermesh (2004), p. 561.
55 Keynes (1936), chapter 19.
56 For example, S. Bowles and R. Boyer (1995) 'Wages, Aggregate Demand and Employment in an Open Economy: An Empirical Investigation', in G.A. Epstein and H.M. Gintis (eds), *Macroeconomic Policy after the Conservative Era* (Cambridge: Cambridge University Press), discuss models of *wage-led* and *profit-led growth*. In the first type of models, increases in wages lead to increases in demand and in employment, while in the second class of models increases in wages lead to a decrease in employment. See also D.K. Foley and T. R. Mich (1999) *Growth and Distribution* (Cambridge, MA: Harvard University Press), chapter 10.
57 Lavoie (2000).
58 Layard *et al.* (1991).
59 All references to this work should cite Lavoie (2000).
60 Ibid.

8
The Impact of Trade Unions: What Do Economists Say?

Zafiris Tzannatos[1]

8.1 Introduction

The effects of trade unions, and of collective bargaining more broadly, on the specific sectors in which they operate or the economy at large vary depending on what unions, employers and governments do or want to do and whether the economy is competitive and open to trade. Various combinations of unions, firms, governments and types of economies can give rise to different economic outcomes of an otherwise identical configuration of organized labour. Even for the same economy, and union characteristics, effects can be different at different points in a country's history. And even if the typology of unions and collective bargaining were clear, there is a multitude of indicators for economic performance: this chapter focuses on more than 30 such indicators (Table 8.1) and this only because it presents a summary of more than one thousand studies on the subject, perhaps omitting as many others.

The aim of the chapter is therefore to attempt to summarize what professional economists have empirically identified to be the relationship between, on the one hand, trade unions and collective bargaining and, on the other hand, key indicators of economic performance. The chapter makes reference to many original studies but also draws on previous surveys on this issue notably (though not exclusively) by Lewis,[2] Ulph and Ulph,[3] Booth,[4] Sapsford and Tzannatos,[5] Flanagan[6] and especially Aidt and Tzannatos.[7] Unavoidably, most of the evidence and discussion draws on evidence from countries that have developed some form of unionization. This implies that developing countries are underrepresented, also for the reason that, even when unions exist therein, quantitative research is still embryonic as good data are often lacking.

The next section briefly outlines the economic theory of trade unions with reference to the role of employers as well as governments in unionized labour markets characterized by collective bargaining and dispute resolution mechanisms. Sections 8.3 and 8.4 summarize the empirical findings from a micro and macro perspective and section 8.5 concludes.

Table 8.1   Selected indicators of economic performance in studies assessing the effects of trade unions

Microeconomic	Macroeconomic
Wage mark-up (wage premium of unionized workers – versus non-union members) **Differences in the mark-up among different groups of workers** (for example, public/private, ethnicity, gender) **Efficiency loss of the wage mark-up** **Wage dispersion/inequality** (by industry or occupation) **Economic environment** (for example, product competition) **Employment level** **Employment growth** **Hours worked** **Voluntary turnover, lay-offs and job tenure** **Profitability** **Productivity** (levels or rate of growth) **Implementation of new technology** **Physical investments** **Research and development** **Training/schooling** **Fringe benefits/health and safety regulations** **Individual performance pay and seniority** **Pensions**	**Employment rate** (the employed as % of the population) **Adjustment speed** (the mean adjustment speed of employment to a shock) **Unemployment rate** **Persistence** (how long it takes for unemployment to return to its original level) **Hysteresis** (the extent to which past unemployment determines current unemployment) **Search effectiveness** (no. of vacancies at a given level of unemployment) **Labour supply** **Inflation** **Compensation (wage) growth** **Real wage flexibility** (responsiveness of aggregate wages to unemployment) **Aggregate earnings inequality** **Total factor productivity** **Economic growth** **Okun's Index** (the sum of unemployment and inflation) **Open Economy Index** (the sum of the unemployment rate and current account deficit as % of GDP) **Job Quality Index** (the difference between the employment rate and the coefficient of variation in wages) **Growth/Inflation Index** (the sum of the slowdown in real GDP growth per capita and the rise in inflation between periods)

8.2   You need three to tango: workers, employers and governments

What do unions do?

It is evident that unions and collective bargaining can have either a positive or a negative effect on economic performance. Though much depends on the specific conditions in which the social partners operate, much also depends on what unions do. The economic views on what unions do can be classified in three main groups.

First, the traditional 'monopoly view' focuses on the social costs of union-ization arising from distortions when unions succeed in obtaining more favourable pay and better general work conditions for their members than non-unionized workers in an assumed *perfectly competitive* economy (not just the labour market).[8] When unions succeed in securing benefits that would not have been possible under competitive conditions, they impose costs on society which are called *the monopoly costs* of unions.[9]

A second view also considers unions to be detrimental to economic out-comes as they create *rent-seeking costs*. In this view, unions are seen as representatives of the special interests of their members in the collective bargaining and political process.[10] Unions can promote policies that reduce competition in labour *and product* markets.[11] This includes support for minimum wage legislation or trade protection. Unions support such poli-cies if they increase the surplus available for sharing with the firm (the effect of less competitive product markets)[12] or increase the union's bargain-ing power (less competition from non-union labour markets). In addition, unions can engage in political activities and can generally involve three types of (static) costs.[13] First, to the extent that the union is successful in getting government regulation, an economic distortion is created, and the resulting inefficiency creates a deadweight loss to society. Secondly, real resources are withdrawn from production to be used in rent-seeking: to the extent that the shadow price of these resources is positive, this consti-tutes another loss to society. Thirdly, since the union's distributive success typically comes at the expense of non-union workers and consumers, a union's political activities may be associated with large distributional costs. In addition to these static costs, rent-seeking can lead to dynamic costs: rent-seeking can be harmful to innovations and thus hampers economic growth.[14]

The third and final view, which is called the 'organizational view' of unions, counters the two previous views and acknowledges that unions can have economic benefits. For example, unions can facilitate worker partici-pation and worker–manager cooperation in the workplace. This can have efficiency-enhancing effects that jointly benefit workers and management and are called the *participatory benefits of unions*.[15] Such benefits can arise because, first, unions are institutions with a collective voice and can com-municate worker preferences to management, as well as participating in the establishment of work rules and seniority provisions in the firm's internal labour market.[16] This changes the 'exit–voice' trade-off of workers by pro-viding a channel through which they can express their grievances ('voice') without having to leave the firm ('exit'). By reducing turnover ('voting with their feet'), this channel increases the incentive of employers to provide firm-specific training, and facilitates long-term working relationships that can benefit all parties.[17] From their side, unions may help to enforce con-tracts between workers and management and thus increase productivity by providing a channel through which labour can draw management's attention to changes in working methods or production techniques that may be beneficial to both parties.[18] This channel also offers a mechanism by which the union can 'shock' management into better practices and reduce X-inefficiency.[19]

What do employers' organizations do?

The members of an employers' organization are individual firms, typically within a particular industry. Each employers' organization may, in turn, be a member of a national employers' organization. A firm may decide to join an employers' organization in order to improve its bargaining position with workers (possibly organized in a union). Firms derive their bargaining power from their ability to lock out workers. From the point of view of an individual firm the cost of an industrial conflict is larger than the cost to the industry as a whole. This is because an individual firm involved in a strike is likely to lose its market share to other firms in the industry that produce close substitutes. Accordingly, whereas each firm has an incentive to give in to wage demands (called 'wage drift') to avoid a local conflict, the industry as a whole has less incentive to do so, and by joining forces, it is easier for firms to resist wage demands from unions.

Employers' organizations can also help to reduce 'leap frogging', which occurs when individual firms increase their wage rate to extract more effort from existing workers or to attract skilled workers from other firms.[20] When all firms engage in this kind of behaviour, the net result may well be that relative wages are unchanged, but the level of all wages can increase substantially. A strong employers' organization that coordinates the behaviour of individual firms can be helpful in internalizing this 'efficiency wage externality' and prevent the wage drift (as discussed above).

In addition, employers' organizations play an important role in providing training: since general training is a public good, firms are unlikely to provide much unless they are subject to external pressure.[21] A strong employers' organization can provide training facilities for firms and can impose sanctions if a firm does not pay its share of the costs.

On the negative side, employers' organizations could engage in cartels and rent-seeking (such as regulatory capture). These activities do not necessarily have a direct impact on labour relations, but certainly expand the surplus available for sharing. Capture is not always the result of the power of private employers but may well arise from the government as an employer. For example, it may occur in some sectors dominated by professionals, such as education and health, and also productive sectors – such as electricity, water or communications. This can of course be the result of trade unions operating in these sectors. Thus there can be adverse consequences of employer power on equity and efficiency in the form of monopolistic practices by private employers' organizations or the nearly monopsonistic position of a government that acts *de facto* as an organized employer by its mere size in centrally delivered services.

Social partnerships: workers, employers and the role of government

Social partnerships had some successes in the early postwar era. Though tripartism has continued to play a role in some European countries, it has come under questioning, especially with the intensification of globalization. And in some transition countries (such as the Czech Republic, Hungary and the Russian Federation) tripartism does not exhibit obviously promising prospects. In other cases, from Zambia in the mid-1980s to Venezuela at the beginning of the 1990s, various macro programmes have failed because they did not gain sufficient popular backing.[22] On the other hand, while corporatism has generally declined (and, in some cases, disappeared), the Netherlands seems to have moved in the opposite direction in the form of the 'Dutch employment miracle,'[23] a phenomenon also observed in most Scandinavian countries, which have achieved relatively low unemployment rates and growth at various periods in recent times. In other parts of the world such as in Latin America, tripartism has helped to ensure the implementation of stabilization programmes.[24] Likewise, Israeli unions played an important role in designing a politically acceptable stabilization programme in the mid-1980s.[25]

There is little systematic evidence about the impact of social partnerships on economic performance. One interesting hypothesis, however, considers how unions interact with governments of different persuasions, for example, a conservative government or a left-wing one.[26] For example, if unions are powerful and the government is left-wing, economic performance can be 'good' to the extent that the pursuit of welfare policies by left-wing parties is likely to lead to voluntary wage moderation as unions are less likely to engage in wasteful rent-seeking.[27]

In the reverse case (weak unions and right-wing government) economic performance may also be 'good' because unions are restricted in their wage demands by competitive pressure from product markets arising from the unwillingness of the right-wing government to regulate.

In the other two remaining combinations (strong unions against a conservative government or weak unions with a left-wing government) 'bad' economic performance may arise because there is a mismatch between the power of the labour movement and the political orientation of the government. If, for instance, a right-wing government coexists with powerful unions, the unions are unlikely to restrict their wage demands voluntarily because the government cannot be expected to deliver welfare goods in return. Likewise, a left-wing government coexisting with weak unions cannot count on any voluntary wage moderation because individual unions

Table 8.2 Aspects of bargaining coordination

A. Union centralization	The capacity of the national union confederation to influence wage levels/patterns across the economy.
B. Union concentration	Union concentration is high if 'few' unions at the relevant level of bargaining are representing workers.
C. Employer centralization	The capacity of the national employers' confederation to influence wage levels/patterns across the economy.
D. Level of bargaining	Collective bargaining takes place at different levels: the firm level, the industry level, and the regional/national level.
E. Informal coordination	1) Informal consultations at the industry, regional, or national level among unions and firms. 2) Pattern bargaining (an agreement in a dominant sector is mimicked by others).
F. Corporatism	A combination of 1) High union density (% of workers who are union members) and bargaining coverage (% of workers who are affected by collective agreements) and high degree of union and employer centralization/concentration and 2) Social partnership between national workers' and employers' organizations and government.
G. Other aspects	This include different types of dispute resolution procedures, the proportion of unionized workers employed in sectors that are subject to international competition, and union density.

Source: Quoted from Aidt and Tzannatos[29] based on Cameron;[30] Tarantelli;[31] and Crouch.[32]

are likely to pursue their own interests (wage pressure) without taking into account the economy-wide consequences of their actions.

These eventualities centre around the so-called 'hypothesis of coherence' which some researchers have confirmed as relevant but others not. As a general observation such a hypothesis is extremely difficult to test empirically as it involves assessing practically all (national) outcomes against all national *and international* determinants at country level.[28] Our simplified exposition between 'blue and red' governments and 'strong and weak' unions is in practice much more multifaceted and subject to (at times, opportunistic) political judgments.

To illustrate the complexity of the social partners' interaction, Table 8.2 provides a typology of various types of bargaining coordination. Thus, the tango the two main protagonists may want to dance can critically depend on a third factor: the kind of music that is being played by the government. This, in turn, affects not only how collective agreements are reached but also, as the next section discusses, how disputes can arise and are resolved.

Dispute resolution

One specific role of the government in the area of collective bargaining is that of regulation with the aim of reducing, if not completely eliminating, industrial conflict. Some conflict is inevitable when wages and other employment conditions are set by negotiation (either collective or individual), rather than by the 'invisible hand' of the market. And, of course, the above view that trade unions are well-informed bodies that look after the interests of their members may not always be true: there have been examples when union leaders have genuinely misjudged the actual situation or have escalated conflict more for their own personal reasons.[33] Recognizing this fact, there are grounds for believing that a well-run centralized, union-based system of wage bargaining may be less costly to society than an individually based negotiating system in terms of both total transaction costs and dispute costs. However, miscalculations or mistakes in a centralized system may have more pandemic effects than those that would arise in a decentralized framework.

The breakdown of negotiations between individual workers and their employers can take various forms, ranging from poor relations in the workplace (with potential costs including decreased levels of labour productivity through poor morale) to labour turnover (the 'exit' option, with the potential loss to the employer of previous investments in the workers' human capital). At the level of collective contracting, the stakes are arguably much higher for both workers (and their unions) and employers, with the ultimate cost of a negotiation breakdown being lost incomes for the workers and lost profits for employers. Given the potentially high level of these costs to both contracting parties, it is likely that workers and employers have a strong incentive to achieve a solution in preference to conflict. Like all good threats, the employer's threat of a lockout and the union's threat of a strike are best if they ensure that an agreement is reached before they are implemented.

In reality, collective bargaining does sometimes break down, and production, labour earnings and profits are lost. It is certainly not safe to assume that the total of such costs is greater under the collective bargaining system than under the individual contracting system. We simply do not know whether these costs to society are greater or less than those that would arise from a breakdown in individual employer–employee pay negotiations. Indeed, the given economies of scale in the production and dissemination of information provide grounds for some to believe that the collective system, through its ability to resolve disputes, may be a less costly option from a social point of view than individual contracting. This point is further illustrated in Table 8.3 which challenges the conventional proposition that the terms of contracts in the labour market should be left to either individual agents (workers and firms) or, in a fully unionized labour market, to their representatives at firm-level bargaining on the assumption that the invisible hand will do the rest.[34] Though many externalities can persist even with centralized bargaining – or any form of labour contracting – Table 8.3 suggests

Table 8.3 Externalities associated with decentralized wage setting

The input price externality	Decentralized wage gains are passed on as higher product prices, thus increasing the real cost of inputs for other firms.
The fiscal externality	Decentralized wage gains lead to unemployment. The cost in terms of unemployment benefits is born by all taxpayers, not only those involved in wage setting.
The unemployment externality	Decentralized wage gains increase overall unemployment, making it more difficult for all unemployed workers to find a new job.
The envy externality	Decentralized wage gains create envy among other workers.
The consumer price externality	Decentralized wage gains are passed on as higher product prices, thus lowering the real wage of all workers.
Efficiency wage externality	At the decentralized level, firms have an incentive to try to increase the relative wage of their workers to increase their motivation.

Source: Calmfors.[35]

that there can *potentially* be a number of significant externalities associated with decentralized wage setting.

There is a strong presumption that when disputes do occur under conditions of collective bargaining, it is because of asymmetries in the information possessed by the involved parties.[36] A common example is when the trade union 'misjudges' the maximum wage that the employer is willing or able to pay. Under such circumstances, the existence of regulation can prove decisive in resolving disputes through its information-gathering and disseminating roles.

To understand the process, it is important to recognize the distinction between the union proper (sometimes called the official union) and its rank and file membership. Under this tripartite framework, the official union (often as a well-informed professional body) acts as an intermediary between the union membership and the employer. As such, its role is to reconcile the aspirations of the former against what it judges (on the basis of its more complete knowledge of the overall situation than that possessed by the union member) that the employer would agree to pay. This reconciliation between worker aspirations and labour market realities may be achieved without either party having to resort to its no-trade sanction. However, should negotiations break down and a dispute occur, the role of the official union as a purveyor of information continues, with information being disseminated in both directions regarding concessions acceptable to each party and any new information that may materialize as the dispute progresses. This transmission of information continues until demands fall into balance with offers, at which time a settlement is achieved.

Viewing a union as an information-gathering and disseminating body suggests that governments might want to adopt policies that increase the effectiveness with which unions fulfil this role. The introduction of so-called cooling-off periods (during which all parties take time to assess the situation fully before implementing no-trade strategies) is one example. Other such policies might require that the employer (generally seen as the party in possession of more complete information) divulge to the union and its members certain types of information, perhaps in a standard form, to minimize the possibility that disputes will arise because workers incorrectly estimate the employer's ability to pay.

Summary

We can summarize the above discussion of the costs and benefits of unions arising from the interaction of the social partners in the labour market using the following simple equation:

Net benefit of unions = participatory and dispute resolution benefits – monopoly costs – rent-seeking costs.

Alternatively, one can talk of cost and rewrite this equation as:

Net cost of unions = monopoly costs + rent-seeking costs – participatory and dispute resolution benefits.

From a theoretical perspective, the net benefit/cost of unions is ambiguous and dependent on the relative size of the three components. These, in turn, depend significantly on the economic, political, and organizational environment in which collective bargaining takes place. The *economic environment* affects both the monopoly costs and the participatory benefits. The *political environment* determines the rent-seeking activities of unions (and employers). The *organizational environment* (bargaining coordination, social partnership, and dispute resolution) affects all three components. In addition, the effects of unions can extend beyond the unionized sector due to the so-called 'spillover' effects, that is, employers may decide to offer concessions to non-union members similar to those demanded by unions in an attempt to limit the organizational and political economy costs associated with increased unionization.[37]

Thus, judging the contribution of unions and, more generally, collective bargaining to the achievement of economic and social outcomes is, ultimately, an empirical question as unions are only one agent in the labour market which is thought to be tripartite (workers, employers, governments). Much depends also on what the other two social partners do and how all three interact in an attempt to determine wages, employment and work conditions. Eventually, all three are constrained by the state of the national economy (whether or not it is competitive) and its relationship to the rest of the world (trade openness). In other words, it is the coordination between the social partners that determine outcomes, not just simply the membership of unions or employers' associations.

These empirical issues are addressed in the next two sections.

8.3   Empirical evidence: microeconomic

There is a large body of empirical literature on the economic effects of unions derived from microeconomic data on individual workers and establishments. It covers the union/non-union wage mark-up, both overall and also in terms of skills, gender, occupation as well as the underlying economic conditions and the institutional environment. It also examines the effect of unions on other economic variables such as employment growth, hours worked, productivity, job mobility, the implementation of new technology, physical investments, spending on research and development, training of workers, profitability, fringe benefits, mode of pay, and pension schemes. Some of these areas are examined below.[38]

The wage mark-up in different countries

The union/non-union wage mark-up (the 'wage mark-up') is defined as the difference between the average wage of unionized and non-unionized workers (with similar individual and workplace characteristics) divided by the average wage of a non-unionized worker.[39] The mark-up can be estimated in different ways. First, it can be estimated as a *membership mark-up*. The membership mark-up is based on information about an individual's union status and calculates the difference in wages between individual unionized and non-unionized workers. Secondly, it can be estimated as a *recognition mark-up*. Here workers are being categorized according to whether or not their pay is determined by a collective agreement between a recognized union and a firm. In the latter case, individual union membership is not crucial. What matters is whether the workers' pay is determined by a collective agreement. The distinction between the membership and the recognition mark-up is important when not all of the workers whose wages are determined by a collective agreement are union members. For example, when many workers are covered by collective agreements although they are not members of a union (such as in France where the two figures stand at around 90 per cent and 10 per cent), estimates based on the membership mark-up underestimate the 'true' mark-up, and it is preferable to use the recognition mark-up to measure the impact of unions on wages.[40]

In all countries where the wage mark-up has been estimated, it has been found to be non-negative; that is, it is found at times to be statistically zero. There are, however, significant cross-country variations as well as variations of estimates within countries and over time. There is also some evidence, albeit weak, that the wage mark-up is, on average, lower in high-income countries than in low and middle-income ones.

The most reliable picture comes from the United Kingdom and the United States by virtue of the many studies that have been carried out and the broad consistency of the results. The wage mark-up in the United States has been estimated in more than 200 studies and is generally found to range from 12 to 22 per cent.[41] Though there is consensus that the *average* mark-up is approximately 15 per cent, this may significantly overestimate the wage gain and the true impact of unions on wages may be around or less than 10 per cent. In the case of the United Kingdom, more than 20 studies have estimated the mark-up to be in the range of 3 to 19 per cent and the average is probably also around 10 per cent.[42]

The evidence for other industrialized economies is sparser, but some generalizations are possible. The conventional view is that the wage mark-up for Australia is in the range of between 7 and 17 per cent.[43] Similarly, the Canadian wage mark-up has been estimated to be in the range of 8 to 25 per cent, although this has decreased over time – reaching 7 to 10 per cent in more recent periods.[44] In (West) Germany, where most unions are industry unions and work and pay conditions contained in collective agreements are largely extended to non-unionized workers, the wage mark-up is found to be small, especially for male workers.[45] Similarly, studies on Japan have found a small average wage mark-up of about 5 per cent.[46]

The evidence is even more limited for low- and middle-income economies. In the Republic of Korea, estimates of the mark-up for male workers in manufacturing industries were found to be below 4 per cent in 1988 but higher in later years (7 per cent in 1991).[47] The union membership wage mark-up in South Africa is among the highest (around 24 per cent for black blue-collar workers)[48] as is also for Malaysia (in the range of 15 to 20 per cent depending on the type of union involved).[49] For Mexico, the mark-up is found to be around 10 per cent[50] but for Ghana it rises to more than 20 per cent.[51]

The mark-up can vary depending upon the percentage of wage and salary earners that are unionized or covered by collective agreements.[52] While union density per se appears to be largely unrelated to the wage mark-up, bargaining coverage is negatively correlated with the mark-up. In other words, when more workers are covered by collective agreements (all other things being equal), the smaller the wage mark-up appears to be. This may be the case because the labour supply in the non-covered sector decreases when more workers become covered, pushing the non-union wage up. Taking this argument one step further, one may say that unions are able to secure a high mark-up only where the marginal cost to society (in terms of impact on the macro economy) is small. In effect, unions are ultimately constrained by the wage share in the total economy: they can have wide coverage and a small mark-up or a high mark-up at the cost of coverage.

An interesting additional question is whether the mark-up is stable over time or if it fluctuates in line with economic conditions. This question has been investigated primarily in only two countries – the United Kingdom and the United States. The conclusion from these studies is that the wage mark-up in the United States has moved pro-cyclically but does not have a distinct trend over the period 1983–95.[53] For the United Kingdom the mark-up declined a little during the 1980s probably due to a fall in the wage mark-up for female workers.[54] These results suggest that union power has not been curtailed significantly, despite the reduction in union density observed over the same period in the two countries.

The efficiency cost of the wage mark-up

When unions are successful in achieving a wage mark-up, workers tend to be displaced from the unionized sectors to non-union sectors, which creates a deadweight loss. A number of studies have estimated this deadweight loss and found, somewhat surprisingly, that it is quite small. For the United States estimates of the welfare loss is found to be less than 0.5 per cent of GDP.[55] The simulated welfare loss associated with a 15 per cent union/non-union wage mark-up is similarly found to be no larger than 0.2–0.4 per cent of GDP.[56] Interestingly, the results for the United States are similar to those for Australia, where the average mark-up is 7 to 17 per cent[57] and where 80 per cent of the workforce is covered by collective agreements (compared to 15 per cent in the United States).

The difference in the mark-up for women and men

Unions are just one of many determinants of the gender wage gap, which is the percentage difference between the wage of a female worker and a male worker who otherwise have the same personal and workplace characteristics. The effect of unions arises in three ways: first, from different unionization rates among men and women; secondly, from the ability of unions to influence wages in some sectors or workplaces but not in others; and thirdly, from differences in the wage mark-up for men and women. In principle, the net effect of unions upon female wages relative to male wages is uncertain: though a higher wage mark-up for women than for men can reduce the gender wage gap, it can also decrease the wages of non-unionized women to such an extent that the gender wage gap actually increases.

In the US literature there is little, if any, difference between the mark-up for female and male workers.[58] The same result emerges from Australian studies.[59] However, most studies in Britain show that the impact of unions on women's wages is greater than that on men's wages: a typical estimate is that the mark-up for women is 4 to 6 percentage points larger than that for men[60] though a few studies find the opposite result.[61] In any case, taking into account the fact that female workers are less likely to be unionized than male workers, the net effect on the average gender wage gap is likely to be small.[62] Evidence from other OECD and middle-income countries unambiguously supports the view that the wage mark-up is greater for women (for example, in Canada,[63] Japan,[64] West Germany,[65] Mexico,[66] and Malaysia[67]).

Differences in the mark-up by ethnic group

Discrimination among workers with different ethnic backgrounds but otherwise similar productivity characteristics can lead to a wage differential. In the United States it is not clear whether there is a substantial difference between the wage mark-up for white and non-white workers. Some studies fail to find any difference, whereas others find that the mark-up is 5 to 10 percentage points higher for blacks than it is for whites.[68] In the United Kingdom, the sparse available evidence shows that a non-white unionized worker has a higher mark-up than a similar white worker.[69] In Canada, unions are found to reduce discrimination marginally (but other variables such as education and experience are much more important).[70] In South Africa, in one study white workers were found to enjoy a mark-up of about 30 per cent, whereas the mark-up for black workers was in the range of 16 to 20 per cent[71] but, after controlling for worker heterogeneity, the mark-up for both groups is somewhat smaller, in particular for white workers (10 per cent).[72] And in Mexico a worker who lives in a county with a large indigenous population gets a bigger wage mark-up than a similar worker living in a less 'indigenous' county.[73]

The economic environment and the wage mark-up

The economic realities facing firms can make it difficult for unions to achieve a high wage mark-up. Competitive pressure from both the product market and the non-union labour market can be particularly effective in serving this role. A number of studies have investigated the effect of competitive pressure on the wage mark-up. Most of these studies use industry concentration (the small number of firms controlling most of the output in a given industry) as a proxy for a firm's market power.

The results of these studies do not support the theoretical predictions. However, the relationship between monopoly power and the wage mark-up can be masked in these estimates if wages are high in concentrated industries even in the absence of unions. For example, this would be the case if firms in these industries wish to forestall unionization. It would similarly come about if firms in concentrated sectors would like to escape possible enforcement of competitive laws or they want to avoid the bad press associated with high profits and low wages. These reasons may be more apparent than real. For example, the fear of provoking the response of the competitive authorities is hypothetical in many countries where there is little faith in competition laws and little effort is spent on enforcing them. Furthermore, firms may receive better press coverage by spending part of their excess profits on health and safety improvements in the workplace or by donating to charities rather than by paying higher wages. One interpretation of the evidence is that firms in concentrated industries use their monopoly rent to withstand the wage demands of unions. This may induce workers to be content with greater job security and other non-monetary benefits as a substitute for high wages. Finally, but not less importantly, the industry concentration ratio may not be a good proxy for a firm's monopoly power in the product market.

This suspicion seems to be confirmed by a few studies that have used indicators other than industry concentration to measure the monopoly power of firms. These studies find that the wage mark-up is larger in firms with monopoly power than in those without it. For example, the use of a mixture of industry concentration ratios and a subjective measure of entry barriers to the industry as a proxy for monopoly power in a sample of unionized manufacturing firms in the United States suggested that the wage mark-up is significantly higher in noncompetitive industries than in competitive ones.[74] In the United Kingdom the use of subjective indicators of competition (such as asking the management within firms about the number of competitors that they are facing in the product market) suggests that competition in the product market significantly reduces the average wage mark-up.[75] In particular, in firms that operate in a competitive product market, the wage mark-up is, on average, zero. On the other hand, firms that have little or no competition in the product market grant a wage mark-up in the range of 8 to 10 per cent. Moreover, unions are unable to create a wage mark-up in firms that operate primarily in international markets. In short, unions are able to create a mark-up only in industries that are sheltered from foreign competition *and* in which the whole industry is heavily unionized.

The design of collective bargaining

The evidence generally suggests that workers, on average, get a wage mark-up if they are members of a union or otherwise have their pay conditions determined by collective agreements. However, the size of the mark-up may depend on how collective bargaining is organized. The institutional framework can be organized into four groups:

- The extent of unionism (average union density in the industry or the percentage of firms in the industry that recognizes a union).
- The level at which bargaining takes place (the firm, industry or national level).

- Multi-unionism (when more than one union represents similar workers in the same workplace).
- Closed shops (a worker can obtain or retain a particular job only if he or she is a member of a particular union).

The extent of unionism: There seems to be a strong relationship between the extent of unionism in an industry (or occupation) and the wage mark-up. In industries where unionization is low in terms of either density or the percentage of firms that recognize a union, unions generally have little impact on wages. This is because attempts to raise the wages paid by a few unionized employers (above what their competitors pay) places union employers at a severe disadvantage in the product market. This increases employers' resistance to union wage pressure and encourages the union to moderate its wage demands. On the other hand, in industries where almost all firms are unionized, unions will have more bargaining power and will, therefore, be able to secure a higher wage mark-up. This is known as the 'extent of unionism' effect and in the United States increases the membership mark-up, although there is substantial disagreement about the magnitude of this effect.[76] A few studies for Canada confirm the positive effect.[77] In the United Kingdom the wage mark-up is larger in industries with more than the 70 per cent threshold for union density.[78]

In the United States, there is no significant difference between union density and coverage of collective agreements (both come to about 15 per cent of the workforce). In the United Kingdom, on the other hand, a large number of workers have their pay conditions determined by collective agreements without actually being members of a union. Therefore, focusing on the membership wage mark-up may bias not only the estimate of the wage mark-up itself but also the estimate of the extent of the unionism effect. More recent British studies take this into account and analyse the relationship between the recognition wage mark-up and union density at the establishment level. The recognition wage mark-up (for semi-skilled manual workers) is significant only for firms where more than 95 per cent of the workforce is unionized. In these circumstances, the mark-up is in the range of 7 to 10 per cent.[79] In firms where a smaller fraction of semi-skilled workers are union members, the wage mark-up is insignificant. This suggests that workers in a workplace where management does recognize a union benefit in terms of higher wages only if almost all of the workers in the workplace are actually organized in unions.

The level at which collective bargaining takes place: The level at which collective bargaining takes place affects how workers and employers interact, and this has implications for the size of the wage mark-up. One would expect the wage mark-up to be higher when collective bargaining is at the industry level rather than at the firm level. In Malaysia, the average wage mark-up paid by a firm that deals with an industrial union is 20 per cent, compared to 15 per cent in firms that deal with a company union.[80] In India, members of independent plant-based unions (unions run and managed by workers employed in the plant) get significantly higher wages and bonuses than workers affiliated with external unions (unions that are explicitly affiliated with a trade union federation).[81]

Multi-unionism: The prime source of information on the effect of multi-unionism is the United Kingdom, a country where multi-unionism plays an important role. In the 1980s, about 30 per cent of all unionized plants in the private sector recognized more than one union for collective bargaining purposes. The 1998 Workplace Employee Relations Survey reported that about 38 per cent of all workplaces still have multiple unions. Under multi-unionism, the unions may bargain together (multiple bargaining) or separately (separate bargaining) with management. Multi-unionism is generally associated with a higher wage mark-up.[82] Some studies have refined this result and show that it is not multi-unionism *per se* that is associated with the additional wage mark-up but rather *the combination of multi-unionism and separate collective bargaining that produces the additional wage mark-up*. If all of the unions that represent workers at a given workplace bargain together, then the wage mark-up is no larger than in firms where workers (of the same type) are represented by a single union.[83]

Closed shops: A closed shop exists when an employee can obtain or retain a particular job only if he or she is a member of a particular union. The closed shop can be either pre- or post-entry. A pre-entry closed shop requires that the employee is accepted as a member of the relevant union ('holds a union card') *before* he or she can be employed in the particular trade. Historically, craft unions have managed to run a pre-entry closed shop. From a theoretical point of view, a closed shop increases a union's control over labour supply and, as a result, its bargaining power. The question, therefore, is whether the presence of a closed shop increases the wage mark-up over and above the basic recognition or membership effect. Post-entry closed shops have been found not to increase the wage mark-up above what it would have been had the majority of the firm's workers been unionized.[84] On the other hand, pre-entry closed shops can increase the wage mark-up by as much as 100 per cent. However, subsequent research finds that the premium associated with the pre-entry closed shop has been reduced and is roughly the same as that found in firms where management recommends union membership.[85]

Unions and employment

The wage mark-up reduces total employment as long as the demand curve of labour in the unionized sector of the economy is sloping downwards and the management of unionized firms retains the right to manage (that is, management independently decides on employment after wages have been agreed with the union). However, the adverse employment effect of an increase in wages can be reduced and even be reversed if (a) unions and firms bargain over wages *and* employment and agree on what is called 'efficient contracts'[86] or (b) firms have monopsony power in the absence of collective bargaining. Some empirical evidence on whether unions and firms bargain over employment suggests that this is rarely the case in either the United Kingdom or the United States.[87] In the United States, many contracts explicitly state that the right to determine employment remains with the management. While this is not true in the United Kingdom, British unions do not generally bargain over employment.

However, although the employment level *per se* is not subject to formal bargaining, recruitment, staffing norms, redundancy pay and deployment can be included in formal bargaining, and this can have indirect effects on employment.[88] It is possible to test econometrically the *right to manage model* (unions push up wages and reduce employment) against the *efficient bargaining model* (unions push up wages and employment).[89] The results often reject both models and one is tempted to conclude that 'on the whole neither theory seems to be able to account satisfactorily for the data on negotiated wages and their associated employment levels'.[90] Although it is tempting to argue that the truth should lie somewhere in the middle, the clear answer may be constrained by data limitations and flawed econometric procedures.[91]

Another way to assess the impact of unions on employment is to consider employment growth, noting that permanent employment growth differences between unionized and non-unionized firms are unlikely to represent *long-run* equilibrium positions. With this in mind, the available evidence from Canada, Jamaica, Malaysia, the United Kingdom and the United States suggests that employment grows more slowly in unionized firms than in non-unionized ones.[92] Some argue, however, that the difference in the growth rate of employment in unionized and non-unionized firms can be partly due to the fact that unionized firms experienced a reduction in restrictive practices during the sample period 1980–84. This implies that unionized firms were more likely than non-unionized firms to lay off workers during this period. This suggests that the estimated effect is associated with an adjustment to a long-run equilibrium rather than with an equilibrium position *per se*.[93]

Studies from Canada, the United Kingdom and the United States typically find a growth differential in the range of 3 to 5 percentage points per year in favour of non-unionized firms.[94] There are a number of possible explanations for the observed employment growth differential:

- It takes time and effort to organize a union. Consequently, at a given point in time, old firms are more likely to be covered by unions than newer firms are. If newer firms expand faster than old firms, we would expect to observe higher employment growth in the newer, non-unionized firms.
- Unions are more likely to be concentrated in sectors that enjoy large rents. If these sectors are less dynamic because of monopoly inefficiencies and

their activities are limited by the size of the domestic market, employment would tend to grow more slowly in these sectors.

- Unions may encourage labour hoarding by increasing hiring and firing costs. This would make unionized firms more reluctant to hire new workers during a boom, thus reducing employment growth over the cycle.
- Labour costs may grow faster in unionized firms than in non-unionized ones.
- Productivity grows slower in unionized firms than in non-unionized ones.

Voluntary turnover, layoffs, and job tenure

The evidence from Australia, Malaysia, the Republic of Korea, the United Kingdom and the United States shows unanimously that voluntary turnover (measured by the 'quit' rate) is lower and job tenure is longer in unionized firms than in non-unionized ones.[95] Perhaps the most convincing recent evidence that unions reduce job separations comes from Japan: the job separation rate is significantly lower in unionized firms than in non-unionized ones. Importantly, the Japanese experience has been attributed to mechanisms that provide 'voice' for the employees and thus reduce separations in unionized firms. All this gives support to the 'collective voice' view of unions and points to one of the key channels through which unions can add to workplace productivity, namely by increasing the length of job tenure.

The welfare gain associated with a reduction in labour turnover has been found to be equivalent to a 0.2 to 0.3 per cent increase in GDP in the United States in the 1980s.[96] For unionized firms, the gain is estimated to be equivalent to a 1 to 2 per cent reduction in costs. While these estimates are usually crude, it is interesting to notice that the welfare gain associated with participatory benefits of this kind is of the same order of magnitude as the estimated monopoly cost of unions. However, the participatory benefit accrues to organized workers (and firms) only, whereas the monopoly cost of unions is borne by society at large.

Unions and hours worked

The effect of unions on the total number of hours worked by their members (compared to non-unionized workers) is not clear *a priori*. On the one hand, unions typically demand lower normal hours, more holidays and so on. Conversely, they may be able to secure overtime work at higher rates of pay.

Overall, the finding is that the presence of unions reduces the total number of hours worked.[97] In particular, the evidence suggests that workers in unionized firms work fewer normal hours. Moreover, unions reduce the number of unpaid overtime hours and, in some cases, increase the amount of paid overtime work.[98] Furthermore, unions increase the likelihood that workers receive paid holidays and unionized workers get, on average, additional weeks of holidays compared to non-unionized workers.[99] While these results are relatively robust and the union/non-union total hours differential in OECD countries is negative, union workers seem to work more in Spain and Switzerland.[100] The estimates range from a one- to two-hour differential per week in the United Kingdom and the United States to a four- to six-hour differential per week in Austria and Ireland.

Unions and profitability

A large number of studies have estimated the impact of unions on profitability. These studies use a number of different measures of profitability such as price/cost margins, net (of wages) return to capital, Tobin's q (the market value of the firm relative to the replacement costs of the firm's assets), and subjective profitability judgements by management. Such studies estimate the union impact using industry, firm, or stock market data. Overall, the earlier empirical evidence from Japan,[101] the Republic of Korea,[102] the United Kingdom,[103] and the United States[104] generally indicated a negative impact on operating profitability. More recent studies are less clear on this effect. Furthermore, some studies looking at the late 1990s in the United Kingdom and the United States find that unions can have positive effects on profits.[105] On balance, the evidence therefore may indicate that the negative influence of unions on profits identified in the 1980s has diminished in the 1990s.

Productivity differentials

Evidence on union productivity-level differentials derives mainly from Australia, Canada, Germany, Japan, the United Kingdom and the United States. In the United States, unionized industries in which firms are subject to substantial product market competition tend to have higher productivity levels than non-unionized ones, while firms with high-quality industrial relations are associated with higher productivity levels and higher product quality than firms with low-quality industrial relations.[106] On the other hand, the observed higher absenteeism among union workers can have a negative effect on productivity.

A negative effect on productivity levels is generally observed in the United Kingdom, but this conclusion is far from robust, and the average estimates hide a lot of variation.[107] Similarly, empirical studies from Japan find that unions have mixed effects on productivity. Some note that unions had a positive impact on productivity levels in the 1970s when technology and labour-quality variables are held constant,[108] while others find that productivity in unionized firms was 15 per cent lower than in similar non-unionized firms.[109] In Germany, unions appear to have a negative, but quantitatively small impact on productivity.[110] The evidence on the impact of works councils suggests that such councils have a positive impact on productivity, but only for larger firms.[111] A similar result is found in the Republic of Korea where unions seem to have no impact on labour productivity in manufacturing firms, while the presence of mandatory works councils has a positive impact.[112] In Australia and Canada the limited evidence available has found a negative effect of unions on productivity.[113]

With respect to developing countries, in Malaysia using the value of total sales relative to the total workforce to proxy productivity suggests that unionized firms have higher productivity levels than non-unionized firms and that the positive productivity differential is primarily associated with industrial rather than company unions.[114] Furthermore, a comparative study into the productivity impact of unions in nine Latin American countries concluded 'The union effects on perhaps the most interesting and controversial outcome, productivity, these [comparative country] results mirror those in the UK and the US: both positive and negative effects are observed in different industries and at different times. A blanket case, either for or against unions, cannot be made on productivity grounds on the basis of the evidence presented in this volume.'[115]

Unions and training

Unions are likely to affect the amount and quality of training that employees receive in the workplace through a number of channels. First, unions might bargain over these issues with employers and demand that training takes place. Secondly, the fact that unions decrease turnover can have a positive impact on the amount of firm-specific human capital in which workers are willing to invest. The empirical evidence from the United States on the relationship between training and unionism is mixed. Some studies find that the amount of work-related and on-the-job training that workers receive in unionized firms is higher than in non-unionized ones.[116] Others cannot find any differences with regard to specific programmes such as computer literacy numeracy, and sales training.[117]

In the United Kingdom, the evidence is rather clear-cut: unionized workers receive more training and benefit more from participating in such programmes than do non-unionized workers (as measured by post-training wages relative to pre-training wages).[118] These effects can partly offset the negative impact on investments in physical capital and R&D.

Unions, fringe benefits and health and safety regulations

Unions do significantly increase wages. While this can be interpreted as evidence that unionized workers earn substantial rents, some have argued that as much as two-fifths of the wage mark-up is compensation for an inflexible and employer-controlled work environment.[119] In addition to their monthly pay, however, unionized workers may be concerned with other issues, such as bonuses, severance pay, health and safety regulations and paid sick leave.

The evidence suggests that workers in unionized firms are more likely to receive these benefits than workers in non-unionized firms. Firms with unions are more likely to provide paid sick leave, retirement benefits, cheap loans and transportation. Unions do increase the likelihood of improved health and safety measures in the United Kingdom.[120] And in Japan unions increase the use of severance payments and the size of the yearly bonus.[121]

Some of these benefits obviously contribute to increasing labour costs in general and turnover costs in particular. On the other hand, cheap loans, free transportation, paid sick leave, and safety regulations may improve worker motivation and pay off in terms of higher productivity. Moreover, to the extent that inadequate safety and health provisions generate a suboptimal allocation of labour, union-sponsored (as well as government-sponsored) safety and health regulations may increase not only individual worker's welfare but also aggregate welfare.

Some studies have considered the issue of disclosure of information in the context of the risk attributes of different jobs.[122] Commodities produced in different sectors use production technologies that expose workers to different levels of physical risks, such as exposure to toxins and industrial accidents. Safety is desirable from the point of view of workers. Therefore, safety has an opportunity cost and safer jobs pay a lower wage. In an unregulated labour market workers may be unable to appreciate the dangers inherent in different jobs. As a consequence, firms would not be required to compensate workers fully for the hidden risks involved in their jobs. This would lead to an inefficient allocation of labour across sectors, with too many workers doing jobs that are too dangerous. A labour market reform that induces full disclosure of safety levels would remove this distortion. An estimate for the Mexican economy of the welfare effects of a labour market reform of this type found that the well-being of workers would increase by 0.5 per cent of baseline GDP per year. Moreover, the real income of the owners of the firms would increase as well because the reform increases the demand for capital for risk-abatement purposes. The total gain is estimated to be 0.6 per cent of baseline GDP per year.[123] This is a substantial gain and is of the same order of magnitude as the estimated monopoly cost of unions.

Individual performance pay and seniority

Individual performance pay is much more prevalent among non-unionized firms in the United States than among unionized firms by as much as 16 to 23 per cent.[124] Similar results are found in Great Britain, where the most significant difference between unionized and non-unionized firms is that individual performance is important in wage determination only in the case of non-unionized firms.[125] While the beneficial link between rewards and productivity cannot be overemphasized, the fact that unions are able to reduce the use of individual performance pay could be seen as evidence that the presence of unions reduces the need for this control instrument. Seniority-based wages can be interpreted as an efficiency wage that is designed to motivate workers to stay with the same firm for a longer period of time. Therefore, unions can increase productivity by extending seniority-based systems to smaller firms.[126]

Unions and pensions

Evidence from many countries shows that unions increase the likelihood that workers are enrolled in pension schemes.[127] If union-sponsored pension plans do not replace private saving, national saving can increase. At the macroeconomic level, the implied reduction in the real interest rate will increase investment demand and may even have a (temporary) impact on economic growth.

8.4   Empirical evidence: macroeconomic

The macroeconomic impact of collective bargaining is hard to disentangle from other determinants of economic performance.[128] While the available evidence from comparative studies of the OECD countries is fragile, two general features should be emphasized.[129] First, the impact of collective bargaining on various aspects of macroeconomic performance depends on the economic, legal and political environment in which collective bargaining takes place and can vary over time. Secondly, important complementarities exist between the many different aspects of the bargaining system. Therefore, the impact of individual aspects such as union density or centralization of bargaining cannot be assessed in isolation. It is the package of institutions that matters.[130]

Methodology

The impact of collective bargaining on macroeconomic performance has usually been assessed through comparative studies where the performance of countries with (very) different bargaining systems is compared systematically. Most studies look at the economic performance of the OECD countries during the period from 1960 to the present and ask how the framework of collective bargaining affects a large number of macroeconomic performance indicators (such as unemployment and inflation) and labour market flexibility indicators (such as real wage flexibility) in an environment in which workers' rights can be taken as granted.[131] It should be pointed out that this approach does not allow us to address the question of causality. At best, cross-country studies of this type can help us identify important correlations between measures of key aspects of labour market institutions and economic outcomes.

In addition to the conventional measurements of unionization (union density and the union coverage), economists have attempted to summarize institutional data on collective bargaining across different economies (see Table 8.2) by constructing qualitative indexes of bargaining coordination. Table 8.4 presents country rankings derived from different assessments of various indicators of bargaining coordination.

Table 8.4 Country rankings based on alternative valuations of bargaining coordination

Country	Calmfors Driffill	OECD-1			Soskice	OECD-2		
	1985–90	1980	1990	1994	1980s	1980	1990	1994
	Based on formal coordination				Based on informal coordination			
	(1)	(2)	(3)	(4)	(5)	(6)	(7)	(8)
Australia	10	3	1	14	—	7	5	15
Austria	1	3	1	1	2	1	1	1
Belgium	8	3	1	1	—	10	10	9
Canada	17	17	17	16	—	18	17	16
Denmark	4	3	8	5	—	4	5	6
Finland	5	2	4	4	—	7	5	6
France	11	8	8	5	9	13	10	9
Germany	6	8	8	5	6	1	1	1
Italy	13	15	14	5	8	15	15	4
Japan	14	17	17	16	1	1	1	1
Netherlands	7	8	8	5	7	10	10	9
New Zealand	9	8	16	16	—	15	17	16
Norway	2	8	1	1	4	4	4	4
Portugal	—	15	1	5	—	13	10	9
Spain	—	3	8	5	—	10	10	9
Sweden	3	1	1	5	5	4	5	9
Switzerland	15	8	8	5	3	7	5	6
United Kingdom	12	8	14	14	10	15	16	16
United States	16	17	17	16	11	18	17	16

— Not available.
Source: quoted from Aidt and Tzannatos[132] based on Calmfors and Driffill;[133] Soskice;[134] OECD.[135]
Note: A *low* rank is an indication of a *high* degree of bargaining coordination.

The first four columns report two sets of rankings that only take the *formal* aspects of bargaining coordination, such as the centralization of collective bargaining and the level of bargaining, into account. The last four columns, on the other hand, report two sets of rankings that attempt to measure *informal* aspects of bargaining coordination. The strikingly different rankings of countries according to different indexes are indicative of the variation in the degree of bargaining coordination that arises from using different indicators.

Although the correlation between the rankings is high, a detailed comparison of the rankings reveals a number of interesting differences. First, some countries, such as Austria, Norway and Sweden, are consistently judged to have highly coordinated bargaining systems. Other countries such as Canada, the United Kingdom, and the United States are consistently classified as having uncoordinated bargaining systems.

Secondly, it makes a considerable difference whether or not informal coordination is taken into account. Comparing the rankings of Soskice and OECD-2 that take informal coordination into account with those of Calmfors and Driffill and OECD-1 that do not, we see that Japan switches from being among the most coordinated countries in the sample to being among the least coordinated ones. Other countries, such as Belgium, become less coordinated when informal bargaining coordination is taken into account.

Thirdly, it is evident from the two OECD rankings that coordination in some countries has changed over time. For instance, Australia, New Zealand and the United Kingdom have become less coordinated and less centralized between 1980 and 1994, whereas Italy and Portugal have moved in the opposite direction.

Union density and union coverage

The importance of collective bargaining as opposed to other ways of organizing contracting in the labour market can be measured by union density (the proportion of workers who are union members) or bargaining coverage (the proportion of the workforce that is covered by a collective agreement). With respect to these two indicators of collective bargaining, the evidence suggests that, first, union density *per se* has a very weak association, or perhaps no association, with economic performance indicators such as the unemployment rate, inflation, the employment rate, real compensation growth, labour supply, adjustment speed to wage shocks, real wage flexibility, and labour and total factor productivity.[136] There is, however, one significant exception: union density correlates negatively with labour earnings inequality and wage dispersion.

Secondly, bargaining coverage tends to be associated with higher real wage growth (with no impact on productivity growth), lower employment rates, higher unemployment rates, and higher inflation. As with union density, bargaining coverage correlates negatively with labour earnings inequality and wage dispersion.

Labour market coordination

Collective bargaining is potentially a powerful means to facilitate *bargaining coordination* irrespective of union density and bargaining coverage. Various types of coordination were shown earlier in Table 8.2 and summarized in Table 8.4. Each can affect the wage-setting procedures and scope of bargaining differently (for example, working conditions, holidays and leave provisions and so on). Bargaining coordination can therefore be an influential determinant of labour market and macroeconomic performance. For example, the Japanese system of wage setting is decentralized (firm-based) but coordinated in the sense that it follows company rules based on seniority (hence, they are transparent) rather than individual contracting. In this system workers are not paid wages equal to their individual reservation wage (that is, the wage level below which the worker will not supply his or her labour), as would have been the case under individual contracting, but this difference does not necessarily affect efficiency adversely. The Netherlands and Germany also have coordinated systems through strong employer organizations, coordination among giant companies or across industries, and coordination among unions. In France the government provides coordination in the form of exercising control over critical sectors such as public services, utilities and large nationalized industries. In Italy there is informal employer coordination (via the big firms and regional employers' associations) and between some union confederations. Finally, Sweden has a centralized employers' organization as well as centralized union confederations.

The comparative literature focuses on two hypotheses about the relationship between bargaining coordination and economic performance. The first hypothesis postulates that coordinated collective bargaining leads to better economic outcomes compared to semi-coordinated collective bargaining, which, in turn, performs better than uncoordinated collective bargaining. The second hypothesis (the 'hump' hypothesis) postulates that semi-coordinated collective bargaining leads to worse economic outcomes than both coordinated and uncoordinated bargaining.[137]

The evidence suggests that bargaining coordination did have a beneficial impact on macroeconomic performance in the 1970s and 1980s, but the evidence is fragile and in the 1990s the impact seemed to have disappeared.[138] More specifically, countries with highly coordinated collective bargaining tend to be associated with lower and less persistent unemployment, less earnings inequality and wage dispersion, and fewer and shorter strikes compared to countries with semi-coordinated (for example, industry-level bargaining) or uncoordinated (for example, firm-level bargaining or individual contracting) collective bargaining.

In terms of productivity growth and real wage flexibility, countries with highly coordinated collective bargaining tend to perform slightly better than countries with semi-coordinated collective bargaining, but may not perform differently than countries with uncoordinated collective bargaining. This lends some support to the first hypothesis, but only for the 1970s and 1980s. For most economic indicators, the differences disappear in the 1990s. Two exceptions are earnings inequality and wage dispersion. These indicators are comparatively low in countries with highly coordinated collective bargaining throughout the whole period.

Although countries with either uncoordinated or coordinated collective bargaining tend to be associated with lower and less persistent unemployment and higher productivity growth than semi-coordinated collective bargaining during the period 1960 to 1990, the evidence in favour of the hump hypothesis is, in general, very weak, particularly for the 1990s. In terms of inflation and the employment rate, there seems to be little difference between coordinated, semi-coordinated, and uncoordinated collective bargaining.

Union density and union coverage versus labour market coordination

These conclusions refer to one dimension of industrial relations and take other dimensions as given (either by controlling for them or by inappropriately ignoring them). This overlooks the possibility of complementarities between union density/bargaining coverage and bargaining coordination.

Such complementarities are important for the impact of collective bargaining on economic performance, and it can therefore be misleading to focus on one particular aspect in isolation. However, one can make some generalizations though with a wide margin of error:[139]

- High union density and bargaining coverage do not contribute to poor unemployment performance so long as they are complemented by high bargaining coordination (particularly among employers);
- Informal coordination of wage bargaining (informal consultations between firms and/or unions or pattern bargaining) tends to mitigate the potential disadvantage (in terms of relative high unemployment) associated with semi-coordinated (such as industry-level) wage bargaining, and can arise in countries with relatively low union density and bargaining coverage;
- Coordination among employers tends to be more important in producing low unemployment than coordination among employees. This suggests that employers' organizations are more effective than union confederations in controlling the wage drift.
- Countries that have competing unions and many different union confederations (multi-unionism) tend to perform worse (in terms of unemployment and inflation) than other countries;
- The relationship between bargaining coordination and industrial disputes is rather clear: bargaining coordination reduces strike activity;[140] in turn, a high level of strikes impacts negatively on economic outcomes (in the sense of higher rates of inflation, unemployment and growth in earnings);[141]
- The effects of coordination can be compromised or accentuated depending upon the political orientation of the government. 'Good' economic outcomes (in terms of economic growth) may arise either when strong, centralized unions are paired with a strong left-wing government or when weak, decentralized unions are paired with a right-wing government. A mismatch (weak unions paired with a strong left-wing government or strong unions paired with a right-wing government) can lead to poor economic outcomes.

Specifically regarding the strength of the evidence on the effects of labour market institutions and regulations on unemployment, the empirical results can be considered to be largely inconclusive, often showing estimates of opposite theoretical sign.[142] In fact, a rather robust relationship is found between stronger labour market institutions and lower unemployment. Ireland and the Netherlands are often highlighted as two countries with strong coordination of bargaining and low unemployment. While there are cases of lower unemployment and weak labour market institutions (such as the United Kingdom and the United States), there are also cases of strong institutions and low unemployment (such as in Austria, Denmark, Norway and Sweden). If a conclusion is in order, this must be that there is a wide range of labour market institutions compatible with the same rate of unemployment.

The evidence summarized above focuses on the relationship between aspects of collective bargaining and specific economic outcomes and provides us with important information as to whether or not particular bargaining institutions are systematically associated with good economic outcomes. However, by taking an essentially static view of the nexus between collective bargaining and economic performance perhaps one of the most important benefits of bargaining coordination is ignored, namely the capacity of the bargaining system to help the economy to adjust to shocks in an effective way.

International trade

To the extent that international trade increases competition in product markets (and non-unionized labour markets), union behaviour can be affected. Theoretical reasoning suggests that competitive product markets can be an important determinant of wage restraint (see earlier discussion on microeconomic performance). In other words, those employed in the exposed sector are likely to be more concerned with problems of international competitiveness than those in the protected sector. In terms of empirical evidence, strike activity, inflation and the unemployment rate tend to be relatively low in countries where unions are concentrated in sectors exposed to international competition.[143] Furthermore, exposure to foreign competition reduces the performance difference between countries with semi-coordinated bargaining systems and coordinated ones. In other words, when import penetration is high, countries with semi-coordinated collective bargaining (at the industry or sector level) perform as well as countries with fully coordinated collective bargaining, provided that import penetration is high (high import ratio). In turn, both perform better than countries with uncoordinated bargaining systems.[144] Overall, it seems that exposure to foreign competition can help to remove the disadvantage (if any) associated with semi-coordinated wage bargaining. What all this means is that the economic environment in which collective bargaining takes place can be an important determinant of economic performance.

Social insurance

An interesting, but often overlooked feature of collective bargaining is its capacity to provide some form of social insurance against shocks arising from international markets. An important source of uncertainty about future wages and employment derives from a country's openness to international trade and the process of globalization. In theoretical terms, a risk-averse worker who is uncertain about his or her future wage would have an incentive to buy insurance against the wage risk. Although this kind of insurance is not privately provided, different types of labour market institutions reduce the uncertainty of future labour earnings, like collective bargaining around minimum wages and unemployment insurance. There is some, albeit limited support of this insurance argument: countries that are more exposed to external risks tend to have a more compressed wage structure, more centralized systems of collective bargaining, a higher replacement ratio, and a higher relative minimum wage.[145]

Bargaining coordination and monetary policy

The organization of collective bargaining can affect economic outcomes in ways other than through the direct impact on wages and employment. An important indirect link is the interaction between the bargaining structure and monetary policy. The establishment of the European Monetary Union and the move towards central bank independence in many OECD countries in the past ten years have spurred an interest in this link. It is clear that under a regime of decentralized collective bargaining, unions are unlikely to take into account how wage settlements might affect monetary policy. However, when collective bargaining is coordinated, unions can act strategically and take into account how the central bank might react to different wage settlements. Broadly speaking, this can affect economic outcomes through two channels.

The first approach takes as its starting point the inflation bias in monetary policy when the central bank is tempted to print money to expand aggregate demand once the private sector has locked itself into nominal wage contracts. If unions anticipate this, all attempts to reduce unemployment below the equilibrium level will fail and inflation will be suboptimally high. Importantly, the higher the equilibrium level of unemployment is, the higher the inflation bias would be because this makes the temptation to create surprise inflation so much bigger. Now, under a regime of coordinated bargaining unions realize that their wage strategy affects the level of equilibrium unemployment and thus the size of the inflation bias. If unions care about inflation per se (independently of their concern for real wages and employment), they have an incentive to moderate their wage demands in order to reduce the equilibrium level of unemployment and the inflation bias. Thus, coordinated bargaining may lead to lower unemployment and inflation.

The second approach focuses on the interaction between the degree of bargaining coordination and the monetary policy regime. It is argued that equilibrium unemployment is lower, the fewer the number of unions and the more non-accommodating the monetary regime is. The logic is that unions might realize that their wage settlements will lead to a larger reduction in real demand when the central bank is committed to a fixed nominal money supply than when it is anticipated that the central bank will accommodate (by increasing the money supply) whatever wage settlement is reached in the labour market. Consequently, unions have an incentive to lower their wage demands when monetary policy is non-accommodating and this leads to high levels of (equilibrium) employment. This mechanism is not operating if collective bargaining is completely uncoordinated because in that case the price effect is too small to be internalized by the unions. Nor does the monetary regime matter, if bargaining is completely centralized or fully coordinated: in this case, the unions can coordinate their wage policies perfectly and choose full employment irrespectively of the monetary regime. Thus, the argument is that semi-coordinated collective bargaining combined with non-accommodating monetary policy is likely to lead to higher levels of employment than semi-coordinated bargaining with accommodating monetary policy. If true, this suggests that semi-coordinated collective bargaining is not associated with poor economic outcomes, as otherwise suggested by the reasoning behind the hump hypothesis.

The hump hypothesis claims that economies with either uncoordinated or completely coordinated wage-setting should have lower unemployment than economies with semi-coordinated wage-setting, but, as discussed above, the evidence in support of this hypothesis is weak. In fact, some (but not all) of the OECD economies with semi-coordinated wage-setting systems have been very successful in sustaining low levels of unemployment throughout the postwar period. More recent evidence takes into account the interaction between monetary policy and collective bargaining regimes to understand these facts. In particular, semi-coordinated collective bargaining combined with non-accommodating monetary policy (as measured by the degree of central bank independence) is found to be able to sustain comparably low levels of unemployment and inflation.[146] While the data confirm that unemployment is comparably low in countries with highly centralized bargaining systems *if* monetary policy is accommodating, we see that the countries with an intermediate level of centralization and a non-accommodating monetary policy regime have the lowest rate of unemployment.[147]

A study of unemployment in 15 OECD countries during the period 1972–93 found that centralization has a dampening effect on unemployment under a regime of accommodating monetary policy, but that the relationship under a regime of non-accommodating policy is *U-shaped*; that is, both decentralized and centralized bargaining are associated with higher unemployment than semi-centralized bargaining.[148] However, a subsequent study found that the relationship is monotonic also under non-accommodating monetary policy (conducted by an independent central bank) and hump-shaped under accommodating monetary policy.[149] Still, another study of 16 OECD countries during the period 1953–92 argued that the unemployment cost of achieving this outcome depends on the nature of wage-setting institutions: the unemployment cost of central bank independence is lower under coordinated bargaining than under uncoordinated bargaining. If their estimates are taken at face value, then a shift from a completely dependent central bank to a completely independent one would increase unemployment by almost 10 percentage points under uncoordinated wage bargaining. Under semi-coordinated wage bargaining, the cost would be about 4 percentage points, but under a regime of completely coordinated wage bargaining unemployment will actually fall by about 1 percentage point.[150]

In conclusion, the evidence points to the importance of the interaction between monetary policy regime and bargaining coordination. Although the literature has not yet settled down, there is some support for the notion that central bank independence (or non-accommodating monetary policy) works relatively well in conjunction with systems of semi-coordinated collective bargaining. However, more research would be needed before firm conclusions can be drawn.

8.5   Summary and conclusions

The international empirical literature on the subject covers thousands of published articles and books and utilizes dozens of micro and macro indicators that are affected by many and diverse combinations of collective bargaining, operating under different political regimes. Theory is often ambiguous and the indicators, even when measured without errors, may exhibit different behaviour in different countries or at different times or even within the same country in different periods. And even if unions have certain objectives, they need to take into account how the economy is structured and how employers conduct their business, including the treatment of their workers. At the end, much depends on the environment in which the unions operate. Is the national economy open to international competition? If an open one, is it still a protected one? What are the colours of the government?

For a long time economists have bravely confronted the 'Trade Union Hydra', with its many different and evolving faces (of economic performance). If economists agree on something, it is that there is no single variable capturing how 'good' or 'bad' trade unions are.

Some indicators seem to be affected favourably by the presence and conduct of unions and the form that collective bargaining takes, while others seem to be affected negatively. It is often hard to determine whether the positive effects outweigh the negative ones without prior judgements.

Even in the case of single indicators, the evidence shows at times a favourable outcome and at times an unfavourable one often within the same country and for the same sector studied during the same period.

Furthermore, the whole idea of a positive or negative effect needs to be clarified: 'for whom?' Obviously a wage decrease is bad news for workers, but welcome news for employers. Similarly, while workers benefit from full employment, employers may get little joy out of it if it decreases their ability to control workers through the threat of dismissal.[151]

Finally, there is a double disjoint when one moves from the micro evidence to the macro evidence. First, microeconomic approaches tend to be theoretically cleaner (though not always) and their empirics tend to be more robust (though, again, not always). Second, macroeconomic approaches are subject to (often ideological) conceptual differences as well as measurement complications while the evidence tends to be much more country and time specific.

This does not lead to an agnostic position. Some patterns have emerged from research on this area of economics and were summarized, unavoidably with omissions, in this chapter.[152] And though the evidence is generally too weak and fragile to warrant grand generalizations about the performance of specific labour market institutions, it suggests that there is a relationship between collective bargaining and economic performance, but this relationship is *too complex* in the first instance and *may change* over time. Findings like this have made researchers increasingly recognize the importance of policy complementarities – that is, that the effectiveness of one policy depends on the implementation of other policies.[153] This is also shown in a more recent survey of unions and collective bargaining where it is argued that it is 'the total package of formal and informal institutions that matters for economic performance'.[154]

In addition, economic theory is a lot more flexible than its practitioners in the policy domain have generally given it credit. For example, many first-order economic principles (such as market-based competition, fiscal discipline, competitive currencies, trade and financial liberalization, privatization, deregulation and so on) do not lead into unique policy packages.[155] In turn, successful economic outcomes may correspond to different combinations of policies, of which some may be conventional and others 'unorthodox'.

In short 'there is no unique correspondence between the *functions* that good institutions perform and the *form* that such institutions take. Reformers have substantial room for creatively packaging these principles into institutional designs that are sensitive to local constraints and take advantage of local opportunities. Successful countries are those that have used this room wisely'.[156] One should therefore be careful not to infer that institutional forms of the labour market that work poorly in some settings (and some times) should not be replicated in other countries at other times. Alternatively, arrangements that may work well in one environment may not work well in other, often very different, ones.

In all, and especially from the perspective of *developing* countries, there are three key areas that would benefit from more attention.

First, at the empirical level, one needs to have a much better understanding of union/non-union differentials as well as their spillover effects. Both effects need to be examined against efficiency gains or losses for the economy at large, not just for the sectors to which they apply.

Secondly, at the theoretical level, one needs to take into consideration the 'reverse causation' and examine not only the effects of institutions upon the economy (as this chapter has done), but also the effects of the economy upon institutions. For example, can a coordinated labour market play a useful social insurance function in the presence of globalization and increasing openness?

Finally, at the policy level, one needs to be aware that introducing new laws in a piecemeal way is not in itself sufficient for creating overall favourable labour market outcomes.[157] Additional broader regulations need to be developed in tandem to ensure that the transition into a new industrial relations system promotes long-term efficiency without short-term adversarial costs.[158]

Notes

1 Adviser, The World Bank Institute, The World Bank. The author wishes to thank participants at the ILO Seminar on Labour Market Institutions and Employment in Developing Countries, November 2005 as well as Toke S. Aidt (University of Cambridge) for useful comments and suggestions. The views and findings in this paper are those of the author and do not necessarily represent those of the World Bank, its member governments, its Executive Directors, or the countries they represent.

2 H.G. Lewis (1986) *Union Relative Wage Effects: A Survey* (Chicago: University of Chicago Press).

3 A. Ulph and D. Ulph (1990) 'Union Bargaining: A Survey of Recent Work', in D. Sapsford and Z. Tzannatos (eds), *Current Issues in Labour Economics* (London: Macmillan Press).

4 A. Booth (1995) *The Economics of the Trade Union* (Cambridge: Cambridge University Press).

5 D. Sapsford and Z. Tzannatos (1993) *The Economics of the Labour Market* (London: Macmillan Press).

6 R. Flanagan (1999) 'Macroeconomic Performance and Collective Bargaining: An International Perspective', *Journal of Economic Literature*, 37(4).

7 T. Aidt and Z. Tzannatos (2002) *Unions and Collective Bargaining: Economic Effects in a Global Environment* (Washington, DC: World Bank).

8 This is a strong assumption that is unlikely to be met in practice in the real world. But it serves as a useful theoretical point for benchmarking variations of economic models.

9   A. Rees (1963) 'The Effects of Unions on Resource Allocation', *Journal of Law and Economics*, 6(1).

10 J.H. Pencavel (1995) 'The Role of Labor Unions in Fostering Economic Development', Policy Research Working Paper No. 1469 (Washington, DC: World Bank).

11 M. Rama (1997) 'Organized Labor and the Political Economy of Product Market Distortions', *World Bank Economic Review*, 11(2), and M. Rama and G. Tabellini (1998) 'Lobbying by Capital and Labor over Trade and Labor Market Policies', *European Economic Review*, 42(7).

12 Note that this proposition (that unions share the firm's profits) ignores the point that rents are capitalized in the value of the firm and so are not available for sharing. For example, assume a monopoly situation is established as a result of an innovation. If the prospect for high profits is real, the inventor is likely to sell the right and make a large capital gain instantaneously. Thereafter, sales grow and the firm reverts to a public company. The monopoly power of the company is now reflected in the value of its shares, not in the rate of operating profit. It is the rate of return to the shares (in the form of dividends and capital gains) that is relevant for collective bargaining and this is determined competitively in the stock market. Hence, the firm's ability to provide high wages to its labour force has disappeared. See Sapsford and Tzannatos, op. cit.

13 Ulph and Ulph (1990).

14 K.M. Murphy, A. Schleifer and R.W. Vishny (1993) 'Why Is Rent-Seeking So Costly to Growth?', *American Economic Review*, 83(2).

15 R. Freeman and J.L. Medoff (1979) 'The Two Faces of Unionism', *Public Interest*, 57, and R.B. Freeman (1980) 'The Exit–Voice Tradeoff in the Labor Market: Unionism, Job Tenure, Quits, and Separations', *Quarterly Journal of Economics*, 94(4).

16 R.L. Faith and J.D. Reid (1987) 'An Agency Theory of Unionism', *Journal of Economic Behavior and Organization*, 8.

17 Whereas individual firms have an incentive to give in to union demands (to avoid a local conflict), the industry as a whole has less incentive to do so, and by joining forces, it is easier for firms to resist union demands. See S. Dowrick (1993) 'Wage Bargaining Systems and Productivity Growth in OECD Countries', Background Paper No. 26 (Canberra: Australian Government Publishing Service).

18 J.M. Malcomson (1983) 'Trade Unions and Economic Efficiency', *Economic Journal*, 93 (Conference Papers Supplement).

19 X-inefficiency refers to a situation in which a firm's total costs are not minimized because the actual output from given inputs is less than the maximum feasible level.

20 R. Layard, S. Nickell and R. Jackman (1991) *Unemployment* (Oxford: Oxford University Press).

21 D. Soskice (1990) 'Wage Determination: The Changing Role of Institutions in Advanced Industrialized Countries', *Oxford Review of Economic Policy*, 6(4).

22 R. Freeman (1993b) 'Labor Markets and Institutions in Economic Development', *American Economic Review*, 83(2).

23 J. Visser (1998) 'Two Cheers for Corporatism, One for the Market: Industrial Relations, Wage Moderation and Job Growth in the Netherlands', *British Journal of Industrial Relations*, 36(2).

24 ILO (International Labour Organization) (1997) *World Labour Report: Industrial Relations, Democracy and Social Stability* (Geneva: ILO).

25 Pencavel (1995).

26 P. Lange and G. Garrett (1985) 'The Politics of Growth: Strategic Interaction and Economic Performance in the Advanced Industrial Democracies, 1974–80', *Journal of Politics*, 47(3); G. Garrett and P. Lange (1986) 'Economic Growth in Capitalist Democracies', *World Politics*, 38(4); and R.M. Alvarez, G. Garrett and P. Lange (1991) 'Government Partisanship, Labour Organization, and Macroeconomic Performance', *American Political Science Review*, 85(2).

27 M. Olson (1982) *The Rise and Decline of Nations: Economic Growth, Stagflation, and Social Rigidities* (New Haven: Yale University Press).

28 For example, an increasingly important determinant of economic performance today is foreign direct investment and this depends in turn on how union legislation, and more broadly core labour standards, are observed in specific countries. See D. Kucera (2002) 'Core Labour Standards and Foreign Direct Investment', *International Labour Review*, 141(1–2), and Aidt and Tzannatos (2002), Chapter 2.

29 Aidt and Tzannatos (2002).

30 D.R. Cameron (1984) 'Social Democracy, Corporatism, Labour Quiescence, and the Representation of Interest in Advanced Capitalist Society', in J.H. Goldthorpe (ed.), *Order and Conflict in Contemporary Capitalism* (Oxford: Oxford University Press).

31 E. Tarantelli (1986) 'The Regulation of Inflation and Unemployment', *Industrial Relations*, 25(1).

32 C. Crouch (1990) 'Trade Unions in the Exposed Sector: Their Influence on Neo-corporatist Behavior', in R. Brunetta and C. Dell'Aringa (eds), *Labour Relations and Economic Performance* (New York: New York University Press).

33 Such reasons may be personal ambition, but need not always be so: they may, for example, relate to the unions leaders' political belief that the time is ripe for conflict in a broader political context.

34 This proposition has solid theoretical foundation in perfectly competitive markets and has been favoured by many researchers, both early and more recent ones. For example, see World Bank (1995) *World Development Report: Workers in an integrating World* (Washington DC: Oxford University Press and the World Bank).

35 L. Calmfors (1993) 'Centralization of Wage Bargaining and Macroeconomic Performance: A Survey', Seminar Paper No. 536, Stockholm University, Institute for International Economic Studies.

36 J.R. Hicks (1932) *The Theory of Wages* (London: Macmillan Press).

37 Rees (1963); D. Mazumdar (1989) 'Microeconomic issues of the Labor Markets in Developing Countries: Analysis and Policy Implications', Economic Development Institute Seminar paper No. 40 (Washington, DC: The World Bank) and J.H Pencavel (1991) *The Origins of Trade Union Power* (Oxford: Oxford University Press).

38 There are effects in other areas that are not examined in this chapters such as wage dispersion, returns to schooling, voluntary turnover, profitability levels and growth differential, speed of implementation of new technology and implementation of physical investments, research and development and so on. These are coved in Aidt and Tzannatos (2002) and, more recently, in Aidt and Tzannatos (2006) 'Unions and Microeconomic Performance: A Look at What Matters for Hard Core Economists (and Employers)', *International Economic Review*, 125(4), 257–78.

39 See, for example, Tzannatos (1987) 'Union versus Non-union Wages, Arithmetic versus Geometric Means and Grouped Data Revisited', *Bulletin of Economic Research*, 39(1).

40 Extensive discussion on methodological issues on the estimation of the wage mark-up can be found in Lewis (1986); Pencavel (1991); Sapsford and Tzannatos (1993); Booth (1995).

41 For 'summary best guess' see the seminal review by Lewis (1986) and more recent studies by D.G. Blanchflower (1996a) 'Product Market Competition, Wages, and Productivity: International Evidence from Establishment-Level Data', *Annals d'Economie et de Statistique*, 41/42(2), 219–54; D.G. Blanchflower (1999) 'Changes over Time in Union Relative Wage Effects in Great Britain and the United States', in S. Daniel, P. Arestis and J. Grahl (eds), *Essays in Honour of Bernard Corry and Maurice Peston, vol. 2: The History and Practice of Economics* (Cheltenham: Edward Elgar); R.K. Filer, D.S. Hamermesh and A.E. Rees (1996) *The Economics of Work and Pay* (New York, NY: HarperCollins College).

42 Pencavel (1991); Sapsford and Tzannatos (1993); Booth (1995); Blanchflower (1999).

43 V. Christie (1992) 'Union Wage Effects and the Probability of Union Membership', *Economic Record*, 68(200); R. Kornfeld (1993) 'The Effects of Union Membership on Wages and Employee Benefits: The Case of Australia', *Industrial and Labor Relations Review*, 47(1); C. Mulvey (1986) 'Wage Levels: Do Unions Make a Difference?', in J. Niland (ed.), *Wage Fixation in Australia* (Sydney: Allen and Unwin).

44 G.M. MacDonald and J.C. Evans (1981) 'The Size and Structure of Union/Non-union Wage Differentials in Canada', *Canadian Journal of Economics*, 14; M. Gunderson (1982) 'Union Impact on Wages, Fringe Benefits, and Productivity', in M. Gunderson and J. Anderson (eds), *Union–Management Relations in Canada* (Toronto: Addison-Wesley); MacDonald (1983) 'The Size and Structure of Union/Non-union Wage Differentials in Canadian Industry: Corroboration, Refinement and Extensions', *Canadian Journal of Economics*, 16; C. Robinson and N. Tomes (1984) 'Union Wage Differentials in the Public and Private Sectors: A Simultaneous Equation Specification', *Journal of Labor Economics*, 2(1); W. Simpson (1985) 'The Impact of Unions on the Structure of Canadian Wages: An Empirical Analysis with Microdata', *Canadian Journal of Economics*, 18(1), 164–81; E.K. Grant, R. Swidinsky and J. Vanderkamp (1987) 'Canadian Union/Non-union Wage Differentials', *Industrial and Labor Relations Review*, 41(1), 93–107; D.A. Green (1991) 'A Comparison of Estimation Approaches of Union/Non-union Wage Differentials', Discussion Paper No. 91–13. Department of Economics, University of British Columbia, Vancouver; M. Gunderson, A. Ponak and D.G. Taras (eds) (2000) *Union–Management Relations in Canada*, 4th edn (Toronto: Addison-Wesley Longman).

45 C. Schmidt and K.F. Zimmermann (1991) 'Work Characteristics, Firm Size, and Wages', *Review of Economics and Statistics*, 73(4); J. Wagner (1991) 'Gewerkschaftmitgliedschaft und Arbeitseinkommen in der Bundesrepublik Deutschland', *Ifo Student*; C. Schmidt (1995) 'Relative Wage Effects of German Unions' (Selapo: University of Munich) Processed.

46 K. Nakamura, H. Sato and T. Kamiya (1988) *Do Labour Unions Really Have a Useful Role?* (Tokyo: Sago Rodo Kenkyujo).

47 Y. Park (1991) 'Union/Non-union Wage Differentials in the Korean Manufacturing Sector', *International Economic Journal*, 5(4); H. Kim (1993) 'The Korean Union Movement in Transition', in S. Frenkel (ed.), *Organized Labor in the Asia-Pacific Region: A Comparative Study of Trade Unionism in Nine Countries*, Cornell International Industrial and Labor Relations Report No. 24 (Ithaca, NY: ILR Press).

48 P. Moll (1993) 'Black South African Unions: Relative Wage Effects in International Perspective', *Industrial and Labor Relations Review*, 46(2); A. Dabalen (1998) 'The Effect of Unions on Wages in South Africa: Repeated Cross-section Estimates', Working Paper (University of California, Berkeley); K. Butcher and C. Rouse (2001) 'Wage Effects of Unions and Industrial Councils in South Africa', *Industrial and Labor Relations Review*, 54(2).

49 G. Standing (1992) 'Do Unions Impede or Accelerate Structural Adjustment? Industrial versus Company Unions in an Industrializing Labour Market', *Cambridge Journal of Economics*, 16(3).

50 A. Panagides and H.A. Patrinos (1994) 'Union/Non-union Wage Differentials in the Developing World: A Case Study of Mexico', Policy Research Working Paper 1269 (Washington, DC: World Bank).

51 F. Teal (1996) 'The Size and Source of Economic Rents in a Developing Country Manufacturing Labour Market', *Economic Journal*, 106.

52 Union density is higher in OECD countries than in developing ones. For example, it averages about 35–40 per cent in the former but is less than half that figure (15 per cent) in Latin America. See J. Heckman and C. Pagés (2004) *Law and Employment: Lessons from Latin America and the Caribbean* (Chicago: University of Chicago Press). Other regions (especially Africa and Asia) have even lower rates. Union coverage is typically higher than union density and often by much. For example, it is on average around 65 per cent in OECD countries (but more than 90 per cent in France where union density is only around 10 per cent). See Aidt and Tzannatos (2002).

53 H.S. Farber and A.B. Krueger (1992) 'Union Membership in the United States: the Decline Continues', National Bureau of Economic Research, Working Paper No. 4216 (Cambridge, MA: NBER); D.G. Blanchflower and R. Freeman (1992) 'Unionism in the United States and Other Advanced OECD Countries', *Industrial Relations*, 31(1); Filer, Hamermesh and Rees (1996); D.G. Blanchflower (1996b) 'The Role and Influence of Trade Unions in the OECD', Discussion Paper No. 310 (London: London School of Economics, Centre for Economic Performance); Blanchflower (1999).

54 M.B. Stewart (1991) 'Union Wage Differentials in the Face of Changes in the Economic and Legal Environment', *Economica*, 58(1); M.B. Stewart (1995) 'Union Wage Differentials in an Era of Declining Unionization', *Oxford Bulletin of Economics and Statistics*, 57(2).

55 Rees (1963); H.G. Johnson and P. Mieszkowski (1970) 'The Effects of Unionisation on the Distribution of Income: A General Equilibrium Approach', *Quarterly Journal of Economics*, 84(4).

56 R. Freeman and J.L. Medoff (1984) *What do Unions Do?* (New York: Basic Books).

57 Christie (1992).

58 Lewis (1986); B. Main and B. Reilly (1992) 'Women and the Union Wage Gap', *Economic Journal*, 102; D.G. Blanchflower and R. Freeman (1996). 'Growing into Work', Discussion Paper No. 296 (London: London School of Economics Centre for Economic Performance).

59 Christie (1992); Mulvey (1986).

60 Blanchflower (1996b; 1999); Blanchflower and Freeman (1996); B. Main (1991) 'The Union Relative Wage Gap', in D. Gallie, R. Penn and M. Rose (eds) (1991), *Trade Unionism in Recession* (Oxford: Oxford University Press).

61 F. Green (1988) 'The Trade Union Wage Gap in Britain: Some Recent Estimates', *Economics Letters*, 27, 183–7; G. Yaron (1990) 'Trade Unions and Women's Relative

Pay: A Theoretical and Empirical Analysis Using UK Data', Applied Economics Discussion Paper No. 95 (Oxford: Oxford University, Institute for Economics and Statistics).

62   D.J. Doiron and W.C. Riddell (1994) 'The Impact of Unionization on Male–Female Earnings Differences in Canada', *Journal of Human Resources*, 29(2), 504–34.

63   Simpson (1985); Doiron and Riddell (1994).

64   Nakumura, Sato and Kamiya (1988); T. Tachibanaki and T. Noda (2000) *The Economic Effects of Trade Unions in Japan* (London and Basingstoke: Macmillan Press).

65   Schmidt (1995).

66   Panagides and Patrinos (1994).

67   Standing (1992).

68   See survey by Lewis (1986).

69   Blanchflower (1999).

70   H.A. Patrinos and C. Sakellariou (1992) 'North American Indians in the Canadian Labour Market: a Decomposition of Wage Differentials', *Economics of Education Review*, 11(3).

71   Dabalen (1998).

72   Butcher and Rouse (2001).

73   Panagides and Patrinos (1994).

74   L. Mishel (1986) 'The Structural Determinants of Union Bargaining Power', *Industrial and Labor Relations Review*, 40(1).

75   M.B. Stewart (1990) 'Union Wage Differentials, Product Market Influence, and the Division of Rents', *Economic Journal*, 100.

76   Lewis (1986).

77   Robinson and Tomes (1984).

78   M.B. Stewart (1983) 'Relative Earnings and Individual Union Membership in the UK', *Economica*, 50, and Green (1988).

79   D. Metcalf and M. Stewart (1992) 'Closed Shops and Relative Pay: Institutional Arrangements or High Density', *Oxford Bulletin of Economics and Statistics*, 54(4).

80   Standing (1992).

81   D. Bhattacherjee (1987) 'Union-Type Effects on Bargaining Outcomes in Indian Manufacturing', *British Journal of Industrial Relations*, 22(2).

82   M.B. Stewart (1987) 'Collective Bargaining Arrangements, Closed Shops, and Relative Pay', *The Economic Journal*, 97.

83   S. Machin, M.B. Stewart and J. Van Reenen (1993) 'The Economic Effect of Multi-unionism: Evidence from the 1984 Workplace Industrial Relations Survey', *Scandinavian Journal of Economics*, 95(3).

84   Metcalf and Stewart (1992).

85   Stewart (1987; 1991; 1995).

86   I.M. McDonald and R.M. Solow (1981) 'Wage Bargaining and Employment', *American Economic Review*, 71(5).

87   A.J. Oswald and P.J. Turnbull (1985) 'Pay and Employment Determination in Britain: What Are Labour Contracts Really Like?', *Oxford Review of Economic Policy*, 1(1); Oswald (1993) 'Efficient Contracts Are on the Labour Demand Curve: Theory and Facts', *Labour Economics*, 1(1), 85–113.

88   Booth (1995).

89   G.S. Alogoskoufis and A. Manning (1991) 'Tests of Alternative Wage Employment Bargaining Models with an Application to the UK Aggregate Labour Market', *European Economic Review*, 35(1), 23–37; C.R. Bean and P.J. Turnbull (1988) 'Employment in the British Coal Industry: A Test of the Labour Demand

Model', *Economic Journal*, 98, 1092–104; J.N. Brown, and O. Ashenfelter (1986) 'Testing the Efficiency of Employment Contracts', *Journal of Political Economy*, 94 (Supplement), S40–S87; D. Card (1986) 'Efficient Contracts with Costly Adjustment: Short-Run Employment Determination for Airline Mechanics', *American Economic Review*, 76, 1045–71; T.E. MacCurdy and J.H. Pencavel (1986) 'Testing between Competing Models of Wage and Employment Determination in Unionized Markets', *Journal of Political Economy*, 94 (Supplement), S3–S39.

90 Ulph and Ulph (1990).

91 Pencavel (1991); Oswald (1993).

92 See R. Freeman and M.M. Kleiner (1990) 'The Impact of New Unionization on Wages and Working Conditions', *Journal of Labor Economics*, 8(1); J.S. Leonard (1992) 'Unions and Employment Growth', *Industrial Relations*, 31(1); W.M. Boal and J.H. Pencavel (1994) 'The Effects of Labour Unions on Employment, Wages, and Days of Operation: Coal Mining in West Virginia', *Quarterly Journal of Economics*, 109(1); S.G. Bronars, D.R. Deere and J. Tracy (1994) 'The Effects of Unions on Firm Behavior: An Empirical Analysis Using Firm-level Data', *Industrial Relations*, 33(4); T. Dunne and D. MacPherson (1994) 'Unionism and Gross Employment Flows', *Southern Economic Journal*, 60(3); and R.J. Lalonde, G. Marschke and K. Troske (1996) 'Using Longitudinal Data on Establishments to Analyze the Effects of Union Organizing Campaigns in the United States', *Annales d' Economie et de Statistique*, 41/42, 155–86 for the United States; R.J. Long (1993) 'The Effect of Unionization on Employment Growth of Canadian Companies', *Industrial and Labor Relations Review*, 46(4), 81–93 for Canada; D.G. Blanchflower, N. Millward and A.J. Oswald (1991) 'Unionism and Employment Behaviour', *Economic Journal*, 101, 815–34 for the United Kingdom.

93 S. Machin and S. Wadhwani (1991) 'The Effect of Unions on Organizational Change and Employment', *Economic Journal*, 101, and Leonard (1992).

94 D.G. Blanchflower and S. Burgess (1996) 'New Technology and Jobs: Comparative Evidence from a Two-Country Study', in B. Hall, M. Doms and F. Kramarz (eds), *Economics of Innovation and New Technology* (Washington, DC: National Academy Press) find that unions have a negative effect on employment in the United Kingdom but not in Australia.

95 Freeman (1980); K. Muramatsu (1984) 'The Effect of Trade Unions on Productivity in Japanese Manufacturing Industries', in M. Aoki (ed.), *The Economic Analysis of the Japanese Firm* (Amsterdam: Elsevier Science Publishers, North-Holland); P. Elias and D.G. Blanchflower (1989) 'Occupations, Earnings, and Work Histories of Young Adults: Who Gets the Good Jobs?', Research Paper No. 68 (London: Department of Employment); M. Kupferschmidt and R. Swidensky (1989) 'Longitudinal Estimates of the Union Effect on Wages, Wage Dispersion, and Pension Fringe Benefits', University of Guelph, Ontario, Canada, Processed; M. Osawa (1989) 'The Service Economy and Industrial Relations in Small and Medium-Size Firms in Japan', *Japan Labor Bulletin*, 1; Standing (1992); P. Miller and C. Mulvey (1991) 'Australian Evidence on the Exit/Voice Model of the Labor Market', *Industrial and Labor Relations Review*, 45(1); P. Miller and C. Mulvey (1993) 'What Do Australian Unions Do?', *Economic Record*, 69(206); M.M. Kleiner and Y.M. Lee (1997) 'Work Councils and Unionization: Lessons from South Korea', *Industrial Relations*, 36(1).

96 Freeman and Medoff (1984).

97 Lewis (1986); J.M. Perloff and R.C. Sickles (1987) 'Union Wage, Hours, and Earnings Differentials in the Construction Industry', *Journal of Labor Economics*, 5,

174–210; J.S. Earle and J. Pencavel (1990) 'Hours of Work under Trade Unionism', *Journal of Labor Economics*, 8(1); J. DiNardo (1991) 'Union Employment Effect: an Empirical Analysis', Discussion Paper No. 90-92-06, University of California, Department of Economics, Irvine; A.J. Oswald and I. Walker (1993) 'Rethinking Labour Supply: Contract Theory and Unions', London: London School of Economics, Centre for Economic Performance, Processed; Trejo (1993).

  98   Oswald and Walker (1993).

  99   F. Green (1995) 'Union Recognition and Paid Holiday Entitlement', Discussion Paper No. E95/13. University of Leeds, School of Business and Economic Studies, Leeds.

100   Blanchflower (1996b).

101   G. Brunello (1992) 'The Effect of Unions on Firms in Japanese Manufacturing', *Industrial and Labor Relations Review*, 45(3).

102   Kleiner and Lee (1997).

103   See survey of British studies in Booth (1995).

104   See survey of American studies in D. Bellman (1992) 'Unions, the Quality of Labor Relations, and Firm Performance', in L. Mishel and P.B. Voos (eds), *Unions and Economic Competitiveness* (New York: M.E. Sharpe).

105   R. Batt and T. Welbourne (2002) 'Performance Growth in Entrepreneurial Firms: Revisiting the Union–Performance Relationship', in J. Katz and T. Welbourne (eds), *Research Volume on Entrepreneurship*, vol. 5 (Saint Louis, MN: JAI Press).

106   H.C. Katz, T.A. Kochan and K.R. Gobeille (1983) 'Industrial Relations Performance, Economic Performance, and QWL Performance: An Interplant Analysis', *Industrial and Labor Relations Review*, 37(1).

107   Booth (1995); J. Kennan (1986) 'The Economics of Strikes', in O. Ashenfelter and R. Layard (eds), *Handbook of Labour Economics*, vol. 2, Handbooks in Economics series, No. 5 (Amsterdam: North-Holland); D. Metcalf (1993) 'Industrial Relations and Economic Performance', *British Journal of Industrial Relations*, 31(2).

108   Muramatsu (1984).

109   Brunello (1992).

110   C. Schnabel (1991) 'Trade Unions and Productivity: the German Evidence', *British Journal of Industrial Relations*, 29(1).

111   J.T. Addison, W.S. Siebert, J. Wagner and X. Wei (2000) 'Worker Participation and Firm Performance: Evidence from Germany and Britain', *British Journal of Industrial Relations*, 38(1).

112   Kleiner and Lee (1997).

113   R. Drago and M. Wooden (1992) 'The Austalian Workplace Industrial Relations Survey and Workplace Performance', *Australian Bulletin of Labour*, 18(2); D.R. Maki (1983) 'The Effects of Unions and Strikes on the Rate of Growth of Total Factor Productivity in Canada', *Applied Economics*, 15.

114   Standing, (1992).

115   P. Kuhn and G. Marquez (eds) (2005) *What Difference Do Unions Make? Their Impact on Productivity and Wages in Latin America* (Washington, DC: Inter-American Development Bank), pp. 11–12. The authors go further and conclude like others (see Aidt and Tzannatos, 2002) that 'careful attention to industry conditions, the structure of bargaining and the nature of industrial relations is required to assess the effects of unions on the productivity of Latin American firms' (ibid., p. 12).

116   L.M. Lynch (1992) 'Private Sector Training and the Earnings of Young Workers', *American Economic Review*, 81(1).

117 L.M. Lynch and S.E. Black (1998) 'Beyond the Incidence of Employer-provided Training', *Industrial and Labour Relations Review*, 52(1).
118 A. Booth (1991) 'Job-related Formal Training: Who Receives it and What is it Worth?', *Oxford Bulletin of Economics and Statistics*, 53(3); A. Booth, M. Francesconi and G. Zoega (2003) 'Unions, Training and Wages: Evidence for British Men', *Industrial and Labor Relations Review*, forthcoming.
119 G.J. Duncan and F.P. Stafford (1980) 'Do Union Members Receive Compensating Wage Differentials?', *American Economic Review*, 70(3).
120 F. Green, G. Hadjimatheou, and R. Smail (1985) 'Fringe Benefit Distribution in Britain', *British Journal of Industrial Relations*, 23(2).
121 Nakumura, Sato and Kamiya (1988).
122 E. Maskus, T.J. Rutherford and S. Selby (1995) 'Implications of Changes in Labor Standards: A Computational Analysis for Mexico', *North American Journal of Economics & Finance*, 6(2).
123 Ibid.
124 Freeman and Medoff (1984).
125 D.G. Blanchflower and A.J. Oswald (1988) 'Internal and External Influences upon Pay Settlements', *British Journal of Industrial Relations*, 26(3).
126 C. Brown (1990) 'Firms' Choice of Method of Pay', *Industrial and Labor Relations Review*, 43(3).
127 R. Freeman (1985) 'Unions, Pensions, and Union Pension Funds', in D. Wise (ed.), *Pensions, Labor, and Individual Choice* (Chicago: University of Chicago Press); Kupferschmidt and Swidensky (1989); Standing (1992).
128 More generally the relationship between labour policies (of which unions are a part) and economic outcomes is rather difficult to measure, for example, according to Heckman and Pagés (2004), 'Overall, there is no empirical relationship between labour reforms and labour market outcomes driven by economic performance ... the existing evidence regarding the impact of employment protection is abundant but inconclusive ... the evidence on the effects of job security on unemployment is equally ambiguous ... from a policy standpoint summarizing many features of a regulatory system in one indicator makes it impossible to distinguish which components, if any, have an adverse effect,' pp. 14, 46, 24.
129 See, for example, C.R. Bean, P.R.G. Layard and S.J. Nickell (1986) 'The Rise in Unemployment: A Multi-country Study', *Economica*, 53; R. Freeman (1988) 'Labour Market Institutions and Economic Performance', *Economic Policy*, 3(1); Layard, Nickell, and Jackman (1991); R. Jackman (1993) 'Mass Unemployment: International Experience and Lessons for Policy', Discussion Paper No. 152 (London: Centre for Economic Performance, London School of Economics); S. Scarpetta (1996) 'Assessing the Role of Labour Market Policies and Institutional Settings on Unemployment: A Cross-Country Study', *OECD Economic Studies*, 26; S.J. Nickell (1997) 'Unemployment and Labour Market Rigidities: Europe versus North America', *Journal of Economic Perspectives*, 11(3); OECD (1997) *Employment Outlook* (Paris: OECD); S.J. Nickell and P.R.G. Layard (1999) 'Labour Market Institutions and Economic Performance', in O. Ashenfelter and D. Card (eds), *Handbook of Labour Economics*, vol. 3C (Amsterdam: North-Holland).
130 T. Aidt and Z. Tzannatos (2008) 'Trade Unions, Collective Bargaining and Macroeconomic Performance: A Review', *Industrial Relations Journal*.
131 See also J. McCallum (1983) 'Inflation and Social Consensus in the 1970s', *Economic Journal*, 93(372); Cameron (1984); M. Bruno and J. Sachs (1985)

Economics of Worldwide Stagflation (Cambridge, MA: Harvard University Press); C. Crouch (1985) 'Conditions for Trade Union Wage Restraint', in L.N. Lindberg and C.S. Maier (eds), *The Politics of Inflation and Economic Stagflation* (Washington, DC: The Brooking Institution); J. McCallum (1986) 'Unemployment in OECD Countries in the 1980s', *Economic Journal*, 96(384); Tarantelli (1986); Heitger (1987); Calmfors and Driffill (1988); W. Carlin and D. Soskice (1990) *Macroeconomics and the Wage Bargain* (Oxford: Oxford University Press); Crouch (1990); Soskice (1990); R.E. Rowthorn (1992a) 'Centralization, Employment, and Wage Dispersion', *Economic Journal*, 102(412); R.E. Rowthorn (1992b) 'Corporatism and Labour Market Performance', in J. Pekkarinen, M. Pohjola and R. Rowthorn (eds), *Social Corporatism: A Superior Economic System* (Oxford: Clarendon Press); Dowrick (1993); M. Golden (1993) 'The Dynamics of Trade Unionism and National Economic Performance', *American Political Science Review*, 87(2); C.R. Bean (1994) 'European Unemployment: A Retrospect', *European Economic Review*, 38(3–4); J. Zweimuller and E. Barth (1994) 'Bargaining Structure, Wage Determination, and Wage Dispersion in Six OECD Countries', *Kyklos*, 47; F.D. Blau and L.M. Kahn (1996) 'International Differences in Male Wage Inequality: Institutions versus Market Forces', *Journal of Political Economy*, 104(4); M. Bleaney (1996) 'Central Bank Independence, Wage-Bargaining Structure, and Macroeconomic Performance in OECD Countries', *Oxford Economic Papers*, 48(3); OECD (1988); Flanagan (1999).

132   Aidt and Tzannatos (2002).

133   L. Calmfors and J. Driffill (1988) 'Bargaining Structure, Corporatism, and Macroeconomic Performance', *Economic Policy*, 6(1).

134   Soskice (1990).

135   OECD (1997).

136   See summary in Aidt and Tzannatos (2002), Chapter 1.

137   The hump hypothesis has been explicitly tested in more than 60 studies including Cameron (1984); Tarantelli (1986); Calmfors and Driffill (1988); Freeman (1988); Dowrick (1993); Calmfors (1993); OECD (1997).

138   Though some still find that differences persisted till the end of the 1990s (see, for example, T. Boeri, A. Brugiavini and L. Calmfors (2001) *The Role of Unions in the 21st Century* (Oxford: Oxford University Press)).

139   P.C. Schmitter (1981) 'Interest Intermediation and Regime Governability in Contemporary Western Europe and North America', in S. Berger (ed.), *Organising Interests in Western Europe* (Cambridge: Cambridge University Press); Cameron (1984); Bruno and Sachs (1985); Bean, Layard and Jackman (1986); Tarantelli (1986); McCallum (1986); A. Newell and J.S.V. Symons (1987) 'Corporatism, Laissez-faire, and the Rise of Unemployment', *European Economic Review*, 31(3); Calmfors and Driffill (1988); G.S. Alogoskoufis and A. Manning (1988) 'Wage-Setting and Unemployment Persistence in Europe, Japan, and the USA', *European Economic Review*, 32(2–3); Layard, Nickell and Jackman (1991); R. Jackman, C. Pissarides and S. Savouri (1990) 'Labour Market Policies and Unemployment in the OECD', *Economic Policy*, 11(23); Jackman (1993); OECD (1997); Nickell (1997); Nickell and Layard (1999); O. Blanchard and J. Wolfers (2000) 'The Role of Shocks and Institutions in the Rise of European Unemployment: The Aggregate Evidence', *Economic Journal*, 110(462).

140   Strike activity is typically measured as the number of days lost because of strikes per 1,000 workers in the labour force per year or the log of the number of workers involved in conflict per 1,000 workers; see Cameron (1984); Crouch (1985,

1990), and D. Hibbs (1978) 'On the Political Economy of Long-Run Trends in Strike Activity', *British Journal of Political Science*, 8.

141 Reverse causality can be important for these findings.

142 D. Baker, A. Glyn, D. Howell and J. Schmitt (2004) 'Unemployment and Labour Market Institutions: The Failure of the Empirical Case for Deregulation', Working Paper No. 43, Policy Integration Department, Statistical Development and Analysis Unit (Geneva: ILO).

143 Crouch (1990).

144 OECD (1997).

145 J. Agell and K.E. Lommerud (1992) 'Union Egalitarianism as Income Insurance', *Economica*, 59, 295–310; J. Agell (1999) 'On the Benefits from Rigid Labour Markets: Norms, Market Failures, and Social Insurance', *Economic Journal*, 109(453).

146 T. Iversen (1998) 'Wage Bargaining, Central Bank Independence and Real Effects of Money', *International Organization*, 52(3).

147 D. Soskice and T. Iversen (2000) 'The Nonneutrality of Monetary Policy with Large Price or Wage Setters', *Quarterly Journal of Economic*, 114(1).

148 Iversen (1998).

149 Cukierman and Lippi (1999).

150 P.A. Hall and R.J. Franzese (1998) 'Mixed Signals: Central Bank Independence, Coordinated Wage Bargaining and European Monetary Union', *International Organization*, 52(3).

151 M. Kalecki (1943) 'Political Aspects of Full Employment', reprinted in M. Kalecki *Selected Essays on the Dynamics of the Capitalist Economy, 1933–70* (Cambridge: Cambridge University Press).

152 No need to remind the reader that political, sociological and related aspects of unionism are notably absent from the current review.

153 Z. Tzannatos (1996) 'Labor Policies and Regulatory Regimes', in C. Frischtak (ed.), *Regulatory Policies and Reform: A Comparative Perspective* (Washington, DC: World Bank); J.M. Orszag, P.R. Orszag, D.J. Snower and J.E. Stiglitz (1999) 'The Impact of Individual Accounts: Piecemeal vs. Comprehensive Approaches', Mimeo, Birkbeck College.

154 T. Aidt and Z. Tzannatos (2005) 'The Costs and Benefits of Collective Bargaining', Cambridge Working Papers in Political Economy No. 0541 (Cambridge University).

155 J. Williamson (1990) 'What Washington Means by Policy Reform', in J. Williamson (ed.), *Latin American Adjustment: How Much Has Happened?* (Washington: Institute for International Economics).

156 Rodrik (2005) 'Growth Strategies', in P. Aghion and S. Durlauf (eds), *Handbook of Economic Growth* (Amsterdam: North-Holland).

157 History suggests that the introduction of more liberal trade union laws, unless swiftly accompanied by supportive industrial relations regulations, can lead to more or less generalized industrial conflict as was the case of Greece and South Europe more generally in the 1970s, and of the Republic of Korea in the early 1990s. Similar experiences were observed in Latin America at the time of change of the political regimes.

158 Such regulations go beyond the basic recognition that workers and employers can act through their representatives in the labour market and cover, for example, membership and representation requirements, definition of strikes, conflict resolution mechanisms, penalties and so on.

9
Labour Standards and Informal Employment in Latin America

Rossana Galli and David Kucera[1]

9.1 Introduction

In recent decades Latin America has experienced a steady and substantial increase in the share of workers characterized by informal employment status. From 1990 to 1997, for instance, the share of informal employment for a group of 14 Latin American countries increased from 51.8 to 57.7 per cent, based on a definition of informal employment used by the International Labour Organization which includes non-agricultural employment in small firms, self-employment and domestic service.[2] One reason for concern regarding the growing share of informal employment in Latin America is that such employment is often characterized by poor work conditions, including low labour standards.

A number of explanations have been offered for the rise in informal employment. Portes and co-authors provide a dynamic view of the growth of informal employment in the context of import substitution and export-oriented development strategies.[3] They argue that the policies of import substitution industrialization adopted from the 1950s to the 1970s led to the concentration of industry in just one or two cities in each country in Latin America. Together with a lack of prospects in rural areas, the urban concentration of industrialization led to a massive rural to urban migration, with the share of the population living in urban areas increasing from less than half to three-quarters between 1950 to 1990. Although a large number of industrial jobs were created in cities, these were insufficient to provide formal employment for all migrants. It was this labour surplus that contributed to the rise in informal employment. In the 1980s, the debt-induced crises led countries in the region to implement export promotion strategies. The decline in formal employment that followed was partly absorbed by informal employment as large formal firms decentralized production through subcontracting to small firms, but also resulted in a steep rise in open unemployment as 'masses of citydwellers found themselves lacking access to even the meager earnings once drawn from odd-jobbing, street vending, and other informal activities'.[4]

Other studies similarly describe the linkages between export-oriented and multinational firms and informal employment through, for instance, sub-contracting arrangements and export-processing zones, and thus the linkages more generally between globalization and informality.[5] Among the other fac-tors argued to contribute to growing informal employment are the decline in public sector employment, the increase in the female supply of labour, and the growth of the service sector in which a large share of informal workers are employed.[6]

Another explanation for the growing share of informal employment is that higher labour standards may lead to a higher share of informal employment. This view has been advanced in a number of studies. For instance, a World Bank report argues that the extent of informal employment in Latin America is partly determined by 'labor policies that overlooked the role of wages and working conditions as incentives and market signals, reducing the number of formal jobs and encouraging the development of the informal sector'.[7] This view, however, is not backed by a theoretical consensus nor by systematic empirical evidence.

First of all, in addressing these issues, it is useful to distinguish between different labour standards that may well have different effects on formal and informal employment. Valuable in this regard are categories of labour stand-ards proposed by Portes as regards 'basic rights', 'survival rights', 'security rights' and 'civic rights', elaborated in Table 9.1.[8] Portes' view is that while stronger 'security rights' may result in increased informalization, stronger 'civic rights' by themselves do not have this effect, even if stronger 'civic

Table 9.1 Types of labour standards

Type	Examples
Basic rights	Right against use of child labour Right against involuntary servitude Right against physical coercion
Survival rights	Right to a living wage Right to accident compensation Right to a limited work week
Security rights	Right against arbitrary dismissal Right to retirement compensation Right to survivors' compensation
Civic rights	Right to free association Right to collective representation Right to free expression of grievances

Source: Portes (1994).

rights' result in higher wages. Summarizing his view in reference to prior studies, Portes writes:

> Studies in several Latin American countries indicate that the drive to infor-malize by modern firms is motivated primarily by the desire to avoid adding to a regular plant of workers that, once hired, can seldom be let go. Hence, apart from basic and civic rights that may become amenable to internationally enforced standards, the implementation of others also requires fine tuning, lest they act as a brake on economic development or on the extension of minimal protection to greater numbers. ... The Latin American studies cited previously indicate that it is not high wages per se, but rather high wages to an immobile labour force regardless of business conditions, that constitute the main incentive for widespread informalization.[9]

Our primary interest is with 'civic rights', particularly regarding free-dom of association and collective bargaining rights and civil liberties more generally. In contrast with Portes, Singh and Zammit argue that stronger freedom of association and collective bargaining (FACB) rights may hin-der economic development and lead to increased informalization.[10] They write:

> [I]f in accordance with the advanced countries' proposals, the two labour conventions under discussion [Freedom of Association and Protection of the Right to Organise convention, 1948 (No. 87) and Right to Organise and Collective Bargaining Convention, 1949 (No. 98)] are imposed in a 'big bang' manner in a developing economy (through, for example, inter-national trade sanctions), it is more than likely that this would lead not to conflict resolution, but rather to strikes and consequent economic dis-ruption. ... The consequent economic and social disruption discourages investment, both foreign and domestic, and therefore does not help the cause of economic development. ... Further, to the extent that formal sec-tor unions succeed in getting higher wages and employment guarantees for their members, this is likely to reduce, other things being equal, the demand for labour in that sector, forcing the unemployed to seek work in the informal sector ... where labour standards hardly apply.[11]

In other words, the authors describe a scenario in which a rapid introduc-tion of freedom of association and collective bargaining rights might lead to more informality through two channels: first, a macroeconomic channel with stronger rights contributing to 'economic and social disruption' and thus discouraging foreign and domestic investment and hindering economic development and leading to increased informality; secondly, a microeco-nomic channel with stronger rights leading to higher wages in the formal sector and thus reducing the demand for formal employment and leading to increased informality.

Regarding Singh and Zammit's macroeconomic channel, a contrasting perspective is suggested by the 'comprehensive development paradigm' put forward by Stiglitz.[12] Summarizing this viewpoint, Stiglitz writes:

> The central argument of this paper has been that open, transparent, and participatory *processes* are important ingredients in the development transformation – important both for sustainable economic development and for *social development* that should be viewed as an end in itself and as a means to more rapid economic growth.[13]

The 'processes' that Stiglitz refers to are very similar to Portes' definition of 'civic rights'. These include a strengthening of civil society, for which Stiglitz specifically refers to labour unions.[14] Stiglitz defines 'social development' as 'the ability of a society to peacefully resolve conflicts and to address amicably sources of common concern when interests differ'.[15] A similar view is put forth by Rodrik in a study providing empirical evidence that countries with stronger civil liberties and political rights experience greater stability in economic performance and adjust better to adverse shocks.[16] As one possible hypothesis to account for these findings, Rodrik writes that 'institutionalized forms of political participation allow for greater voice without the need for conflict and civil strife'.[17] Both Stiglitz and Rodrik suggest a scenario in which stronger 'civic rights' lead to less rather than more conflict and instability. This, in turn, may give rise to more foreign and domestic investment, contributing to economic growth and the creation of formal employment.[18] Regarding formal wages, moreover, the microeconomic channel proposed by Singh and Zammit might be offset by a macroeconomic channel in which higher wages boost aggregate demand (in scenarios of wage-led growth) and thus contribute to economic growth and the creation of formal employment.

These considerations show how contrasting theories can be used to predict different effects of stronger 'civic rights' on formal and informal employment. This chapter investigates the empirical evidence for the hypothesis that stronger 'civic rights' – including FACB rights – and higher wage shares (wages relative to value added) in the formal sector reduce employment in that sector and thereby contribute to informalization. This issue is explored using panel data on specific categories of formal and informal employment for 14 Latin American countries in the 1990s, evaluating both cross-country and time series variation.

The remainder of this chapter is structured as follows. Section 9.2 provides a survey of relevant empirical studies on the effects of labour standards on formal and informal employment in Latin America. Section 9.3 provides definitions of formal and informal employment and general information on data sources and also describes trends in both formal and informal employment. Section 9.4 presents our findings on the effects of labour standards on formal and informal employment. Section 9.5 concludes.

9.2   Prior empirical evidence for Latin America

The empirical literature on the effects of labour standards on formal and informal employment focuses largely on 'security rights', particularly regarding job security regulations. This literature addresses two sets of issues: first, the effects of job security regulations on formal employment cyclical variability and on turnover rates for formal workers; and, secondly, the effects of job security regulations on shares of formal and informal employment.

As suggested by Bertola, tight job security regulations may discourage formal firms from dismissing workers during downturns and from hiring workers during upturns, as they take into account the possibility of incurring high costs of dismissal in the following downturn.[19] As a result, the variability of formal employment in response to output fluctuations is expected to be lower in periods and countries where job security regulations are tighter. This prediction is confirmed by a study on Peru that finds a more strongly pro-cyclical movement of formal employment in the period following the reforms which reduced workers' security rights starting in 1991.[20] More generally, there is strong evidence that the reductions in job security regulations implemented in several Latin American countries in the 1990s led to higher turnover rates for formal workers (especially those with short job tenure), which suggests that formal employment may have become more strongly pro-cyclical.[21]

The evidence is less conclusive regarding the effects of security rights on formal and informal shares of employment, most studies being concerned with the impact of job security regulations either on overall employment levels – without distinction between formal and informal employment – or on formal employment alone. Moreover, the little available evidence on the relation between job security and informal employment addresses only self-employment and provides inconclusive results. A cross-country study on Latin American and OECD countries by Márquez and Pagés finds a strong positive correlation between an index of employment protection (constructed by Márquez) and self-employment controlling for GDP per capita, suggesting that in highly protected labour markets more workers tend to be self-employed.[22]

More ambiguous results are found by Heckman and Pagés-Serra based on a sample of 16 Latin American countries.[23] Consistent with Márquez and Pagés, they find a positive and statistically significant cross-country relationship between their index of job security and self-employment (estimated by pooled OLS), but a negative and statistically significant relationship when only the time-series variability of the sample is evaluated (with the fixed effects estimator). Thus, while countries with weak job security regulations tend to have lower rates of self-employment, the weakening of job security regulations tends to be associated with increases in self-employment. The authors consider these contrary cross-country and over-time relationships to be a puzzle requiring more research.

These results can be reconciled, however, in that weakening job security regulations might involve an adjustment process and therefore have different effects in the short and long run, for instance as firms seek to restructure the skills composition of their workforces. That is, the immediate effect of weakening job security relations could be a greater increase in firing than hiring of formal sector employees and, therefore, an increase in the share of informal employment. After this initial round of firing, however, the effect of reduced hiring and firing costs could result in a net gain in formal employment as hiring and firing rates adjust to their long-run equilibrium position. An analogous point is made by Kugler regarding the *a priori* ambiguous effect of a reduction in firing costs on shares of formal and informal employment.[24]

While there are a fair number of studies looking at the effects of 'security rights' on formal and informal employment, we were able to find only one study concerned with informal employment and 'civic rights', more specifically with the nature of the collective bargaining process. This is a study by Carneiro and Henley, which provides insights into how this relationship changed in Brazil in the mid-1980s as the wage bargaining process shifted from being state-determined and highly centralized to being bargained collectively by unions at an intermediate level of centralization.[25] The authors find that the relationship between the extent of informal employment (measured by the number of workers without labour cards) and formal employment real wages (proxied by industrial employment real wages) changed from positive during the period of state-determined wages to negative during the more liberalized collective bargaining regime of the 1990s. They interpret this as resulting from a change in the direction of causality between formal wages and informal employment. During the period of state-determined wages, informal employment is argued to have been determined partly by the level of formal wages on the grounds that if formal wages are set too high, workers will be displaced from their formal jobs and end up in informal employment. During the more liberalized collective bargaining regime of the 1990s, by contrast, informal employment is argued to have influenced formal wages because a larger share of informal employment weakened formal employees' fallback position and, therefore, their bargaining power. This effect of informal employment on formal wages is estimated to be smaller in the short run than in the long run.

Carneiro and Henley (1998) argue that the shift from a state-regulated wage policy towards a more liberalized collective bargaining regime allowed the growth of powerful groups of wage bargainers at the sectoral level, reducing formal wage flexibility and causing a growing displacement of workers into informal employment. The authors conclude that, 'the liberalisation of collective bargaining in a developing economy can be potentially damaging for economic performance in that this facilitates rent-seeking behaviour by powerful wage bargainers, leading to inflationary wage settlements. In developing countries, where unemployment insurance is either sparse or non-existent, the consequences may be structural growth in the informal sector'.[26]

The empirical literature on the effects of labour standards on formal and informal employment can be summarized as follows. Studies on the effects of job security regulations on job turnover show, overall, that a weakening of such regulations is associated with higher job turnover rates, particularly for formal workers with short tenure. The findings on the effects of job security regulations on the extent of self-employment are more ambiguous, indicating that across countries, weaker job security regulations tend to be associated with lower levels of self-employment, but that within countries over time the weakening of job security regulations tends to be associated with increases in self-employment. Finally, a study on collective bargaining and informal employment finds a positive relationship between the extent of informal employment and formal employment real wages during a period of state-determined wage bargaining process and a negative relationship during a period of liberalized collective bargaining.

9.3   Employment data definitions, sources and overview

The literature contains multiple contending definitions of formal and informal employment. Because of data availability, we have adopted the definition used in the International Labour Office's publication *Panorama Laboral*. According to this definition, informality is associated with employment in small firms (fewer than five or ten workers, depending on the country-specific definition), with self-employment (own-account workers – excluding administrative, professional and technical workers – and unpaid family workers) and with domestic service. Formality is associated with employment in large private firms (five or more, or ten or more workers) and in the public sector. In the following analysis we consider each of these five employment categories separately, rather than aggregating them into formal and informal employment categories, thus enabling us to better address the heterogeneity of formal and informal employment.

Two of the most obvious shortcomings of this definition of formal and informal employment are that workers may actually belong to more than one employment category in a given period, and that many of those employed in large private firms may be informal in that, for instance, they are not covered by social security or do not have a written contract. If one were to employ a definition of informal employment based on a lack of social security coverage or a written contract, studies suggest that the share of informal employment would be larger than using the definition based on firm size.[27] For instance,

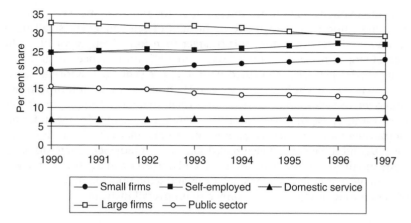

Figure 9.1 Non-agricultural employment shares for 14 Latin American countries, 1990–97
Source: PREALC (1998).

Marcouiller *et al.* (1997) find 47.9 per cent of the urban labour force in El Salvador to be informal as defined by firm size, compared with 62.8 per cent as defined by social security coverage (in 1990), with corresponding figures of 57.5 and 61.8 per cent for Peru (in the mid-1980s) and 30.8 and 43.2 per cent for Mexico (in 1990). The authors nonetheless come to broadly similar conclusions using either definition of informality in their analysis of returns to human capital in formal and informal employment. For Peru from 1990 to 1995, Saavedra and Chong also come to similar findings based on two different definitions of informal employment regarding changes in shares of informal employment over business cycles.[28] In a study of worker mobility in Mexico between formal and informal employment, Gong and van Soest again come to similar conclusions defining informality by either firm size or job type (the latter including own-account workers, those who manage a firm without employees, and piece-workers).[29]

The data employed in this chapter are taken from *Panorama Laboral* (1998) and cover a period of eight years, from 1990 to 1997, for 14 Latin American countries: Argentina, Bolivia, Brazil, Chile, Colombia, Costa Rica, Ecuador, Honduras, Mexico, Panama, Paraguay, Peru, Uruguay and Venezuela.[30] These data are measured as employment shares and refer to total (versus urban) non-agricultural employment. The exceptions are Peru, where the data are for the Lima metropolitan area, and Uruguay, where the data are for Montevideo. Additional information on data sources is provided in an appendix.

Figure 9.1 shows employment shares for 14 Latin American countries. The ranking of employment shares does not change over these years, with employment in large firms representing the largest share, followed by self-employment, small firms, the public sector and domestic service. If one measures informal employment as the sum of self-employed, small firms and domestic service shares, this is larger than formal employment as the sum of large firms and the public sector. In 1997, for instance, the informal share is 57.7 per cent, compared with 42.3 per cent for the formal share. Note that even excluding domestic service from the definition of informal employment yields larger shares for informal than formal employment. Figure 9.1 also shows that over the 1990s there was a relative decline in formal employment and an increase in informal employment. This was driven by the four and three percentage point declines in employment shares for large firms and the public sector respectively, and the reverse image three- and two-percentage point increases for small firms and self-employment, respectively, with domestic service showing only a slight overall increase.

9.4   Labour standards and formal and informal employment

Descriptive statistics

This section shifts to a consideration of the effects of labour standards on formal and informal employment. In order to explore these relationships across countries and over time, we make use of various indicators of 'civic rights' and 'security rights' and consider their relationship with categories of formal and informal employment. These rights have changed substantially in most Latin American countries since the 1980s, making the region particularly interesting for studying the impact of changing labour standards. For 'civic rights' – particularly the right to unionize, the right to bargain collectively, and the right to strike – there was a strengthening in most countries in the past two decades. For 'security rights' – particularly employment protection regulations – in contrast, there was a weakening in several countries.[31] This latter pattern is confirmed by the job security index constructed by Heckman and Pagés-Serra for Latin American countries for the 1990s.[32] In general, for countries experiencing a strengthening of 'civic rights', this tended to be concentrated in the 1980s, reflecting the resurgence in democracy in these countries.[33] This suggests the political nature of 'civic rights', for which changes in Latin America were discontinuous rather than gradual. For 'security rights', in contrast, changes were concentrated in the 1990s.

Table 9.2 shows various measures of interest for 14 countries as period averages for 1990 to 1997, whenever the data permit (with exceptions described in the notes to the table). Columns 1 through 5 show employment shares in our five employment categories. Columns 6 through 13 provide measures related to labour standards. Columns 14 and 15 provide data related to GDP per capita (in current international prices) as an indicator of economic development.

Table 9.2 Non-agricultural employment shares and labour market and development indicators for 14 Latin American countries, 1990–1997

	1 Small firms	2 Self-employed	3 Domestic service	4 Large firms	5 Public sector	6 Civil liberties*	7 Political rights*	8 Unionization rate	9 FACB unweighted*	10 FACB weighted*	11 Employment protection index#	12 Job security index#	13 Manuf. wage share	14 GDP per capita (PPP, current)	15 GDP per capita, % of Argentina
1 Argentina	17.1	26.3	7.8	33.0	15.8	6.7	8.7	25.4	2.4	2.6	24.0	2.977	40.9	10,324.2	100.0
2 Bolivia	16.2	37.5	5.7	27.2	13.4	6.5	8.5	16.4	0.5	1.4	35.5	4.756	11.1	2,072.6	20.1
3 Brazil	24.8	22.6	8.8	33.9	10.0	5.6	7.9	32.1	3.3	3.8	13.0	1.785	19.8	6,255.9	60.6
4 Chile	20.3	23.2	7.1	41.9	7.6	8.3	8.3	15.9	4.8	5.9	25.5	3.380	18.6	6,832.3	66.2
5 Colombia	26.3	24.2	4.6	36.2	8.7	5.0	6.7	7.0	0.0	0.0	34.0	3.493	16.8	5,519.7	53.5
6 Costa Rica	21.1	18.2	5.3	36.2	19.2	9.0	10.0	13.1	2.4	2.6	27.0	3.121	41.4	6,277.5	60.8
7 Ecuador	18.6	32.7	5.0	28.1	15.7	6.7	8.1	9.8	2.4	2.8	31.0	4.035	19.1	3,078.1	29.8
8 Honduras	11.9	34.4	6.2	33.9	13.6	6.7	7.5	4.5	2.4	3.1	33.0	3.530	47.6	2,303.6	22.3
9 Mexico	21.0	31.1	5.5	19.2	23.3	5.4	5.2	31.0	1.9	2.6	30.0	3.126	20.2	7,168.2	69.4
10 Panama	13.4	19.9	7.7	33.8	25.3	7.1	6.9	14.2	4.8	5.2	n.a.	2.718	39.9	4,858.1	47.1
11 Paraguay	30.4	23.2	10.8	23.2	12.4	6.7	5.6	9.3	1.9	2.3	21.0	2.168	21.8	4,354.1	42.2
12 Peru	14.5	35.6	4.8	35.7	9.5	4.6	4.2	7.5	1.4	2.0	32.0	3.796	16.2	3,914.6	37.9
13 Uruguay	10.7	20.4	6.1	45.0	17.8	8.3	9.4	11.6	8.6	8.6	19.5	2.232	23.5	7,554.4	73.2
14 Venezuela	14.1	25.4	3.1	37.5	20.0	6.7	7.9	14.9	6.7	6.9	37.0	2.955	17.3	5,806.1	56.2
Mean	18.6	26.8	6.3	33.2	15.2	6.7	7.5	15.2	3.1	3.6	27.9	3.1	25.3	5,451.4	52.8
Standard deviation	5.75	6.30	1.96	6.89	5.44	1.26	1.64	8.61	2.36	2.32	7.05	0.79	11.74	2,242.20	21.72
Coeff. of variation	0.31	0.24	0.31	0.21	0.36	0.19	0.22	0.57	0.76	0.65	0.25	0.25	0.46	0.41	0.41

Notes: "*" = indices range in value from 0 to 10, worst to best, respectively.
FACB = freedom of association/collective bargaining.
"#" = higher index values mean greater employment protection and job security.
"n.a." = not available.

Among 'civic rights' measures, columns 6 and 7 provide civil liberties and political rights indices as constructed by the non-profit organization Freedom House. The civil liberties index is based partly on a consideration of freedom of association and collective bargaining rights. Of the 14 sets of questions addressed in the construction of the index, one is: 'Are there free trade unions and peasant organizations or equivalents, and is there effective collective bargaining? Are there free professional and other private organizations?'[34] These questions come under the category of 'association and organizational rights', and the other three categories considered in the construction of the civil liberties index are 'freedom of expression and belief', 'rule of law and human rights', and 'personal autonomy and economic rights'. The political rights index addresses questions relating to free and fair elections, the competitiveness of political parties, self-determination and discrimination.

Additional 'civic rights' measures are presented in columns 8 through 10. Column 8 shows the number of union members as a percentage of the non-agricultural labour force. Columns 9 and 10 provide indices of violations of freedom of association and collective bargaining (FACB) based on coding textual sources for 37 evaluation criteria that address *de jure* as well as *de facto* problems, leaning in emphasis toward the latter.[35]

Columns 11 and 12 show two 'security rights' measures, the employment protection and job security indices drawn from Márquez and Pagés and Heckman and Pagés-Serra, respectively.[36] Column 13 shows UNIDO data on manufacturing wages as a percentage of manufacturing value-added. According to UNIDO, 'The manufacturing data refer to the formal sector only. They refer to the establishments that were registered at the National Statistical Offices' (personal correspondence). We therefore take this as a proxy for wage shares in formal employment to address the hypothesized effects of 'civic rights' on formal and informal employment through wages, similar to Carneiro and Henley,[37] who use wage data for industrial employment.

Finally, column 14 shows each country's GDP per capita, and column 15 shows each country's GDP per capita as a percentage of Argentina, which had the highest GDP per capita during this period. This shows that countries in the sample vary considerably in terms of per capita income, with Bolivia, Honduras and Ecuador having the lowest per capita incomes, ranging between 20 and 30 per cent that of Argentina.

Table 9.3 shows correlation coefficients (Pearson) for the above measures, with critical values of the correlation coefficients for two-tailed statistical significance (at the 10, 5 and 1 per cent levels) shown in the notes to the table. In discussing Table 9.3, we focus on correlations that are statistically significant or are otherwise of interest. Shaded areas indicate more direct relevance to issues of labour standards and formal and informal employment, in that they address relationships between our measures of labour standards and self-employment and employment in small and large firms. We leave aside employment in domestic service and the public sector, as we have no

Table 9.3   Correlation coefficients (Pearson) for non-agricultural employment shares and labour market and development indicators for 14 Latin American countries, 1990–97 period averages

	1 Small firms	2 Self-employed	3 Domestic service	4 Large firms	5 Public sector	6 Civil liberties*	7 Political rights*	8 Unionization rate	9 FACB unweighted*	10 FACB weighted*	11 Employment protection index#	12 Job security index#	13 Manufacturing wage share	14 Manufacturing GDP per capita
1 Small firms	1.00													
2 Self-employed	−0.27	1.00												
3 Domestic service	0.46	−0.33	1.00											
4 Large firms	−0.42	−0.43	−0.24	1.00										
5 Public sector	−0.38	−0.21	−0.16	−0.23	1.00									
6 Civil liberties*	−0.21	−0.54	0.12	0.43	0.26	1.00								
7 Political rights*	−0.23	−0.38	−0.07	0.47	0.11	0.76	1.00							
8 Unionization rate	0.20	−0.12	0.24	−0.30	0.22	−0.13	0.08	1.00						
9 FACB unweighted*	−0.49	−0.50	−0.05	0.60	0.36	0.55	0.39	0.04	1.00					
10 FACB weighted*	−0.51	−0.44	−0.03	0.58	0.33	0.55	0.36	0.07	0.99	1.00				
11 Employment protection index#	−0.34	0.60	−0.76	−0.14	0.16	−0.25	−0.20	−0.44	−0.31	−0.30	1.00			
12 Job security index#	−0.26	0.74	−0.56	−0.17	−0.16	−0.17	−0.03	−0.34	−0.51	−0.46	0.80	1.00		
13 Manufacturing wage share	−0.28	−0.27	0.22	0.12	0.39	0.40	0.29	−0.09	0.08	0.05	−0.13	−0.21	1.00	
14 GDP per capita (PPP, current)	0.08	−0.57	0.15	0.27	0.18	0.22	0.26	0.57	0.36	0.31	−0.47	−0.53	0.18	1.00

Notes: * = indices range in value from 0 to 10, worst to best, respectively.

FACB = freedom of association/collective bargaining.

= higher index values mean greater employment protection and job security. Shaded areas indicate direct relevance to labour standards and informalization. In terms of two-tailed statistical significance, the critical values for 14 observations are 0.458, 0.532 and 0.661 for the 10, 5 and 1% levels, respectively; the critical values for 13 observations (regarding the employment protection index) are 0.476, 0.553 and 0.684 for the 10, 5 and 1% levels, respectively.

a priori reason to expect labour standards to affect employment in these sectors. Among our three employment categories of main interest, we would expect labour standards to have the most direct effect on formal employment in large firms, with less direct effects on informal employment in small firms and self-employment, largely a consequence of formal employment effects.

For employment shares in large firms and the civil liberties and political rights indices, there is a positive relationship, though statistically significant at the 10 per cent level only for the political rights index, indicating that countries with stronger rights by these measures tend to have higher shares of formal employment. A similar result holds for the FACB indices, with stronger positive and statistically significant correlations. These results suggest that stronger 'civic rights' are associated with more formal employment.

For employment shares in small firms and self-employment, we see a rough mirror image of the relationship between employment shares in large firms and our measures of 'civic rights'. That is, we see negative correlations with the civil liberties and political rights indices and the FACB indices, some of which are statistically significant. Regarding the civil liberties index, there is a statistically significant correlation with self-employment but not with employment in small firms.

For the employment protection and job security indices, the strongest relationships are with self-employment, with positive and statistically significant correlation coefficients of 0.60 and 0.74 respectively. These strong positive correlations are consistent with studies by Márquez and Pagés and Heckman and Pagés-Serra, who find a strong significantly positive cross-country relationship between these same measures and self-employment shares.[38]

The last row of Table 9.3 shows the relationship between our measures and GDP per capita. For employment shares, the most noteworthy result is for self-employment, for which there is a statistically significant negative correlation, showing that poorer countries tend to have higher shares of self-employment. On the flip side, there are weakly positive, statistically insignificant correlations for employment in large firms and the public sector, with the positive sign consistent with more formal employment in richer countries. All measures of 'civic rights' as well as manufacturing wage shares are positively correlated with GDP per capita, though generally insignificantly, with the positive signs suggesting that richer countries generally enjoy stronger rights by these measures. However, the two measures of 'security rights' are negatively correlated with per capita income, significantly so for the job security index, indicating weaker employment protection regulations in richer countries. As with correlations with employment shares, we see that 'civic rights' and 'security rights' have broadly opposite patterns.

Econometric results

We more fully explore the relationships between employment shares and those measures of labour standards for which time series are available, that is, the Freedom House indices and manufacturing wage shares, in econometric panel data models of specific categories of formal and informal employment. We first investigate these relationships by running panel data regressions for each of the five employment categories on the civil liberties index controlling for GDP per capita.[39] Though both Freedom House indices on civil liberties and political rights are available as time series, we use the former as it is more closely tied to freedom of association and collective bargaining rights and Portes' notion of 'civic rights'. We first address the trend relationship between civil liberties and employment shares by transforming the data as the Hodrick-Prescott trend of the variables. There are two reasons for this transformation. First, the civil liberties indices are highly volatile for these countries over the period. Second, we do not expect changes in civil liberties to have a direct immediate effect on employment shares, but to operate in a more roundabout manner, such as through increasing wage shares.[40] Given the transformation of the data, what we call trend regressions in the chapter are driven by cross-country variation. We include GDP per capita in the model to control for certain income-related aspects of 'civic rights', suggested by the positive correlation between GDP per capita and our 'civic rights' indicators.

Table 9.4 shows the results of pooled OLS regressions described above estimated in two model specifications, with and without time dummies. For small firms and self-employment, we find highly significant negative coefficient estimates on the civil liberties index in both model specifications. For large firms, we find the opposite, a highly significant positive coefficient estimate on the civil liberties index in both model specifications. This confirms the findings suggested by Table 9.3 that stronger civil liberties are associated with less informal employment and more formal employment, even while controlling for GDP per capita. For these three sectors of main interest, the sign and significance of the coefficient estimates on the civil liberties index is robust with respect to the exclusion of one country at a time from the sample (these and other results referred to but not shown are available from authors on request).[41] In domestic service employment regressions, not surprisingly, coefficient estimates on the civil liberties index are statistically insignificant for both model specifications. In public sector employment regressions, coefficient estimates on the civil liberties index are stably positive, but not consistently statistically significant with respect to excluding one country at a time from the sample.

We also test these regressions including six additional control variables, introduced into the regressions one at a time, addressing labour market tightness and structural aspects of the economy. These variables are the urban

Table 9.4 Trend regressions of employment shares on civil liberties indices and GDP per capita for 13 Latin American countries, 1990–97

Estimation method		Small firms	Self-employed	Domestic service	Large firms	Public sector
Pooled OLS	Civil liberties	−1.3026**	−1.8598**	0.0425	2.1994**	0.9195*
		(0.4044)	(0.3001)	(0.1120)	(0.4959)	(0.4409)
	GDP per capita	3.8520**	−7.8697**	0.6733*	2.5416*	0.8144
		(0.7012)	(0.8024)	(0.2655)	(1.1254)	(0.7767)
	Adj. R-squared	0.1809	0.5643	0.0271	0.2398	0.0342
Pooled OLS with time dummies	Civil liberties	−1.2297**	−1.7483**	0.0151	2.1981**	0.7645#
		(0.4274)	(0.3143)	(0.1140)	(0.5184)	(0.4379)
	GDP per capita	3.5436**	−8.3409**	0.7889**	2.5473*	1.4694*
		(0.6866)	(0.8165)	(0.2506)	(1.1811)	(0.6943)
	Adj. R-squared	0.1389	0.5584	−0.0186	0.1832	0.0267
Pooled 2SLS with political rights as an instrumental variable for civil liberties	Civil liberties	−0.5755	−1.9969**	0.1764	2.2124**	0.1807
		(0.3606)	(0.3333)	(0.1225)	(0.4484)	(0.4486)
	GDP per capita	3.4331**	−7.7907**	0.5961#	2.5341*	1.2400
		(0.9706)	(0.8974)	(0.3297)	(1.2071)	(1.2075)
	Adj. R-squared	0.1465	0.5636	0.0155	0.2398	0.0076
Pooled 2SLS with political rights as an instrumental variable for civil liberties with time dummies	Civil liberties	−0.5552	−1.9715**	0.1706	2.2121**	0.1412
		(0.3723)	(0.3394)	(0.1268)	(0.4693)	(0.4531)
	GDP per capita	3.1077**	−8.1967**	0.6884*	2.5383*	1.8722
		(1.0161)	(0.9263)	(0.3462)	(1.2810)	(1.2368)
	Adj. R-squared	0.1077	0.5563	−0.0352	0.1832	0.0067

Notes: #, * and ** indicate significance at 10, 5 and 1% levels, respectively.
White heteroskedasticity-consistent standard errors in parentheses.
Data are transformed as the Hodrick–Prescott trend of the variables.
Hodrick–Prescott trend is based on the years 1984–1997 and a smoothing parameter of 100.
GDP per capita is measured in PPP current international dollars in log form.
Paraguay is excluded from the sample for the sake of comparability with wage share results (see Tables 9.6 and 9.7); Including Paraguay in the sample does not substantively change results (results available from authors on request).

unemployment rate, the urban population as a percentage of total population, and value-added as a percentage of GDP for agriculture, industry, manufacturing and services. Introducing these variables does not substantively alter coefficient estimates on the civil liberties index, which remain significantly negative for small firms and self-employment and significantly positive for large firms.

The finding that stronger 'civic rights' are associated with lower levels of informal employment and higher levels of formal employment might be thought to result from reverse causality – particularly given that we define formal employment as employment in large firms. That is, 'civic rights' for workers might tend to be stronger in large firms because organizing costs are lower, given the spatial concentration of workers, and thus the collective power of workers might tend to be greater. Moreover, 'civic rights' for workers established by legislation are likely to be more easily monitored and enforced in large firms. One way in which we address the possibility of reverse causality is by re-evaluating the above relationships using the political rights index as an instrument for the civil liberties index in two-stage least squares regressions. The political rights index appears to be a suitable instrumental variable in that it is strongly correlated with the civil liberties index but does not address workers' right directly. These results are shown in the lower panel of Table 9.4. Results remain substantively the same for employment in large firms and self-employment, with a significantly positive coefficient estimate on the civil liberties index for the former and a significantly negative coefficient estimate for the latter. For employment in small firms, the coefficient estimates on the civil liberties index remain negative but fall in value by roughly half and are no longer statistically significant. Overall, estimation using instrumental variable methods does not yield substantive evidence that the positive relationship between 'civic rights' and formal employment results from reverse causality.

We also test the causality of 'civic rights' with respect to employment shares, by using the lagged instead of the contemporaneous civil liberties index. For this we do not use the civil liberties data transformed as the Hodrick–Prescott trend, since the smoothed series is computed on the basis of all observations, including contemporaneous values. Given the volatility of the raw civil liberties data, moreover, we do not include the lags of the indices as separate explanatory variables, but calculate the average value of the civil liberties index over the previous five years or ten years and lag this by one period with regard to the employment shares. We choose a period of at least five years because we expect that the impact of civil liberties on the structure of employment to be of a medium to long-run nature.

The results of these estimations are shown in Table 9.5. For self-employment and employment in large firms, the results do not differ substantially from those presented in Table 9.4. The estimated coefficient on lagged civil liberties is in fact significantly negative for self-employment and significantly positive for large firms, with both the five- and ten-year averages, with and without time dummies. For employment in small firms, the coefficient estimate on lagged civil liberties is negative, but lower in value and statistically significant only in the specification based on five-year averages. As for robustness with respect to excluding one country at a time from the sample, the coefficient on lagged civil liberties is consistently negative and significant for self-employment; consistently positive for large firms but statistically insignificant when Mexico is excluded from the sample; and consistently negative for small firms but statistically insignificant in two cases.[42] Overall, then, we find evidence that stronger civil liberties over the previous five or ten years are associated with less informal employment (particularly self-employment) and more formal employment (particularly employment in large firms), suggesting that this relationship may be causal.

Table 9.5 Regressions of employment shares on lagged civil liberties indices and GDP per capita for 13 Latin American countries, 1990–1997

Estimation method		Small firms	Self-employed	Domestic service	Large firms	Public sector
Pooled OLS	Civil liberties (lagged 5 year avg.)	−0.7077*	−1.3578**	−0.0047	1.3930**	0.6750
		(0.3210)	(0.3506)	(0.0952)	(0.4639)	(0.4389)
	GDP per capita	3.5804**	−8.0223**	0.7009**	2.8660*	0.8874
		(0.7386)	(0.8106)	(0.2536)	(1.2198)	(0.7878)
	Adjusted R-squared	0.1122	0.5214	0.0260	0.1515	0.0214
Pooled OLS with time dummies	Civil liberties (lagged 5 year avg.)	−0.6251#	−1.2415**	−0.0340	1.3845**	0.5145
		(0.3303)	(0.3629)	(0.0903)	(0.4969)	(0.4537)
	GDP per capita	3.2295**	−8.5165**	0.8248**	2.9037*	1.5680*
		(0.7156)	(0.8393)	(0.2391)	(1.3111)	(0.7442)
	Adjusted R-squared	0.0693	0.5132	−0.0178	0.0885	0.0139
Pooled OLS	Civil liberties (lagged 10 year avg.)	−0.3277	−1.0710*	−0.1755*	0.9937#	0.5774
		(0.2938)	(0.3933)	(0.0846)	(0.5459)	(0.4708)
	GDP per capita	3.2732**	−8.3801**	0.7896**	3.2882*	1.0417
		(0.7601)	(0.8297)	(0.2428)	(1.2747)	(0.8219)
	Adjusted R-squared	0.0783	0.4791	0.0481	0.0996	0.0110
Pooled OLS with time dummies	Civil liberties (lagged 10 year avg.)	−0.3214	−1.0627**	−0.1783*	0.9930#	0.5664
		(0.3045)	(0.3723)	(0.0813)	(0.5659)	(0.4674)
	GDP per capita	2.9193**	−8.9075**	0.8932**	3.4416*	1.6633*
		(0.7275)	(0.8292)	(0.2275)	(1.3427)	(0.7337)
	Adjusted R-squared	0.0433	0.4851	0.0057	0.0363	0.0152

Notes: #, * and** indicate significance at 10, 5 and 1% levels, respectively. White heteroskedasticity-consistent standard errors in parentheses. Employment shares and GDP per capita are transformed as the Hodrick–Prescott trend of the variables. Hodrick–Prescott trend is based on the years 1984–97 and a smoothing parameter of 100. GDP per capita is measured in PPP current international dollars in log form. Paraguay is excluded from the sample for the sake of comparability with wage share results (see Tables 9.6 and 9.7); Including Paraguay in the sample does not substantively change results (results available from authors on request).

Based on the same model specification, estimation methods and variable construction, Table 9.6 presents the results of trend regressions of employment shares on manufacturing wage shares and GDP per capita. Regressions for small firms and self-employment show a highly significant negative coefficient estimate on the wage share in both model specifications, analogous to the results for the civil liberties index. Regressions for large firms yield positive but not strongly significant coefficient estimates on the wage share in both model specifications. This is consistent with the results for the civil liberties index and is contrary to the expectation that higher manufacturing wage shares, a proxy for formal sector wage shares, have a negative impact on formal sector employment. Regressions for domestic service and public sector employment yield a highly significant positive coefficient on the wage share in both model specifications. Given that we had no *a priori* expectations about the effects of manufacturing wage shares on employment in domestic service and the public sector, these results are somewhat surprising. For all employment categories except employment in large firms, the sign and the statistical significance of these estimated coefficients are robust with respect to excluding one country at a time from the sample.

As with the regressions using the civil liberties index, we also test these wage share regressions introducing the same six control variables, one at a time. For employment in small firms, coefficient estimates on wage shares remain significantly negative at the 1 per cent level in all cases. For self-employment, coefficient estimates on wage shares remain negative but become statistically insignificant when controlling for the urbanization rate. For employment in large firms, coefficient estimates on wage shares remain positive but become statistically insignificant when controlling for the agricultural share of value-added or the urban unemployment rate.[43]

We also explore the relationship between employment shares and manufacturing wage shares by regressing the difference in employment shares on the log difference of manufacturing wage shares and GDP.[44] These regressions more directly address the shorter-run effects of higher wage shares – possibly resulting from strengthening worker rights in the formal sector – on formal and informal employment. The upper panel of Table 9.7 presents the results of these regressions estimated in two fixed effects model specifications, with and without time dummies. Fixed effects regressions with time dummies reflect variation over time within countries whereas fixed effects regressions without time dummies reflect overall variation over time (with neither of the two reflecting cross-country variation).[45]

The results are generally quite different from those obtained from the trend regressions described in Table 9.6. Regressions for small firms do not yield a statistically significant coefficient estimate on the wage share in any of the two model specifications, and regressions for self-employment now show a positive and significant coefficient on the wage share (the significance being stronger in the specification including time dummies). Regressions for large

Table 9.6 Trend regressions of employment shares on wage share and GDP per capita for 13 Latin American countries, 1990–97

Estimation method		Small firms	Self-employed	Domestic service	Large firms	Public sector
Pooled OLS	Wage share	−0.1223**	−0.1451**	0.0389**	0.0580#	0.1708**
		(0.0304)	(0.0386)	(0.0101)	(0.0331)	(0.0436)
	GDP per capita	3.4254**	−9.2971**	0.3553	4.5274**	1.0024
		(0.7759)	(0.9921)	(0.2204)	(1.3139)	(1.0080)
	Adj. R-squared	0.1586	0.5400	0.1065	0.0903	0.1198
Pooled OLS with time dummies	Wage share	−0.1235**	−0.1501**	0.0394**	0.0603#	0.1743**
		(0.0306)	(0.0377)	(0.0102)	(0.0343)	(0.0432)
	GDP per capita	3.0430**	−9.9589**	0.4758*	4.8327**	1.6185
		(0.7502)	(0.9825)	(0.2163)	(1.3718)	(0.9942)
	Adj. R-squared	0.1111	0.5467	0.0669	0.0222	0.0924

Notes: #, * and ** indicate significance at 10, 5 and 1% levels, respectively.
White heteroskedasticity-consistent standard errors in parentheses.
Data are transformed as the Hodrick–Prescott trend of the variables.
Hodrick–Prescott trend is based on the years 1984–97 and a smoothing parameter of 100.
GDP per capita is measured in PPP current international dollars in log form.
Paraguay is excluded from the sample due to data unavailability.

Table 9.7 Difference regressions of employment shares on wage share and GDP for 13 Latin American countries, 1990–97

Estimation method		Small firms	Self-employed	Domestic service	Large firms sector	Public
Fixed effects	Wage share	-0.0544	1.0368#	-0.3467*	-0.5845	-0.0092
		(0.6313)	(0.5667)	(0.1603)	(0.6760)	(0.4194)
	GDP	-7.1684	-20.9559**	1.4996	32.3597**	-5.9820
		(4.3273)	(6.0043)	(1.1570)	(6.4341)	(3.7859)
	Adj. R-squared	-0.1455	0.0225	0.0130	0.1462	0.0212
Fixed effects with time dummies	Wage share	-0.1281	2.4794**	-0.4245*	-1.7821*	-0.0959
		(0.7438)	(0.6435)	(0.1854)	(0.8301)	(0.5245)
	GDP	-7.3221	-21.9377**	1.7768	31.0928**	-3.9293
		(4.7382)	(5.5215)	(1.2509)	(6.8004)	(4.1236)
	Adj. R-squared	-0.1028	0.1902	0.0013	0.2142	0.0203
Fixed effects	Wage share (−1)	1.2062	-1.3447#	-0.1079	-0.0875	0.2624
		(0.7808)	(0.7506)	(0.1819)	(1.1380)	(0.5217)
	GDP (−1)	-3.5963	0.2363	-0.3656	7.0657	-3.1389
		(4.3170)	(4.1315)	(1.3789)	(7.0983)	(3.8562)
	Adj. R-squared	-0.1412	-0.1029	0.0159	-0.0787	0.0191
Fixed effects with time dummies	Wage share (−1)	1.1396	-1.4102*	-0.1710	-0.5251	0.8890#
		(0.7285)	(0.6805)	(0.1819)	(0.9675)	(0.4865)
	GDP (−1)	-5.4757	0.5092	0.4961	7.7849	-3.1716
		(4.9923)	(4.2953)	(1.3789)	(6.5699)	(3.4746)
	Adj. R-squared	-0.0534	-0.0235	-0.0116	0.0088	0.1099

Notes: #, * and ** indicate significance at 10, 5 and 1% levels, respectively. White heteroskedasticity-consistent standard errors in parentheses. Paraguay is excluded from the sample due to data unavailability. Based on differencing of employment share variables and log growth rates of wage share and GDP. GDP is measured in constant terms (yielding identical results based on local currency or US dollars). Controlling for inflation (GDP deflator) does not affect the statistical significance nor substantively change the magnitude of the above coefficient estimates.

firms, in turn, yield negative coefficient estimates on the wage share, though significant only in the model with time dummies. Regressions for domestic service and public sector employment yield negative coefficients on the wage share in both model specifications, significant only in the case of domestic service.

These results are consistent with the view that there might be a trade-off in the short run between formal wage shares and formal employment shares within countries, with self-employment increasing as the share of formal employment decreases. The statistical significance of these relationships is not, however, robust with respect to excluding one country at a time from the sample. For self-employment, the coefficient on the wage share is consistently positive, but becomes statistically insignificant when Ecuador is excluded from the sample. For large firms, the coefficient on the wage share is consistently negative, but becomes statistically insignificant in two cases and significant at only the 10 per cent level in three additional cases.

It might be the case that the results on contemporaneous changes in employment and wage shares derive to some extent from reverse causality. For instance, exogenous declines in large firm employment shares would be associated with higher wage shares if lower-paid workers are laid off first. Consequently, we evaluate the model with one-year lags on the independent variables in an attempt to better isolate causality from wage shares to employment shares, as shown in the lower panel of Table 9.7. We find that the positive statistical significance for self-employment and negative statistical significance for large firms is not robust when independent variables are lagged one year. For self-employment, in fact, the coefficient estimate on wage shares changes from positive to negative and is also significant in this opposite direction. This negative statistical significance is not robust, however, with respect to excluding one country at a time from the sample. For large firms, the coefficient estimate remains negative, but is no longer close to significant. Therefore, causality from wage shares to employment shares is not strongly supported by our findings.

9.5   Concluding remarks

This chapter addresses the relationship between 'civic rights' and formal sector wages, on the one hand, and formal and informal employment on the other hand. We explore this relationship using panel data for 14 Latin American countries in the 1990s. Our strongest result is that countries with stronger 'civic rights' have higher shares of formal employment and lower shares of informal employment, even accounting for GDP per capita and other control variables, addressing the possibility of reverse causality using instrumental variable methods, and using lagged indicators of 'civic rights'.

Wage results driven by variation over time within countries are somewhat in contrast to cross-country results but are not found to be statistically robust. In other words, we find evidence that countries can reach a long-run position of stronger 'civic rights' and more formal and less informal employment, but we cannot altogether exclude the possibility of short-run trade-offs, at least with respect to wages.

The introduction to this chapter presented two sets of competing hypotheses as to whether stronger 'civic rights' might lead to more or less informal employment through two causal channels – the first related to economic and social stability and the second related to formal employment wages. Regarding the first, the competing hypotheses differ as to whether stronger 'civic rights' lead to more or less economic and social stability, with Singh and Zammit suggesting less and Rodrik and Stiglitz suggesting more, with attendant macroeconomic implications for foreign and domestic investment, economic growth and the creation of formal employment.[46] Regarding the last, Singh and Zammit hypothesize a microeconomic channel in which stronger 'civic rights' lead to higher wages in formal employment, thereby reducing demand for formal employment and leading to increased informality. This microeconomic effect might be offset by higher wages increasing aggregate demand and thus contributing to the growth of formal employment.

Our main finding that countries with stronger 'civic rights' have higher shares of formal employment and lower shares of informal employment is consistent with the view that the positive developmental effects of stronger 'civic rights' offset the negative. The hypothesized mediating linkages (such as between 'civic rights' and economic and social stability) require, however, further empirical investigation and raise a number of conceptual issues as well. For instance, does the effect of stronger 'civic rights' on formal and informal employment depend on the pace at which these rights are introduced (as suggested by Singh and Zammit)? Given the political nature of 'civic rights', often associated in Latin America with a change from dictatorship to democracy, can countries generally choose the pace at which these rights are implemented?

Resolving these issues would involve investigation that is beyond the scope of this chapter. We therefore interpret our findings cautiously and suggest that an exogenous increase in 'civic rights' would not necessarily result in higher shares of formal employment. Rather, stronger 'civic rights' and higher shares of formal employment may represent different qualitative aspects of economic development for which the causal relationship is dynamic and complex. As such, policies aimed at increasing the share of formal employment may need to consider not only the strengthening of 'civic rights' but also other developmental considerations, particularly policies promoting economic growth and creating the conditions for employment growth in the formal sector.[47]

Notes

1   For their helpful comments, the authors would like to thank Ajit Ghose, Alejandro Portes, Ken Swinnerton and three anonymous referees.

2   ILO (1998) *Panorama Laboral* (Lima).

3   A. Portes (1989) 'Latin American Urbanization in the Years of the Crisis', *Latin American Research Review*, 24(3); A. Portes and R. Schauffler (1993) 'Competing Perspectives on the Latin American Informal Sector', *Population and Development Review*, 19(1); A. Portes (1994) 'When More Can Be Less: Labor Standards, Development, and the Informal Economy', in C.A. Rakowski (ed.), *Contrapunto: The Informal Sector Debate in Latin America* (Albany: State University of New York Press).

4   Portes (1989), op. cit., p. 25. Portes makes clear that, 'This kind of unemployment should not be equated with that endured by workers in advanced countries in view of the fact that Latin American workers have little or no recourse to government relief', ibid., p. 38.

5   O. de Oliveira and B. Roberts (1994) 'The Many Roles of the Informal Sector in Development: Evidence from Urban Labor Market Research, 1940–89', in C.A. Rakowski, op. cit.; W.F. Maloney (1997) 'Labor Market Structure in LDCs: Time Series Evidence on Competing Views', World Bank working paper; M. Carr and M.A. Chen (2001) 'Globalization and the Informal Economy: How Global Trade and Investment Impact on the Working Poor', WIEGO working paper, Women in Informal Employment Globalizing and Organizing.

6   Carr and Chen (2000); de Oliveira and Roberts (1994); J. Saavedra and A. Chong (1999) 'Structural Reform, Institutions, and Earnings: Evidence from the Formal and Informal Sectors in Urban Peru', *The Journal of Development Studies*, 35(4).

7   World Bank (1995) *Labor and Economic Reforms in Latin American and the Caribbean* (Washington, DC: The World Bank), p. 6.

8   Portes (1994).

9   Ibid., p. 125. Portes' hypothesis regarding 'security rights' was formulated in a particular macroeconomic context, during which there were more formal sector firms that could have been benefited from greater flexibility in employment protection regulations. The newer macroeconomic context is characterized by declining public sector employment and by export-oriented development strategies involving firms operating in export-processing zones. In this context, greater flexibility in employment protection regulation may mainly benefit firms in export-processing zones, which may create poor quality jobs such that workers prefer to remain informal. Portes, personal correspondence, 2002.

10 A. Singh and A. Zammit (2000) *The Global Labour Standards Controversy: Critical Issues for Developing Countries* (Geneva: South Centre).

11 Ibid., pp. 32–3.

12 J. Stiglitz (2002) 'Participation and Development: Perspectives for the Comprehensive Development Paradigm', *Review of Development Economics*, 6(2).

13 Ibid., p. 175, emphasis added.

14 Ibid., p. 166.

15 Ibid., p. 171.

16 D. Rodrik (1997) *Democracy and Economic Performance* (Cambridge, MA: Harvard University Press).

17 Ibid., p. 15.

18 Singh and Zammit describe the relationship between economic growth and formal employment as follows: 'Employment in the formal sector increases until a very

high level of per capita income is reached. At that point, the share of employment in industry declines and that of services, particularly informal services (informal in the sense that many labour laws become difficult to apply due to the small size of the enterprise), begins to rise' (Singh and Zammit, op. cit., pp. 31–2). Regarding the relationship between FACB rights and conflict, perhaps also relevant are the findings of several studies providing evidence that greater coordination in collective bargaining is associated with less strike activity (summarized in T. Aidt and Z. Tzannatos (2002) *Unions and Collective Bargaining: Economic Effects in a Global Environment* (Washington, DC: The World Bank)). Interpreting the findings of these studies, Aidt and Tzannatos write: 'This suggests that a coordinated bargaining system can produce social peace because it either helps to institutionalize a distributional norm or improves the flow of information and thereby reduces the risk that a strike would occur because of the workers' misconception about the firm's profitability' (Aidt and Tzannatos, op. cit., p. 116).

19 G. Bertola (1990) 'Job Security, Employment and Wages', *European Economic Review*, 34(4).

20 J. Saavedra and M. Torero (2000) 'Labor Market Reforms and their Impact on Formal Labor Demand and Job Market Turnover: The Case of Peru', Inter-American Development Bank Research Network working paper, R-394. Based on firm-level surveys conducted bimonthly (quarterly since 1996) in Lima. Data refer to a pseudo-panel of about 500 private non-agricultural formal firms employing more than nine workers, pooled into eleven industrial sectors. Output is defined at the sectoral level. Estimates include sector fixed effects and therefore pick up solely within sector variation. The period evaluated is 1987 to 1997.

21 See A. Kugler (2000) 'The Impact of Firing Costs on Turnover and Unemployment: Evidence from the Columbian Labour Market Reform', Inter-American Development Bank Research Network working paper, R-393 for Colombia; H. Hopenhayn (2001) 'Labor Market Policies and Employment Duration: The Effects of Labor Market Reform in Argentina', Inter-American Development Bank Research Network working paper, R-407 for Argentina; R. Paes de Barros and C.H. Corseuil, (2001) 'The Impact of Regulations on Brazilian Labor Market Performance', Inter-American Development Bank Research Network working paper, R-427 for Brazil (on the *increase* in job security beginning in 1988); J. Saavedra and M. Torero (2000) 'Labor Market Reforms and Their Impact on Formal Labor Demand and Job Market Turnover: The Case of Peru', Inter-American Development Bank Research Network working paper, R-394 for Peru and G. Márquez and C. Pagés (1998) 'Ties that Bind: Employment Protection and Labor Market Outcomes in Latin America', Inter-American Development Bank working paper, 373, for a multi-country study on Latin American and OECD countries.

22 Márquez and Pagés (1998).

23 J. Heckman and C. Pagés-Serra (2000) 'The Cost of Job Security Regulation: Evidence from Latin American Labor Markets', *Economia*, 1(1).

24 Kugler (2000).

25 F. Carneiro and A. Henley (1998) 'Wage Determination in Brazil: The Growth of Union Bargaining Power and Informal Employment', *The Journal of Development Studies*, 34(4). Carneiro and Henley's view of the relationship between the centralization of collective bargaining and macroeconomic outcomes builds on the work of Calmfors and Driffill (1988) 'Bargaining Structure, Corporatism and Macroeconomic Performance', *Economic Policy*, 6, who argue that collective bargaining at intermediate levels (such as at the sectoral level as developed in Brazil) is likely

to lead to more negative macroeconomic outcomes than either highly centralized collective bargaining (such as at the national level) or highly decentralized collective bargaining (such as at the firm level). This is argued by Calmfors and Driffill to result from trade unions understanding their considerable bargaining power in highly centralized collective bargaining and moderating their positions accordingly; from trade unions not having significant bargaining power in highly decentralized collective bargaining; and from trade unions having significant bargaining power at intermediate levels but tending to ignore the macroeconomic implications of their positions.

26 Carneiro and Henley (1998), p. 136.
27 D. Marcouiller, V. Ruiz de Castilla and C. Woodruff (1997) 'Formal Measures of the Informal-sector Wage Gap in Mexico, El Salvador, and Peru', *Economic Development and Cultural Change*, 45(2); Saavedra and Chong (1999).
28 The authors maintain that while there is a counter-cyclical movement of the shares of informal employment based on a 'legal' definition of informality (determined, for example, on whether the work has a written contract and is entitled to social security benefits), there is no such movement based on a 'traditional' definition of informality (largely determined by firm size). However, with the exception of the change from 1990 to 1991, year-to-year changes in the shares of informal employment based on either definition always move in the same direction.
29 X. Gong and A. van Soest (2002) 'Wage Differentials and Mobility in the Urban Labour Market: A Panel Data Analysis for Mexico', *Labour Economics*, 9(4).
30 ILO (1998) *Panorama Laboral* (Lima).
31 R. Frisoni and M. Kongolo (2002) 'The Evolution of Labour Law in Latin America since the 1980s', International Institute for Labour Studies (background document).
32 Heckman and Pagés-Serra (2000).
33 This general pattern is also observed in the Freedom House civil liberties indices, which are described below.
34 Freedom House (1999) *Freedom in the World: The Annual Survey of Political Rights and Civil Liberties 1998–99* (New York: Freedom House), p. 548.
35 These evaluation criteria are based on the Freedom of Association and Protection of the Right to Organise Convention, 1948 (No. 87), and the Right to Organise and Collective Bargaining Convention, 1949 (No. 98), and related ILO jurisprudence, as well as problems noted in textual sources. The measures are constructed in unweighted (that is, equally weighted) and weighted form, scaled from 0 to 10, with 0 indicating the worst possible score (most violations observed) and 10 indicating the best possible score (least violations observed). For the weighted measures, each of the evaluation criteria is assigned a weight of 1, 1.25, 1.5, 1.75 or 2, with greater weights indicating what are judged to be more severe problems. The construction of these measures is described more fully elsewhere. See D. Kucera (2001) 'The Effects of Core Worker Rights on Labour Costs and Foreign Direct Investment: Evaluating the "Conventional Wisdom"', International Institute for Labour Studies Decent Work research programme working paper, p. 130.
36 Márquez and Pagés (1998) and Heckman and Pagés-Serra (2000).
37 Carneiro and Henley (1998).
38 Márquez and Pagés, op. cit., and Heckman and Pagés-Serra (2000).
39 Since employment shares sum to 100, a system of equations might yield more precise estimates. For example, one could use the SUR/Parks estimation method.

However, this requires a larger number of years than cross-sections, a condition which our data do not satisfy. Therefore throughout this chapter we run separate regressions for each employment share.

40 A result found in D. Rodrik (1999) 'Democracies Pay Higher Wages', *The Quarterly Journal of Economics*, 114(3).

41 Coefficient estimates on the civil liberties index are also robust to the inclusion in the sample of Paraguay, which was excluded from the benchmark sample of 13 countries for the sake of comparability with results in Table 9.6, given that wage share data are unavailable for Paraguay.

42 Results refer to the specification using the five-year average value of the civil liberties index.

43 There is also the possibility of reverse causality in the above trend regressions regarding wage shares. This is suggested by Carneiro and Henley (1998), who argue that that having a larger share of informal employment weakens the bargaining power of workers in the formal sector, leading to lower wages for formal employment. Our results do not allow us to exclude this possibility, and therefore this remains a possible interpretation. We do not further explore this possibility, however, because trend regressions for wage shares are not robust for two of our three employment categories of main interest, the exception being employment in small firms.

44 We do not explore the shorter-run relationships between employment shares and the civil liberties index because, as explained above, we do not expect changes in civil liberties to have an immediate effect on employment shares.

45 We use fixed effects rather than random effects for two reasons. First, our country sample is drawn exclusively from Latin America and is thus not randomly chosen from a larger population. Second, random effects models evaluate both cross-country and within-country variation and we are interested in addressing these types of variation separately.

46 Singh and Zammit (2000), Rodrik (1999); Stiglitz (2002).

47 Data sources:
Civil liberties and political rights indices: Freedom House, www.freedomhouse.org
Employment protection index: Márquez and Pagés (1998).
Employment shares: ILO (1998).
Job security index: Heckman and Pagés-Serra (2000).
Manufacturing wage share (wages relative to value added): UNIDO (2001) *UNIDO Industrial Statistics Database* (Vienna).
Unionization rate: ILO (1997) *World Labour Report, 1997–98* (Geneva).
Urban unemployment rate: ILO (2000) *Panorama Laboral* (Lima).
All other data: World Bank (2001) *World Development Indicators* (Washington, DC).

10
Legal Determinants of Labour Informality

José Luis Daza Pérez

10.1 Introduction

Evidence that a large part of the working population in developing countries works outside the parameters established by labour and fiscal laws, and that part of the services and goods produced in industrialized countries are produced clandestinely, has made the informal economy the focus of attention of economic and labour policies. Although the informal economy is of universal concern, the definitions used, the perception of the phenomenon, its consequences and the solutions proposed to remedy its associated problems are not the same in all parts of the world. Furthermore, a great difference can be seen between the perception and treatment of informality in developing countries and that in the highly industrialized countries.

A number of arguments have been advanced to account for the existence of informality. There is the view that informality results from over-regulation of labour markets, or regulations that may be appropriate for industrialized countries but are excessive in the case of developing countries. Judith Tendler argues that informality can be caused by an implicit 'devil's deal' between politicians and their constituents in small enterprises, in which votes are effectively exchanged for the non-enforcement of regulations.[1] Then there is Hernando De Soto's well-known argument that informality is created by excessive government regulation of the ownership of private property in developing countries.[2]

The questions surrounding the informal economy can be addressed from many points of view. Demands for rights for informal workers are increasing and the human dimension to informality is emerging, forcing us to think about the conditions of work, including social coverage, of those engaged in informal activities. Other aspects of informality are also important, such as taxation, property rights, credit, the exchange of goods, occupational safety and health, to name but a few. Our focus in this chapter is on the labour aspects of informality, including social protection coverage.

For the International Labour Organization, addressing the issue of informality is intended to improve the working conditions of people worldwide, thus promoting opportunities of decent work for all.[3] This chapter endeavours to contribute to the establishment of a concept of informal work from a legal point of view, differentiating the informal activities from the formal ones, as well as the different categories of workers and companies that, according to the national legislations, can be in one or another situation. This exercise is undertaken because in order to 'eliminate' informality or 'formalize the informal', policy-makers must understand the legal mechanisms available, as well as what aspects of informality they are addressing. This chapter considers whether sizeable numbers of workers are indeed excluded from formal legal protection, as is often thought, as well as the attitude of the state to informality. The main point of the chapter is to argue that informality is primarily due to the lack of enforcement of existing legislation, rather than the exclusion of workers from protection under the law. The main policy solution lies, therefore, in enforcing existing laws rather than extending their scope, as well as better understanding why states may not enforce existing laws with the aim of improving enforcement.

10.2 Concepts and definitions on informality at work

There has been much debate about the concepts and definitions of informality.[4] The concept of informality first originated in a 1972 ILO study entitled *Employment, Income and Equality: A Strategy for Increasing Productive Employment in Kenya*, where the expression 'informal sector' was used to describe the activities of poor workers who were not recognized, recorded, protected or regulated by public authorities. The opposite of informal sector was the 'modern sector of the economy'. Though, like informal sector, this term was also highly ambiguous, with both definitions confusing legal and economic concepts.

Nevertheless, the recognition that an 'informal sector' existed within developing countries led to widespread use of the term, both in ILO documents and also in academic and policy circles outside the ILO. The first attempt to describe the informal sector in international standards can be found in the Employment Policy (Supplementary Provisions) Recommendation, 1984 (No. 169), which refers to the informal sector in terms of 'economic activities which are carried on outside the institutionalised economic structures'.[5] If the formal sector is understood as comprising registered enterprises operating within the law, and thus subject to the control of public administration, then informality can be interpreted, for example, as those activities that do not appear in administrative registries.

The concern to measure the phenomenon of informality led to the adoption of an international definition of the informal sector for statistical purposes at the 15th International Conference of Labour Statisticians in 1993. On that occasion, the informal sector was defined in terms of the characteristics of the 'units of production' (enterprises) in which the activities took place, rather than in terms of the characteristics of the persons concerned or their work. The definition for statistical purposes of the concept of 'enterprises of informal workers' introduced the size of enterprise, measured by the number of workers, as one of the criteria for defining informality. The practical result in many developing countries was that frequently, without taking other criteria into account, the broadest concept of informality focused on the size of enterprise, sometimes combined with the volume of business in monetary terms, but not the scope of the legislation concerning them.

While it is true that in some countries some laws exist, especially on safety and health at work, which do not include small enterprises in their scope (the so-called Factory Acts in common law countries), in the majority of countries there are no exclusions based on size. Nevertheless, in many developing countries 'small' gradually became synonymous in practice with 'informal' when speaking of enterprises and work. This was problematic, as some small enterprises were registered and their workers made regular contributions into the social security system, whereas others were not registered and their workers did not benefit from social security coverage and were thus operating illegally. Also, in the few cases where the enterprise was exempt from the law, there was no incidence of illegality, but the workers might not benefit from social security coverage. All three distinctions had different policy implications, thus the categorization of lumping small enterprises as 'informal' was not particularly useful and often led to much confusion. Moreover, taking into account that the majority of employment in developing countries occurs in various forms of self-employment, in family businesses and in small-scale economic units that are not incorporated (that is not constituted as limited liability companies), usually included in the category of micro and small enterprises, it is no wonder that when employment is quantified, the percentages involved reflect the predominance of the informal over the formal.

At its 90th Session in 2002, the International Labour Conference (ILC) addressed the theme of the informal economy, including the difficulties with its definition, and adopted a resolution on decent work and the informal economy. It stated that:

> the term 'informal economy' refers to all economic activities by workers and economic units that are – in law or in practice – not covered or insufficiently covered by formal arrangements. Their activities are not included in the law, which means that they are operating outside the formal reach of the law; or they are not covered in practice, which means that – although they are operating within the formal reach of the law,

the law is not applied or not enforced; or the law discourages compliance because it is inappropriate, burdensome, or imposes excessive costs.

The resolution also stated that informality was primarily a matter of governance and considered that the difficulty of reducing the decent work deficit is much greater when the work performed is outside the limits of the coverage or scope of the legal and institutional framework. It also emphasized that, 'given that workers and enterprises in the informal economy are often not recognized, regulated or protected by law, a national legal and institutional framework becomes crucial'.

The 2002 ILC resolution considered that the term 'informal economy' was preferable to the term 'informal sector' because the workers and enterprises in question did not fall within any one sector of economic activity, but cut across many sectors. Since then, in the ILO context, the use of 'informal sector' has been systematically replaced by 'informal economy'.[6]

It is essential to understand what formality and informality mean in a practical sense, both for the purposes of labour administration and for the ILO's social partners. In almost all countries, 'formal' means that which conforms to the rules and 'formality' refers to conduct aimed at compliance with the rules or a state of being in compliance with the rules. 'Formalities' usually means the set of procedures and documents which clothe the situation in legality. Their opposites 'informal' and 'informality' would be, respectively: that which does not conform to the rules and an attitude of non-compliance with the rules or a state of not being in compliance with the rules. In practice, however, in some countries, all self-employed workers and micro enterprises, and even small enterprises whose owners are natural persons,[7] are subsumed in the concept of the informal economy or informal sector.

Efforts to define the informal sector in legal terms have been rare. Nonetheless, when it comes to persons engaged in informal work, there are frequent references to obligations or rights, emphasizing the abundance and economic burden of the former and the difficulties involved in implementing the latter. Despite the lack of definition, the term informal sector is found in some legal texts, especially in Africa and Asia, taking their meaning as read.

The concept of informal economy as accepted by the ILC in 2002 needs to be analysed in depth in order to arrive at a practical concept of 'informal work' that might serve as a reference for the activity of the labour administration, as well as for initiatives by the social partners. Not all of the formalities which enterprises are obliged to observe are labour related and not all of the rights claimed by workers in the informal economy refer to labour rights or aspects of social protection. Thus, for example, the typical claim made over the right to occupy urban spaces for street trading that is made to municipal authorities, although essential for exercising an economic activity, does not have a labour law dimension.

If the obligations imposed by laws and compliance with obligations are the essence of formality, informality can only be expressed in a negative way, that is 'not being' or 'not doing'. Two situations of informality can be distinguished:

1. Activities of persons and enterprises that are not covered by the law which means that they operate outside it. There are no obligations to fulfil or rights to be satisfied or claimed.
2. Activities of persons and enterprises where the applicable law is not enforced (i.e. the law is not applied in practice). Obligations are not fulfilled and rights are not recognized.

The difference between these two situations is fundamental. In the first case, informality stems from the lack of a formal reference: there is no applicable law, thus it is not subject to rights or obligations. Thus, for example, a self-employed worker cannot make a claim to earn the minimum wage, as this worker does not have an employer. In the second case, informality stems from not complying with formal requirements; there are applicable labour laws but they are wholly or partially unenforced.

How do these different situations arise? In the first case, when there is no law applicable to a situation, the cause lies in the absence of legal provision for that situation or express legal exclusion. In this situation, one can genuinely speak of informality. The cause, which leads to the second situation, non-compliance, may be ignorance, because the very existence or content of the laws is not known. It may be the will of persons, deliberate behaviour to evade costs, without discounting the fact, recognized by the ILC in 2002, that sometimes the law itself discourages compliance because it is inappropriate, cumbersome and excessively costly. In this situation, one can speak of illegality. As for example, when an employer does not declare some or all of the staff, despite the legal obligation to do so, thus infringing social security laws.

We could establish a third, intermediate category, for those situations insufficiently covered by regulations, although there may be problems of identification. This category could arise, for example, where there are regulations on conditions of work, but not social security or vice versa. The situation of casual workers in some countries, whereby they are included in the labour regulation concerning application of the minimum wage and working hours, but they are excluded from social security, is a typical example of the weak development of social security institutions and is usually associated with the presumption or evidence of the lack of capacity of the worker to contribute to the system. Other situations that could be included in this grey zone are those workers that are not covered by labour laws, but who have the option of voluntarily joining the social security system by making periodic contributions.

10.3 The legal framework of labour: the reality of the scope of labour law regarding inclusions, exclusions and exemptions

In many documents and debates on informal work, it is commonly stated that labour legislation does not apply to the informal economy or that the legislation does not apply to informal enterprises. This assertion, which may be true in some cases, depends both on what is meant by informal economy or informal enterprises and what is meant by the application of labour legislation.

In the informal economy we find both independent and dependent workers (employees or waged workers who work in the informal economy), and the enterprise owners themselves. To analyse the situation of these persons, one must take into account whether they are dependent or independent workers, as different laws apply to each category. For example, workers' protection has mainly been centred on the universal notion of the employment relationship, based on a distinction between dependent and independent workers, also known as own-account or self-employed workers.[8] This is relevant precisely because the majority of the countries have no labour laws for independent workers.

In order to determine to which persons or enterprises the provisions of labour legislation apply, it is necessary to analyse the scope of states' labour legislation. The notion of labour laws should be used in a broad sense, including labour codes or general labour laws, social security laws, laws that govern contracts of employment, employment, small enterprises and occupational safety and health.

In general, labour laws contain clauses that describe their scope. These clauses specify inclusions and exclusions; that is, to whom they apply and to whom they do not apply. In some countries, they only indicate inclusions generically, but exclusions may appear throughout in specific articles. In other countries, only exclusions are indicated. On a few occasions, they are silent as to the scope, in which case it may be necessary to refer to each country's system of interpretation of laws to infer to which persons they apply. In the majority of *common law* countries, the substantive content of the law is preceded by a series of definitions, to which reference must be made to obtain a precise idea of the scope. These definitions can extend to terms such as enterprise, entrepreneur, establishment, worker, contract of employment, subcontractor, domestic work, and home work.

Relationships included in the scope of labour laws

In the majority of countries, all employment situations are included in the scope of labour laws, that is those featuring an employer and an employee. From that starting point, explicit exclusions come into play, as well as those that are implicit, under another separate law, whether or not containing specific provisions. As regards exclusions, there is a whole series of employment relationships which may be excluded from the scope of a general labour law, but which are regulated by a law with similar content, giving them special treatment.

Normally the scope refers to the subjects of the employment relationship – that is including employers, workers or both. The figure of the employer takes various forms, such as entrepreneur or boss, and, frequently, enterprise or establishment. Numerous cases are also found in which inclusion refers to relations between parties to an employment relationship.

Sometimes, the scope of a law is defined by the scope of others. There is no shortage of cases where it is stated that there may be special regulations.

Relationships excluded from the scope of labour laws

Exclusions are also made by reference to the parties and their characteristics, their relationships (or absence of a relationship) or to sectors of the economy. However, some categories of workers excluded from the scope of general labour law have their conditions of work regulated by other labour or administrative legislation. What follows is an attempt to classify true exclusions, which are found in almost all legislations, and exclusions from a general law regulated by a specific law, of which some are very frequent, others frequent only in certain regions and others less frequent.

The first set of exclusions is general exclusions, exclusions that are justified by the absence of one or more of the contractual elements in the employment relationship.

Autonomous work

Normally excluded from the scope of labour laws is autonomous work, that is autonomous or independent (also designated as self-employed workers, own-account workers, and so on) since in these cases no employment relationship of any kind exists. However, in the legislation of industrialized countries, a number of provisions on occupational safety and health also affect this class of workers.

Family work

Members of the family of the entrepreneur or the owner of the business are generally excluded, since it is considered that even though there is a dependent relationship, it is not contractual. The way in which this exclusion is expressed may vary, from the most generic provision to a list of the degrees of parentage covered. In many cases, as well as the family tie, there is a requirement of living in the same household and the absence of a wage.

Cooperatives

Normally excluded are members of producer cooperatives, since there is no dependent relationship, reference being made to the specific regulations on cooperative societies. In some countries, labour legislation is declared applicable on a subsidiary basis to cooperatives.

Religious work

In certain countries, persons exercising an activity of a religious character are excluded, identifying them by their inclusion in the organization of a particular faith or church and the function exercised (Germany, Denmark, Estonia, Finland and Switzerland).

Voluntary work

In several countries, voluntary or charitable work is expressly excluded, as is work on a friendly or good neighbour basis performed on a casual and unpaid basis.

The second set of exclusions is relatively frequent. In these cases, despite the existence of contractual elements, some countries have chosen to exclude them from the scope of labour legislation. Many more countries, however, instead of excluding them, have given them special treatment with exceptions to the application of certain rules. In one group, special consideration is paid to the place where the work is carried out, whether at the worker's home (home work) or the employer's family home (domestic service, 'au pair' work). Another group primarily concerns work referred to as precarious work (part-time, temporary or casual work use to be considered as non-standard or precarious work in many countries). Finally, in a separate group, exclusions are found based on the size of the enterprise.

Exclusions based on the place of work

- Although home work[9] is almost always included in the scope of labour laws, a number of countries exclude it. Several European countries have excluded home work from the scope of their labour codes (Latvia, Lithuania and Switzerland) or from some labour laws (Belgium and Luxembourg – working hours). Nevertheless, other countries have recently included home work in their labour laws. For example, the new Labour Code of 2004 in Morocco includes homework and qualifies its interpretation, with the aim of avoiding the situation whereby homeworkers are treated as independent contractors. Regarding telework, which can be regarded as a variant of home work, no legal definitions for labour purposes or express exclusions from the scope of general labour legislation have been found.
- Domestic service is normally the subject of special treatment in the majority of countries, falling only partly within the scope of labour law or a special regulation. There are also many countries which have left this activity totally unregulated.[10]

Precarious work

- Some countries exclude casual workers (Zambia) or short-term temporary contracts (Bahrain and Kuwait) from the scope of their labour laws.[11] The problem that arises with these situations is that they are not always defined, nor defined with sufficient precision. Moreover, in many legislations, temporary contracts are not required to be in writing when their duration is less than a given period.
- The term part-time worker, according to the Part-Time Work Convention, 1994 (No. 175), means an employed person whose normal hours of work are less than those of comparable full-time workers. Some countries (Austria, Denmark, Germany) exclude part-time workers whose income and length of work are less than determined minimum limits from the scope of social security schemes (except for work-related accidents). In these cases, it is also usual to exclude them from the scope of protective measures relating to termination of the employment relationship, paid annual holidays and paid public holidays, maternity protection and sick leave.

Exclusions based on size of enterprise

Although in many developing countries there is a widespread view that labour law does not apply to micro enterprises and small enterprises, in fact, in only a very small number of legislations are enterprises outside the scope of the general regulations. Exclusions of this type are very rare in labour codes and labour laws. Only 10 per cent of the 178 ILO member States have legislated such exclusions. Furthermore, some of these exclusions only affect enterprises in certain sectors, such as agriculture (as is the case in Costa Rica and Honduras).

Somewhat more frequent are exclusions of micro and small enterprises from the scope of legislation on occupational safety and health, especially in countries where such legislation is laid down for industrial establishments. The majority of exclusions occur in African and Asian countries which followed the Factory Acts model, and it is almost impossible to find such exclusions in other regions of the world.

With respect to social security, exclusions from the scope of social security laws can be found in a number of developing countries, at least for certain contingencies, concerning enterprises of up to 5, 10 or 20 workers. The exclusions are found in less than 10 per cent of the countries.[12]

Artisans

The category of artisan (producers of handicrafts or traditional goods) appears in some legislations, usually referring to the self-employed and owners of micro and small enterprises, with full or partial exemption from labour legislation or subject to special regulations. By extension, the artisanal workshop can receive the same treatment as is given to micro and small enterprises.

Legally regulated employment classified as being something other than work

'Au pair' placement. This type of relationship is regulated in many European States along the lines of the European Agreement (Council of Europe) of 24 November 1969. The Agreement considers that this type of placement does not imply an employment relationship and defines it as 'the temporary reception by families, in exchange for certain services, of young foreigners who come to improve their linguistic and possibly professional knowledge as well as their general culture by acquiring a better knowledge of the country where they are received'.

Unpaid work experience in enterprises (for example, internships, apprenticeships)

This type of activity, where those involved are usually young students, is considered part of their education and may, to some extent, be covered through legislation on education or vocational training. To facilitate its acceptance in enterprises, the relationship has been deprived of its work character and responsibilities normally remain with educational establishments.[13] However, apprenticeship contracts are normally regulated as a contract having the nature of work, with special characteristics (qualities of the employer, formalities, teaching a job, lower wages, defined duration, and so on).

The third set of exclusions is exclusions from general labour laws which do not imply a lack of protection, since there is a special regulatory framework.

State employees

In the majority of countries, the following categories of workers whose employer is the State are explicitly excluded from the scope of labour laws: members of the armed forces and police; civil servants; and judges. As this exclusion is made because such workers are included in the scope of other laws which govern their conditions of work, normally of an administrative character, it is obvious that they could in no way be regarded as informal. Furthermore, in some developing countries these workers, together with those in state corporations and large private firms, are almost the only ones considered as formal workers.

Sectoral exclusions

In some labour codes and laws, whole economic sectors or parts of sectors are excluded from the scope. The most common exclusion is agriculture, in totality or in part, as well as maritime work and, sometimes, air transport. This exclusion in many cases does not mean a total absence of regulation, since the exclusion is frequently followed by reference to another regulatory act, at least with respect to certain maritime activities and air transport.

It is fairly common to find countries in which some agricultural workers in cross-cutting occupations (such as mechanics or managers) or certain types of agricultural or livestock production fall within the scope of labour law, while manual workers are excluded. In some cases, the scope of labour standards can be extended by regulatory act to certain categories of agricultural workers and to certain agricultural enterprises.

Sometimes labour provisions can be found in laws that seek to cover many aspects of a particular economic sector. Thus, the situation of workers in those sectors may be protected in another equivalent way; equally, they may not be protected. In any case, it can be seen that when the agricultural sector has its own separate regulations, the level of protection is lower.

Exemptions and exceptions in the application of legal concepts

In numerous countries, labour laws have set up exemptions or exceptions for several standards, while other laws that proclaim to be of universal application have allowed the Ministries of Labour to establish exemptions or exceptions. These refer either to enterprises or workers.

Most countries do not exclude small and medium-sized enterprises from the application of labour law; however, many labour laws and regulations have set up exceptions or exemptions from a number of precepts for those categories of enterprises. The areas in which the exceptions and exemptions can be observed are very varied but refer mainly to conditions of work and labour relations. In several legislations, exemptions refer to obligations on registration of employers, declaration of establishment, recruitment, documentation and reporting. Exceptions are usually related to representation of personnel and consultation. However, one can consider that, instead of exceptions, in some cases there is in reality special treatment of a situation, replacing one obligation for another which is supposed to have a similar, but not always equivalent effect. In several countries, for example, the costs related to the dismissal or severance pay are fewer for micro, small and medium-sized enterprises than those established for the largest.

In spite of these generalized exemptions, the situation of workers in small enterprises cannot always have the consideration of being short of protection. Moreover, exemptions should be (and are usually) thought of as the adaptation of an ideal legal framework of labour to the possibilities of enterprises with weak administrative structure and low level of investment, both inherent to their size.

10.4   Attitude of states towards informality

The legal framework of labour legislation and social security determines the obligations, mandated by the state, which employers and their dependent workers as well as the self-employed, have. At the same time this legal framework recognizes a series of rights that shall be guaranteed by the state through its labour administration services, such as the minimum wage and safety and health regulations. The state may also manage, sometimes through autonomous agencies, social security benefits. Yet in order for workers to benefit from this system, their employers must have complied with the obligation to register them and to make regular payments on their behalf and on the behalf of their workers.

The recognition of a right or the imposition of an obligation can only be done with respect to natural persons or legal entities, such that in order to carry out its mission, the labour administration must know the identity, location and activities of the firm, as well as the identity of the workers who carry out their activities for the firm or on their own account. The daily working of the labour administration depends, to a large extent, on the accuracy of its information, in census or registries, obtained as a result of declarations or applications. Without the maintenance of this information, its accuracy is compromised. It is thus the act of declaration that brings about formality, regardless of whether there is an extension in the scope of coverage of labour law or a greater presumption regarding the existence of an employment relationship.

The differing visions on informality from region to region around the world determine different attitudes on the part of the public authorities. In countries where informality is regarded as a breach of the rules of the market, the attitude of public administrations has tended to be to try and enforce the law. State resources, including public awareness campaigns, persuasion and repression, have been set in motion to regularize situations that do not comply with the law.

In general, efforts to enforce existing legislation in developing countries have been scant. Governments have been overwhelmed by the growth of informality and have not seen the need to adopt firm or repressive measures, especially when the administrative control mechanisms have traditionally been ineffective. The cost of legality is considered too high, particularly by small business owners who in many cases do not abide by the obligation to declare their establishment, or the contracting of labour or the registration of their staff in the social security system, and, in consequence, do not pay social security contributions or taxes. Inspection services are often poorly organized and suffer from a chronic lack of resources, both in staff and materials, which limit them from the frequency needed to ensure the application of laws.

Nevertheless in some countries, such as Argentina, a variety of programmes have been put forward since 2000 to regularize non-registered work in response to the dramatic increase in the number of uncovered workers during the 1990s. Through its programmes the national government seeks to combat the non-registration of work, ensure conditions of work that guarantee respect for fundamental rights at work and the entitled social protection, and incorporate excluded workers into the social security system. Through the collaboration of different government agencies and under the guidance of the Ministry of Labour, Employment and Social Security, the government hopes to achieve better efficiency in the detection and rectification of non-compliance with labour and social security laws. The programme also includes measures to raise awareness of the problems associated with non-registration of employment and the benefits of having regulated contracts so that employers voluntarily correct their situation.

Treating informal activities as a means of subsistence and inadequate regulation of the labour market or large segments of that market, has led to tolerance or ignorance on the one hand and policy proposals to procure or facilitate some degree of protection on the other, though many of these policies have not been carried out in practice. Nevertheless, some countries, such as Thailand, have developed policies to extend social security. Thailand's Social Security Law of 1990 instituted a general system of social security to be implemented progressively. Initially, the programme was only to cover workers in firms with 20 or more employees with the provision that in three years workers in firms with 10 or more employees would be included. A progression in contributions and benefits was also envisaged, including the introduction in 1998 of retirement benefits. Contributions to the retirement fund equal 9 per cent of the salary, paid in equal parts by the employer and the worker; the government provides a subsidy equal to 2.5 per cent of the salary. The system covers 9.5 million workers in 1.3 million enterprises. Finally, the Royal Decree of 2002 established that all employers, with one or more workers, were subject to application of the Social Security Law. This extension to microenterprises implies the extension of coverage to an additional 3.5 million workers in 1.2 million enterprises.

Subject to the risk inherent in generalizations, we can summarize the attitude of public administrations to informality as follows:

- In industrialized countries, informality is equivalent to illegality. Thus, ministries of labour are obliged to combat it, irrespective of the size of the enterprises or sectors in which it is found. The labour administration, in collaboration with other government agencies, spreads its activities with the aim of detecting non-declared work. Inspection programmes have established priorities in relation to geographical zone, economic sector, and those firms who, by their size or economic activity, have a high incidence of non-compliance.
- In developing countries, the labour administration tends to limit labour inspection to registered large and medium-sized firms. In practice, the labour administration tends to regard micro and small enterprises as outside the scope of regulation, without exerting any pressure to enforce existing laws, to the detriment of workers in those firms as well as firms that abide by the laws. In some countries, however, the labour administrations have been concerned with select groups (such as self-employed workers or artisans) establishing promotional programmes that provide training on becoming self-employed and, in some cases, offering credit for the creation of microenterprises. This is the case in Burkina Faso, where a

Fund to Support the Informal Sector (FASI, in French) has been operating since 1997 providing assistance to various sectors including agricultural, trade, construction, transport, craft production, services and art.

10.5   Conclusion: policies to incorporate workers and informal activities into the formal economy

In conclusion, and always from a legal approach, the desired process of moving from informality to formality can only be understood as:

- the extension of the scope of application of labour norms to employment relationships, categories of wage-earning workers and enterprises that are presently excluded; avoiding ambiguity when considering a worker as salaried or independent;
- the extension of the scope of application of the norms of social security to the categories of wage-earning workers that are presently excluded;
- the establishment or adaptation of the regulating norms of the social security system for non-salaried workers or own-account workers who lack protection, taking into consideration the possibility of voluntary schemes; and
- the enforcement of the effective norms in the cases of illegal work or work that is not declared.

It is not sufficient, and certainly not useful, simply to make the claim often heard in policy debates that labour regulations and social protection policies should be made available to informal workers. As this chapter has demonstrated, despite some very explicit exceptions or modifications, labour laws and the associated social protection policies are applicable to all waged workers. Thus, for most informal workers, especially those under the category of waged workers, the problem is not of a missing juridical framework, but of the lack of application of the laws and policies. In other words, it is a problem of illegality. Thus, in order to 'eliminate' informality or 'formalize the informal' it is necessary to understand why employers and independent workers have chosen to not honour their obligations – be it for reasons that are economic or administrative, or simple negligence – and adopt appropriate policies to remedy the problem. Stating that informal workers should benefit from laws and policies is the first step, as opposed to the solution.

Notes

1   J. Tendler (2002) 'Small Firms, the Informal Sector, and the Devil's Deal', in *IDS Bulletin* 33(3).

2   H. De Soto (2000) *The Mystery of Capital: Why Capitalism Triumphs in the West and Fails Everywhere Else* (New York: Basic Books).

3   *Decent Work*, Report of the Director-General to the 87th Session of the International Labour Conference, Geneva, 1999.

4   The debate has been further complicated by the various connotations of apparently equivalent terms in different languages. For example, translations sometimes use synonyms which are not common and which, in certain national or local usage, confer on them particular nuances or make them dissimilar.

5   Employment Policy (Supplementary Provisions) Recommendation, 1984 (No. 169), paragraph 27.

6   Since the 2002 ILC, labour statisticians have agreed on the value of supplementing statistics on the informal sector with statistics on informal employment. As a result, the 17th International Conference of Labour Statisticians in 2003 drew guidelines for a statistical definition of employment, which identified informal employment by the characteristics of the job.

7   'Natural persons' is a legal term that distinguishes people from corporations, which are considered 'corporate persons' under the law.

8   This is how it is indicated in the document, *The Scope of the Employment Relationship*, which was discussed at the ILC in 2003. The report also states that 'This is still the basic approach in many countries, with some variations' and 'the same approach is also reflected in many international labour standards: some ILO Conventions and Recommendations cover all workers, without distinction, while others refer specifically to independent workers or self-employed persons and others apply only to dependent workers' (Report V, Chap. II, International Labour Conference, 91st Session, Geneva, 2003).

9   For the purposes of the Home Work Convention, 1996 (No. 177), Article 1, the term home work means work carried out by a person, to be referred to as a homeworker: (i) in his or her home or in other premises of his or her choice, other than the workplace of the employer; (ii) for remuneration; (iii) which results in a product or service as specified by the employer, irrespective of who provides the equipment, materials or other inputs used, unless this person has the degree of autonomy and of economic independence necessary to be considered an independent worker under national laws, regulations or court decisions.

10 Bahrain, Cambodia, Japan, Jordan, Kuwait, Lebanon, Oman, Qatar, Saudi Arabia, Singapore, Sweden and Yemen.

11 In Bahrain and Kuwait, exclusions apply to persons employed in temporary and casual work which is outside the scope of the employer's business and for a duration not exceeding three months.

12 Exclusions based on the size of the enterprise have been found in Liberia, Nigeria, Sudan and Uganda in Africa, and in Bahrain, Bangladesh, India, Indonesia, Iraq, Jordan, Kiribati, Laos, Pakistan and Viet Nam in Asia.

13 Article 6 of the Minimum Age Convention, 1973 (No. 138), took this into account when it stated that it would not apply to work done by children and young persons in schools for general, vocational or technical education or in other training institutions, or to work done by persons at least 14 years of age in undertakings, where such work is carried out in accordance with conditions prescribed by the competent authority.

11
New Trends in Latin American Labour Reforms: The Law, its Reform and its Impact in Practical Terms

María Luz Vega Ruíz

11.1 Introduction

Labour law concerns a body of laws whose aim is to provide fair solutions to social issues. Some authors identify the sole purpose of labour law as being to improve workforce productivity,[1] which is primarily an economic objective with a social component. In order to facilitate the smooth running of a business, labour law provides employers with tools for dealing with personnel management that are not available under common law, such as managerial and disciplinary powers, principles of personnel participation in the workplace and collective bargaining in the company.

This point of view notwithstanding, national labour legislations are sometimes criticized for their supposed failure to adapt to economic and social contexts. There are repeated claims that labour law constitutes a restraint to competition and the free use of economic laws, in that it limits the discretionary authority of the employer, although the arguments presented each time vary somewhat and are presented from different perspectives. This is in addition to the present line of thought that labour law protects only an ever-decreasing minority of the labour market (the wage-earners) and 'forgets' the rest of the active population, both employed and unemployed (in essence, wide sections of the informal economy).

It is as a result of this argument that for more than a decade the concepts of deregulation and flexibility have been evoked, with various meanings, by governments, social partners and international institutions, and that labour law is considered by certain sectors to be restrictive and interventionist.[2] Moreover, the expression *labour law* has frequently been substituted by *regulation of the labour market*, even though the difference between both concepts, at least in terms of origin, goes beyond the simple question of terminology.

One radical result of such questioning is that labour legislation is sometimes perceived as anachronistic, and that eliminating or reducing the minimum protection of the rights of workers – particularly those rights that guarantee livelihood and well-being – is advocated (the often-asked question: should a labour market be regulated?). Critics argue that deregulation would benefit economic openness since businesses would be able to operate with fewer institutional restrictions and would be less burdened with costs. Such a position (fortunately not very widely expressed and increasingly less adopted) does not adequately take into account that labour law is not unrelated to the economic context; on the contrary, it is a product of practical experience and of the demands of workplace relations. It reflects the very essence of productive work and is by nature flexible. This does not exclude, however, the existence of gaps or contradictions in the legislations which need amending, or legislative rights that need to be revised, in years to come.

Labour law is a useful tool both for business management and for workers' protection, in that it can strike an appropriate balance between social, economic and political concerns. It is ultimately about blending economic progress with respect for the most minimal, basic protection, in order to ensure that business proceeds and prospers peacefully and to allow for individual development, for the human being as much as for the worker.

In the 1990s, a clear international position was developed concerning the need for minimum labour laws, particularly in the context of globalization and international trade, giving rise to a series of related labour reforms, often concerning collective rights. This trend has been reaffirmed since 2000, as seen in the recent free-trade agreements in Latin America, which take a firm stand on the four fundamental rights of the International Labour Organization's (ILO) Declaration on Fundamental Principles and Rights at Work: the freedom of association; the right to collective bargaining; elimination of child and forced labour; and anti-discrimination. The fundamental principles are at the heart of the agreements, but the agreements are not limited by them, as they also include national legislation to respect 'acceptable working conditions with respect to minimum wages, working hours and occupational health and safety'.

Nevertheless, the interests of employers and workers and the relationships between the various social and professional groups fluctuate according to the pace of political, economic, technological, social and ideological change. These interests and relationships have changed as a result of the crises of the 1980s and 1990s, and of the process and consequences of globalization. The changing perceived role of the state in the economy and in society, in international trade, and in innovation in technology and business, has greatly influenced views about labour standards and their role within the national and international environment. The necessary (though sometimes under-used) participation of social partners during the process of legislative amendments and reforms, as legitimate representatives of their own interests, itself brings new insights about their influence in the workplace.[3] Work carried out by trade unions on behalf of their members can affect a company's efficiency,[4] even if dialogue is not often given priority. A 2004 Inter-American Development Bank (IDB) study points out that trade union intervention has very clear, positive effects, such as the reduction in the salary gap between skilled and unskilled workers, and also between men and women. Furthermore, the greater the affiliation to trade unions, the better the distribution of income. Indeed, the study finds that a 10 per cent increase in trade union affiliation is linked to a drop in wage inequality of between 6 per cent and 10 per cent.[5]

Latin America, particularly over the past 15 years, has not been immune to this debate between protection and flexibility. There has been a series of reforms during this time spanning efforts to 'lessen' some of the rights traditionally recognized in labour legislation as well as towards the reduction of labour costs, all under the banner of greater competition and job creation, to reforms aimed at consolidating or improving workers' rights as well as modernizing institutions.[6] Since 2000, and to a certain degree following the reforms initiated in some industrialized countries, the central discussion has shifted towards more specific issues within the wider debate. Thus, the regularization of underground or illegal workers and the quest for more comprehensive legal coverage for the various types of labour relations, as well as the need to develop forms of contracts that are sufficiently adaptable to the changing needs of the market but also of the labour force, are issues of high priority in the national and international debate. Put another way, the central issue today is the generation of employment, but as governments have been coming to recognize, the employment in question must meet certain criteria – specifically, what the ILO has classified as decent work.

It should be pointed out that in recent years criticism of the excessive protectionism of the region's standards has been modified to some degree. The tendency today is to point out that, even if Latin American labour legislation is excessively regulated and long-winded, this is not its main problem. Rather, its greatest failure lies – as Daza Pérez discusses in Chapter 10 of this volume – is the lack of efficient means to guarantee that legislation is applied, a situation that is detrimental to the very workers it should be protecting.[7] The problem today is what form the reform should take, its boundaries, its characteristics and its scope, bearing in mind that labour law has a duty towards matters of general interest.

Some authors argue that the amendments already made to the region's labour legislation are insufficient.[8] In fact, when looking through the reform laws, most labour codes have undergone, at least once, far-reaching amendments in some of their basic institutions. Although this is not the case in Bolivia, Cuba, Costa Rica, Mexico, Honduras and Uruguay, the labour laws in these countries have undergone partial amendments or reforms are in the pipeline.[9] Even reforms that are classified as being more protectionist-oriented (Brazil and Venezuela) reveal elements of flexibility, undertaken to better adapt labour relations to economic changes.[10]

In general terms, these reforms only deal with substantive aspects of the legislation and have not changed administrative functions, which would allow the regulations to be better applied and more effective. One particular and pertinent exception is the recent Argentine Act of 2004, which included a reform of labour inspection, with both orderly internal structure and performance improvement in mind, together with the substantive amendments of individual and collective relations. In addition to reforms of the procedural codes of Venezuela and Ecuador, other amendments have been promulgated in Peru and, to lesser extent, in Brazil, Chile, Guatemala and Nicaragua.

Even though there has been a notable reduction in the general rate of labour law promulgation since 2000, reforms have continued to take place in a number of countries.[11] In some instances, however, the reforms have been in contradiction to the reforms previously undertaken, in response to inefficiencies revealed from some of the initial changes – particularly in terms of job creation – along with the need to make corrections in order to re-establish rights that had been temporarily reduced.[12]

Amendments to labour legislation are thus controversial not just for technical reasons, but also for ideological, philosophical and political ones. The debates revolve around the economic 'model' of openness and the demands it brings, but also on the need to preserve workers' values and rights, independent of the prevailing economic model. The controversies, however, are further complicated by different interpretations of the legislation's scope and of its reforms even if only because the parties concerned have different examples or even different periods of time in mind. Therefore, in order to engage in a dialogue that will lead to more uniform criteria and conclusions, it is essential to establish a clear definition of the discussion's aim, in terms of the legislation and the reforms that the debate is founded on.

Does a concept of flexibility exist?[13]

There is no doubt that since 1990, Latin America's big debate has centred on the issue of flexibility. At the international level, the general definition of flexibility most frequently invoked has been the one quoted in a report of a group of Organization for Economic Co-operation and Development (OECD) experts (the Dahrendorf Report), and that, from a sociological and psychological point of view, is defined as 'the ability of individuals in the economy, and in particular in the labour market, to let old habits die and to adapt to new circumstances.'[14]

From a strictly legal perspective, perhaps the only way to approach a definition is to start with the evidence: the apparent clash that exists between the protective principle – the essence of labour law that assumes that certain rights confirmed by economic laws cannot be repealed or waived – and the principles of free competition and maximum performance as dictated by economic laws. In effect, as distinct from other branches of the law (such as in civil law, where contractual freedom rules supreme), in labour law the respect of certain essential rights is the 'minimum indispensable principle' for guaranteeing workers' protection. Thus, the right to place limits on the working day, to establish a minimum wage and work breaks, and to guarantee health and safety in the workplace are, among others, fundamental rights (therefore, minimum rights that cannot be changed). These rights in turn guarantee unquestionable legal rights, such as human health, dignity and life, pertaining to all workers. However, and without prejudice to these conditions (in contrast with other issues), labour legislators need to take into account that their role places them in a position where the survival of the business is essential, thus inflexibility and failure to adapt can destroy the very source of the contract.

According to the logic of labour law, flexibility needs to be defined on the basis of being able to count on the legal means that enable a company to adjust its production and its employment and working conditions to the fast and continuous fluctuations of the economic system, without endangering the basic minimal principles of social protection.

In its various publications, the ILO has been the driving force behind concerns over flexibility, without expressly specifying what such a concept implies in relation to the work environment, exhibiting perhaps an uncertainty about the definition of this concept. Various writings on the subject have been based on the different elements considered to be key in the flexibility debate (that is, the work contract, working time, termination of contract, scope of collective bargaining, and so on), placing more emphasis on the study of types of application and their effects, rather than attributing global characteristics to the phenomenon.

Nevertheless, the general issue of flexibility in policy framework has been under discussion within the ILO, in the context of international labour standards (hereafter referred to as ILS), for a number of years. A significant number of documents have dealt with this subject.[15] For example, at the 81st Session of the International Labour Conference (ILC) in 1994,[16] when analysing general issues relating to international standards, some members of the Committee on the Application of Conventions and Recommendations referred to flexibility problems in legislative review processes. According to the Committee's report, trade unions were not against the issue of flexibility *per se*, provided that the 'equilibrium between workers' and employers' interests is not damaged to the detriment of the former'.[17] 'Flexibility must not just mean applying certain standards or not, nor must it mean that they are interpreted entirely at will.' On the subject of collective relations, the same report cites the workers' opposition to accepting changes that, under the banner of flexibility, 'aimed specifically at altering the power of unions'.[18] In this sense, workers question if the arguments made in favour of flexibility are no more than 'a device to reduce the bargaining power of unions'.

Equally, policy formulation itself reflects in its evolution the need for compliance and change, symptomatic of structural and economic modifications regarding basic minimum rights. The ILO and its constituents are doubtless aware that concepts of labour change over time, and for that reason the ILC is developing new proposals based on the same topics but with different backgrounds. Good examples of such an ability to adapt include the Night Work Convention, 1990 (No. 171),[19] and in particular the Private Employment Agencies Convention, 1997 (No. 181). Convention No. 181 fundamentally modified the Conference's perspective on the issue of the monopoly of public employment agencies (provided for by the Fee-Charging Employment Agencies Convention, 1949 (No. 96)), on the basis, as pointed out in its Preamble, of 'the importance of *flexibility* in the functioning of labour markets'; 'considering the very different environment in which private employment agencies operate, very different to the existing conditions when Convention No. 96 was adopted' and, 'recognising the role that private employment agencies may play in the smooth running of the labour market' (italics added). Although the Conference states that such criteria are of a general nature, the actual Preamble introduces and pinpoints restrictions that indicate, while recognising the need for flexibility, that it is essential '*to protect workers* against abuses … to guarantee the right to freedom of association and to promote collective bargaining and social dialogue as necessary components of a well-functioning industrial relations system' (italics added). The text bases its argument on a key number of Conventions that guarantee necessary protection in the framework but with a basis of flexibility.[20] The way forward is clear: adapt where necessary, but take protection founded on fundamental rights and principles as a starting point.

As has gradually come to be recognized, flexibility, though not specifically regulated and existing only in pockets, is widely acknowledged as being a polemical undercurrent in the ILO's framework. Flexibility is thus considered to be necessary in the role of market laws, provided the need is genuine and well founded and that minimum protection is guaranteed. How can this assertion be verified and vouched for?

While no standards as such exist to regulate or deal with this concept, the means available to the ILO when facing possible issues and challenges concerning flexibility, are:[21]

(i) the international standards arising from the Conference. By their very nature, these international standards are flexible and have a wide scope, and are not only able to adapt to the market needs themselves, but are also able to guarantee the protection of fundamental basic human rights. Moreover, many of the labour-related topics dealing with the issue of flexibility are subject to an individual Convention (for example, Termination of Employment Convention, 1981 (No. 158), Freedom of Association Convention, 1948 (No. 87), or the different Conventions relating to minimum working hours);

(ii) the means of consultation and information, set out in international instruments, that favour the players concerned being fully informed on the subject; and

(iii) technical assistance, that through analysis of the facts will enable the actual and current needs of each country to be pinpointed.

From this perspective, it can be supposed that flexibility in the workplace is a fact of life in the working environment, and as such the ILO must approach it by weighing up its need against its acceptability. Could a concept of flexibility that is socially acceptable to the ILO be promoted? In principle, while taking the prescriptions and standards laid down at the heart of the ILO into account, all legislative change carried out on the basis of economic criteria, in order to be socially acceptable according to the parameters set out by the ILO, should respect the fact that:

(i) the work is free and open, and offered under equal conditions;

(ii) all workers are remunerated justly and fairly on the basis of the work they perform;

(iii) all workers enjoy adequate protection against unfair dismissal and, in case of dismissal due to economic or technology-related reasons, workers are guaranteed a fair termination deal, with sufficient economic and administrative guarantees;[22]

(iv) the period of work and rest time are guaranteed, in order to allow for personal development, and adequate health and safety conditions;

(v) workers are able to exercise freely their right of association and collective bargaining; and

(vi) prescriptions of minimum age for admittance to employment are not contravened.

From this perspective, flexibility can be approached from various angles, and could indeed be accepted. However, the main issue continues to be whether or not this topic is in fact the greatest obstacle to necessary reforms, or put another way, to an amendment that will cater for the need to protect workers, within the context of progress.

Let us re-examine some facts.

11.2 Main amendments to labour relations

The employment contract

The beginning (or signing of the employment contract) and its termination are the two key events in the evolution of individual employment relations and, therefore, two of the main areas of focus of Latin American legislative reforms over the past decade.

An employment contract's duration is the conventional and most used criterion in drawing up guidelines for terms and conditions. In fact, part of the current debate regarding flexibility is based on the conflicts of interest surrounding this issue. On the one hand, claims are made for workers' protection through stability of employment (which in practice generally means restrictions on and demands for justification of temporary recruitment); on the other hand is the issue of looking after the interests of the enterprise or company (interpreted as the businessperson having the greatest autonomy of will in this decision).

The rule applied by legislations in Latin America originally favoured the open-ended contract, which has corresponded historically to the intent of those who are bound by an agreement in relation to employment. This preference for open-ended contracts has been expressed within the assumption that the employment contract is for an indefinite period, unless proven to the contrary, and where the requirement of the supposed restrictions in which conditions imposed on the duration of the contract are defined by time or nature of the work.

Some reforms relating to employment contracts, such as those initially undertaken in Argentina,[23] as well as Colombia, Chile, Peru and to a lesser extent Brazil and Panama, have eased or eliminated the rules that made open-ended contracts the 'preferred' type of employment contract. In these cases, the prevailing notion has been that fixed-term contracts are better adapted to the needs of the business, allow for the mobility of the workforce and significantly reduce labour costs.

The use of fixed-term contracts or, more generally, temporary contracts in their various guises, has traditionally been attractive to employers, partly because of the opportunity that such contracts offer for letting workers go without having to compensate them. Most of the recent reforms have eased the ability of employers to issue and renew temporary contracts, as well as extend their duration, with a view to generating jobs, encouraging training for first-time employees, as well as for responding to businesses' economic, production or organizational needs.[24]

In terms of the possible controversial effects of the use of fixed-term contracts, the Argentine experience is noteworthy. From 1991, and influenced by Spanish legislation, public incentives of total or partial exemption from social security contributions were granted for the first time to employers using fixed-term contracts to launch new enterprises, for contracts offered to the unemployed, and for work experience and apprenticeships for young people. Thus, fixed-term contracts were no longer the exception but became the norm, as the result of state incentives. Reforms put in place in 1995 completed the flexible arrangement, introducing new types of fixed-term contracts and exemptions and, for small businesses, eliminating registration requirements at the start of the contract. But after three years of negotiations, the 1998 reform removed these new types of temporary employment contracts. And Act 25.250 of 2000 further modified the reform by offering partial exemption from social security contribution payments as an incentive for issuing contracts of indefinite duration, thus reintroducing (and perhaps taking into account the Spanish influence of 1997) a preference for open-ended contracts.

It is difficult to get a precise measure of the general impact of these new contracts, due both to the speed with which they came out and to the lack of reliable statistical data. Nevertheless, perhaps in the most illustrative cases of Argentina and Peru (the latter has nine types of special contracts), the effects on the labour market are not particularly encouraging. Rather than reducing the number of workers without contracts, non-regular employment actually increased.[25] This occurred despite the reforms being justified as a means of improving the competitive nature of businesses by overcoming the inflexibility that 'discouraged employment creation, insofar as it hindered dismissal or increased its cost'.[26] In Argentina, because non-regular work actually increased, questions were raised concerning the need for these new laws in the first place, especially considering that the Law on Contract of Employment (Ley de Contrato de Trabajo – LCT) was perhaps not as rigid as initially thought, in that it allowed, for dismissal on just grounds, without just grounds, or with no grounds at all.[27] Even though the social partners negotiated new types of flexibility – authorized at all times by the relevant industry's collective agreements in the Framework Agreement for Employment, Productivity and Social Fairness in 1994, from 1997 job security appeared to have worsened. Inspired by new trends in the Spanish model, attempts were made to radically reduce fixed-term contracts by effectively rationalizing them.[28]

In this sense, official statistics offer the best indicator of the effects of the changes in Argentine legislation. In May 1991, fixed-term contracts made up 3.2 per cent of all employment contracts subject to pension contributions (in other words, all contracts excluding workers employed during the probation period or unregistered or illegal workers). This percentage increased to 4.1 per cent between October 1996 and May 1998. But even more significant than this change in the structure of paid employment under contract is that in an important sector such as manufacturing industry, while open-ended contracts dropped by 15.1 per cent during the period 1991–98, temporary contracts rose by 49.8 per cent, and non-registered contracts by 5.3 per cent.

A similar trend could be observed where in Chile, in 1994 the total percentage of employed people with a temporary contract of employment in the manufacturing industry was 6 per cent. By 1996 this figure had risen to 9.6 per cent. During the same period the percentage in the construction industry also increased, from 28.7 per cent to 34.9 per cent; and that in the services industry rose from 5.6 per cent to 11 per cent.

In Peru, the use of fixed-term contracts has also been on the increase,[29] in even greater numbers than in the above cases. In 1989, 20.4 per cent of wage-earners in metropolitan Lima were working under fixed-term contracts and

30.5 per cent of wage-earners did not have a contract. After the 1993 reform, these percentages increased to 24.5 per cent and 35.1 per cent respectively, and in 1997, to 32.5 per cent and 41.2 per cent respectively. This means that in 1997, 74 per cent of total wage earners were working either without a contract or on a fixed-term contract as opposed to 51 per cent before the reforms.

In reality, regulations in Peru are extremely detailed, but permissive. For example, fixed-term contracts authorized in response to *market needs*, in order to comply with 'one-off' increases in production originating from substantial variations in market demands, can last as long as five years, which is evidently not quite in tune with the notion of 'one-off'. Even though the reform was an attempt to tackle a labour market with high levels of informal and unofficial activity, where permanent employment contracts were something of a utopia, the creation of these new contracts and the flexibility attached to them have not reduced the employment problems. Nor would it appear that they have helped to formalize employment relations. On the contrary, the main problem that still exists, according to the statistics, appears to be unregistered employment.[30]

From this perspective, the end results sought by the large-scale use of fixed-term contracts are questionable, from the point of view not only of social protection, but also of economic effectiveness. Moreover, excessive use of fixed-term contracts can lead to complications of internal personnel management, and can act as a disincentive to investment in training workers. At some stage this may inevitably place limits on the technical abilities of businesses and on their ability to cope with the technical demands made by international markets.

Interestingly, changing the duration of probation to promote flexibility has not been practiced as widely in Latin America as in some European countries, where it can be included through collective agreement. The probation period is intended as a 'test-bed of the employment relationship', which allows both parties to rescind the contract at any time, with no further obligation. This is typical of open-ended contracts, though there is no reason why it cannot also be applied to fixed-term contracts. Generally speaking, the maximum probation period in the region is two months in Colombia, Paraguay, Honduras and Guatemala, three months in Bolivia, Brazil, Ecuador and Panama,[31] and six months in Peru and, in certain cases, Argentina.[32]

In conclusion, it seems clear that the increased availability of fixed-term contracts in almost all the reforms in the region has been used as a way of encouraging employment, at times in novel forms, but with questionable results. For this reason, the latest reforms tend to limit these types of contracts and to guarantee a certain degree of stability, in order to ensure productivity. On the other hand, the region has not seen a trend of extending the probation period, perhaps due to the prevalence of temporary contracts and the flexibility it brings.

Termination of the employment contract

Preference for open-ended contracts is manifested in the law through restrictions imposed on employers for terminating employment. These restrictions are based on the principle of employment stability, which in most countries in the region is of a constitutional nature.[33] This principle translates in practice by protecting the worker against arbitrary or unfair dismissal or in any situation where he or she is not at fault. This is the intended meaning of ILO Convention No. 158 concerning the termination of employment, which requires claims of justified cause (related to the conduct or ability of the workers or the needs of the business) in order to set a dismissal in motion, and which, in order to be valid, stipulates certain requirements in terms of notice, method and procedure.

Because of its economic and social implications, termination of employment at the initiative of the employer continues to be one of the most widely debated issues. For workers, protection against dismissal is a key element of their employment rights. From the employers' point of view, strict regulation of termination of employment can limit opportunities for adapting the business to an ever-changing market and to the challenge of competition.

Discussion on issues linked to termination of employment is generally confined to that of dismissal – termination of the contract of employment at the initiative of the employer – in that the cessation by mutual consent (at the initiative of the worker or at the end of the contract of employment) does not present specific problems because it does not generate additional costs for the business.[34] The debate is therefore centred on: the causes of dismissal; the length of notice period and the possible substitution of this notice with financial compensation; the compensation or severance payment owed by the employer on terminating the contract and, to a lesser degree, the cost of reinstatement,[35] which has a lower incidence. National reforms relating to these aspects signal changes to dismissal and firing procedures.

Termination of employment has been subject to reforms in most countries across the region, where significant changes have taken place. However, there has been no specific modification since 1999. In general, the idea has been to simplify procedures, extend the causes justifying dismissal, and reduce severance payment. Some reforms have been met with strong social opposition, which in turn has led to further revisions. The changes to the system in certain countries have included setting up a system of unemployment funds in order to guarantee minimum protection, even in the instance that the employer becomes insolvent.

In 1966, Brazil was the first country to deregulate and make dismissal more flexible.[36] However, that flexibility was then mitigated by the country's 1988 Constitution, which ordered that while the principles of the Guarantee Fund for Time of Service (FGTS) would not be regulated, a worker who was unfairly dismissed had the right to an additional compensation equivalent to 40 per cent of the value of the funds accumulated, in addition to the sums deposited in the Fund. The law also mandated a 30-day notice period by the employer which included time off to search for work.

Since then, there have been a number of reforms in the region aimed at creating unemployment funds in order to ease the obligation of paying severance (such as in Colombia) as well as for allowing economic and structural change as grounds for dismissal (in Chile and Peru) with fewer procedural requirements and lower severance payments.[37] Changes to collective dismissal legislation have not been far-reaching and have been limited to better precision of the motive, in certain cases, allowing economic and organizational reasons (such as in Argentina, Chile, Panama and Peru). In the case of Colombia, Act 50 introduces a new concept of collective dismissal that relates not to specific reasons (although these are applicable to other types of dismissal) but to numerical criteria (percentage of workers affected in relation to the size of the business). As to the procedure for actually carrying out a dismissal, the reform has tended to simplify it enormously. The most prominent case is without doubt that of Peru, where an employer can obtain, at the request of the party involved and in a short space of time, administrative authorization. Moreover, even without an administrative response, the request for dismissal is taken as approved.

Conditions of employment

In addition to the commencement and the termination of a contract of employment, the law also regulates its content, which does not prevent the parties from changing or finalizing the contract, provided they are not in conflict with the obligatory regulations. Most recent reforms have seen some changes in terms of working hours and wages.

Working hours

The law contains a basic concept of working hours. This is understood to be the daily, weekly or annual period of time that a worker must devote to fulfil his or her contract. The period of working hours is intended to define the services rendered by the worker in terms of time.

Legislation has evolved along the general lines of a restriction and gradual reduction of working hours, partly for reasons of social justice but also because excessively long periods of work have been shown to be unproductive, often affecting the health of the worker, but also risking damage to the business (in terms of equipment or services provided). Since the beginning of the twentieth century, state intervention to guarantee the health and livelihood of workers resulted in the introduction of regulations concerning basic and obligatory rights (in other words, laws no party can change) restricting working hours. The idea of working hours is likewise linked to wages, which are calculated on the basis of an ordinary day's work. They provide for extra charges or additional payments for night work or public holidays, or for hours worked over and above the maximum number of hours of work permitted, as well as for special working days relating to various categories and sectors of work.

In general terms, working hours' regulations do not show large differences from one country to another across the region. The reason for this is probably that restricting working hours has been a traditional social claim, advocated since the beginning of the labour standard movement and adopted in international conventions and national legislation. The large majority of countries stick to legal working hours of eight hours per day and between 44 and 48 hours per week, with variants incorporated mostly through collective agreements. Rest time between working days or shifts is a minimum of nine or ten hours.

Without prejudice to the prescription of the law, there has been a trend in countries such as Argentina, Brazil, Colombia, Chile and Mexico towards an increase in the number of hours actually worked (exceeding, in some sectors, the legal working hours).[38] This could be related to the low cost of overtime and a failure of supervisory controls.

Advocates of reforming working hours legislation claim that removing restrictions on working hours is necessary in order to allow companies to adapt to market demands, and also to promote employment.[39] In Latin America, working hours reforms are still in their initial stages, even though they appear with increasing frequency and even feature in texts considered to be protective. In Venezuela, for example, conventionally accepted changes to the maximum working hours are allowed, without administrative authorization and with an average limit of 44 hours per week in an eight-week period.[40] In Argentina, collective agreements are able to establish calculation methods for working out maximum working hours based on averages 'in line with the characteristics of each industry'. These methods allow for the calculation of working hours per week, month or year. In fact, 50 per cent of collective agreements include clauses concerning working hours.[41] Some agreements even provide for minimum working hours.

The Brazilian Constitution allowed for compensating working hours and for the reduction of working hours through a collective arrangement or agreement. Similarly, it established a reduced working day of six hours in broken shifts, unless collectively bargained, which no doubt opened up opportunities. Changes introduced in January 1998 added to the flexible system, incorporating the legal recognition of accumulated working hours, or banked hours, already included in some collective agreements.[42] This system allows for reducing working hours during periods of low activity (over a period of 120 days) without any salary reduction, but keeping hours in credit to be used during periods of high activity, without exceeding a limit of ten hours per working day. If the worker's contract ends before the accumulated hours are used, the employer will compensate by paying overtime.

The law tends to authorize overtime work in exceptional circumstances (in Bolivia and the Dominican Republic), or by establishing quantitative limits (in Paraguay and Venezuela) and even the reforms undertaken contain certain guarantees to protect the worker. However, working overtime over the legal limit is common practice in the region 'at the expense of job creation and despite that extended working hours feed off the lack of industrial development and technology', and in spite of extended working hours not promoting increased production.[43] The fundamental reason is the low cost of overtime for employers, given the low level of salaries and the need for workers to work over and above the ordinary working hours in order to earn indispensable additional income.

With respect to night work, there have been few novel reforms and the trend has been to improve the percentage of compensation.[44] Only Paraguay has a system whereby night work is subject to authorization by management. Shift work has not been regulated in a number of countries, such as Bolivia, Brazil, Ecuador, Guatemala and Mexico. In Argentina and Brazil, regulation is through collective agreement in line with the company's specific needs.

The Colombian reform of shift work defined, in more detail and with more flexibility, shift work without interruption every day of the week (during a given period of time or indefinitely), setting a limit of six hours per day or 36 hours per week. In Peru, an employer is allowed to alter shifts, and to introduce new shifts with workers on a fixed-term contract. In other countries, such as the Dominican Republic and Venezuela, regulation of shift work is carried out along the lines of compensating working hours, with weekly limits, and in the case of the Dominican Republic, with payment of extra time as overtime.

Wages

Wages are the remuneration or earnings owed by the employer to the worker by virtue of the contract of employment.[45] They are in this sense the object of the main obligation of the employer and, correspondingly, a fundamental right of the worker.

Whilst wages reward a service, they also secure the maintenance and subsistence of the worker and his or her family. For this reason, most Latin American constitutions stipulate the right to just or fair remuneration. As such, legislation, or the Constitution itself, contains a system of wage protection, with rules governing wage fixing – particularly with respect to minimum wages. It also includes terms for how, when and where payment should take place and the means of protecting the system, such as legal protection, secured debt, protection against default, and collateral funds, should the employer become insolvent. Some of these have been subject to reform.

Some reforms have chosen to clarify the legal concept of wages, in order to determine which concepts should be used as a basis for working out severance payments or other wage-based benefits, and contributions to social security or for professional training. In 1992, the law in Panama excluded from the concept of wages 'incentive payments based on production and other bonus payments'. And the 1991 Reform in Ecuador eliminated the 'use of lodgings and in-kind benefits'. In 1997, Venezuela succeeded by tripartite consensus in introducing a reform that was centred on wage issues and benefits, and on severance payments to be paid at the termination of an employment contract. Its objective was to resolve the irregularities that had occurred following the application of the Act of 1990. This reform stipulated that a series of incentive payments and subsidies, which had previously proliferated by being excluded from wages, should become an integral part of them. Such payments and subsidies would not have been taken into account when re-adjusting benefits for time-in-service.[46] The intention is thus to create a more rational wage structure and to make its reassessment more viable in practice.

Initial reforms in Colombia and Peru introduced the concept of comprehensive wage systems.[47] This is a formula that allows for the accumulation of all entitlement payments due for different reasons during the course of the year. The exceptions to this are paid holidays in Colombia and profit-sharing in Peru. In Colombia, however, this is only applicable to workers whose wages are at least ten times the minimum legal wage.[48] In Peru, it applies to workers whose remuneration is not below two taxation units.

The minimum wage, which is another important chapter in the legislation, stipulates a restriction on negotiation between the parties, in that they are not allowed to agree on wages that are below the minimum wage. The purpose of this minimum wage is, above all, to protect the most vulnerable groups of workers, to establish a socially fair wage and to determine a point of reference in the wage structure. But in general terms, the region has seen a reduction in the value of the minimum wage through a 'conservative' wage policy. In the 1990s minimum wages had fallen in real terms compared with the level reached in 1980, particularly in Mexico, but also in other countries of the region, thus widening the gap between minimum wages and average wages. The decline in minimum wages is partly because they are used as a tool to fight inflation. This led Nicaragua, for instance, to no longer consider criteria for fulfilling the basic needs of workers and their families as a reason for adjusting the minimum wage upwards. Instead, adjustments are based on a minimum threshold of acceptable income for a worker.[49]

The few legal reforms concerning minimum wages focus on particular points. In Chile, the 1978 Reform stipulated different minimum wage structures for workers under the age of 21 and for those above the age of 65. This restriction for older workers was abolished in 1990, but not for workers under the age of 21. In Ecuador, the national minimum wage must now be reviewed every six months, and the minimum wage per occupation must be renewed on an annual basis, not every two years as previously. In the Dominican Republic, since 1991, wages for individual industries must be reviewed every two years.

The conventional flexibility of the wage structure is a growing phenomenon, particularly in countries with a predominantly industry-based collective bargaining structure, such as in Argentina, Brazil and Uruguay. However, this has still not been explicitly contained in the law (as in some European countries), with the possible exception of Argentina where, as a result of the economic crisis, the law does provide for the possibility of collective agreement in establishing a reduction in wages. In general terms, current labour codes make it impossible to change wages agreed via collective agreement,[50] with only a few variations allowed, related to payment of certain non-wage benefits or to the breaking up of supplementary wages.[51]

In Brazil in 1994, during the policy of stabilization and wage de-indexation, various provisional measures were introduced, granting an essential role to collective agreements in the process of determining wages.[52] This new strategy required companies to negotiate with the trade unions of the relevant industries employee profit-sharing, or sharing in any other profit-related company results, which, added to an exemption from paying employers' contributions on the said amounts, was aimed at guaranteeing reduced labour costs and at converting profit-sharing to a variable component of remuneration. In practice, however, the measures have not been applied by all companies, partly because the norms did not specify sanctions or terms of compliance.

Labour legislation and small businesses

Equality of working conditions is an imperative concerning workers as much as it is a regulator of business. For this reason, labour legislation in Latin America dictates a uniform treatment of labour relations for all workers. Nevertheless, there exist several exceptions relating to the size of a business. Some exceptions appeared in the initial labour codes of the region, posing legal and economic difficulties, but have since disappeared in recent reforms. In Colombia, for example, unemployment relief payments excluded 'craftsmen who, working in their own business, did not employ more than five workers, who were not family members, on a permanent basis'. This provision was repealed in 1990, as the notion of protecting and preventing discrimination against workers employed in micro-businesses prevailed.

However, there is still a body of regulations relating to shift work, promotion, suspension, and so on, which apply only to labour relations, in a workplace or factory setting. Some social benefits, or the treatment of collective dismissals or trade union activities (that is, the number of representatives with authority), are also regulated, from time to time, according to the criteria of the type of business.

The current practice is to remove inappropriate provisions for small and medium-sized businesses, or to replace them with others which smooth the way of administrative procedures.[53] In fact, some ILO Conventions allow for exclusions or exceptions relating to small businesses.[54] Such simplifications must not, however, affect workers' minimum rights, especially if one bears in mind that any differentiation based purely on the number of workers in a company can lead to clear, counterproductive simplifications. Furthermore, it is difficult to assess the impact of a legislation that makes a distinction of this nature in favour of small businesses, given the absence of data that is specific or broken down into type of business.

In countries such as Argentina, Brazil and Peru, laws or bodies of regulations aimed at regulating labour relations in small businesses have been adopted. However, most legal references in the region appear to be incorporated into general laws, or are implicit in the regulations of labour codes.

The definition of a small business, in labour terms, does not always exist or is not clear, and in any case is not uniform across the region, let alone internationally. Argentine law regards a small business as one that does not exceed 40 workers and whose annual turnover is below the limit determined by the Follow-up Special Commission.[55] Brazil does not define a small business, and instead confines itself to regulating micro and small businesses as a separate issue.[56] In Peru, some of the regulations included in the Act Concerning Productivity and Competition are geared towards promoting the setting up of small businesses.

However, the range of application of some provisions is determined by the number of workers or by the company's assets, with smaller-sized businesses clearly in mind, although with different criteria. In Argentina, regulation relating to companies at crisis point applies only to companies employing more than 50 workers.[57] In Colombia, registration of workers only applies to companies employing five or more on a permanent basis.[58] In other countries, the application of the law is determined by the company's capital (such as in Bolivia for workers employed in the hotel and printing industries), or by the nature of the business itself (such as in Colombia, in relation to the regulation of certain sectors that typically fall under the category of craft industry sectors or small-scale enterprises such as hairdressing salons, florists, bread shops and small restaurants, and so on). In practice the regulation is reserved for small-scale industry or business.

The employment system for small businesses is not homogenous across the region, and is still in its early stages. Some reforms prescribe particular rules concerning working conditions, especially the working day and pay that are more flexible and less onerous for the employer. In particular, in Argentina the law not only facilitates a system of registration for small businesses, but it also enables them to use temporary contracts of employment without any entitlements or prior confirmation by collective agreement. This keeps the rules non-specific and general in nature (new regulation concerning the probation period has brought with it new developments, as discussed above). With regard to working conditions, the law also allows, under certain conditions and through collective agreement, amendment of standard practice, qualifications, notice, and timing of basic annual leave. This throws open virtually unlimited space for flexibility on these matters. Brazilian law, while supporting the company's obligation to control the periods of leave of its employees, has similar leanings, in liberating small businesses from the obligation of reporting to the authorities the start and finish dates of holidays.[59]

The simplification of dismissal procedures is another feasible objective of the reforms, the reasoning being that small businesses need simpler procedures for taking on labour. In various countries, the general provisions for termination of employment do not apply to small businesses, for historical reasons as well as those of flexibility and/or simplification.[60] In Latin America there are some examples of this, but no provision exempts small businesses from the regulations concerning dismissal. Instead, the effects of termination, and compensatory severance payments in particular, are the main focus.[61]

In Colombia, reduced severance payments for companies with a taxable net worth below 1,000 times the minimum wage applies. However, in Colombia as well as in Brazil and Peru, small businesses fall under the regulation of the general system. But in Venezuela and Peru, special limits have been set on the obligation to reinstate workers in some types of small companies. According to Venezuelan law, businesses employing fewer than ten workers are not obliged to reinstate them, but are obliged to pay their entitlements. Peruvian law, on the other hand, allows employees in businesses employing up to 20 workers to claim compensatory severance pay, but does not give them the right to be re-employed by the same company.

Similarly, Mexican law tacitly exempts the employer from reinstating a worker if the employer can prove to the relevant authority (Council of Conciliation and Arbitration) that the worker 'for reasons of the work carried out or by the nature of his/her tasks, is in direct and permanent contact with the employer'. This is typical of small businesses, where working relationships are of an almost inter-family nature. In Panama, the Labour Code does not regard the reinstatement of workers employed in small businesses to be compulsory. This is the case for agricultural enterprises employing 10 or fewer workers, agribusiness enterprises employing 20 or fewer workers, and manufacturing enterprises employing 15 or fewer workers. This is also the case for retail establishments and enterprises in the services industry who employ five or fewer workers, as long as they are not to do with financial services, insurance, or real estate. These limits also apply to grounds for dismissal, where these small businesses are able to carry out a dismissal without any need for justification, by way of a provision of exception. Although similar rules used to apply in Colombia, at present, except for a transitional implementation of the traditional system, the derogation of reinstatement gives the same results.

11.3 Main amendments to collective labour relations

Effective social dialogue requires a minimum set of conditions, ranging from a certain degree of social organization to a climate of civil liberty. These minimum conditions have, however, been difficult to achieve in any uniform way in Latin America. This is due to repeated upheavals that have without doubt generated a climate of social instability, undermining the foundation of a stable system of labour relations.

Since 1990, and in some cases beforehand, the countries in the region have undergone policies of economic adjustment, privatization, and a general opening up of their economies, including regional integration. The new economic environment has reawakened the debate on labour relations, which has fallen back on the law as almost the sole regulator of labour relations. This trend is borne out in Argentina, with the so-called 'collective availability', which provides the means for making flexible adjustments (revoking or reducing rights) to the conditions regulated by the law. Nevertheless, alongside this process there is also a movement towards encouraging collective bargaining as a means of guaranteeing an agreed and stipulated flexibility (in Argentina and Brazil).

The legislative development of collective labour relations in the region have thus been positioned somewhere between the notion of collective autonomy and a tendency towards state intervention and control. Nevertheless, the reforms have generally been undertaken via unilateral regulation by the government, enforced by law, resulting in a detailed set of norms.[62] Most of these revisions have been based on the high ratification rates[63] of the Freedom of Association and Protection of the Right to Organize Convention, 1948 (No. 87), and the Right to Organize and Collective Bargaining Convention, 1949 (No. 98), supported by the return to democracy in many countries in the region.[64] Yet this is at a time when in some countries total compliance with the Conventions in question is still an unattained goal.[65] However, the comments made by the Commission of Experts in the Application of Conventions and Recommendations, in relation to both Conventions, are numerous, and complaints to the Committee on Freedom of Association are on the increase, thus indicating the manifold difficulties surrounding this issue.

It is important to keep in mind, however, that freedom of association and collective bargaining rights are core labour rights, acknowledged in numerous international treaties. Presently, these rights constitute a minimum essential requirement in negotiations over trade agreements, acting as a reference point in international trade. Moreover, as illustrated in the ILO's Reports under the Follow-up to the Declaration on Fundamental Principles and Rights at Work,[66] respect for the rights of freedom of association and collective bargaining can bring commercial success to a company, by encouraging innovation and flexibility in production and in the organization as a whole. Moreover, such rights are also instrumental in fighting poverty and in resolving the wealth distribution problems that threaten social stability. Indeed, countries with better developed systems of labour relations produce better results in terms of employment, and better global economic results.[67]

Freedom of association

Recent reforms are levelled, in general and official terms, at strengthening the right to organize, either by gradual modification of the legislation or, as is the case in Chile, by an attempt to restore the old system – still only halfway complete. The sole exception to this trend within the region is in Venezuela following the adoption of its 1999 Constitution. Articles 95 and 293 of the Constitution contain stipulations that allowing for interference in the management of trade unions, their elections, and the handling of their funds. Subsequent regulations have followed in the same vein.

In addition to lifting the restrictive regulations concerning freedom of association (as in El Salvador), some reforms have been aimed at facilitating the exercising of such rights. This can be done by reducing the minimum number of members required to constitute a trade union (in El Salvador and Panama), or by simplifying the requirements for registering a trade union and obtaining legal status, to the point of declaring registration of full rights in the face of administrative inaction and with no administrative intervention (in Colombia, El Salvador, Panama and Paraguay). Other reforms extend the freedom of association to new categories of workers (farmers in El Salvador, and civil servants in Chile, Nicaragua and Panama). They can also facilitate the creation of company unions, or unions for casual, temporary or independent workers (Peru); of trade unions by area of activity (Chile); of unions for foreign workers (in Panama and, to a certain extent, Colombia); or of federations and confederations of trade unions (in Chile and El Salvador). The Colombian amendment of Act 584 likewise contains derogations that remove management's control of trade unions.

The institution of the 'trade union charter', that is, the special protection of the right of tenure given to any worker with union responsibilities, except in cases of justified dismissal for a serious offence, has been introduced or extended in a number of countries (Colombia, Costa Rica, the Dominican Republic, El Salvador, Guatemala, Panama, Paraguay, Venezuela). In Costa Rica, legislation includes rules to protect trade unions against anti-trade union activities, specifically in relation to solidarity organizations.[68] In general terms, the Venezuelan Organic Labour Law (Ley Orgánica del Trabajo – LOT) now contains more detailed trade union protection, and the reform made prior to the new Constitution repealed any managerial dissolution of a trade union.

However, the practical results are a long way from the theoretical objectives. Trade union organizations in many countries are weaker than before and show low membership levels. Could this be as a direct result of the reform?

It is difficult to explain this somewhat regressive result of what is essentially a progressive reform. It is certainly true that the reform fits into the overall picture of strengthening labour relations at company level. Countries where the average number of small and medium-sized businesses is very high show a significant decrease in the role of sectoral trade union organizations and, therefore, limited numbers of workers joining the trade union structure. In fact, the minimum number of workers required to constitute a trade union (20 on average), owing to the fragmentation already mentioned, makes it difficult for workers to join an organization, given that in practice (and indirectly by limits imposed in the legislation),[69] there are no industry-based trade unions.

Another unresolved issue concerns unionization in the public sector, which is generally either ignored by the law, underdeveloped or is bound by restrictions that obstruct any development – as is the case in Bolivia, Colombia, El Salvador and Paraguay.

Collective bargaining

In the case of collective bargaining, the main thrust of labour law has been to encourage organized workers to engage in dialogue with their employers, and, as a result of these conversations, to reach collective agreements for defining working conditions and for regulating relations between workers and employers. In this context, regulation on this subject has also been renewed, and in some cases has been the result of agreements or accords between governments, workers and employers, as is the case in Argentina.

In other cases, attempts at reform – for example, in Ecuador in the Trolley Bus Act 2 ('Ley trolebús 2') – included topics such as a worker's contract without an Agreement of Collective Employment, some aspects relating to security provisions in case of a strike, and minimum services that could affect freedom of association. However, any grey areas were resolved by most of the proposed articles being declared unconstitutional.

Reforms of this type essentially cover some of the following main issues: development of collective bargaining, accreditation, and encouraging flexibility of one-to-one employment relations through negotiation. A number of reforms in Chile, the Dominican Republic and Venezuela tend to favour the development of collective bargaining as a good way of increasing the number of issues the reforms can deal with (as in Panama and Peru), as well as the scope of these issues, such as public responsibilities (as in Argentina, Paraguay and Venezuela). In the case of Chile, it relates to the increased scope given to so-called 'non-regulated negotiations'.

In the same way, the value of collective conventions is underlined, as is the case in Chile, by re-establishing the principle that their clauses prevail over those of the individual contract of employment. Moreover, attempts have been made to consolidate collective bargaining as a trade union activity, in the light of some countries – such as Costa Rica and El Salvador – banning collective agreements of groups of workers when a trade union is involved. On the other hand, the law in Peru, Ecuador and Colombia permits collective agreements with non-union workers. In Colombia, collective compacts (agreements without trade union intervention) have increased by 10 per cent since 1990, while collective agreements have proportionally decreased.

There is a general move towards strengthening the role of trade unions, and also extending compulsory union fees to workers who benefit from a collective convention but are not members of the trade union (as in Chile, Colombia, Ecuador and Venezuela). There is also a move towards opening up opportunities of collective bargaining for trade union federations and confederations (El Salvador).

In what might be considered, on the other hand, as stipulations obstructing the signing of collective agreements, Argentina, as mentioned previously, has two new policy criteria regarding the registration mechanism of the collective convention. It is through this convention that the competent administrative authority recognizes the legality of the content of the collective convention and grants authority for its official registration (which is necessary for the collective convention to take effect). The first of these criteria states that the collective convention must not contain clauses of salary indexation that cannot be justified by an increase in productivity, on the grounds that they are contrary to the country's monetary policy. The second criterion sets out the binding nature of including clauses for regulating relations in small businesses unless a specific collective agreement for these already exists. Moreover, the law allows the administrative authority to intervene in the renewal of collective agreements for small businesses, by summoning the parties to the negotiating table.

Some reforms underscore the role of collective bargaining in regulating employment contracts, including inserting clauses that alter the minimum legal requirement or reduce workers' benefits. In this way, collective bargaining can lead more easily to fixed-term contracts or can regulate the standard working day, and work during hours traditionally considered as overtime, through the creation of a system of an accumulated bank of hours, such as in Brazil. Collective bargaining can also link wages to productivity (in Panama and Venezuela) or 'modernize' workers' benefits according to the current circumstances of the business, by substituting benefits, renewing or revising the collective convention (in Panama and Paraguay), possibly with a reduction of benefits (Venezuela).

Equally, and as pointed out previously, despite the whole of the region recognising the plurality of negotiation levels in principle, the absence of negotiation procedures by area of activity in most countries evidently obstructs that plurality, as is the case in Bolivia and Colombia. In Venezuela, this procedure is no less complex, but it has at least been separated from the arbitration procedure for cases of disagreement, and dissatisfied trade unions are now able to resort to strike action.

A number of countries (for example, Peru) have opted for company-level negotiation and the new Argentine regulation appears to operate on the same lines. As previously pointed out, Argentine law promotes the decentralization of collective bargaining and adapting it to the small business with rules concerning 'collective availability'. According to these rules, it is possible – through a collective contract clause – to 'entitle' an employer to employ workers for a specific period of time under certain conditions, without the collective contract needing to be authorized in this respect. The clause can also alter the legal set of rules on annual leave, break up the periods of payment of the end-of-year bonus, and modify the rules for terminating employment. The clause can also redefine jobs as they correspond to the categories outlined in the collective contracts, and can modify collective or statutory regulations applicable in the event of the workplace being restructured for technological, organizational or market reasons. At the same time it safeguards small businesses' covenants in respect of covenants drawn up elsewhere, which cannot be modified during their term of validity.

Working at company level (with the employer so close at hand) has its advantages as well as its limitations. A trade union may feel more at ease, but can also run into serious difficulties, with the risk of conflict, or, quite the reverse, find itself controlled by the employer. At the same time, for workers, putting the right to organize into practice can be more difficult at this level, although there are much better opportunities for one-to-one communication. Moreover, negotiation at company level has the particular virtue of regulating working conditions in a specific context, in keeping with the company's current circumstances and with the workers' needs. However, the power to make such working conditions uniform is necessarily less effective than in a negotiation that is specific to a particular industry.[70]

Prevention or resolution of conflicts

Legislation in Latin America has typically granted governments a strong interventionist and controlling role in collective labour relations in general and, in particular, in situations of conflict. Paradoxically, legislation has tended to focus more on conflict than on dialogue, with regulations that are not conducive enough to negotiation or to finding means of avoiding or resolving conflict. This could perhaps be due to a mistrust of collective organizations or of the trade union movement *per se*.

The handful of reforms introduced in recent years appear to confirm a trend of reduced state intervention in matters of conflict. These reforms relate as much to the issue of strikes as to the means of preventing and resolving collective conflicts. The new regulations take a broader view of regulating the concepts and reasons for strikes (as seen, for example, in Chile, Colombia and Nicaragua), to include public service strikes and sympathy strikes. At the same time, some legislations affect exercising the right to strike, either by introducing advance notice of an impending strike (as in Paraguay), or a deadline for calling the strike, or a maximum period of duration of a strike (as in Colombia). When a strike is called, there are differing provisions regarding hiring replacement workers. The practice is accepted in Chile and Ecuador, if the strike affects minimum basic services, but it is not allowed in either Colombia or Paraguay, unless the strike is illegal (in Paraguay). Greater openness is noted in the state's presumption of whether a strike is legal (El Salvador), in defining the assumptions of illegality (Colombia, El Salvador and Peru), and in a more toned-down effect given to the statement of illegality (Nicaragua). Even so, the use of strikes tends to be subject to serious preconditions that act as a disincentive, and many strikes are declared illegal. Finally, some reforms relate to essential services, where strikes are either banned or restricted, and to the provision of minimum services in case of a strike.

Five of the new pieces of legislation concern the structures in place for addressing conflicts – in particular, conciliation and optional or compulsory arbitration. Chile, for example, provides for the free use of mediation and optional mediation. Peru has adopted a special law concerning arbitration. In Argentina, an act in 1998 stipulates that the Ministry of Labour will establish a mediation and arbitration service in order to resolve collective conflicts. In any case, in general terms, the state reserves the right to order compulsory arbitration and the resumption of work in certain circumstances.

11.4   Conclusions

Tracing the course of labour legislation introduced over the last decade of the twentieth century allows us to reach certain conclusions concerning the reforms and their scope.

Firstly, it is worth noting that, to a greater or lesser degree, there have been reforms in most countries in Latin America. Some countries have tried to update laws that had remained immutable for many years. Others have wanted to bring labour relations in line with the re-establishment or the consolidation of public liberties. Certain reforms have been general in nature, while others have introduced specific changes to certain institutions or structures. Amendments have been carried out in various ways. Most amendments have been passed by law, but others have derived directly from the Constitution and from decrees, terms of reference or guidelines.[71] In general terms, a reform is made through an instrument that deals with labour issues. However, in Argentina for example, there have also been important instances of legal texts dealing with economic issues and texts on small and medium-sized companies that directly amend the rights of significant groups of workers. In this way, not only can labour relations stagnate, by being shackled to the whims of economic and financial regulation, but the sporadic and dispersed nature of regulations can also complicate the legal system and make its application more cumbersome. Some reforms are the result of external factors, for instance, by limiting credit or assistance from international banks, or by the

ILO's Committee of Experts on the Application of Conventions and Recommendations requesting a member State to harmonize its legislation with a certain ratified instrument.[72]

Secondly, some reforms respond to attempts to make labour relations more flexible.[73] In this sense, Panama tried 'to seek fair return for the capital it had invested', quite distinct from the Code of 1971, whose aim was 'to introduce special state protection in favour of workers'. In Colombia, the Preamble to the Colombian Reform points out that 'modernising the economy requires a more flexible labour system, in order to make our products more competitive, promote investment and increase the generation of employment'. The dominant aim was to deregulate certain aspects of labour relations in order to allow the parties more room to manoeuvre, or, which amounts to the same thing, to have a freer hand in terms of supply and demand of labour. These changes are noticeable, above all, in certain regulations concerning individual labour relations.

Thirdly, one of the main guiding principles behind the most important reforms has been the promotion of employment. Starting from the premise that the traditional model of an employment contract and the cost of dismissal are rigid and costly (constituting a disincentive to employment), new formulas have been designed to simplify the commencement and the termination of a contract, and to reduce wage costs, including severance payments. However, flexibility in an employment contract and a reduction of its costs have not resulted in an increase in gainful employment, nor have the structural reforms that inspired them. The link between labour legislation and labour costs and productivity is obvious, but it is difficult to estimate the impact of labour legislation on employment, given that other elements come into play. It is a basic legal teaching that the law must always take the social environment it regulates into account. Given this fact, all efforts to continually adapt labour legislation to the current and changing circumstances of employer–employee relations can be considered legitimate, provided that the fundamental principles and values upon which the law has been structured are not sacrificed in the process. Nevertheless, it does not appear that labour regulations can be included among the variant factors curbing employment in Latin America, or at least they are not seen to be on the same level as factors such as inadequate investment, foreign debt, currency imbalance, political problems, violence, poverty and inequality, restricted generation of technology and modern enterprises, and deficiencies in professional training.

Fourthly, the reform's objective have in some cases served to strengthen the position of workers and their organizations, particularly concerning the treatment of collective labour relations and the search for greater collective autonomy. However, in some of these assumptions the practice of individualizing labour relations and the distancing from the state have seriously reduced workers' protection. This seems to have offset the progress made by legislative reforms in terms of trade union guarantees and the promotion of collective bargaining. This would be a crucial point in any rigorous summing up of the economic and labour effects brought about by labour legislation reforms that have taken place since 1990.

It is very difficult, for many reasons, to assess accurately the scope of a labour reform, unless radical changes are involved. At the beginning of the 1990s, national legislative situations varied greatly, making the value of a reform and its true scope dependent upon what it represented for each individual country. There is also the issue of the likely interval, either temporary or drawn out, between a regulation and its effective application. From this perspective, reforming willpower would certainly find plenty of opportunities in terms of the administrative and legal structures surrounding labour. Many problems that are attributed to substantive law can in fact be put down to an inadequate application of the law, and to long, complex and costly administrative and legal procedures. The quest for immediacy, simplicity and transparency, under the watchful eyes of social partners, may well lead to a new, more productive and rewarding phase in the regulation of labour relations.

In the end, some key problems remain unresolved. How useful is it to talk about a reform that only extends to 30 per cent of the economic active population? Where do they fit in, and how do the systems of minimum protection for the poorest people interconnect with each other? How can inequality be fought through a more comprehensive system of law? And, finally, what reform is most needed today?

Notes

1 M. Valverde, R. Sañudo and G. Murcia (2000) *Derecho del trabajo*, 9th edn (Madrid: Tecnos), p. 61.
2 Refer to G. Márquez and C. Pagés (1998) 'Ties that Bind: Employment Protection and Labor Market Outcomes in Latin America', in *Employment in Latin America: What is the Problem and How to Address It?*, Inter-American Development Bank and Inter-American Dialogue Seminar (Washington, DC: Inter-American Development Bank); ILO (1970) *Towards Full Employment* (Geneva: ILO), pp. 210–11.
3 The tripartite pacts have in fact facilitated the development of some reforms (the Dominican Republic, 1991; El Salvador, 1994).
4 IDB (2004) *Informe de Progreso económico y social. Se buscan buenos empleos. Los mercados de trabajo en América Latina* (Washington: Advance), p. 4.
5 Ibid., p. 18.
6 E. Lora and C. Pagés (1996) *Legislación laboral en el proceso de reformas estructurales de América Latina: y el Caribe* (Inter-American Development Bank), p. 2.
7 IDB (2004), p. 4.
8 Lora and Pagés note that labour reforms have been few and not far-reaching, contrasting with structural reforms carried out in the region. They point out that while 23 countries have introduced radical trade reforms, 24 countries have considerably liberalized their financial sectors, and 14 countries have introduced privatisation,

which in a given year exceeded 1 per cent of GDP. Since the 1980s, only five countries have made significant reforms: Argentina (1991), Colombia (1990), Guatemala (1990), Panama (1995) and Peru (1991). Both authors conclude that labour reforms have not only been scarce but limited. Or to put it less bluntly, they have been adopted as a means of gradual, not shock, therapies. Lora and Pagés (1996) pp. 7–8.

9   Despite maintaining its Code since 1939, Bolivia has made ongoing partial amendments and its 1975 Reform on Termination on Employment can be considered substantive. Costa Rica passed the Act 7360 in 1993, for example, amending the *Ley de Asociaciones Solidaristas*; the Labor Code; and the Organic Law of the Ministry of Labour. In Honduras, much work has been done over a number of years to reform the Labour Code, and some partial amendments do exist. The same has applied to Cuba since 1999. In Uruguay, the 1985 labour reforms were intended to annul the labour laws introduced during the era of dictatorship, but have never been replaced by new legislation.

10 In Venezuela there are talks concerning 17 new policy declarations on the issue of flexibility contained in its Organic Labour Law, in addition to the reforms already undertaken in 1997. O. Hernández Álvarez (1993) 'La evolución del Derecho del Trabajo en Venezuela', *Venezuela's Legal Seminar at the Threshold of the 21st Century* (Barquisimeto).

11 The most recent reforms of significant impact and weight are those enacted in Argentina (a range of issues), Brazil (equality of treatment and maternity), Colombia (social protection and small enterprise), Chile (Labour Code and agricultural workers), Ecuador (amendments to the Labour Code), Guatemala (various reforms to the Labour Code, namely, collective labour relations), Peru (collective labour relations, small and medium-sized enterprises and cooperatives), notwithstanding other minor reforms in Honduras, Paraguay, Uruguay, and so on. There are also revision projects and reform discussions in Mexico, Peru, Uruguay (collective labour relations) and Venezuela.

12 In Peru, for example, severance payments were first amended in October 1996 (reducing their maximum ceiling to six months) and later in November 1996 (resetting it to 12 months). In Venezuela, in 1990, there was also a broad reform to the Act. A new reform in 1997 dealt specifically with the issue of severance payment for unfair dismissal, with a maximum ceiling as in Peru. The Argentine experience is especially significant, given that the 2004 Reform amends issues, such as the compulsory inclusion of clauses of productivity in collective bargaining, introduced in the early 1990s.

13 For the preparation of this section, the contribution of the discussions held with my colleague D. Martínez of the ILO Regional Office for the Americas, on the possible concept of socially acceptable flexibility should deservedly be acknowledged. His comments were most valuable in writing this section.

14 OECD (1986), *Labour Market Flexibility: Report by a High-level Group of Experts to the Secretary-General* (Paris), p. 6.

15 A sample of this is ILO: *Decent Work*, Report of the Director-General to the International Labour Conference, 87th Session (Geneva: ILO, 1999), where, when discussing the international normative policy, the Director-General stresses the need to guarantee certain flexibility in line with the Organization's criteria (pp. 20–1).

16 ILO: General Report of the Committee on the Application of Conventions and Recommendations, International Labour Conference, 81st Session, Geneva, 1994.

17 See paragraph 15 of the General Report.

18 See paragraph 160 of the General Report.

19 In effect, based on the new criteria of equality and lack of discrimination, and taking into account the specific need to protect maternity as a matter of course and not to treat women as if they were a 'different category of worker', Convention No. 171 stipulates criteria of restrictions for night work based on a woman's procreative role, taking into account the legal status of the 'nasciturus', and not the woman for the mere fact of her gender.

20 Employment Service Convention, 1948 (No. 88); Forced Labour Convention, 1930 (No. 29); Freedom of Association and Protection of the Right to Organise Convention, 1948 (No. 87); Right to Organise and Collective Bargaining Convention, 1949 (No. 98); Discrimination (Employment and Occupation) Convention, 1958 (No. 111); Employment Policy Convention, 1964 (No. 122); Minimum Age Convention, 1973 (No. 138); Employment Promotion and Protection against Unemployment Convention, 1988 (No. 168), as well as other provisions on recruitment and placement entered in the Migration for Employment Convention (Revised) (No. 97), 1949; and Migrant Workers Convention (Supplementary Provisions), 1975 (No. 143).

21 It should not be forgotten that the decisions made by the ILO's Governing Body, the resolutions made at the Conference, and the decisions of any of the ILO's non-policy bodies, can have a major impact on the development of this concept of socially acceptable flexibility. In general, all standard activities pass through the above stages of consideration and prior study.

22 Protection against the negative effects of a termination of employment encompasses different areas collected from different standard texts: severance payment, unemployment insurance, properly administered unemployment funds, consultation with workers, participation of the administrative authority in the processes, and so on.

23 However, Act 25.013 takes into account the derogation of promotion contracts (notwithstanding a transitional arrangement in force). This situation was ratified in the Act 25.250, article 2, which promotes stable employment.

24 The first legislative amendment of this kind took place in Chile in 1978. Ecuador (1980), Peru (1986) and Argentina (1991) followed suit and reforms are still ongoing. At present, Argentina and Peru record the largest number of temporary contracts. In 1998, Brazil allowed liberalized fixed-term contracts though authorized through collective bargaining.

25 On Argentina, see A. Marshall (2004) 'Labour Market Policies and Regulations in Argentina, Brazil and Mexico: Programmes and Impacts', Employment strategy paper, no. 2004/13 (Geneva, ILO).

26 Preamble of the Argentinian National Employment Act.

27 A. Bronstein (1998) *Avances y retrocesos en la evolución de la legislación laboral en América Latina*, XII Ibero-American Congress of Labour Law and Social Security, Panama 27–30 April.

28 The new Act of 1998 has its origin in the *Acta de Coincidencias* signed by the (Argentinian) General Labour Confederation and the Argentinian Government in May 1997, which proposed eliminating most fixed-term contracts of employment.

29 In Peru, since 1995, fixed-term contracts do not require administrative authorization (thus eliminating tax costs). Moreover, the presumption of indefinite term contracts was abolished in the event where the work performed does not correspond to the type of work the worker was contracted to do.

30 According to a household survey undertaken in metropolitan Lima in 1997, of the total paid employment in the private sector, 26 per cent of contracts

were for an indefinite period; 16 per cent temporary; 1 per cent employment training agreements; 4 per cent services and cooperatives; 11 per cent commissions and contract work; and 41 per cent did not have a written or signed contract.

31 In Panama, restrictions were placed in 1995 on any abuse of the probation period, not applicable to workers previously employed by the same company.

32 In Argentina, in 1998, the probationary period for open-ended contracts was limited to 30 days, with the possibility of an extension to 180 days through approved agreement. Act 25.250 of 2000 stipulated the general probation period as three months (to be extended through collective agreement to a maximum of six months). For small businesses, the period is six months, to be extended through collective agreement to 12 months for skilled workers, as defined by such agreement.

33 For example, where there is an important constitutionalization in Latin America (labour law region) only 13 texts, out of a total of 20 countries, recognized them. They are: Argentina, Bolivia, Brazil, Colombia, Costa Rica, El Salvador, Guatemala, Honduras, Mexico, Panama, Paraguay, Peru and Venezuela.

34 Furthermore, payment of severance or accumulated funds is anticipated during the course of the employment, for example, in Brazil and Colombia.

35 Reinstatement exists in Cuba, Honduras, Mexico, Nicaragua, Panama, Peru and Venezuela. However, it is subject to certain conditions, such as a minimum of one year of employment (in Mexico), a minimum number of workers employed in a business (in Venezuela), and so on.

36 In effect, Act 5.105 introduced the Guarantee Fund for Time of Service; it limited the absolute prohibition of unfair dismissal established in the Consolidation of Labour Laws; and gave workers the opportunity to opt for the system of absolute stability or the new Guarantee Fund for Time of Service, which did not require notice and compensatory severance payment. In practice, employers did not employ any workers not opting for the Fund, which led to the old system becoming defunct.

37 The system of severance payment has been amended in Argentina, Chile, Colombia, Ecuador, El Salvador, Guatemala, Nicaragua, Panama, Peru and Venezuela.

38 See ILO (2000) *Labour Statistics Yearbook 2000* (Geneva: ILO).

39 See, for example, the Doing Business Index of the International Finance Corporation (www.doingbusiness.org) which penalizes countries that impose working hours restrictions.

40 The present version of the Venezuelan Constitution provides for a daytime working week of 48 hours (November 1999).

41 Ministerio de Trabajo y Seguridad Social – MTSS (Ministry of Labour and Social Security – MLSS) (1997): *Report on Employment Conditions*, June 1997.

42 For example, the 1996 agreement between the Ford Motor Company and the Union of Metallurgy in the ABC Region of Sao Paulo established a four-day working week (38 hours per week) over a period of six months. It was agreed that the reduction could be compensated in 1997 once production levels recovered. This agreement was based on the need for trade unions need to prevent imminent dismissals and on the need for management to reduce costs.

43 FIDE (Fundación de Investigaciones para el Desarrollo) (1981) *Cambios en la estructura productiva y el empleo. Coyuntura y desarrollo*, No. 33, May (Buenos Aires: FIDE), p. 50.

44   In Peru, the percentage of compensation is 30 per cent; Venezuela increased it from 20 per cent to 30 per cent; and the Dominican Republic introduced it for the first time at a rate of 15 per cent.

45   It is necessary to distinguish between remuneration and wage. Remuneration is the full earnings or receipts (wages are part of this) that a worker receives in exchange of his or her work, from the employer.

46   The value of the benefit was readjusted on the basis of the amount of wages earned at the time of termination, or on the date the wage was paid. From here came the idea of classifying a series of authorized payments from the government, or agreed to by the employer, in a different way – which were, in fact, wages in another guise.

47   This is a monthly wage that includes all the economic payments made by the employer. A worker who chooses this method does not receive legal or extra-legal payments, such as severance or Christmas bonuses. Instead, all payments received are accumulated in an improved monthly wage. In other words, the worker receives in advance and on a monthly basis all the other payments owed to him/her by the employer together with his/her wage.

48   It must also include compensatory payment of at least 30 per cent of the reference salary.

49   Prior to the reform, the Code stipulated that the minimum wage had to be consistent with the cost of subsistence, and with the conditions and needs of the various regions in the country, thus ensuring the worker the minimum well-being compatible with human dignity. It is now defined as the minimum remuneration a worker must receive for services rendered for an ordinary day's work, to ensure that the basic and vital needs of the breadwinner are fulfilled.

50   This is a point being stressed after the reform, for example in Colombia and Peru, which previously did not contain standard clauses in this respect.

51   In this sense, Act 24.467 of 1995 in Argentina provides for the free provision through collective agreement of the breaking up of periods of payment of supplementary wages, provided they do not exceed three periods in one given year.

52   Provisional measures Nos 794 of 1994 and 1593-34 of 1997. The decree laws are standards introduced in cases of urgent need, legal in character, which must be submitted within 30 days to the special processing unit.

53   ILO, *Development of Small and Medium-size Enterprises*, Report VI, International Labour Conference, 72nd Session (Geneva: ILO, 1986). Equally, the Job Creation in Small and Medium-Sized Enterprises Recommendation, 1998 (No. 189), adopted at the 86th Session of the ILC, stipulates the need to eliminate administrative requirements that act as a disincentive for employing workers, and which hinder the development of small and medium-sized businesses (para. 5 (h)).

54   For example, the Termination of Employment Convention, 1982 (No. 158) stipulates those exceptions (of the entire Convention or some of the stipulations) concerning certain categories that present problems that take on significant importance, especially in consideration of the size of the business that employs them.

55   Act 24.467 of 1995.

56   Act 8.864 of 28 March 1994.

57   Decree 2072/94 25 November 1994.

58   Labour Code.

59   Act 8.864.

60   ILO: Committee of Experts on the Application of Conventions and Recommendations, General Study on the Protection against Unfair Dismissal, International Labour Conference, 82nd Session, Geneva, 1995, para. 69.

61 In terms of procedures, Act 24.467 in Argentina stipulates in a class by itself a specific notice period of one month, to be calculated from the day after the notice has been given. This provision is in response to the notion of simplification being needed for such companies.

62 The main exception is Uruguay, where labour relations have developed through voluntary collective bargaining, imposed exclusively by the employer or de facto. (See, for example, R.J. Rosenbaum (2001) *Tendencias y Contenidos de la Negociación Colectiva en el Cono Sur de América Latina* (Lima: ILO).)

63 As of April 2007, Convention No. 87 has been ratified by 19 member States in the region; and Convention No. 98, by 17.

64 Revisions have occurred in 14 countries of the region: Argentina, Brazil, Chile, Colombia, Costa Rica, the Dominican Republic, Ecuador, El Salvador, Guatemala, Nicaragua, Panama, Paraguay, Peru and Venezuela.

65 The case of Chile is revealing. The recent ratification of Convention Nos 87 and 98 has not entailed a parallel alignment with the national legislation.

66 ILO (2000) *Your Voice at Work* (Geneva) and ILO (2004) *Organizing for Social Justice* (Geneva).

67 See P. Auer (2000) *Employment Revival in Europe: Labour Market Success in Austria, Denmark, Ireland and the Netherlands* (Geneva: ILO).

68 In 1993, a number of anti-union practices were prohibited in Costa Rica, although they were enforced with absolutely no legal force. A trade union charter was introduced in favour of the founders of trade unions and trade union leaders who, until then, had been unprotected against unfair dismissal. Likewise, the number of workers required to establish a trade union was reduced. It was also forbidden for employers to enter into collective agreements with non-unionized groups of workers in cases where there was no trade union within the company.

69 Actually, in Colombia for example, the procedure of sectoral collective bargaining is not regulated. In Peru the law defines the pre-eminence of negotiation on a company by company basis.

70 *Acerca de las ventajas y desventajas de la descentralización de la negociación colectiva,* see Márquez and Pagés, (1998), p. 43.

71 This is the case in Brazil, with the constitutional reform and the repeated use of interim measures to deregulate negotiations concerning public benefits; or in Peru, through its legislative decrees. In February 1998, the Labour Ministry in Costa Rica tried to introduce flexible amendments. While hierarchically the Code cannot be contravened, its legal effectiveness has been negligible, but it has at least served to re-launch the importance of the subject and the possible need to amend the legislation.

72 M.L. Cook attributes the changes in the legislation to a number of factors. These are opportunity issues, the former characteristics of the system of professional relations, the strength and direction of the trade union movement, the unity and the direction of employer groups, the strategies used by government leaders, and external factors, such as the International Monetary Fund and the ILO (op. cit., pp. 323–8).

73 The authors of the National Employment Act in Argentina pointed out in 1991 that the model of contract provided by the Law on Contract of Employment imposed restrictions that affected competition among businesses, and discouraged employment creation, in as much as they hindered dismissal or made the cost of termination more expensive. Nevertheless, dismissal without cause in Argentina is not more difficult than in Chile, Colombia or Mexico.

Bibliography

Abowd, J.M., F. Kramarz and D.N. Margolis (1999) *Minimum Wages and Employment in France and the United States*, NBER Working Paper No. 6996 (Washington, DC: National Bureau of Economic Research).

Acemoglu, D. and J.S. Pischke (1998) 'Why Do Firms Train? Theory and Evidence', *The Quarterly Journal of Economics*, 113(1): 79–118.

ADB (Asian Development Bank) (2003) 'Competitiveness in Developing Asia', in *Asian Development Outlook* (Manila: Asian Development Bank).

Addison, J.T., W.S. Siebert, J. Wagner and X. Wei (2000) 'Worker Participation and Firm Performance: Evidence from Germany and Britain', *British Journal of Industrial Relations*, 38(1): 7–49.

Adler, W.M. (2000) *Mollie's Job: A Story of Life and Work in the Global Assembly Line* (New York: Touchstone).

Agell, J. (1999) 'On the Benefits from Rigid Labour Markets: Norms, Market Failures, and Social Insurance', *Economic Journal*, 109(453): F143–64.

Agell, J. and K.E. Lommerud (1992) 'Union Egalitarianism as Income Insurance', *Economica*, 59: 295–310.

Aidt, T. and Z. Tzannatos (2002) *Unions and Collective Bargaining: Economic Effects in a Global Environment* (Washington, DC: World Bank).

Aidt, T. and Z. Tzannatos (2005) 'The Costs and Benefits of Collective Bargaining', Cambridge Working Papers in Political Economy No. 0541 (Cambridge University).

Aidt, T. and Z. Tzannatos (2008) 'Trade Unions, Collective Bargaining and Macroeconomic Performance: A review, *Industrial Relations Journal*.

Akerlof, G. and W. Dickens (1984) 'The Economic Consequences of Cognitive Dissonance', in *An Economic Theorist's Book of Tales* (Cambridge: Cambridge University Press).

Alber, J. (1981) 'Government Responses to the Challenge of Unemployment: The Development of Unemployment Insurance in Western Europe', in P. Flora and A. Heidenheimer (eds), *The Development of Welfare States in Europe and America* (New Brunswick, NJ: Transaction Books).

Alchian, A.A. and S. Woodward (1988) 'The Firm is Dead; Long Live the Firm: A Review of O.E. Williamson's The Economic Institutions of Capitalism', *Journal of Economic Literature*, 26(1): 65–79.

Alcock, A. (1971) *History of the International Labour Organization* (London: Macmillan).

Alogoskoufis, G.S. and A. Manning (1988) 'Wage-Setting and Unemployment Persistence in Europe, Japan, and the USA', *European Economic Review*, 32(2–3): 698–706.

Alogoskoufis, G.S. and A. Manning (1991) 'Tests of Alternative Wage Employment Bargaining Models with an Application to the UK Aggregate Labor Market', *European Economic Review*, 35(1): 23–37.

Alston, P. and J. Heenan (2004) 'Shrinking the International Labor Code: An Unintended Consequence of the 1998 ILO Declaration on Fundamental Principles and Rights at Work?', *New York University School of Law Journal of International Law and Politics*, 36: 221–64.

Álvarez, O. Hernández (1993) 'La evolución del Derecho del Trabajo en Venezuela', *Venezuela's Legal Seminar at the Threshold of the 21st Century* (Barquisimeto).

Alvarez, R.M., G. Garrett and P. Lange (1991) 'Government Partisanship, Labor Organization, and Macroeconomic Performance', *American Political Science Review*, 85(2): 539–56.

Anti-Slavery International and International Working Group for Indigenous Affairs (1997) *Enslaved Peoples in the 1990s: Indigenous Peoples, Debt Bondage and Human Rights* (London and Copenhagen: Anti-Slavery International and International Working Group for Indigenous Affairs).

Auer, P. (2000) *Employment Revival in Europe: Labour Market Success in Austria, Denmark, Ireland and the Netherlands* (Geneva: ILO).

Baker, D. (2005) 'Labour Market Institutions and Unemployment: A Critical Assessment of the Cross-Country Reference', in D.R. Howell (ed.), *Fighting Unemployment: The Limits to Free Market Orthodoxy* (New York: Oxford University Press).

Baker, D., A. Glyn, D.R. Howell and J. Schmitt (2004) 'Unemployment and Labour Market Institutions: The Failure of the Empirical Case for Deregulation', Working Paper No. 43, Policy Integration Department, Statistical Development and Analysis Unit (Geneva: ILO).

Barnard, D. and R. Hobbs (2003) 'Opting Out of the 48-Hour Week: Employer Necessity or Individual Choice?', *Industrial Law Journal*, 32(4): 223–52.

Barnes, G.N. (1926) *History of the International Labour Office* (London: Williams and Norgate).

Batt, R. and T. Welbourne (2002) 'Performance Growth in Entrepreneurial Firms: Revisiting the Union-Performance Relationship', in J. Katz and T. Welbourne (eds), *Research Volume on Entrepreneurship*, vol. 5 (Saint Louis: JAI Press).

Bean, C.R. (1994) 'European Unemployment: A Retrospect', *European Economic Review*, 38(3–4): 523–34.

Bean, C.R., P.R.G. Layard and S.J. Nickell (1986) 'The Rise in Unemployment: A Multi-country Study', *Economica*, 53: S1–S22.

Bean, C.R., and P.J. Turnbull (1988) 'Employment in the British Coal Industry: A Test of the Labour Demand Model', *Economic Journal*, 98: 1092–104.

Becker, G.S. (1975) *Human Capital* (Chicago: University of Chicago Press).

Bellman, D. (1992) 'Unions, the Quality of Labor Relations, and Firm Performance', in L. Mishel and P.B. Voos (eds), *Unions and Economic Competitiveness* (New York: M.E. Sharpe).

Belser, P. (2001) *Four Essays on Trade and Labour Standards*, unpublished Ph.D. dissertation, University of Sussex.

Berg, J. and S. Cazes (2008) 'Policymaking Gone Away: The Labour Market Regulations of the Doing Business Indicators', in *Comparative Labor Law and Policy Journal*, 29(3).

Bernstein, J. and J. Schmitt (1998) *Making Work Pay: The Impact of the 1996–97 Minimum Wage Increase* (Washington, DC: Economic Policy Institute).

Bertola, G. (1990) 'Job Security, Employment and Wages', *European Economic Review*, 34(4): 851–79.

Bertola, G. (2005) 'Distribution, Efficiency, and Labor Market Regulation: In Theory, in OECD Countries, and in Latin America', in J. Restrepo and A. Tokman (eds), *Labor Markets and Institutions* (Santiago: Central Bank of Chile).

Bertola, G., T. Boeri and S. Cazes (2000) 'Employment Protection in Industrialized Countries: The Case for New Indicators', *International Labour Review*, 139(1): 57–72.

Besley, T. and R. Burgess (2004) 'Can Labor Relations Hinder Economic Performance? Evidence from India', *Quarterly Journal of Economics* (1): 91–134.

Bhattacherjee, D. (1987) 'Union-Type Effects on Bargaining Outcomes in Indian Manufacturing', *British Journal of Industrial Relations*, 22(2): 247–66.

Blanchflower, D.G. (1996a) 'Product Market Competition, Wages, and Productivity: International Evidence from Establishment-Level Data', *Annals d'Economie et de Statistique*, 41/42(2): 219–54.

Blanchflower, D.G. (1996b) 'The Role and Influence of Trade Unions in the OECD', Discussion Paper No. 310 (London: London School of Economics, Centre for Economic Performance).

Blanchflower, D.G. (1999) 'Changes over Time in Union Relative Wage Effects in Great Britain and the United States', in S. Daniel, P. Arestis and J. Grahl (eds), *Essays in Honour of Bernard Corry and Maurice Peston, Vol. 2: The History and Practice of Economics* (Cheltenham, UK: Edward Elgar).

Blanchflower, D.G. and S. Burgess (1996) 'New Technology and Jobs: Comparative Evidence from a Two-Country Study', in B. Hall, M. Doms and F. Kramarz (eds), *Economics of Innovation and New Technology* (Washington, DC: National Academy Press).

Blanchflower, D.G. and R. Freeman (1992) 'Unionism in the United States and Other Advanced OECD Countries', *Industrial Relations*, 31(1): 56–79.

Blanchflower, D.G., N. Millward and A.J. Oswald (1991) 'Unionism and Employment Behaviour', *Economic Journal*, 101: 815–34.

Blanchflower, D.G. and A.J. Oswald (1988) 'Internal and External Influences upon Pay Settlements', *British Journal of Industrial Relations*, 26(3): 363–70.

Blanchard, O. and J. Wolfers (2000) 'The Role of Shocks and Institutions in the Rise of European Unemployment: The Aggregate Evidence', *Economic Journal*, 110(462): 1–33.

Blau, F. and L. Kahn (2002) *At Home and Abroad: US Labor Market Performance in International Perspective* (New York: Russell Sage).

Blaustein, S. (1993) *Unemployment Insurance in the United States: The First Half Century* (Kalamazoo, MI: W.E. Upjohn Institute for Employment Research).

Bleaney, M. (1996) 'Central Bank Independence, Wage-Bargaining Structure, and Macroeconomic Performance in OECD Countries', *Oxford Economic Papers*, 48(3): 20–38.

Boal, W.M. and J.H. Pencavel (1994) 'The Effects of Labor Unions on Employment, Wages, and Days of Operation: Coal Mining in West Virginia', *Quarterly Journal of Economics*, 109(1): 267–98.

Boeri, T., A. Brugiavini and L. Calmfors (2001) *The Role of Unions in the 21st Century* (Oxford: Oxford University Press).

Bollen, K.A. (2001) 'Indicator: Methodology', in N. Smeler and P. Baltes (eds), *International Encyclopedia of the Social & Behavioural Sciences*, vol. 11 (Amsterdam: Elsevier).

Booth, A. (1991) 'Job-related Formal Training: Who Receives it and What is it Worth?', *Oxford Bulletin of Economics and Statistics*, 53(3): 281–94.

Booth, A. (1995) *The Economics of the Trade Union* (Cambridge: Cambridge University Press).

Booth, A., M. Francesconi and G. Zoega (2003) 'Unions, Training and Wages: Evidence for British Men', *Industrial and Labor Relations Review*, 57(1): 68–91.

Borjas, G.J. (2005) *Labor Economics* (New York: Irwin McGraw-Hill).

Bosch, G. and S. Lehndorff (2001) 'Working-time Reduction and Employment: Experiences in Europe and Economic Policy Recommendations', *Cambridge Journal of Economics*, 25(2): 209–43.

Botero, J., S. Djankov, R. La Porta, Lopez-de-Silanes, and A. Shleifer (2004) 'The Regulation of Labour', *Quarterly Journal of Economics*, 119(4): 1339–82.

Botwinick, H. (1993) *Persistent Inequalities: Wage Disparity under Capitalist Competition* (Princeton, NJ: Princeton University Press).

Boulin, J.Y., M. Lallement, F. Michon and J. Messenger (eds) (2006) *Decent Working Time: New Trends, New Issues* (Geneva: ILO).

Bowles, S. and R. Boyer (1995) 'Wages, Aggregate Demand and Employment in an Open Economy: An Empirical Investigation', in G.A. Epstein and H.M. Gintis (eds), *Macroeconomic Policy after the Conservative Era* (Cambridge: Cambridge University Press).

Braithwaite, J. and P. Drahos (2005) *Global Business Regulation* (New York: Cambridge University Press).

Brodsky, M. (1994) 'Labor Market Flexibility: A Changing International Perspective', *Monthly Labor Review*, 117(11): 53–60.

Bronars, S.G., D.R. Deere and J. Tracy (1994) 'The Effects of Unions on Firm Behaviour: An Empirical Analysis Using Firm-level Data', *Industrial Relations*, 33(4): 426–51.

Bronstein, A. (1998) *Avances y retrocesos en la evolución de la legislación laboral en América Latina*, XII Ibero-American Congress of Labour Law and Social Security, Panama, 27–30 April.

Brooks, R. (2002) 'Why is Unemployment High in the Philippines?', IMF Working Paper 02/23 (Washington, DC: IMF).

Brown, C. (1990) 'Firms' Choice of Method of Pay', *Industrial and Labor Relations Review*, 43(3): 165–82.

Brown, C., C. Gilroy and A. Kohen (1982) 'Times-series Evidence of the Effect of the Minimum Wage on Youth Employment and Unemployment', *Journal of Human Resources*, 18(1): 3–31.

Brown, J.N. and O. Ashenfelter (1986) 'Testing the Efficiency of Employment Contracts', *Journal of Political Economy*, 94 (Supplement): S40–S87.

Brown, P. (1957) 'The Meaning of the Fitted Cobb–Douglas Function', *Quarterly Journal of Economics*, 71: 546–60.

Browne, J., S. Deakin, and F. Wilkinson (2002) 'Capabilities, Social Rights and European Market Integration', ESRC Centre for Business Research Working Paper 253 (Cambridge: University of Cambridge).

Brunello, G. (1992) 'The Effect of Unions on Firms in Japanese Manufacturing', *Industrial and Labor Relations Review*, 45(3): 471–87.

Bruno, M. and J. Sachs (1985) *Economics of Worldwide Stagflation* (Cambridge, MA: Harvard University Press).

Burkhauser, R. and A. Finegan (1993) 'The Economics of Minimum Wage Legislation Revisited', *Cato Journal*, 13(1): 123–9.

Burkhauser, R., K.A. Couch and D.C. Wittenburg (2000) 'A Reassessment of the New Economics of the Minimum Wage Literature with Monthly Data from the Current Population Survey', *Journal of Labor Economics*, 18: 653–701.

Busse, M. (2001) 'Do Labour Standards Affect Comparative Advantage?: Evidence for Labour-intensive Goods', Centre for International Economic Studies Discussion Paper No. 0142 (Adelaide).

Butcher, K. and J. DiNardo (2002) 'The Immigrant and Native-born Wage Distributions: Evidence from United States Censuses', *Industrial and Labor Relations Review*, 56(1): 97–121.

Butcher, K. and C. Rouse (2001) 'Wage Effects of Unions and Industrial Councils in South Africa', *Industrial and Labor Relations Review*, 54(2): 349–74.

Calmfors, L. (1993) 'Centralization of Wage Bargaining and Macroeconomic Performance: A Survey', Seminar Paper No. 536 (Stockholm: Stockholm University, Institute for International Economic Studies).

Calmfors, L. and J. Driffill (1988) 'Bargaining Structure, Corporatism, and Macroeconomic Performance', *Economic Policy*, 6: 13–62.

Camargo, J.M. (1998) 'Minimum Wages in Brazil: Theory, Policy and Empirical Evidence', *Labour Management Relations Series*, No. 67 (Geneva: ILO), 55–80.

Cameron, D.R. (1984) 'Social Democracy, Corporatism, Labour Quiescence, and the Representation of Interest in Advanced Capitalist Society', in J.H. Goldthorpe (ed.), *Order and Conflict in Contemporary Capitalism* (Oxford: Oxford University Press).

Card, D. (1986) 'Efficient Contracts with Costly Adjustment: Short-Run Employment Determination for Airline Mechanics', *American Economic Review*, 76(5): 1045–71.

Card, D. and A.B. Krueger (1994) 'Minimum Wages and Employment: A Case Study of the Fast-food Industry in New Jersey and Pennsylvania', *American Economic Review*, 84(4): 772–93.

Card, D. and A.B. Krueger (1995) *Myth and Measurement. The New Economics of the Minimum Wage* (Princeton, NJ: Princeton University Press).

Card, D. and A.B. Krueger (2000) 'Minimum Wages and Employment: A Case Study of the Fast-food Industry in New Jersey and Pennsylvania: Reply', *American Economic Review*, 90: 1397–420.

Cárdenas, M. and R. Bernal (2004) 'Determinants of Labor Demand in Colombia 1976–96', in J. Heckman and C. Pagés (eds), *Law and Employment: Lessons from Latin American and the Caribbean* (Chicago: University of Chicago Press).

Carlin, W. and D. Soskice (1990) *Macroeconomics and the Wage Bargain* (Oxford: Oxford University Press).

Carneiro, F. and A. Henley (1998) 'Wage Determination in Brazil: The Growth of Union Bargaining Power and Informal Employment', *Journal of Development Studies*, 34(4): 117–38.

Carr, M. and M.A. Chen (2001) 'Globalization and the Informal Economy: How Global Trade and Investment Impact on the Working Poor', WIEGO working paper.

Castro, C. de Maura, K. Kempner and D. Bas (2000) 'Apprenticeship: The Perilous Journey from Germany to Togo', in C. de Maura Castro, K. Schaack and R. Tippelt (eds), *Vocational Training at the Turn of the Century* (Frankfurt am Main).

Chimerine, L., T. Black and L. Coffey (1999) 'Unemployment Insurance as an Automatic Stabilizer: Evidence of Effectiveness Over Three Decades', Occasional Paper 99–8 (Washington, DC: US, Department of Labor).

Christiansen, N.F. and K. Petersen (2001) 'The Dynamics of Social Solidarity: The Danish Welfare State, 1900–2000', *Scandinavian Journal of History*, 26(3): 177–96.

Christie, V. (1992) 'Union Wage Effects and the Probability of Union Membership', *Economic Record*, 68(200): 43–56.

Cobb, C. and P. Douglas (1928) 'A Theory of Production', *American Economic Review* Papers and Proceedings of the Fortieth Annual Meeting of the American Economic Association, 18 (Supplement).

Cohen, A. and G. Harcourt (2003) 'Whatever Happened to the Capital Controversies?', *Journal of Economic Perspectives*, 17(1): 199–214.

Crouch, C. (1985) 'Conditions for Trade Union Wage Restraint', in L.N. Lindberg and C.S. Maier (eds), *The Politics of Inflation and Economic Stagflation* (Washington, DC: The Brookings Institution).

Crouch, C. (1990) 'Trade Unions in the Exposed Sector: Their Influence on Neocorporatist Behaviour', in R. Brunetta and C. Dell'Aringa (eds), *Labour Relations and Economic Performance* (New York: New York University Press).

Curry, J. (1993) 'The Flexibility Fetish: A Review Essay on Flexible Specialisation', *Capital & Class*, 50(3): 99–126.

Dabalen, A. (1998) 'The Effect of Unions on Wages in South Africa: Repeated Cross-section Estimates', Working Paper (University of California, Berkeley).

Dasgupta, P. (1988) 'Trust as a Commodity', in D. Gambetta (ed.), *Trust: Making and Breaking Cooperative Relations* (New York: Basil Blackwell).

De Oliveira, O. and B. Roberts (1994) 'The Many Roles of the Informal Sector in Development: Evidence from Urban Labor Market Research, 1940–89', in C.A. Rakowski (ed.), *Contrapunto: The Informal Sector Debate in Latin America* (Albany, NY: State University of New York Press).

De Soto, H. (2000) *The Mystery of Capital: Why Capitalism Triumphs in the West and Fails Everywhere Else* (New York: Basic Books).

Deakin, S. (2001) *Renewing Labour Market Institutions* (Geneva: International Institute for Labour Studies).

Deere, D., K.M. Murphy and F. Welch (1995) 'Employment and the 1990–91 Minimum-wage Hike', *American Economic Review*, 85(2): 232–7.

Dembe, A.E., J.B. Erickson, R.G. Delbos and S.M. Banks (2005) 'The Impact of Overtime and Long Work Hours on Occupational Injuries and Illnesses: New Evidence from the United States', *Occupational and Environmental Medicine*, 62(9): 588–97.

DiNardo, J. (1991) 'Union Employment Effect: An Empirical Analysis', Discussion Paper No. 90-92-06 (California: Department of Economics, University of California, Irvine).

Doiron, D.J. and W.C. Riddell (1994) 'The Impact of Unionization on Male–Female Earnings Differences in Canada', *Journal of Human Resources*, 29(2): 504–34.

Dolado, J., F. Kramarz, S. Machin, A. Manning, D. Margolis and C. Teulings (1996) 'The Economic Impact of Minimum Wages in Europe', *Economic Policy*, 23: 318–57.

Dowrick, S. (1993) 'Wage Bargaining Systems and Productivity Growth in OECD Countries', Background Paper No. 26 (Canberra: Australian Government Publishing Service).

Drago, R. and M. Wooden (1992) 'The Australian Workplace Industrial Relations Survey and Workplace Performance', *Australian Bulletin of Labour*, 18(2): 142–69.

Dumlao, L. (2002) 'Lowering Unemployment by Hiking Minimum Wage', *Business World*, 7 May.

Duncan, G.J. and F.P. Stafford (1980) 'Do Union Members Receive Compensating Wage Differentials?', *American Economic Review*, 70(3): 355–71.

Dunne, T. and D. MacPherson (1994) 'Unionism and Gross Employment Flows', *Southern Economic Journal*, 60(3): 727–38.

Earle, J.S. and J. Pencavel (1990) 'Hours of Work under Trade Unionism', *Journal of Labor Economics*, 8: 151–74.

Eastern Economic Journal (2005) 'Symposium: Aggregate Production Functions', 31(3).

Elias P. and D.G. Blanchflower (1989) 'Occupations, Earnings, and Work Histories of Young Adults: Who Gets the Good Jobs?', Research Paper No. 68 (London: Department of Employment).

European Commission, Directive 2003/88/EC of the European Parliament and of the Council of 4 November 2003 concerning certain aspects of the organization of working time, Preamble. Hours of Work (Industry) Convention, 1919 (No. 1); Hours of Work (Commerce and Offices) Convention, 1930 (No. 30).

Eyraud, F. and C. Saget (2005) *The Fundamentals of Minimum Wage Fixing* (Geneva: ILO).

Faith, R.L. and J.D. Reid (1987) 'An Agency Theory of Unionism', *Journal of Economic Behavior and Organization*, 8: 39–60.

Farber, H.S. and A.B. Krueger (1992) 'Union Membership in the United States: the Decline Continues', NBER, Working Paper No. 4216 (Cambridge, MA: National Bureau of Economic Research).

Feldstein, M. and D. Altman (1998) 'Unemployment Insurance Savings Accounts', NBER Working Paper No. 6860 (Cambridge, MA: National Bureau of Economic Research).

Felipe, J. and G. Adams (2005) '"A Theory of Production". The Estimation of the Cobb–Douglas Function: A Retrospective View', *Eastern Economic Journal*, 31(3): 427–45.

Felipe, J. and F.M. Fisher (2003) 'Aggregation in Production Functions: What Applied Economists Should Know', *Metroeconomica*, 54(2–3): 208–62.

Felipe, J. and R. Hasan (eds), (2006) *Labor Markets in Asia: Issues and Perspectives* (Basingstoke: Palgrave).

Felipe, J. and L. Lanzona (2006) 'Unemployment, Labour Laws and Economic Policies in the Philippines', in J. Felipe and R. Hasan (eds), *Labor Markets in Asia: Issues and Perspectives* (Basingstoke: Palgrave).

Felipe, J. and J.S.L. McCombie (2001) 'The CES Production Function, the Accounting Identity and Occam's Razor', *Applied Economics*, 33: 1221–32.

Felipe, J. and J.S.L. McCombie (2002) 'A Problem with Some Recent Estimations and Interpretations of the Mark-up in Manufacturing Industry', *International Review of Applied Economics*, 16(2): 187–215.

Felipe, J. and J.S.L. McCombie (2003) 'Methodological Problems with the Neoclassical Analyses of the East Asian Economic Miracle', *Cambridge Journal of Economics*, 27(5): 695–721.

Felipe, J. and J.S.L. McCombie (2005) 'How Sound are the Foundations of the Aggregate Production Function?', *Eastern Economic Journal*, 31(3): 467–88.

Felipe, J. and J.S.L. McCombie (2007) 'Are Estimates of Labor Demand Functions Mere Statistical Artefacts?', *International Review of Applied Economics*. Forthcoming.

Fields, G. (2004) 'A Guideline to Multisector Labor Market Models', Paper prepared for the World Bank Labor Market Conference, Washington DC, 18–19 November.

Filer, R.K., D.S. Hamermesh and A.E. Rees (1996) *The Economics of Work and Pay*, 6th ed. (New York: HarperCollins College).

Fisher, F.M. (1971) 'Aggregate Production Functions and the Explanation of Wages: A Simulation Experiment', *Review of Economics and Statistics*, 53(4): 305.

Fisher, F.M. (1993) *Aggregation, Aggregate Production Functions and Related Topics* (London: Harvester Wheatsheaf).

Flanagan, R. (1999) 'Macroeconomic Performance and Collective Bargaining: An International Perspective', *Journal of Economic Literature*, 37(4): 1150–75.

Flanagan, R. (2003) 'Labor Standards and International Competitive Advantage', in R. Flanagan (ed.), *International Labor Standards: Globalization, Trade and Public Policy* (Stanford, CA: Stanford University Press).

Flora, P. and J. Alber (1981) 'Modernization, Democratization and the Development of Welfare States in Western Europe', in P. Flora and A. Heidenheimer (eds), *The Development of Welfare States in Europe and America* (New Brunswick, NJ: Transaction Books).

Flora, P. and A. Heidenheimer (1981) 'The Historical Core and Changing Boundaries of the Welfare State', in P. Flora and A. Heidenheimer (eds), *The Development of Welfare States in Europe and America* (New Brunswick, NJ: Transaction Books).

Fluitman, F. and X. Oudin (1992) 'Skill Acquisition and Work in Micro-enterprises: Evidence from Lomé, Togo', Discussion Paper, Vocational Training Branch (Geneva: ILO).

Fluitman, F. and A.K. Sangré (1989) 'Some Recent Evidence of Informal Sector Apprenticeship in Abidjan, Cote d'Ivoire', in *Training for Work in the Informal Sector* (Geneva: ILO).

Foley, D.K. and T.R. Mich (1999) *Growth and Distribution* (Cambridge: Harvard University Press).

Freeman, D.G. and R. Freeman (1996) 'Growing into Work', Discussion Paper No. 296 (London: London School of Economics Centre for Economic Performance).

Freeman, R. (1980) 'The Exit–Voice Tradeoff in the Labor Market: Unionism, Job Tenure, Quits, and Separations', *Quarterly Journal of Economics*, 94(4): 643–74.

Freeman, R. (1984) *What do Unions do?* (New York: Basic Books).

Freeman, R. (1985) 'Unions, Pensions, and Union Pension Funds', in D. Wise (ed.), *Pensions, Labor, and Individual Choice* (Chicago: University of Chicago Press).

Freeman, R. (1988) 'Labour Market Institutions and Economic Performance', *Economic Policy*, 3: 64–78.

Freeman, R. (1993a) 'Labor Market Institutions and Policies: Help or Hindrance to Economic Development?', *World Bank Annual Conference on Development Economics, 1992* (Washington, DC: World Bank).

Freeman, R. (1993b) 'Labor Markets and Institutions in Economic Development', *American Economic Review*, 83(2): 403–8.

Freeman, R. (2005) 'Labour Market Institutions Without Blinders: The Debate Over Flexibility and Labour Market Performance', NBER Working Paper No. 11286 (Cambridge, MA: National Bureau of Economic Research).

Freeman, R. and M. Kleiner (1990) 'The Impact of New Unionization on Wages and Working Conditions', *Journal of Labor Economics*, 8(1): 8–25.

Freeman, R. and J.L. Medoff (1979) 'The Two Faces of Unionism', *Public Interest*, 57: 69–93.

Frisoni, R. and M. Kongolo (2002) 'The Evolution of Labour Law in Latin America since the 1980s', Background Document (Geneva: International Institute for Labour Studies).

Fudenberg, D. and J. Tirole (1993) *Game Theory* (Cambridge, MA: MIT Press).

FIDE [Fundación de Investigaciones para el Desarrollo] (1981) *Cambios en la estructura productiva y el empleo. Coyuntura y desarrollo*, 33 (Buenos Aires: FIDE).

Garrett, G. and P. Lange (1986) 'Economic Growth in Capitalist Democracies', *World Politics*, 38: 517–45.

Gasparini, L. (2004) 'América Latina: Estudio de la Protección Social y el Empleo sobre la base de Encuestas de Hogares', in F. Betranou (ed.), *Protección Social Mercado Laboral* (Santiago de Chile: OIT).

Gersbach, H. and A. Schmutzler (2001) 'A Product Market Theory of Training and Turnover in Firms', Discussion Paper No. 327, IZA (Bonn: Institute for the Study of Labor).

Ghosh, R., Singh, N. Raj and H. Sekar (eds) (2002) *Hard Labour at a Tender Age: Child Labour in the Home-based Industries in the Wake of Legislation* (Noida: V.V. Giri National Labour Institute).

Gibbon, I. (1911) *Unemployment Insurance: A Study of Schemes of Assisted Insurance* (Westminster: P.S. King and Son).

Gill, I.S., F. Fluitman and A. Dar (2000) *Vocational Education and Training Reform: Matching Skills to Markets and Budgets* (Washington, DC: World Bank and Oxford University Press).

Gill, I.S. and N. Ilahi (2000) 'Economic Insecurity, Individual Behavior and Social Policy', Paper prepared for the regional study, *Managing Economic Insecurity in Latin America and the Caribbean* (Washington, DC: World Bank).

Golden, M. (1993) 'The Dynamics of Trade Unionism and National Economic Performance', *American Political Science Review*, 87(2): 439–54.

Gong, X. and A. van Soest (2002) 'Wage Differentials and Mobility in the Urban Labour Market: A Panel Data Analysis for Mexico', *Labour Economics*, 9(4): 513–29.

Grant, E.K., R. Swidinsky and J. Vanderkamp (1987) 'Canadian Union/Non-union Wage Differentials', *Industrial and Labor Relations Review*, 41(1): 93–107.

Green, D.A. (1991) 'A Comparison of Estimation Approaches of Union/Non-union Wage Differentials', Discussion Paper No. 91-13 (Vancouver: Department of Economics, University of British Columbia).

Green, F. (1988) 'The Trade Union Wage Gap in Britain: Some Recent Estimates', *Economics Letters*, 27.

Green, F. (1995) 'Union Recognition and Paid Holiday Entitlement', Discussion Paper No. E95/13, University of Leeds, School of Business and Economic Studies, Leeds.

Green, F., G. Hadjimatheou and R. Smail (1985) 'Fringe Benefit Distribution in Britain', *British Journal of Industrial Relations*, 23(2): 261–80.

Grimshaw, D. and M. Miozzo (2003) *Minimum Wages and Pay Equity in Latin America: Identifying the Employment and Pay Equity Effects*, DECLARATION Working Paper 12/2003 (Geneva: ILO).

Gunderson, M. (1982) 'Union Impact on Wages, Fringe Benefits, and Productivity', in M. Gunderson and J. Anderson (eds), *Union–Management Relations in Canada* (Toronto: Addison-Wesley).

Gunderson, M., A. Ponak, and D.G. Taras (eds) (2000) *Union–Management Relations in Canada*, 4th edn (Toronto: Addison-Wesley).

Hall, P.A. and R.J. Franzese (1998) 'Mixed Signals: Central Bank Independence, Coordinated Wage Bargaining and European Monetary Union', *International Organization*, 52(3): 505–35.

Hall, P.A. and D. Soskice (2001) 'An Introduction to Varieties of Capitalism', in P. Hall and D. Soskice (eds), *Varieties of Capitalism: The Institutional Foundations of Comparative Advantage* (Oxford: Oxford University Press).

Hamermesh, D.S. (1993) *Labor Demand* (Princeton, NJ: Princeton University Press).

Hamermesh, D.S. (2004) 'Labor Demand in Latin America and the Caribbean: What Does It Tell Us?', in J. Heckman and C. Pagés (eds), *Law and Employment: Lessons from Latin American and the Caribbean* (Chicago: University of Chicago Press).

Harhoff, D. and T.J. Kane (1997) 'Is the German Apprenticeship System a Panacea for the U.S. Labor Market?', *Journal of Population Economics*, 10: 171–96.

Heckman, J. and C. Pagés (2000) 'The Cost of Job Security Regulation: Evidence from Latin American Labor Markets', *Economia*, 1(1): 109–54.

Heckman, J. and C. Pagés (2004) *Law and Employment: Lessons from Latin America and the Caribbean* (Chicago: University of Chicago Press).

Heckman, J., M. Ljunge and K. Ragan (2006 (June 1 draft)) 'What are the Key Employment Challenges and Policy Priorities for OECD Countries', *Paper for Presentation on Boosting Jobs and Incomes: Lessons from OECD Country Experiences*, Toronto, 15 June.

Hibbs, D. (1978) 'On the Political Economy of Long-Run Trends in Strike Activity', *British Journal of Political Science*, 8: 153–75.

Hicks, J.R. (1932) *The Theory of Wages* (London: Macmillan Press).

Hopenhayn, H. (2001) 'Labor Market Policies and Employment Duration: The Effects of Labor Market Reform in Argentina', Inter-American Development Bank Research Network Working Paper, R-407 (Washington, DC: IDB).

Howell, D.R. (ed.) (2004) *Fighting Unemployment: The Limits of Free Market Orthodoxy* (Oxford: Oxford University Press).

ICFTU (2005) 'Comments by ICFTU/Global Unions on the World Bank's *Doing Business in 2005*: "Hiring and Firing of Workers"', mimeo.

IDB (2004) *Informe de Progreso económico y social. Se buscan buenos empleos. Los mercados de trabajo en América Latina* (Washington, DC: IDB).

ILO (International Labour Organization) (1925) 'Unemployment Insurance: Study of Comparative Legislation', Studies and Reports Series C No. 10 (Geneva: ILO).

ILO (1944) *Declaration of Philadelphia*, 1944, Annex to the Constitution of the ILO (Geneva: ILO).

ILO (1986) *Development of Small and Medium-size Enterprises*, Report VI, 72nd Session, International Labour Conference, Geneva, 1986.

ILO (1995) *General Study on the Protection against Unfair Dismissal*, Committee of Experts on the Application of Conventions and Recommendations, International Labour Conference, 82nd Session, Geneva, 1995.

ILO (1997) *World Labour Report, Industrial Relations, Democracy, and Social Stability* (Geneva: ILO).

ILO (1998) *Panorama Laboral* (Lima: ILO).

ILO (1999a) *Decent Work*, Report of the Director-General, International Labour Conference, 87th Session, Geneva, 1999.

ILO (1999b) *World Employment Report 1998–99* (Geneva: ILO).

ILO (2000a) *Your Voice at Work* (Geneva: ILO).

ILO (2000b) *Labour Statistics Yearbook 2000* (Geneva: ILO).

ILO (2003a) 'Active Labour Market Policies', GB.288/ESP/2, Paper prepared for the 288th Session of the Governing Body, Geneva, 2003.

ILO (2003b) 'Learning and Training for Work in the Knowledge Society', Resolutions concerning Human Resources Training and Development, International Labour Conference, 91st Session, Geneva, 2003.

ILO (2004) *Organizing for Social Justice* (Geneva: ILO).

ILO (2005) *Hours of Work: From Fixed to Flexible?* General Survey of the Reports concerning the Hours of Work (Industry) Convention, 1919 (No. 1), and the Hours of Work (Commerce and offices) Convention, 1930 (No. 30), Report of the Committee of Experts on the Application of Conventions and Recommendations, International Labour Conference, 93rd Session, Geneva.

Ince, G.H. (1937) *Report of Unemployment Insurance in Australia*, The Parliament of the Commonwealth of Australia, 22 February.

Infante, R., A. Marinakis and J. Velasco (2003) *Minimum Wage in Chile: An Example of the Potential and Limitations of this Policy Instrument*, Employment Paper 2003/52 (Geneva: ILO).

International Monetary Fund (IMF) (1999) 'Chronic Unemployment in the Euro area: Causes and Cures', *World Economic Outlook*, May (Washington, DC: IMF).

International Monetary Fund (IMF) (2003) 'Unemployment and Labor Market Institutions: Why Reforms Pay Off', *World Economic Outlook*, May (Washington, DC: IMF).

Iversen, T. (1998) 'Wage Bargaining, Central Bank Independence and Real Effects of Money', *International Organization*, 52(3): 469–504.

Jackman, R. (1993) 'Mass Unemployment: International Experience and Lessons for Policy', Discussion Paper No. 152 (London: Centre for Economic Performance, London School of Economics).

Jackman, R., C. Pissarides and S. Savouri (1990) 'Labour Market Policies and Unemployment in the OECD', *Economic Policy*, 11(23): 449–90.

Johnson, H.G. and P. Mieszkowski (1970) 'The Effects of Unionisation on the Distribution of Income: A General Equilibrium Approach', *Quarterly Journal of Economics*, 84(4): 539–61.

Jorgenson, D.W. (1963) 'Capital Theory and Investment Behavior', *American Economic Review*, 53(2): 247–59.

Journal of Economic Perspectives (1998) 'Symposium on Globalization in Perspective', 12(4).

Kahn, L.M. (1996) 'International Differences in Male Wage Inequality: Institutions versus Market Forces', *Journal of Political Economy*, 104(4): 791–837.

Kalecki, M. (1943) 'Political Aspects of Full Employment', reprinted in M. Kalecki, *Selected Essays on the Dynamics of the Capitalist Economy, 1933–70* (Cambridge: Cambridge University Press).

Kaplan, R. (ed.) (1999) *Freedom in the World: The Annual Survey of Political Rights and Civil Liberties 1998–99* (New York: Freedom House).

Kapur, D. *et al.* (1997) *The World Bank: Its First Half Century*, vol. 1 (Washington, DC: Brookings).

Katz, H.C., T.A. Kochan and K.R. Gobeille (1983) 'Industrial Relations Performance, Economic Performance, and QWL Performance: An Interplant Analysis', *Industrial and Labor Relations Review*, 37(1): 3–17.

Katz, L.F. and A.B. Krueger (1992) 'The Effect of the Minimum Wage on the Fast-food Industry', *Industrial and Labor Relations Review*, 46: 6–21.

Keen, S. (2001) *Debunking Economics: The Naked Emperor of the Social Sciences* (Annandale and London: Pluto Press and Zed Books).

Kennan, J. (1986) 'The Economics of Strikes', in O. Ashenfelter and R. Layard (eds), *Handbook of Labor Economics*, vol. 2, Handbooks in Economics Series, No. 5 (Amsterdam: North-Holland).

Kennan, J. (1995) 'The Elusive Effects of Minimum Wages', *Journal of Economic Literature*, 33(4): 1950–65.

Keynes, J.M. (1936) *The General Theory of Employment, Interest and Money* (London: Macmillan).

Kim, H. (1993) 'The Korean Union Movement in Transition', in S. Frenkel (ed.), *Organized Labor in the Asia-Pacific Region: A Comparative Study of Trade Unionism in Nine Countries*, Cornell International Industrial and Labor Relations Report no. 24 (Ithaca, NY: ILR Press).

King, K. (1977) *The African Artisan: Education and the Informal Sector in Kenya* (London: Heinemann).

Kleiner, M.M. and Y.M. Lee (1997) 'Work Councils and Unionization: Lessons from South Korea', *Industrial Relations*, 36(1): 1–16.

Kornfeld, R. (1993) 'The Effects of Union Membership on Wages and Employee Benefits: The Case of Australia', *Industrial and Labor Relations Review*, 47(1): 114–28.

Korpi, W. (2004) 'Changing Class Structure and the Origins of Welfare States: The Break-Through of Social Insurance 1860–1940', Presented at the EPSAnet Conference on European Social Policy, University of Oxford, 9–11 Sept. 2004.

Kreps, D.M. (1990) 'Corporate Culture and Economic Theory', in J.E. Alt and K.A. Shepsle (eds), *Perspectives on Positive Political Economy* (Cambridge: Cambridge University Press).

Kucera, D. (2001) 'The Effects of Core Worker Rights on Labour Costs and Foreign Direct Investment: Evaluating the "Conventional Wisdom"', Decent Work research programme working paper (Geneva: International Institute for Labour Studies).

Kucera, D. (2002) 'Core Labour Standards and Foreign Direct Investment', *International Labour Review*, 141(1–2): 31–70.

Kugler, A. (2000) 'The Impact of Firing Costs on Turnover and Unemployment: Evidence from the Columbian Labour Market Reform', Inter-American Development

Bank Research Network working paper, R-393 for Colombia (Washington, DC: IDB).

Kuhn, P. and G. Marquez (eds) (2005) *What Difference Do Unions Make? Their Impact on Productivity and Wages in Latin America* (Washington, DC: IDB).

Kupferschmidt, M. and R. Swidensky (1989) 'Longitudinal Estimates of the Union Effect on Wages, Wage Dispersion, and Pension Fringe Benefits', mimeo (Ontario: University of Guelph).

Lalonde, R.J., G. Marschke and K. Troske (1996) 'Using Longitudinal Data on Establishments to Analyze the Effects of Union Organizing Campaigns in the United States', *Annales d' Economy et de Statistique*, 41/2: 155–86.

Lange, P. and G. Garrett (1985) 'The Politics of Growth: Strategic Interaction and Economic Performance in the Advanced Industrial Democracies, 1974–80', *Journal of Politics*, 47(3): 792–827.

Langille, B. (2005) 'What is International Labour Law For?' (Geneva: International Institute for Labour Studies).

Lavoie, M. (2000) 'Le Chômage d'équilibre: Réalité on artefact statistique?', *Revue Economique*, 52(6).

Lawrence, R., D. Rodrik, and J. Whalley (eds) (1996) *Emerging Agenda for Global Trade: High Stakes for Developing Countries* (Washington, DC: Overseas Development Council).

Layard, R., S. Nickell and R. Jackman (1991) *Unemployment* (Oxford: Oxford University Press).

Lee, F. (1999) *Post Keynesian Price Theory* (Cambridge: Cambridge University Press).

Lee, S. (2004) 'Working-hour Gaps: Trends and Issues' in J. Messenger (ed.), *Working Time and Workers' Preferences in Industrialized Countries: Finding the Balance* (London: Routledge).

Lee, S. and D. McCann (2006) 'Working Time Capabilities: Towards Realizing Individual Choice', in J.Y Boulin, M. Lallement, J. Messenger, and F. Michon (eds), *Decent Working Time: New Trends, New Issues* (Geneva: ILO).

Lee, S., D. McCann and J. Messenger (2007) *Working Time Around the World* (London and Geneva: Routledge and ILO).

Leonard, J.S. (1992) 'Unions and Employment Growth', *Industrial Relations*, 31(1): 80–94.

Lewis, H.G. (1986) *Union Relative Wage Effects: A Survey* (Chicago: University of Chicago Press).

Lindert, P. (2004) *Growing Public: Social Spending and Economic Growth since the Eighteenth Century*, vol. 1 (New York: Cambridge University Press).

Long, R.J. (1993) 'The Effect of Unionization on Employment Growth of Canadian Companies', *Industrial and Labor Relations Review*, 46(4): 81–93.

Lora, E. and C. Pagés (1996) *Legislación laboral en el proceso de reformas estructurales de América Latina y el Caribe* (Washington, DC: Inter-American Development Bank).

Lorenz, E.C. (2001) *Defining Global Justice: The History of U.S. International Labour Standards Policy* (Notre Dame: University of Notre Dame Press).

Lynch, L.M. (1992) 'Private Sector Training and the Earnings of Young Workers', *American Economic Review*, 81(1): 299–312.

Lynch, L.M. and S.E. Black (1998) 'Beyond the Incidence of Employer-provided Training', *Industrial and Labour Relations Review*, 52(1): 64–81.

MacCurdy, T.E. and J.H. Pencavel (1986) 'Testing between Competing Models of Wage and Employment Determination in Unionized Markets', *Journal of Political Economy*, 94 (Supplement): S3–S39.

MacDonald, G.M. (1983) 'The Size and Structure of Union/Non-union Wage Differentials in Canadian Industry: Corroboration, Refinement and Extensions', *Canadian Journal of Economics*, 16(3): 480–85.

MacDonald, G.M. and J.C. Evans (1981) 'The Size and Structure of Union/Non-union Wage Differentials in Canada', *Canadian Journal of Economics*, 14(2): 216–31.

Machin, S. and A. Manning (1996) 'Employment and the Introduction of a Minimum Wage in Britain', *Economic Journal*, 106(436): 667–76.

Machin, S., M.B. Stewart and J. Van Reenen (1993) 'The Economic Effect of Multi-unionism: Evidence from the 1984 Workplace Industrial Relations Survey', *Scandinavian Journal of Economics*, 95(3): 279–96.

Machin, S. and S. Wadhwani (1991) 'The Effect of Unions on Organizational Change and Employment', *Economic Journal*, 101(407): 835–54.

MacIsaac, D. and M. Rama (2001) 'Mandatory Severance Pay: Its Coverage and Effects in Peru', mimeo (Washington, DC: World Bank).

Maddison, A. (2003) *The World Economy: Historical Statistics* (Paris: OECD).

Main, B. (1991) 'The Union Relative Wage Gap', in D. Gallie, R. Penn and M. Rose (eds), *Trade Unionism in Recession* (Oxford: Oxford University Press).

Main, B. and B. Reilly (1992) 'Women and the Union Wage Gap', *Economic Journal*, 102(410): 49–66.

Maki, D.R. (1983) 'The Effects of Unions and Strikes on the Rate of Growth of Total Factor Productivity in Canada', *Applied Economics*, 15(1): 29–33.

Malcomson, J.M. (1983) 'Trade Unions and Economic Efficiency', *Economic Journal*, 93 (Conference Papers Supplement): 52–65.

Maldonado, C. and G. Le Boterf (1985) 'L'Apprentissage et les apprentis dans les petits métiers urbains. Le cas de l'Afrique francophone', Working Paper, WEP (Geneva: ILO).

Maloney, W.F. (1997) 'Labor Market Structure in LDCs: Time Series Evidence on Competing Views', World Bank working paper (Washington, DC: World Bank).

Maloney, W.F. and J. Nuñez Mendez (2004) 'Measuring the Impact of Minimum Wages', in J.J. Heckman and C. Pagés (eds), *Law and Employment Lessons from Latin America and the Caribbean* (Chicago: University of Chicago Press).

Marcouiller, D., V. Ruiz de Castilla and C. Woodruff (1997) 'Formal Measures of the Informal-sector Wage Gap in Mexico, El Salvador, and Peru', *Economic Development and Cultural Change*, 45(2): 367–92.

Mares, I. (2000) 'Strategic Alliances and Social Policy Reform: Unemployment Insurance in Comparative Perspective', *Politics and Society* 28(2): 223–44.

Mares, I. (2001) 'Firms and the Welfare State: When, Why and How Does Social Policy Matter to Employers?' in P.A. Hall and D. Soskice (eds), *Varieties of Capitalism: The Institutional Foundations of Comparative Advantage* (Oxford: Oxford University Press).

Márquez, G. and C. Pagés (1998) 'Ties That Bind: Employment Protection and Labor Market Outcomes in Latin America', Inter-American Development Bank Working Paper 373 (Washington, DC: IDB).

Marshall, A. (2004) 'Labour Market Policies and Regulations in Argentina, Brazil and Mexico: Programmes and Impacts', Employment Strategy Paper 2004/13 (Geneva, ILO).

Maskus, E., T.J. Rutherford and S. Selby (1995) 'Implications of Changes in Labor Standards: A Computational Analysis for Mexico', *North American Journal of Economics & Finance* 6(2): 171–88.

Mazumdar, D. (1989) 'Microeconomic Issues of the Labor Markets in Developing Countries: Analysis and Policy Implications', Economic Development Institute Seminar Paper 40 (Washington, DC: The World Bank).

Mazza, J. (1999) 'Unemployment Insurance: Case Studies and Lessons for Latin America and the Caribbean', Inter-American Development Bank Working Paper, May (Washington, DC: IDB).

McCallum, J. (1983) 'Inflation and Social Consensus in the 1970s', *Economic Journal*, 93(372): 784–805.

McCallum, J. (1986) 'Unemployment in OECD Countries in the 1980s', *Economic Journal*, 96(384): 942–60.

McCann, D. (2004) 'Regulating Working Time Needs and Preferences', in J. Messenger (ed.), *Working Time and Workers' Preferences in Industrialized Countries: Finding the Balance* (London and Geneva: Routledge and ILO).

McCombie, J.S.L. (1998) 'Are there Laws of Production?: An Assessment of the Early Criticisms of the Cobb-Douglas Production Function', *Review of Political Economy*, April: 141–73.

McDonald, I.M. and R.M. Solow (1981) 'Wage Bargaining and Employment', *American Economic Review*, 71(5): 896–908.

McLaughlin, S.D. (1979) *The Wayside Mechanic: An Analysis of Skill Acquisition in Ghana* (Amherst, MA: Centre for International Education).

Metcalf, D. (1993) 'Industrial Relations and Economic Performance', *British Journal of Industrial Relations*, 31(2): 255–83.

Metcalf, D. (1999) 'The British National Minimum Wage', *British Journal of Industrial Relations*, 37(2): 171–201.

Metcalf, D. and M. Stewart (1992) 'Closed Shops and Relative Pay: Institutional Arrangements or High Density', *Oxford Bulletin of Economics and Statistics*, 54(4): 503–16.

Miller, P. and C. Mulvey (1991) 'Australian Evidence on the Exit/Voice Model of the Labor Market', *Industrial and Labor Relations Review*, 45(1): 44–7.

Miller, P. and C. Mulvey (1993) 'What Do Australian Unions Do?', *Economic Record*, 69(206): 315–42.

Ministerio de Trabajo y Seguridad Social – MTSS (Ministry of Labour and Social Security – MLSS) (1997) *Report on Employment Conditions*, June 1997.

Mishel, L. (1986) 'The Structural Determinants of Union Bargaining Power', *Industrial and Labor Relations Review*, 40(1): 90–105.

Mitchell, A.G. (1998) 'Strategic Training Partnerships between the State and Enterprises', Employment and Training Paper 19, Training Policies and Systems Branch (Geneva: ILO).

Mitchell, B.R. (1982a) *International Historical Statistics: Africa and Asia* (London and Basingstoke: Macmillan).

Mitchell, B.R. (1982b) *European Historical Statistics 1750–1975* (London and Basingstoke: Macmillan).

Moll, P. (1993) 'Black South African Unions: Relative Wage Effects in International Perspective', *Industrial and Labor Relations Review*, 46(2): 245–62.

Montenegro, C.E. and C. Pagés (2004) 'Who Benefits from Labour Market Regulations?: Chile 1960–98', in J. Heckman and C. Pagés (eds), *Law and Employment: Lessons from Latin America and the Caribbean* (Chicago: University of Chicago Press).

Mulvey, C. (1986) 'Wage Levels: Do Unions Make a Difference?', in J. Niland (ed.), *Wage Fixation in Australia* (Sydney: Allen and Unwin).

Muramatsu, K. (1984) 'The Effect of Trade Unions on Productivity in Japanese Manufacturing Industries', in M. Aoki (ed.), *The Economic Analysis of the Japanese Firm* (Amsterdam: Elsevier Science Publishers, North Holland).

Murphy, K.M., A. Schleifer and R.W. Vishny (1993) 'Why Is Rent-Seeking So Costly to Growth?', *American Economic Review*, 83(2): 409–14.

Murray, J. (2001) *Transnational Labour Regulation: the ILO and EC Compared* (Hague: Kluwer Law International).

Nakumura, K., H. Sato and T. Kamiya (1988) *Do Labor Unions Really Have a Useful Role?* (Tokyo: Sago Rodo Kenkyujo).

Neri, M., G. Gonzaga and J.M. Camargo (2001) 'Salário mínimo, "efeito-farol" e pobreza', *Revista de economia política*, 21(2): 78–90.

Neumark, D. and W. Wascher (2000) 'Minimum Wages and Employment: A Case Study of the Fast-food Industry in New Jersey and Pennsylvania: Comment', *American Economic Review*, 90: 1362–96.

Newell, A. and J.S.V. Symons (1987) 'Corporatism, Laissez-faire, and the Rise of Unemployment', *European Economic Review*, 31(3): 567–614.

Nickell, S.J. (1997) 'Unemployment and Labor Market Rigidities: Europe versus North America', *Journal of Economic Perspectives*, 11(3): 55–74.

Nickell, S.J. and R. Layard (1999) 'Labour Market Institutions and Economic Performance', in O. Ashenfelter and D. Card (eds), *Handbook of Labor Economics*, vol. 3C (Amsterdam: North Holland).

North, D. (1990) *Institutions, Institutional Change and Economic Performance* (Cambridge: Cambridge University Press).

Nunziata, L. (2003) 'Labour Market Institutions and the Cyclical Dynamics of Employment', *Labour Economics*, 10(1): 31–53.

Nyambara, P. (2003) 'Rural Landlords, Rural Tenants, and the Sharecropping Complex in Gokwe, Northwestern Zimbabwe, 1963–79', in M. Roth and F. Gonese (eds), *Delivering Land and Securing Livelihoods: Post-Independence Land Reform and Resettlement in Zimbabwe* (Harare: CASS).

OECD (Organisation for Economic Co-operation and Development) (1994) *The OECD Jobs Study: Facts, Analysis, Strategies* (Paris: OECD).

OECD (1994) 'Labour Standards and Economic Integration', in *OECD Employment Outlook* (Paris: OECD).

OECD (1997) *Employment Outlook* (Paris: OECD).

Olson, M. (1982) *The Rise and Decline of Nations: Economic Growth, Stagflation, and Social Rigidities* (New Haven, CT: Yale University Press).

Orszag, J.M., P.R. Orszag, D.J. Snower and J.E. Stiglitz (1999) 'The Impact of Individual Accounts: Piecemeal vs. Comprehensive Approaches', mimeo (London: Birkbeck College).

Osawa, M. (1989) 'The Service Economy and Industrial Relations in Small and Medium-Size Firms in Japan', *Japan Labor Bulletin*, 1: 1–10.

Oswald, A.J. (1993) 'Efficient Contracts are on the Labour Demand Curve: Theory and Facts', *Labour Economics*, 1(1): 85–113.

Oswald, A.J. and P.J. Turnbull (1985) 'Pay and Employment Determination in Britain: What Are Labour Contracts Really Like?', *Oxford Review of Economic Policy*, 1: 80–97.

Oswald, A.J. and I. Walker (1993) 'Rethinking Labour Supply: Contract Theory and Unions' (London: London School of Economics, Centre for Economic Performance).

Paes de Barros, R. and C.H. Corseuil (2001) 'The Impact of Regulations on Brazilian Labor Market Performance', Inter-American Development Bank Research Network working paper, R-427 (Washington, DC: IDB).

Panagides, A. and H.A. Patrinos (1994) 'Union/Non-union Wage Differentials in the Developing World: A Case Study of Mexico', Policy Research Working Paper 1269 (Washington, DC: World Bank).

Park, Y. (1991) 'Union/Non-union Wage Differentials in the Korean Manufacturing Sector', *International Economic Journal*, 5(4): 70–91.

Patrinos, H.A. and C. Sakellariou (1992) 'North American Indians in the Canadian Labour Market: A Decomposition of Wage Differentials', *Economics of Education Review*, 11(3): 257–66.

Pencavel, J.H. (1991) *The Origins of Trade Union Power* (Oxford: Oxford University Press).

Pencavel, J.H. (1995) 'The Role of Labor Unions in Fostering Economic Development', Policy Research Working Paper No. 1469 (Washington, DC: World Bank).

Perloff, J.M. and R.C. Sickles (1987) 'Union Wage, Hours, and Earnings Differentials in the Construction Industry', *Journal of Labor Economics*, 5: 174–210.

Piore, M. (2004) 'Rethinking International Labor Standards' in W. Milberg (ed.), *Labor and the Globalization of Production: Causes and Consequences of Industrial Upgrading* (Basingstoke: Palgrave).

Pissarides, C. (2001) 'Employment Protection', *Labour Economics*, 8(2): 131–59.

Portes, A. (1989) 'Latin American Urbanization in the Years of the Crisis', *Latin American Research Review*, 24(3): 7–44.

Portes, A. (1994) 'When More Can Be Less: Labor Standards, Development, and the Informal Economy', in C.A. Rakowski (ed.), *Contrapunto: The Informal Sector Debate in Latin America* (Albany, NY: State University of New York Press).

Portes, A. and R. Schauffler (1993) 'Competing Perspectives on the Latin American Informal Sector', *Population and Development Review*, 19(1): 33–60.

Portugal, P. and A. Rute Cardoso (2006) 'Disentangling the Minimum Wage Puzzle: An Analysis of Worker Accessions and Separations', *Journal of the European Economic Association*, 4(5): 988–1013.

Rama, M. (1997) 'Organized Labor and the Political Economy of Product Market Distortions', *World Bank Economic Review*, 11(2): 327–55.

Rama, M. (2001) 'The Consequences of Doubling the Minimum Wage: The Case of Indonesia', *Industrial and Labor Relations Review*, 54(4): 864–81.

Rama, M. and G. Tabellini (1998) 'Lobbying by Capital and Labor over Trade and Labor Market Policies', *European Economic Review*, 42(7): 1295–316.

Rasmusen, E. (1995) *Game and Information* (Cambridge, MA: Blackwell).

Rees, A. (1963) 'The Effects of Unions on Resource Allocation', *Journal of Law and Economics*, 6(1): 69–78.

Restrepo, J. and A. Tokman (eds) (2005) *Labor Markets and Institutions* (Santiago: Central Bank of Chile).

Robinson, C. and N. Tomes (1984) 'Union Wage Differentials in the Public and Private Sectors: A Simultaneous Equation Specification', *Journal of Labor Economics*, 2(1): 106–27.

Rodgers, G. (1994) 'Institutional Economics, Development Economics and Labour Economics', in G. Rodgers (ed.), *Workers, Institutions and Economic Growth in Asia* (Geneva: International Institute for Labour Studies).

Rodrik, D. (1997) *Democracy and Economic Performance* (Cambridge, MA: Harvard University Press).

Rodrik, D. (1999) 'Democracies Pay Higher Wages', *The Quarterly Journal of Economics*, 114(3): 707–38.

Rodrik, D. (1999) 'Globalization and Labour, or: If Globalization is a Bowl of Cherries, Why Are There So Many Glum Faces Around the Table?' in R. Baldwin, D. Cohen,

A. Sapir and A. Venables (eds), *Market Integration, Regionalism and the Global Economy* (New York: Cambridge University Press).

Rodrik, D. (2005) 'Growth Strategies', in P. Aghion and S. Durlauf (eds), *Handbook of Economic Growth* (Amsterdam: North-Holland).

Rowthorn, R.E. (1992a) 'Centralization, Employment, and Wage Dispersion', *Economic Journal*, 102(412): 506–23.

Rowthorn, R.E. (1992b) 'Corporatism and Labour Market Performance', in J. Pekkarinen, M. Pohjola and R. Rowthorn (eds), *Social Corporatism: A Superior Economic System* (Oxford: Clarendon Press).

Saavedra, J. and A. Chong (1999) 'Structural Reform, Institutions, and Earnings: Evidence from the Formal and Informal Sectors in Urban Peru', *The Journal of Development Studies*, 35(4): 95–116.

Saavedra, J. and M. Torero (2004) 'Labor Market Reforms and Their Impact over Formal Labor Demand and Job Market Turnover: The Case of Peru', in J. Heckman and C. Pagés (eds), *Law and Employment: Lessons from Latin America and the Caribbean* (Chicago: University of Chicago Press).

Sapsford, D. and Z. Tzannatos (1993) *The Economics of the Labour Market* (London: Macmillan Press).

Scarpetta, S. (1996) 'Assessing the Role of Labour Market Policies and Institutional Settings on Unemployment: A Cross-Country Study', *OECD Economic Studies*, 26: 43–98.

Schelling, T. (1960) *The Strategy of Conflict* (Cambridge, MA: Harvard University Press).

Schmidt, C. (1995) *Relative Wage Effects of German Unions*, CPER Discussion Paper 918 (Selapo: University of Munich).

Schmidt, C. and K.F. Zimmermann (1991) 'Work Characteristics, Firm Size, and Wages', *Review of Economics and Statistics*, 73(4): 705–10.

Schmitter, P.C. (1981) 'Interest Intermediation and Regime Governability in Contemporary Western Europe and North America', in S. Berger (ed.), *Organising Interests in Western Europe* (Cambridge: Cambridge University Press).

Schnabel, C. (1991) 'Trade Unions and Productivity: the German Evidence', *British Journal of Industrial Relations*, 29: 15–24.

Sengenberger, W. (1994) 'Protection – Participation – Promotion: The Systematic Nature and Effects of Labour Standards', in W. Sengenberger and D. Campbell (eds), *Creating Economic Opportunities: The Role of Labour Standards in Industrial Restructuring* (Geneva: International Institute for Labour Studies).

Shaikh, A. (1974) 'Laws of Production and Laws of Algebra: The Humbug Production Function', *Review of Economics and Statistics*, 56(1): 115–20.

Shaikh, A. (1980) 'Laws of Production and Laws of Algebra: Humbug II', in E.J. Nell (ed.), *Growth, Profits and Property, Essays in the Revival of Political Economy* (Cambridge: Cambridge University Press), pp. 80–95.

Simpson, W. (1985) 'The Impact of Unions on the Structure of Canadian Wages: An Empirical Analysis with Microdata', *Canadian Journal of Economics*, 18(1): 164–81.

Simon, H.A. (1979) 'On Parsimonious Explanation of Production Relations', *Scandinavian Journal of Economics*, 81: 459–74.

Singh, A. and A. Zammit (2000) *The Global Labour Standards Controversy: Critical Issues for Developing Countries* (Geneva: South Centre).

Solow, R. (1958). 'A Skeptical Note on the Constancy of Relative Shares', *American Economic Review*, 48: 618–31.

Soskice, D. (1990) 'Wage Determination: The Changing Role of Institutions in Advanced Industrialized Countries', *Oxford Review of Economic Policy*, 6(4): 36–61.

Soskice, D. and T. Iversen (2000) 'The Nonneutrality of Monetary Policy with Large Price or Wage Setters', *Quarterly Journal of Economic*, 114(1): 265–85.

Spurgeon, A. (2003) *Working Time: Its Impact on Safety and Health* (Geneva: ILO).

Standing, G. (1992) 'Do Unions Impede or Accelerate Structural Adjustment? Industrial versus Company Unions in an Industrializing Labour Market', *Cambridge Journal of Economics*, 16(3): 327–54.

Standing, G. and D. Vaughan-Whitehead (eds) (1995) *Minimum Wages in Central and Eastern Europe: From Protection to Destitution* (Budapest: Central European University Press).

Stanojevic, M. (2005) 'Slovenia: Rigidity or "Negotiated" Flexibility', in Vaughan-Whitehead (ed.), *Working and Employment Conditions in New EU Member States: Convergence or Diversity?* (Geneva: ILO), pp. 339–81.

Steedman, I. (1985) 'On Input "Demand Curves"', *Cambridge Journal of Economics*, 9(2): 165–72.

Stewart, M.B. (1983) 'Relative Earnings and Individual Union Membership in the UK', *Economica*, 50: 111–25.

Stewart, M.B. (1987) 'Collective Bargaining Arrangements, Closed Shops, and Relative Pay', *The Economic Journal*, 97: 140–56.

Stewart, M.B. (1990) 'Union Wage Differentials, Product Market Influence, and the Division of Rents', *The Economic Journal*, 100: 1122–37.

Stewart, M.B. (1991) 'Union Wage Differentials in the Face of Changes in the Economic and Legal Environment', *Economica*, 58: 155–72.

Stewart, M.B. (1995) 'Union Wage Differentials in an Era of Declining Unionization', *Oxford Bulletin of Economics and Statistics*, 57(2): 143–66.

Stiglitz, J. (2002) 'Participation and Development: Perspectives for the Comprehensive Development Paradigm', *Review of Development Economics*, 6(2): 163–82.

Swepston, L. (1994) 'The Future of ILO Standards', *Monthly Labor Review*, 117(9): 16–23.

Tachibanaki, T. and T. Noda (2000) *The Economic Effects of Trade Unions in Japan* (Basingstoke: Macmillan).

Tarantelli, E. (1986) 'The Regulation of Inflation and Unemployment', *Industrial Relations*, 25(1): 1–15.

Teal, F. (1996) 'The Size and Source of Economic Rents in a Developing Country Manufacturing Labour Market', *The Economic Journal*, 106: 963–76.

Tendler, J. (2002) 'Small Firms, the Informal Sector, and the Devil's Deal', *IDS Bulletin*, 33(3): 98–104.

Thirlwall, A.P. (1993) 'The Renaissance of Keynesian Economics', *Banca Nazionale del Lavoro Quarterly Review*, 186: 327–37.

Tzannatos, Z. (1987) 'Union versus Non-union Wages, Arithmetic versus Geometric Means and Grouped Data Revisited', *Bulletin of Economic Research*, 39(1): 91–4.

Tzannatos, Z. (1996) 'Labor Policies and Regulatory Regimes', in C. Frischtak (ed.), *Regulatory Policies and Reform: A Comparative Perspective* (Washington, DC: World Bank).

Tzannatos, Z. and T. Aidt (2006) 'Unions and Microeconomic Performance: A Look at what matters for Economists (amd Employers)', *International Labour Review*, 125(4): 257–78.

Tzannatos, Z. and S. Roddis (1998) 'Unemployment Benefits', *Social Protection Discussion Paper Series*, No. 9813 (Washington, DC: World Bank).

Ulph, A. and D. Ulph (1990) 'Union Bargaining: A Survey of Recent Work', in D. Sapsford and Z. Tzannatos (eds), *Current Issues in Labour Economics* (London: Macmillan).

US Library of Congress, 'Social Welfare, Health Care, and Education', *Country Studies* 2003. http://countrystudies.us/germany/111.htm.

US Social Security Administration (1999) 'Social Security Programs Throughout the World' (Washington, DC).

Vega Ruíz, M.L. (2004) *La Reforma Laboral en América Latina: 15 años después* (Geneva: ILO).

Visser, J. (1998) 'Two Cheers for Corporatism, One for the Market: Industrial Relations, Wage Moderation and Job Growth in the Netherlands', *British Journal of Industrial Relations*, 36(2): 269–92.

Vodopivec, M. (2006) 'Choosing a System of Unemployment Income Support: Guidelines for Developing and Transition Countries', *World Bank Research Observer*, 21: 49–89.

Vroman, W. (2004) 'International Evidence on Unemployment Compensation Prevalence and Costs', Paper prepared for the International Social Security Association meeting, Beijing, China, September.

Wagner, J. (1991) 'Gewerkschaftmitgliedschaft und Arbeitseinkommen in der Bundesrepublik Deutschland', *Ifo Student*: 109–40.

Waud, R.N. (1968) 'Man-Hour Behavior in US Manufacturing: A Neoclassical Interpretation', *Journal of Political Economy*, 76: 407–27.

Weeks, J. (1971) 'Wage Policy and the Colonial Legacy: A Comparative Study', *The Journal of Modern African Studies*, 9(3): 361–87.

Williamson, J. (1990) 'What Washington Means by Policy Reform', in J. Williamson (ed.), *Latin American Adjustment: How Much Has Happened?* (Washington, DC: Institute for International Economics).

Williamson, O. (1985) *The Economic Institutions of Capitalism: Firms, Market and Relational Contracting* (New York, NY: Free Press).

World Bank (1995) *Labor and Economic Reforms in Latin American and the Caribbean* (Washington, DC: The World Bank).

World Bank (2004a) *Doing Business 2005* (Washington, DC: World Bank).

World Bank (2004b) *The World Development Report: A Better Investment Climate for Everyone* (Washington, DC: World Bank).

World Bank (2005) *Doing Business 2006* (Washington, DC: World Bank).

Yaron, G. (1990) 'Trade Unions and Women's Relative Pay: A Theoretical and Empirical Analysis Using UK Data', *Applied Economics Discussion Paper* 95 (Oxford: Oxford University, Institute for Economics and Statistics).

Yuen, T. (2003) 'The Effect of Minimum Wages on Youth Employment in Canada: A Panel Study', *The Journal of Human Resources*, 38(3): 647–72.

Zweimuller, J. and E. Barth (1994) 'Bargaining Structure, Wage Determination, and Wage Dispersion in Six OECD Countries', *Kyklos*, 47: 81–93.

Index